My Hard Days and Long Nights with The Beatles, The Stones, Bob Dylan, Eric Clapton, and the Women They Loved

MISS O'DELL

CHRIS O'DELL

with

Katherine Ketcham

A TOUCHSTONE BOOK

Published by Simon & Schuster

New York   London   Toronto   Sydney

Touchstone
A Division of Simon & Schuster, Inc.
1230 Avenue of the Americas
New York, NY 10020

First Touchstone hardcover edition October 2009

TOUCHSTONE and colophon are registered trademarks of Simon & Schuster, Inc.

For information about special discounts for bulk purchases,
please contact Simon & Schuster Special Sales at
1-866-506-1949 or business@simonandschuster.com.

The Simon & Schuster Speakers Bureau can bring authors to your live event.
For more information or to book an event contact the Simon & Schuster Speakers Bureau
at 1-866-248-3049 or visit our website at www.simonspeakers.com.

Designed by Ruth Lee-Mui

Manufactured in the United States of America

1   3   5   7   9   10   8   6   4   2

Library of Congress Cataloging-in-Publication Data
O'Dell, Chris.
Miss O'Dell : my life with the Beatles, the Stones, Bob Dylan,
and the women they loved / by Chris O'Dell with Katherine Ketcham
p.   cm.
1. O'Dell, Chris, 1947–   2. Sound recording indusry—Employees—
Biography.   3. Rock musicians—Anecdotes.   4. Concert tours—
Anecdotes.   I. Ketcham, Katherine, 1949–   II. Title.
ML429.O24A3   2009
782.42166092—dc22
[B]   2009014555

ISBN 978-1-4165-9093-4
ISBN 978-1-4165-9675-2 (ebook)

This book is dedicated to my son, William.

I wasn't famous.

I wasn't even almost famous.

But I was there . . .

CONTENTS

1

DEREK TAYLOR

February–March 1968

I was sprawled out on the sofa in my Hollywood apartment, wearing jeans and a sweatshirt, watching a game show on the black-and-white, thirteen-inch TV, smoking a joint, and getting really annoyed. My date was almost two hours late. I was alone in the apartment because my roommates, both high school friends from Tucson, were out partying. Where the hell was he?

When the phone finally rang around 10:00 p.m., I didn't try to hide the fact that I was upset.

"Chris! It's Allan." He sounded a little out of breath, and from the background noise I guessed he was in a restaurant somewhere.

"Allan, where have you been?" I said. "You said you'd be here two hours ago."

"I know, I'm sorry, but look, I'm at the La Brea Inn with some friends and there's someone here you have to meet." Allan was talking fast. "His name is Derek Taylor, he used to work for the Beatles, he's doing publicity for A&M Records, and, Chris, you just have to come down here and meet him."

"I don't want to go out. I thought you were coming over here." I was still annoyed with Allan, and I didn't believe that this guy Derek knew the Beatles. The Beatles! Who knew anyone who worked for the Beatles?

He was probably just one of those people hanging out on the periphery who once met someone who once knew someone who claimed they were once best friends with someone who worked for the Beatles.

"Chris, you'll really like him." Allan sounded pretty excited, actually. He was almost pleading with me. "Just jump in your car and come over. Come on!"

I was torn—should I go or stay? I remember staring at the lamp on the side table, almost as if I thought it might tell me what to do. Allan seemed sincere about wanting me to join him, and whoever Derek was, he had certainly impressed Allan. I'd never seen him act this way about anyone before. Oh, what the heck, whatever happened, it would be better than sitting in my apartment all alone feeling sorry for myself.

"Okay," I said. "I'll be there in half an hour or so."

"Hurry. I'll be watching for you," he said.

I changed into my yellow-striped bell-bottom jeans and white top with puffy sleeves (Cher in her "Sonny and" days was my fashion idol), touched up my makeup, and drove to the La Brea Inn on Sunset Boulevard and North La Brea Avenue. I loved my new beige Mustang, which I'd bought in Tucson for two thousand dollars. My father cosigned the loan. I'll never forget that feeling of driving off the lot in my new car, the windows down, the hot desert air blowing through my hair. Oh, that indescribable feeling of total freedom!

The drive took about fifteen minutes. The streetlights on Sunset Boulevard were so bright it might as well have been day, and under their glare I began to feel exposed and insecure. Maybe I should have stayed home. Really, all I'd wanted to do that night was hang out with Allan in my apartment, two friends talking, no pressure, no stress. I liked it that way. I always tried to take things lightly, not to invest too much, although I have to admit that even at twenty I fantasized a lot about finding the right guy and a relationship that would last a lifetime. *Maybe this is the one,* I'd think when I first became interested in someone. But when the relationship ended, even though it would hurt like hell, I moved on pretty quickly. I went with the flow—one of my great strengths that would also prove, at times in my life, to be a significant weakness.

I parked my car in the crowded lot and took a few deep breaths, trying to force the anxious thoughts out of my mind and put a confident smile on my face. I was always uncomfortable walking into a room where the party was going strong and everyone else seemed to know one another. Never knowing what to expect, I feared I wouldn't fit in, that no one would talk to me, and if they did, I'd say something stupid or inappropriate. So I had learned to put on a "face," smiling confidently, walking with a firm stride, my back straight and head held high while my insides were trembling, whether from fear or excitement I never quite knew.

The restaurant was dimly lit, and a massive two-sided fireplace in the center of the room separated the bar from the dining area. A thin fog of cigarette smoke drifted toward the high ceiling, a pleasant hum of conversation filled the room, and the crackling fire put a pleasant glow over everything. As my eyes adjusted to the light, I saw Allan waving to me from a table by the fireplace.

"Hey, Chris, glad you made it," he said, giving me a hug and introducing me, first, to the two women at the table—a writer named Eve and her friend, whose name I immediately forgot. I wasn't paying attention to them anyway because I couldn't take my eyes off the handsome man who had pushed back his chair, waiting for Allan to introduce us. He was so—well—so English, dressed in a navy blazer with a silk scarf tied loosely around his neck and tucked into an open-collared shirt, a drink in one hand and a cigarette in the other. A well-groomed mustache lined his upper lip, his long hair, layered to look somewhat unkempt, curled up at the ends, and his eyes drooped in a gentle, lazy way. Just like Paul McCartney's eyes, I thought.

"Chris O'Dell, meet Derek Taylor," Allan said.

"Lovely to meet you, Chris," Derek said, standing up and taking my hand in his, all the while looking deep into my eyes. At that moment I felt like the most important person in the world, as if no one else in the room mattered to him. Dashing—that was the word for him. He reminded me of the romantic, swashbuckling Errol Flynn.

I sat down next to Allan and tried not to look like I felt—out of my element. This was clearly the "in" crowd. Eve was talking about her latest writing project, and from the sound of it, she was one of those almost-famous people who really did know a lot of famous people. Dressed in jeans and a flowing silk blouse, with rings on almost every finger and a huge gaudy necklace that was probably worth a fortune, she held her head back at a steep angle, eyes slightly narrowed, looking down the steep cliff of her cheek at me. I'm sure she sensed my insecurity and perhaps that raised the angle of her chin a bit higher.

"What's your sign?" she asked me, her eyes intent and unsmiling.

"Sign?" I had no idea what she was talking about.

"Astrological," she said, raising her chin a little higher.

I smiled, trying to be friendly. "Pisces," I said. And with that, she turned away and didn't speak another word to me for the rest of the evening. Like everyone else, she focused her attention on Derek, and who could blame her? I loved the way his eyebrow lifted in an amused sort of way and how his undulating, often indecipherable English accent cloaked what I would come to know as a Liverpudlian wit, which says one thing and means another, poking fun without being blatantly cruel about it. Derek would tell his stories, spinning his magic with perfectly chosen words, drawing you into his spell, and making you feel as if there were no better place to be in all the world than sitting right next to him. We drank and talked, and after three or four glasses of wine, I was feeling much better about everything, especially when Eve and her friend stood up to leave.

"Deadlines," Eve explained, with a wink at Derek.

Derek, Allan, and I drew our chairs closer together, ordered more drinks, and stayed until the restaurant closed. Something clicked that night between Derek and me. He told me later that he was attracted to the fact that I seemed so unaffected by the Hollywood scene and so innocent about the world. I'm not sure how innocent I was—I'd been in LA for almost two years, and I'd already had several disastrous love affairs, I was drinking too much, smoking too much pot, and discovering the joys of amphetamines. But perhaps it was a sort of youthful naïveté that endeared me to Derek, and later to the Beatles, the Stones, and all the other rock stars, along with my willingness to withdraw into the shadows and let others take center stage.

I was always the listener, the eager helper who wanted more than anything to be liked and accepted, the friend who was content to do what she could to make other people happy. Ever since I was a little girl growing up in Keota, Oklahoma, I'd learned how to put other people's needs above my own. The memories are so strong that I can still picture myself, a six-year-old girl with wavy blond hair and blue eyes who wore plaid dresses with white collars and patent leather Mary Janes with anklets. I'd skip down the sidewalk of the main street, past the sheriff's office, past the winos sitting on the bench in front of Burris's grocery story, past the tiny houses where I waved at people sitting on their porches or working in their yards until I came to my favorite spot, an old oak tree with spreading limbs and acres of grass all around.

Sitting under the leafy branches, my legs splayed out in front of me, I spent hours searching for four-leaf clovers. I had a lot of time after school to explore because my younger sister, Vicki, was sick again with chronic pneumonia—eventually the doctors would remove part of her right lung—and my mother was staying with her in the closest hospital, thirty miles away, across the Oklahoma border in Fort Smith, Arkansas. My father was always busy at school, teaching or coaching, and I had afternoons to myself. I was used to being alone. Loneliness was part of me, as familiar as taking a breath. The message I had internalized was to take care of myself, do the best I could, and no matter what the circumstances, keep a big smile on my face.

I also learned early on that I was not the center of the universe, but that knowledge did not stop me from pursuing my dreams. I never stopped looking for the four-leaf clover that would change my life. It was waiting out there for me, and when I couldn't find it in the shade of the massive oak, I skipped along the dirt road and looked for it elsewhere. I never stopped dreaming that I would discover something precious and beautiful, mine alone to keep and treasure.

After we closed down the La Brea Inn, Derek invited Allan and me to continue the party at his rented home in Laurel Canyon. We sat in the living room, listening, as he rolled a joint and told us stories about how he'd once worked for a local paper in Liverpool and left that job to work as the personal assistant to the Beatles' manager Brian Epstein. After touring with the Beatles in 1964, Derek moved to Hollywood to become a publicist for Paul Revere and the Raiders and, later, the Beach Boys, Captain Beefheart, the Byrds, Tiny Tim, and the Doors. But now, he said as he passed the joint around, he was preparing to leave LA in a few weeks to start his new job in London as press officer for Apple Corps Limited, the Beatles' new company. His wife and four children (soon to be five and eventually six) were already settled in their new home in the country outside London.

That was the strongest pot I'd ever had, some Hawaiian stuff that I think Derek called "Icebox." We listened to the Bonzo Dog Doo Dah Band, playing the Intro and Outro track over and over again, which cracked us up. Derek continued to regale us with stories about his life with the Beatles, and I sat there stoned out of my mind, thinking, Wow, so this is how the in-crowd lives in Hollywood. I felt as if I had stepped into a whole new world. Which, of course, I had.

I look back at that magical evening with one question in mind: What if I had stayed home? We all have those critical junctures in our lives, when we make a seemingly trivial decision that radically alters the direction of our lives. It takes only a second, really, and then everything changes.

When I met Derek I was twenty, a high school graduate with a pleasant personality and an eagerness to please. I didn't have any great ambitions, although I had moved to Los Angeles to get away from Tucson with the dream of something better happening to me. That was the choice—stay in Arizona and go to college (I wanted to major in drama), or leave Tucson with dreams but no plans and see where life took me. But when I got to LA, I realized I was just a small-town girl in a big city—lonely, directionless, insecure, and self-doubting, always waiting, waiting, waiting for a new experience or adventure to come along. I was free to be whatever I wanted to become, but I had no idea what that was.

That night in the La Brea Inn changed everything. I have lived such a storied life, filled with wild adventures and unimaginable opportunities, surrounded by rock stars and celebrities, living in times that were at once magical, thrilling, bewildering, and terrifying. Despite all the craziness and confusion, the bad (some would say stupid) decisions and the good (I would say lucky) choices, the close friendships and the bitter betrayals, the drug highs and the inevitable lows, this is my life and I wouldn't change one tiny piece of it for fear of losing it all.

But back then I had no idea that one chance meeting would completely alter the direction of my life.

"Chris, dear, would you like to join me and some friends for dinner at the La Brea Inn?" I just adored Derek's voice with its soft, sweet tone and the warmth that seemed to wrap around each word. I had to admit it—even though I struggled with the fact that Derek was fourteen years older than me (and married, with four children)—I had a huge crush on him. He was attracted to me, too, but the fact that he was married, with children, stopped anything from happening between us. His conscience got in the way, which was okay with me because I came to see him as more of a father figure than a boyfriend. A boyfriend could always dump me, but a father figure would protect me and stand up for me no matter what.

"I'd love to!" I said. I was sitting at my desk at Ted Randal Enterprises struggling with typing up the latest tip sheet on the mimeograph paper. Ted programmed radio stations in the US and Australia, picking the records he thought would be hits and creating playlists for the stations. I hated that mimeograph paper because it was so unforgiving of typos and so incredibly messy, the blue ink getting all over my hands every time I touched it.

Derek didn't own a car—he didn't even know how to drive, which I found sort of strange—and for the next three weeks I was his driver, chauffeuring him around Los Angeles as he tied up loose ends and prepared to move back to London. I drove him to television and radio interviews, sat in on recording sessions, accompanied him to meetings with lawyers and record producers, and joined him for lunches, dinners, and drinks with people like folksinger Phil Ochs, screenwriter Carl Gottlieb, film producer Fred Roos, and actress Teri Garr.

It was all such a frenetic, fantastic whirlwind, with one event following right on the heels of another, that I didn't have time to go to work. Or so I told myself. For the first few days I phoned in sick, but after a while I didn't even bother to call. All I wanted to do was be with Derek for the few short weeks before he left. When I finally handed in my notice, Ted Randal was clearly irritated with me, but truthfully I didn't care—I was young and carefree, Derek was paying for all my gasoline and meals, and he was introducing me to so many people in the record and entertainment industries that I figured I'd find another job without a lot of trouble. In the meantime, I was having too much fun to worry about much of anything. I was living in the moment, and the moment was all about Derek.

One evening, just a few days before Derek left for London, was particularly memorable. I was in my apartment, getting ready to meet Derek at A&M Records, when he called.

"Chris, dear, tonight we're having dinner with Peter Asher," Derek said.

Peter Asher! I struggled to contain my excitement. Peter Asher, formerly of Peter and Gordon, the British duo! Peter Asher, brother of Jane Asher, Paul McCartney's girlfriend! *Peter Asher!* I thought. *Wow!*

"Okay," I said nonchalantly.

I remember thinking how well-mannered and quintessentially English Peter was as he dabbed at the corners of his mouth with his white linen napkin and talked to Derek about this new business venture called Apple. He had much redder hair than I had imagined from his photographs, and he wore black Buddy Holly–type glasses that might have looked goofy on someone else but made him look cute in a refined sort of way, if that makes any sense at all. Prim and proper and not one for small talk, Peter focused most of his attention on Derek. I assumed he was shy because he didn't look at me very often, even though Derek kept trying to include me in the conversation. When Peter did turn my way, he swiveled his whole body around at the same time he turned his head, which seemed to me a very polite gesture and a way of giving me his full attention.

"Yes, my dear," he said to me at one point, and I liked that, having

Peter Asher call me "dear." He had a really sweet smile. I sipped my wine and listened politely as the two men talked about the Beatles' grand plans for Apple, including separate divisions for publishing, film, electronics, and even an Apple boutique. Peter was already working as head of A&R, the artists and repertoire division of Apple Records.

After we dropped Peter at the airport for his flight to London, Derek said the most amazing thing.

"You should think about coming to London, Chris."

"London?" I wasn't sure what he meant. Was he inviting me to come visit him?

"Apple is going to be huge," Derek said. "It would be a very good time to appear, you know."

I laughed, delighted by the idea of "appearing" at Apple. Would I just walk in and ask for a job? Was Derek serious? It seemed so preposterous. I didn't have any savings, and I didn't know a soul in London except for Derek and now Peter. I couldn't just pack up and move to London without a job or a place to live—it was a fabulous fantasy, a scene that I could play out in my mind or in front of my mirror, picturing myself having tea with Pattie Harrison or chatting with George, Ringo, Paul, or John in a real English pub. And when I listened to Derek, sometimes I even believed the dream might come true.

2

CIRO'S

March 28–29, 1968

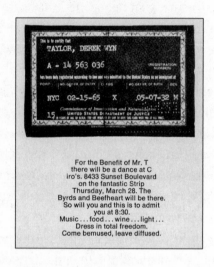

This is to certify that
TAYLOR, DEREK WYN

A - 14 563 036   (REGISTRATION NUMBER)

has been duly registered according to law and was admitted to the United States as an immigrant at

PORT | MO-DAY-YR. OF ENTRY | C. #06 | MO-DAY-YR. OF BIRTH | SEX

NYC 02-15-65   X   .05-07-32 M

Commissioner of Immigration and Naturalization
15   UNITED STATES DEPARTMENT OF JUSTICE

For the Benefit of Mr. T
there will be a dance at C
iro's. 8433 Sunset Boulevard
on the fantastic Strip
Thursday, March 28. The
Byrds and Beefheart will be there.
So will you and this is to admit
you at 8:30.
Music...food...wine...light...
Dress in total freedom.
Come bemused, leave diffused.

Derek threw himself a going-away party, and it cost him a fortune. He charged his guests $5.50 to attend, figuring that wasn't such a bad deal considering it included all the food and white wine they could drink plus a concert by the Byrds, Captain Beefheart and His Magic Band, and even Tiny Tim. He was hoping the entrance fee would pay for his return ticket to London the next day—he owed the IRS a lot of money as he somehow had neglected to pay taxes the entire time he was in the States—but many invited guests walked in without paying, hundreds more crashed the party, and Derek bought way too much white wine, which hardly anybody was drinking because they were all stoned or tripping on acid. He told me later that the party cost him over two thousand dollars.

"Derek has a lot of nerve asking for an admission fee," said a handsome twenty-something-year-old dressed in jeans and with hair down to his shoulders. From the outfit, I figured he was in the promotion or publicity department of some record company. He laughed, then, knowing he was getting a good deal, and I laughed too, stretching out my hand to take his $5.50. Derek's secretary, Jackie, was helping me collect money at the door. The line snaked around the block and by the time people got to us, they were a little antsy and ready to start partying.

I was all dolled up in an outfit I bought at a little clothes shop near the corner of Sunset and Vine. When I saw the lime green minidress with the spaghetti straps and the lacy netting over a skin-tight inner sheath, I couldn't resist it. A new pair of white high-heeled shoes and a long blond fall completed the outfit. Looking at myself in the mirror just before I left to pick up Derek, I couldn't help thinking that I looked a little bit like Twiggy, the London fashion model who was making "skinny" look fashionable. That was fine by me, because no matter how hard I tried, I couldn't seem to gain weight. I'd always been self-conscious about my protruding bones.

I tried checking names off the guest list, but so many people showed up who weren't on the list that I finally gave up. As long as they were willing to pay the $5.50 we let them in. After an hour or so, the line was gone and I left Jackie at the door to deal with the stragglers. We'd already collected what seemed like a lot of money, and I wanted to be inside partying with Derek and his friends.

I filled my wineglass and fought my way through the crowd to Derek, who was entertaining everyone with one of his stories. During a lull in the conversation, he put his arm around me and leaned close to whisper in my ear.

"Chris, luv, I've dropped some acid. Keep an eye on me. Don't let me go over the top, okay?"

I knew Derek did acid—he told me later that the drug transformed his life and saved his marriage while simultaneously making him a true believer in the possibility of world peace, some pretty big claims if you asked me—but I'd never been around him when he was tripping and I'd never taken acid myself. I had no idea what to expect, although I'd heard stories of people freaking out and losing touch with reality. I stayed right next to Derek, feeling grateful that at least on this night I could be his protector.

The hours passed in a kaleidoscopic blur of color, movement, and sound. I took off my shoes and danced until my stockings were full of holes. I felt as if I were tripping on acid, too, because the noise was so intense that it seemed as if the room were pulsating and the walls might explode. At one point I looked around for Derek and couldn't find him. I panicked, fearing that he had wandered off somewhere alone and unguarded, but he showed up a few minutes later with a big grin on his face, cigarette in one hand and wineglass in the other, winking at me as if to say, "I'm doing pretty well here, aren't I?" *Oh Derek,* I thought. *What am I going to do without you?*

It seemed as if the party had just started when everything got quiet and I looked around to find the room empty of everyone but me, Derek, Jackie, and a few bleary-eyed stragglers.

"What time is it, luv?" Derek said, swaying a little on his feet.

I looked at my watch and my eyes got big. "Six-thirty," I said, adding for no real reason, "in the morning."

"Bloody hell, I've got a plane to catch!" Derek said, and suddenly we were all scurrying around the room, searching for our belongings. I couldn't find my shoes. I searched everywhere for them, under the tables and chairs, even under the stage area, but they were nowhere to be found. Losing my pretty new white shoes got all mixed up in my mind with losing Derek and I started to cry, tears just pouring down my face, streaking my already smudged makeup.

"I can't find my shoes," I sobbed.

"There, there, luv, it's okay," Derek said, looking at me with concern. "Jackie will help you find them."

We searched for a few minutes but finally gave up and headed out the loading doors to the side parking area. I blinked my eyes in the bright morning sunshine and took one look back, just to fix that night in my memory. Daylight spilled into the empty room. Chairs were overturned, plates and cups were scattered everywhere, and cigarette smoke drifted like a fog over it all. I turned around, my heart sinking, and began to run across the parking lot to my car.

We drove to Derek's office, where he picked up his bags, and Jackie came running out with an extra pair of shoes. Black and at least two sizes too big, they didn't look so good with my lime green dress but I was grateful to have them. I drove about twenty miles over the speed limit all the way to the airport, dropped Derek and Jackie at the terminal, parked the car, and then ran as fast as I could to the gate in those big black shoes. Several of Derek's friends had come to see him off and they were all standing in a group near the gate area. Looking frazzled for the first time since I had known him, Derek told me he was out of cigarettes.

"Would you be a love and go buy me a carton?" he said, handing me a twenty-dollar bill.

I ran for what seemed like miles, found a store that sold cigarettes, and tore back to the gate. Jackie was still standing by the gate, but the door was closed.

"Derek asked me to say good-bye to you," Jackie said, reaching out to pat my arm. "They were closing the gate, and he had to go."

"But I have his cigarettes," I said, hugging the carton of cigarettes to my chest. "I have to give him his cigarettes."

"Chris, it's okay," Jackie said, trying to reassure me. "He'll be fine without the cigarettes." I understood, then, that Derek had sent me away, knowing the gate would close before I returned and hoping to spare me the pain of saying good-bye.

I couldn't let him leave like that.

"Doesn't he change flights in San Francisco?" I asked Jackie.

"He has a two-hour layover there before he continues on to London," she said.

"I'm flying to San Francisco," I said.

"Chris, please, you'll never make it." Jackie sighed. She knew she wasn't going to talk me out of it.

"I'm going. But I don't have any money—would you buy me a ticket?"

•   •   •

Half an hour later I was on my way to San Francisco. When we landed I pushed my way to the front of the plane and ran down endless corridors until I got to the gate for Derek's flight. I don't know how I didn't fall flat on my face during that mad dash through the airport, flip-flopping around in Jackie's big shoes. What a sight I must have been in my lime green minidress, my makeup smeared all over my face, my fall tilting over to one side of my head, a carton of cigarettes held tight to my chest.

I nearly crashed into the little stand by the gate.

"I have to get on this plane and give these cigarettes to someone," I said, trying to catch my breath.

"I'm sorry, but we can't let you do that," the female gate attendant replied. "We've already had the final boarding call."

"No, you don't understand. You see, I just flew here from Los Angeles because he left these cigarettes behind." I held up the carton of cigarettes as if it would explain my predicament. "He needs them. He's going to London. I have to get on the plane."

I wasn't making any sense. She shook her head firmly, and I knew then that all was lost. I started to cry. I just stood there sobbing.

"All right," she said, not unkindly, "but only for a minute. You must give him the cigarettes and come right back."

"Thank you," I said and ran as fast as I could onto the plane and down the aisle, searching the rows for Derek's face. He was sitting in an aisle seat in the middle of the plane. His eyes were closed. I kneeled down next to him and touched his arm. He opened his eyes.

"You forgot your cigarettes," I said, handing him the carton.

Completely disoriented, he took a moment to reply. "Oh. Chris. What are you doing? How did you get here?"

"I couldn't let you leave without saying good-bye." I took one long last look at him and it seemed that all my hopes and dreams were wrapped up with him and they were deserting me, too. I leaned over and gave him a hug and then I walked, with as much grace as I could muster, down the aisle and into the gate area where I stood at the big windows and watched his plane back up and taxi to the runway. Then I walked to a phone book and dialed my uncle's number. I hadn't seen him for a long time and we weren't particularly close, but he was the only person I knew in the Bay Area. He picked me up at the airport, took one look at me, and drove me to a department store to buy some new clothes.

Derek called several times in the next few months to check on me and fill me in on his new job at Apple. At the end of these conversations he always encouraged me to think about moving to London.

"You know, Chris, things are really moving along here," Derek said one morning when he called. "Are you going to come over?"

Every other time Derek asked that question, it seemed fanciful, teasing, as if to say, "I wish you could be here with us on this fabulous adventure even though I know it's not really in the realm of possibility." But this time Derek sounded more serious, as if he really wanted me to consider the idea.

"I promise I'll think about it," I said, smiling at the thought of seeing Derek again. Just hearing his voice on the phone lifted my spirits. *If only I had some money saved up,* I found myself thinking. *If only I had wings and could just fly there on my own.*

"Derek wants me to come to England and work at Apple." I was having lunch with my friend Jack Nelson, a salesman I worked with at my new job with a record distributor. "What do you think I should do?"

"Are you kidding, Chris?" Jack said, taking a big bite of his cheeseburger. "You'd be crazy not to go."

"But it would cost so much money," I said, moving the French fries around on my plate. "You know, the airplane ticket, cash to get through the first few weeks, hotels, food, taxis." I had no idea what the costs were going to be, but I was sure London was expensive.

"Will Derek help you get a job?"

"Well, he hasn't exactly promised me a job, but I'm sure he'll do what he can."

"Have you got any money saved?"

"I haven't made enough money to save any," I said, feeling a little miserable. I was stuck, and I knew it. "Maybe I could sell something."

"What about your car?"

"I owe more than it's worth." I pondered the seemingly insurmountable obstacles in my way. "The only thing I own of any value is my record collection."

"Why not sell that?"

Sell my records? I was aghast. What would I do without my music? Where would I be without Smokey and the Miracles, Clyde McPhatter, the Supremes, the Four Tops, Elvis, the Beatles, and the Stones to soothe and rock me through the day?

"Look," Jack said, leaning across the table and forcing me to pay attention to him, "I know a guy who buys used records. I bet you could get a couple hundred for them."

So that's what I did. I sold my records for two hundred dollars.

Then I called my parents.

"Hi, Mom," I said, casually, as if this were one of our Sunday afternoon phone calls. We chatted for a while before I broke the news. "Listen, I have a chance to go to London—and maybe even work for the Beatles."

"Are you kidding?" she said. "How did that happen?" Mom and Dad knew I worked in the record business in LA, but they thought the most famous person I'd met so far was Liberace and that was enough to impress them.

I told her about my friendship with Derek and his repeated phone calls asking me to move to London and work for the Beatles' new company, Apple.

"Oh, Chris, England is a long way away," Mom said.

"I know, Mom," I said in a reassuring tone, "but believe me, this is a chance of a lifetime."

My parents had learned a long time ago to turn my life over to me, to suffer their own fears in silence, and to support me in any way they could, as long as they felt I wasn't doing something that might hurt me or harm my future. When my mother adjusted to the idea and actually became excited about my new opportunity, Dad's worries eased. "What can we do to help?" they both asked. Dad sold my life insurance policy, Mom searched for an inexpensive one-way ticket to London, and they agreed to take over my car payments.

And that's how it happened that on May 17, 1968, two months after Derek left LA, I hugged my parents good-bye at the Tucson airport and flew to London.

3

APPLE

May 18–20, 1968

I arrived on a Saturday morning, took a taxi to a bed and breakfast in the Shepherd's Bush district of London, visited all the big tourist sights on Sunday, and called Apple first thing Monday morning.

"Good morning," a cheerful female voice answered. "Apple Corps Limited."

"Hello," I said in my most confident voice, "is Derek Taylor there?"

"One moment, please." I waited for Derek's familiar voice, my heart racing, all sorts of questions running through my mind. Was I dressed right? That was my big question. I'd spent a good hour that morning trying to decide what to wear for my first appearance at Apple. I'd packed four outfits that I considered appropriate for a London work-day, and I tried them all on, finally settling on a shocking pink A-line dress with white tights and pink shoes with chunky block heels. From what I'd seen of London fashion, I felt as if I'd fit right in.

A second female voice came on the line. "Reception. May I help you?"

"Is Derek Taylor there?" I repeated.

"I'm sorry, he hasn't arrived as of yet, but I do believe he's on his way. Would you care to leave a message?"

"Yes, thank you. My name is Chris O'Dell, and I'm a friend of Derek's from Los Angeles."

"Can he phone you back?"

"Well, it's hard to reach me because I'm calling from a pay phone," I said. "Do you think it would be all right if I just came over?"

"Of course," she said in a very chipper voice with a lovely English accent. "If Derek arrives before you, I'll tell him you're in transit."

The "in transit" part was a little unnerving, mostly because they drove on the opposite side of the road, and the taxi driver was so laid back, one hand holding the steering wheel as he turned around to talk to me, then braking or swerving suddenly to avoid a pedestrian or a bus loaded with tourists. But I didn't care, I was in London and I was going to Apple Corps Ltd., headquarters of the Beatle's new business ventures. What would Derek do when he saw me? Would I meet one of the Beatles? Would people at Apple be friendly? So many thoughts were running through my mind and I was so nervous—or was I excited? I've never been good at distinguishing between the two.

"This is 95 Wigmore Street, madam." The taxi driver looked at me in his rearview mirror as I counted out shillings, pounds, and pennies, eventually giving up the attempt to pretend I knew what I was doing and dumping the whole lot in his outstretched hand. When he gave me a huge smile, I realized I had probably given him the biggest tip of his life.

The drab modern building surprised me. I'd imagined that Apple would be housed in an elegant, old, stone London building with gargoyles and graceful arches. The only bright spot was a poster hanging outside the door of the building showing a nerdy-looking man playing a guitar and singing his heart out to a microphone. "THIS MAN HAS TALENT . . ." the poster announced in lime green print. In smaller letters the poster encouraged people to send their tapes, letters, and photographs to Apple Music. "DO IT NOW! THIS MAN NOW OWNS A BENTLEY!"

That poster put a smile on my face. I remembered that Derek had told me about Apple's mission to help all the struggling musicians and artists who couldn't get anyone to pay attention to them at the big record companies. This poster said it all—if that funny-looking man in the poster could make it big at Apple, then so could anyone—even me!

I noticed a group of young women about my age standing off to the side of the entrance, and I knew immediately from their fresh, hopeful faces that they were Beatles fans. Later I'd learn that the Beatles called these ultraloyal fans the Apple Scruffs. Every day they waited outside Apple and EMI's Abbey Road Studios, hoping to see one of the Beatles.

"Good morning, miss. May I help you?" the uniformed doorman asked as I walked in the front door.

"Yes, thank you, I'm meeting Derek Taylor with Apple."

"Fourth floor, madam," he said, showing me to the elevator.

I walked into the Apple reception area, a large windowless room with a half dozen doors leading into various offices. The walls were white and empty except for a few photos of the Beatles and some framed gold records.

"Hi, I'm Chris O'Dell," I said to the receptionist, hoping that my voice didn't betray my nervousness. "I'm here to see Derek Taylor. Has he arrived yet?"

"Yes, he's in a meeting with Neil Aspinall," she said with a warm smile and a welcoming voice. "Why don't you have a seat, and I'll let him know you're here."

Neil Aspinall. Derek had often spoken about Neil, the once-upon-a-time Beatles' road manager who was now the managing director of Apple. I sat down on one of the chairs lined up against the wall (I chose the chair that sat directly under a black-and-white photograph of John and Paul), crossed my legs in a demure way, and tried to look calm and composed. I leafed through a copy of *Billboard* magazine and surreptitiously watched the people walking through the reception area. Who were they and what were they doing at Apple? Feeling a little conspicuous as the only person in the reception area, I buried my nose in the magazine and pretended to be absorbed in the new Top 100 list.

One of the office doors opened, and I looked up from my pretend reading to see Derek walking toward me.

"Chris, my luv!" he said, giving me a big hug. "You made it, my goodness, you really are here, aren't you, don't you look wonderful, I can't believe you are actually here."

I laughed, filled with happiness just to hear Derek's voice and his run-on sentences, hearing the warmth and reassurance in his voice, knowing right then that I had done exactly the right thing by coming to London.

Derek's office was as plain and ordinary as the building itself. Photos of the Beatles appeared in haphazard places on the stark white walls, but there was Derek's high-backed, white wicker chair, shipped all the way from his office in Los Angeles. "The throne of Apple," he lovingly called it. "If you didn't know what it had seen and where it had been," he wrote many years later, "you wouldn't give fifty dollars for it." I wonder where that chair is now. I hope it's somewhere, and I hope whoever owns it appreciates where it's been.

"Sit down, luv, tell me about your trip, did everything go well, how was the flight, when did you arrive, did you find your way around London, how is your room, are people treating you well?" Derek said, lighting up a cigarette, his eyes inviting me to tell him every detail. I was entertaining him with my description of the truly awful bacon served by the Indian couple who owned the B&B when a middle-aged woman dressed in an apron walked into the room pushing a trolley filled with pots of tea and coffee, china cups and saucers, a pitcher of milk, a bowl of sugar, and assorted English tea cookies.

"Would you like a cup of tea?" she asked in the sweetest voice. Imagine! A tea lady! After pouring each of us a steaming cup of strong, dark tea, she disappeared with a little squeak of the trolley wheels.

Derek and I gratefully sipped our milk-filled tea as I continued my story about my first two days in London.

"Very adventurous of you!" Derek said, tapping his cigarette in the ashtray with one hand and playing with the cigarette box with his other hand, flipping it up and over, up and over. "So, Chris, do you really want to work at Apple?"

"Well, yes, of course, I'd love to work here," I said, laughing nervously.

Derek sat back in his throne, lacing his fingers together and smiling, the beneficent Prince of Appledom. "Well, I think we should be able to do something. But first things first—you can't stay in that bed and breakfast, it sounds depressing and besides, it's too far from the office. I'll get one of the secretaries to book you into a hotel nearby."

Derek had work to do, but he invited me to sit in his office and observe the goings-on. The action seemed never to stop. In walked the man from the *"This man has talent!"* poster. His name was Alistair Taylor, and he was Apple's general manager. Derek told me that Alistair had been with the Beatles since 1961 when he was working as Brian Epstein's assistant at NEMS (North End Music Store) in Liverpool and accompanied him to the Cavern to hear a new band called the Beatles play to wildly enthusiastic crowds; weeks later Alistair witnessed the first contract signed between the Beatles and Brian, their new manager.

Following right on Alistair's heels was Peter Brown, an executive director at Apple and personal assistant to the Beatles. Peter Brown (nobody ever called him just Peter) was one of the most distinguished-looking men I had ever met—tall and lean with a full neatly trimmed beard, polished English manners, and eyes that literally twinkled when he laughed, revealing the distinctive human being under the distinguished exterior. Every few minutes he'd pull at the sleeves of his freshly ironed shirt to make sure they extended the perfect inch below the cuffs of his tailor-made Tommy Nutter suit. Everyone at Apple had enormous respect for Peter Brown, who was one of the only people at Apple with direct and immediate access to the Beatles and their wives or girlfriends, and the only person at Apple who knew exactly what they were doing at any particular moment of the day or night.

Sometime in midafternoon I was leafing through a magazine, feeling a little sleepy, when Derek suddenly jumped up from his desk.

"It sounds like Paul's here," he said on his way out of the office. "I need to have a word with him. I'll be right back."

I could hear people talking through the wall, and I had to restrain myself from jumping up and peeking out the door to see who it was. Paul? Was Paul McCartney on the other side of that wall? My heart was thumping and my palms were sweating. I could not believe that I was this close to Paul McCartney. I could hear that famous voice and I couldn't grasp the fact that he was right here, in the same building as me. It seemed so unreal.

"Paul, this just came in the post," a female voice called out. I could sense the excitement in the reception area as doors opened and closed and more people joined the conversation.

"What do you think of this jacket for the Apple Boutique?" someone said.

"Well, that's not bad, is it?" That was Paul's voice. "Yes. Lovely. That will do, eh?"

Several minutes passed before Derek came back into his office chatting amiably with someone, and my heart did a little flip-flop thinking it was Paul. I was sitting with my back to the door, facing Derek's desk, and I kept staring straight ahead at the only wall with a window, not wanting to be rude or presumptuous by turning around and interrupting the conversation.

"Chris, meet Neil Aspinall," Derek said. *Phew,* I thought. I wasn't quite ready to meet one of the Beatles, but I knew from everything Derek had told me that Neil wasn't far removed. He'd been with the band since they were just a local Liverpool group, even before Ringo became the drummer. George Harrison called Neil "the fifth Beatle."

"Any friend of Derek's is a friend of ours," Neil said. A ruggedly handsome man with prematurely thinning hair and gentle eyes, Neil always had a half smile on his face even in the most serious moments. Sometimes I thought it was his way of encouraging the rest of us to loosen up and take things lightly, and other times I wondered if he was masking his real feelings with a disarming grin. I'd soon discover that Neil could be a toughie at times.

Derek was telling Neil how I had helped chauffeur him around Los Angeles when I heard a voice behind me and felt someone brush past my chair.

"Neil, have you any idea if John is coming in today?" Paul said.

"John and Yoko are in my office now," Neil said.

The conversation continued between Derek, Neil, and Paul McCartney, but I can't remember one word of it. All I could think about was the fact that Paul McCartney was standing right in front of me, close enough that I could have reached out and touched him, and John Lennon and Yoko Ono were a few steps away. Was this really happening?

"Paul, this is Chris O'Dell," Derek was saying, "a friend from Los Angeles."

"Hullo, Chris," Paul said, smiling down at me.

"Hi," I said, smiling up at him. As hard as I tried, I couldn't get that stupid smile off my face. It was frozen there.

Paul, Neil, and Derek returned to their conversation while I quietly excused myself, giving Derek a little wave as I left the office. It was all too much for me. I walked into the reception area, expecting to be alone and hoping to pull myself back together, but sitting on a small sofa, as close together as they could be without sitting right on top of each other, were John and Yoko. They both turned at the same time to see who had entered the room. I smiled. They smiled back.

I stayed at the Apple offices until eight o'clock that night, when Derek left to catch the train to his country home and I jumped in a taxi for my last night in the bed and breakfast. I didn't have a job yet, but I had already made up my mind that I would show up for work every day until someone gave me something to do.

I had walked into that building a fan, just like the rest of the world, adoring the Beatles from afar. They had been pictures in magazines, images on the television screen, or at the cinema, voices on vinyl, all fitting into my own little fantasy. But that had all changed in a matter of hours. I had seen them, talked to them, occupied the same space they did. And they, perhaps only for a second, knew who I was. Never again would my life be the same. I had crossed the line and entered into their world. I knew instantly that I belonged there.

4

LUNCH AT THE ARETUSA

May 22, 1968

My third day at Apple was off to a good start.

"Why don't you join me for lunch today?" Derek asked when I walked into his office Wednesday morning around nine. It was May 22, 1968, my fifth day in London.

"Great!" I said with a big smile.

"Are you settled into your hotel?"

"Almost," I said. The night before, I'd moved my two suitcases and my transistor radio into a hotel in the West End. When the bellman opened the door to my room, my mouth fell open and I let out an audible "Oooohhh." The room was the size of a large walk-in closet, with one twin bed cuddled up against the wall and a dresser and mirror hugging the opposite wall. A small window looked out on a narrow alley, and the building across the way blocked all sunlight. But at least I had my own bathroom, a definite improvement over the bed and breakfast, and I'd only be there for a short time, until I found a place of my own.

"Good," he said absentmindedly, already back at work editing a press release.

I wandered down the hallway to see if Richard DiLello needed any help. Everyone called Richard "the house hippie"—he had curly Afro-style hair, he was often stoned on hash, and he definitely had an "everything's cool" attitude. On my second day at Apple, Derek suggested that I could keep myself busy by helping Richard paste news clippings into scrapbooks. When I opened the door to the small unfurnished office Richard was using, he was sitting on the floor, surrounded by hundreds of cut-out newspaper articles, scissors in hand, scrapbooks open. I plunked down on the floor next to him, and as we cut and pasted he told me stories about his days at Apple and offered suggestions about how I might nail down a job. Keep being seen, be helpful, don't get in the way, and try not to make the other girls jealous was the gist of it.

Just before noon I grabbed my purse and walked down the hallway to Derek's office. George Harrison was standing next to Derek's desk, stubbing out his cigarette in the ashtray.

"Oh, hullo there," he said in a curious voice, "and who are you?"

Derek, as always, came to my rescue. "George, this is Chris O'Dell, a friend from LA."

"Are you coming to lunch?" George asked, and without waiting for an answer, he was striding across the room and out the door.

George drove us in his Mercedes to the Club Del'Aretusa on the King's Road where, I learned, we were meeting Don Short, a journalist from the *Daily Mirror*. I sat in the backseat listening to Derek and George banter back and forth, thinking how much alike they were with their witty remarks and quick rejoinders. They could have been brothers. I was surprised, actually, to discover that George was so attractive in person. I'd always thought of Paul as the cute one, but up close George was ruggedly handsome, even striking, with his long hair curling up just above the shoulders, his face smooth and clear, and those dark, intense eyes. But it was definitely his smile that hooked me—this incredibly sexy, crooked grin, almost a friendly sneer (*like Elvis*, I thought) that etched little lines in his cheeks, bringing your attention simultaneously to his heart-shaped face and his slightly crooked teeth.

Every few minutes Derek turned around in his seat. "You okay, luv?" he'd ask, and I'd nod my head and smile, feeling a little dreamy from the incense that seemed to linger around George, permeating the air everywhere he went. I was as happy as I could ever be listening to them talk in their Liverpool accents while taking in all the sights of the King's

Road—the quaint little bookshops with the hanging flower baskets, the fashionable shops and fancy restaurants with their mannequins and daily specials, the wrought-iron gates surrounding the old Georgian buildings, the gargoyles with their tongues hanging out, the double-decker buses packed with tourists, and the London Black Cabs with the large grills and yellow signs on the top. London. Apple. Lunch with Derek and George. I was in heaven.

As the waiter led us to the back of the room, I noticed people staring as we walked past their tables. I felt horribly uncomfortable in my blue-and-orange-checked skirt with its matching cape. My outfit looked like it came right off the rack of J.C. Penney, not from one of the fancy boutiques along the King's Road. I'm definitely going to have to buy some new clothes, I told myself, drawing my cape closer around me. I felt so out of place, so unhip. I might as well have had a sign on my forehead that said "American." Sensing that I was out of my element, Derek put his hand on my back to comfort me and help steer me through the crowd.

I was greatly relieved when we reached our table against the far wall, separated from the other diners. The table, set for four places, was beautifully laid out with silver cutlery and crystal wineglasses. Derek sat next to me and Don took the seat next to George across the table from us. George took a seat across the table. After a while I began to relax—it must have had something to do with the wine bottles that kept getting replaced—and as we ate lunch I listened contentedly to their conversation. I've always liked sitting back and observing people, and George, in particular, fascinated me. I watched him chatting with Derek and Don, his dark eyes intently focused, the thick eyebrows almost touching in the middle, and every so often he'd look over at me and smile; I had the feeling he was reassuring me that I had nothing to fear from this group. At the same time, George had this interesting way of keeping his distance from people. Occasionally his eyes would dart around the room, not so much to see what was happening, it seemed to me, but more as a self-protective, "don't come any closer" look. It was almost as if he were creating boundaries with his eyes. And it worked, because nobody bothered us.

The lunch crowd thinned out, the noise died down, and for a while we were the only people left in that big, bright room. Then, suddenly, as if from nowhere, a whole new crowd spilled into the restaurant, filling up the tables, ratcheting up the noise level, and creating a partylike atmosphere.

"What's going on?" I asked Derek.

"The fashion show is going to start shortly."

"What fashion show?"

"Oh dear, did I forget to mention that?" Derek seemed to find my wide-eyed confusion amusing. "This is the opening of the new Apple Boutique for men."

Photographers and journalists were swarming around the table, taking pictures, asking questions, lightly nudging themselves into position (this was when the press were still civilized) as John and Yoko arrived at the table. Two chairs were hurriedly added to the table, and Yoko sat down next to me.

"This is their first public appearance together," Derek whispered to me, which explained why the press was all over them. John fielded the questions, while Yoko appeared to cling to him even as she sat straight backed in her chair, still as a stone, never saying a word. Her long, black hair was parted in the middle and looked as if it were charged with electricity. I had the feeling that if I reached out and touched her, I'd get shocked.

Over the next few months as I got to know her better, I learned that she wasn't the fearful type, but that day I felt sorry for her. She looked so tiny and helpless, with that deer-in-the-headlights look. Maybe she needs a friend, I thought.

"You're doing great," I said, leaning over and whispering to her. She turned her head slowly, a curious expression on her face, and gave me a vacant smile. Then she turned away from me to focus on John, giving him that adoring look that we would all come to know so well.

Ouch. That didn't go so well. I knew immediately that Yoko was the kind of person who I'd find it difficult to be around—she didn't ask for much, but she didn't give very much either. That's what I was thinking when Pattie Harrison appeared at the table and sat next to George, almost directly across from me. I'm afraid I stared at her for a moment in disbelief. Back in LA, when I was thinking about moving to London, I'd sometimes play a little game in front of my bathroom mirror. I'd imagine that Pattie and I were friends, sitting in her kitchen, laughing and talking about silly things, sharing our secrets. I know it might seem like I'm making all this up after the fact, but it's the truth—I did daydream about being friends with Pattie long before I met her, and I had other dreams that came true, too.

But this was real life. I felt stupid sitting there watching everyone else talking and interacting. I needed to start a conversation and make a connection with someone, if only to justify my place at the table.

"I love the way you do your makeup," I blurted out to Pattie. She looked confused, even a little flustered.

"Thank you," she said after what seemed an eternity. *Well, you're in it now,* I thought. *Might as well keep the conversation going.*

"Do you think you might someday show me how to do my makeup?" I said, stumbling a little over my words. Again she smiled at me, looking more amused than annoyed. Still, I was painfully aware that I was straddling a fine line between making a friend and making a complete fool of myself.

"I'm a friend of Derek's," I said. "I just moved to London last week, so I don't know very many people. Perhaps we could get together sometime." I couldn't believe my own audacity.

"Yes," she said, looking very queenly in her poise and stature. "That's a possibility."

Well, that was enough for me. I didn't need a time, a date, or a place. All I needed was the possibility of spending an hour or two with Pattie Harrison.

The waiters were clearing the lunch plates, wineglasses were refilled, photographers and journalists jockeyed for position, and the hum of conversation died down as we turned our chairs to face the runway.

After the fashion show Derek and I walked down the King's Road to the new Apple Boutique. John and Yoko were walking just ahead of us. When we came to a street corner, John slowed down and whispered something to Derek, who looked at me and smiled.

"He wanted to know who you were," Derek told me a few minutes later. " 'Who is that attractive girl you're with?' were his exact words."

An image flashed in my mind of the night when my sister and I, seated in the far reaches of the balcony at Dodger Stadium, watched the Beatles perform on August 28, 1966. They were so far away that they actually looked like tiny bugs (beetles?) moving around on the stage, but that didn't matter to us because just knowing we were in the same place on earth as the Beatles was enough. And now John was walking just a few steps ahead of me on a London street, hand in hand with Yoko, wondering who I was. Even in my wildest dreams I could never have imagined *this* moment.

5

JAMES TAYLOR

May 22–23, 1968

"Chris, you needn't be alone this evening," Derek said later that day. After the boutique opening, we took a taxi back to Apple where Derek returned dozens of phone calls, and I sat in his office reliving the day in my mind.

The more time I spent with Derek, the more he took on that fatherly role, watching out for me, worrying about me, even hovering over me a bit. In those early days at Apple, I'd spend hours sitting on the chair in his office, leafing through magazines, watching and waiting for my lucky break while he'd carry on with business as usual, answering phone calls, writing press releases, entertaining visitors, and checking in with me every now and then to make sure I was okay.

"I'm fine, Derek, don't worry about me," I said. Actually I couldn't wait to be alone. I was tired and slightly hung over from the wine at lunch, and I still needed to unpack my bags and settle into my new hotel room.

"Let me ring up this nice American lad who's here in London. He would be great company for you."

I didn't want to meet a nice American lad. I wanted to go to bed.

"He's from North Carolina. A songwriter. Wonderful voice. Peter

Asher just signed him to Apple Records." Derek was talking in spurts, conscious of the time and the fact that he had a train to catch.

"An American?" I tried not to sound too disappointed. I really wasn't interested in hanging out with an American—I wanted to meet people from England. I must have been really tired because I was a little irritated with Derek. He was usually so sensitive to my needs, why didn't he realize that the last thing I wanted to do on my fifth night in London was spend a boring evening entertaining a nice American?

"His name is James," Derek said, reaching for the phone and looking again at his watch. "He's rather shy, but I think you'll enjoy one another." I looked at Derek, my expression quizzical, and he gave me a funny little smile. *What does that mean?* I wondered. *Is he playing the matchmaker?*

"James! Hullo there, it's Derek Taylor. Listen, there's a lovely young lady sitting across from me who I'd like you to entertain this evening. She's just arrived from America and doesn't know anyone in London. Would you be free?"

I realized that I had tensed up, hoping the voice on the other end of the line would decline the offer. Maybe he was tired, too. Maybe, like me, he had no desire whatsoever to meet another American.

"That's great!" Derek said. "Her name is Chris O'Dell. Why don't you meet at her hotel around, say, eight o'clock?"

So that's how it happened that exactly at eight o'clock that night there was a knock on my door and I opened it to find a tall, gangly, handsome young man smiling shyly at me. He had long brown hair and carried a guitar case.

"Hi," I said. "I'm Chris O'Dell."

"Hi, I'm James Taylor," he said.

"Come in," I said, stepping aside to make room for him to pass by me. There was barely enough room for him to walk by, even with my back up against the wall. That was the smallest room I'd ever seen.

"I'm really sorry if Derek ruined your evening," I said. "I guess he was worried I'd get lonely."

"No problem. I wasn't doing anything anyway. It's cool." Very gently he laid his guitar case on the floor and then sat down next to it, his back against the wall. I perched on the edge of the twin bed and tried to get a conversation going. He sure was slow to warm up, but once I got him talking about himself, he opened up a little. He told me he'd been vacationing in Formentera, a little island off the southern coast of Spain, and he was recovering from a love affair that had gone bad. He didn't give me many details, but I could tell he was in some kind of pain. What I didn't know then was that he was addicted to heroin and was trying to get clean, so I might have confused his physical distress with emotional torment, although usually they travel together.

"How did you end up in London?" I asked.

"I met Peter Asher through a mutual friend, he liked my material, and he brought me here," James said, his arm draped protectively around his guitar case, his eyes staring at the speckled brown carpet. Every once in a while he'd glance up at me and give me a really nice shy smile before returning his gaze to the floor. He told me that he liked Peter, and he thought signing with Apple would be a good thing. I was surprised that he wasn't more excited about the whole thing, but I soon learned that this was James's style—he wasn't exactly the effusive type.

After dinner at a nearby pub, we spent hours talking in the hotel room, sharing stories about our lives, our experiences in London, and the whirlwind of my days at Apple. It was after midnight when James opened his guitar case and began to play while I listened, absorbing the gentle energy of his music and feeling so relaxed I could have drifted right off to sleep.

Somewhere around two in the morning I began to wonder if he was ever going to leave. I decided to give him a big hint.

"Gosh, it's getting late," I said with a big yawn. "Aren't you tired?"

James stopped his humming and strumming for just a moment and shook his head. "No," he said in his lazy sort of way. "I always stay up late. It's a great time to write."

Shit, I thought, *now what am I supposed to do?* I didn't want to be rude, so I sat on my bed for another half hour or so, listening to him strum his guitar and sing quietly under his breath. How was I going to fall asleep with this guy singing in my room? *Oh man,* I thought, *Derek is going to pay for this.*

"James, I really need to go to bed now," I said finally.

"Oh, sure, go ahead. I'm just going to work on this song a little longer."

Surely he wasn't planning to stay? What did he want from me? Was he expecting to go to bed with me? Nothing even remotely sexual had passed between us the whole night. Why didn't he leave? Maybe he sensed my confusion, because he seemed to emerge from his songwriting fog for a moment.

"Look, you don't mind if I stay the night, do you? It's kinda late and I'd like to finish this song and crash."

"Oh. Well, the bed's not very big." I looked at my twin bed with a "gee, I'm sorry" look and hoped he'd get the message. James was a tall guy—skinny, but really tall—and I was tired. I didn't want to share my bed with him.

"Well," he said, following my lead and looking at the bed, "it's okay for me if you don't mind. I could always sleep on the floor if it's a problem."

What was I going to do, kick him out in the middle of the night? He clearly wasn't going to leave. But what if he came on to me when the lights were out? I didn't trust myself—saying no wasn't exactly in my repertoire of responses at that time of my life. I knew I had to do something to defuse the situation, and I had a secret weapon, the ultimate turn-off—if James had any ideas about having sex with me, I'd instantly eradicate them.

"Okay, you can stay if you like, but I'm getting ready for bed," I said, sitting down at the dressing table. I opened the drawer containing my hair rollers. Now these weren't just any hair rollers. I had packed six jumbo frozen orange juice cans, both ends removed—no wonder I needed two big suitcases—and I began to roll my hair around the cans, securing them with jumbo-sized hairpins.

James was so absorbed in his music that he didn't even notice. I went into the bathroom to change into my nightgown, and when I returned, James was still oblivious to my presence, so I got in bed without a word and turned toward the wall. The rollers were a bit awkward, but I'd gotten used to them and knew how to position my head so they didn't poke into my scalp. I fell asleep to the soft strumming of James's guitar.

I woke up the next morning to discover that James had somehow managed to squeeze himself into the bed, between me and the wall. When he heard me get out of bed, he stretched and yawned.

"I hope you weren't too crowded," he said.

"No, it was fine," I said, and it really was, although I have no idea how either of us managed to get any sleep at all. I sat down at the dressing table to take out my rollers.

"James, I have to leave soon," I said. "Do you want to stay here and sleep in?"

"No," he said, sitting up on the bed and stretching, "I'll leave with you."

I combed my hair and began to tease the top layers to get some height on top, adding lots of hair spray, while James reached for his guitar and started to play the song he'd been working on the night before. Suddenly he stopped.

"Hey, Chris," he said, "why do you wear those orange juice cans in your hair?"

I laughed, a little embarrassed and wondering, too, if he saw through my ploy of the night before.

"Well, they smooth out the curl and add some lift," I said.

"Oh." I think I gave him a little too much information. "Hey, are you done in the bathroom?"

"Yeah, sure," I said. I watched him shuffle into the bathroom, eyes looking at the floor as usual, guitar in hand. He shut the door and began to sing, much louder than the night before. *He really is odd,* I thought. I didn't know then that musicians often like to sing in the bathroom because of the acoustics.

Ten minutes later he opened the door and asked if I would mind coming into the bathroom to listen to the song he was working on. While I put on my makeup in front of the bathroom mirror, he sat on the toilet playing his guitar and singing his new song about missing Carolina, seeing the sunshine, feeling the moonshine.

He was homesick, that much was clear. And I wasn't. In fact, I was a little impatient because I wanted to get to Apple before everyone else arrived. I didn't want to miss anything.

But as I listened and began to relax into the music, my impatience eased. The sound in that tiny bathroom was so rich and full that I didn't want him to stop. I felt as if he were singing straight from the depths of his soul, exposing his loneliness and longing to me and in response, I loosened up, softened, released. Had I made a mistake with the curlers?

"James, that was truly beautiful," I said when he stopped singing and looked up at me.

He thanked me, and I had the feeling that I could say a thousand words of praise about the song and still it might not be enough to still his troubled mind.

"Would you like to come to my rehearsal?" he said as he put his guitar back into its case. I noticed that he had slender, strong, beautiful hands. "I'm meeting the band in an hour. We could get some breakfast on the way."

"I'd like that," I said. And that's how I spent the morning of my sixth day in London, watching James Taylor and his band rehearse at the Apple Publishing office on the floor just above the Apple Boutique.

6

FIRST SESSION

June–July 1968

I wanted a job. I wanted to know everything about Apple, to find my way into the thick of things, and make myself indispensable so someone would notice me and put me to work. I'd show up early and leave late, trying not to get in the way while hoping to be noticed for my helpfulness. I didn't have much of a social life, but that was fine by me because Apple was my social life. I was living now with Dee, a secretary from the office, in a cold, damp basement in Paddington. Every night after we arrived home from Apple, we put coins in two meters outside the flat to turn on the heat and electricity. That seemed quaint at first but got old really fast. One night we were listening to music when all the lights went out, and more than once we ran out of change for the meters and spent the night shivering in the cold and the dark.

I had a few close friends—Leslie Cavendish, the Beatles' hairdresser and now mine (he gave me the most fabulous layered haircut), and Francie Schwartz, an American who had worked for Derek in the press office. Francie was now going out with Paul, who had recently broken up with his fiancée Jane Asher, Peter's sister. That made me jealous, but I wasn't focusing on romance at the time. The only thing that mattered to me in my first month at Apple was figuring out some way to land a steady job. So I continued helping Richard in the press clipping room and I hovered around the reception area, trying to make myself useful. I got a lot of little odd jobs that way.

One day I was hanging out in the hallway off the reception area talking to Laurie in the tiny room where she operated the switchboard.

"You know, I used to work as a switchboard operator back in Los Angeles," I said. "I'd be happy to help if you ever need an extra hand."

Laurie spent a moment thinking about my offer. Slightly overweight and very shy, with rosy cheeks, flawless skin, and a lovely, lilting phone voice, Laurie was fiercely protective of the Beatles. She'd been in charge of the Beatles fan club in Liverpool, and when Brian Epstein moved to London, he brought her with him. I think she liked me well enough, although I suspect she put up with me in part because I was a friend of Derek's, a temporary visitor who was in no danger of becoming a permanent fixture.

"Thanks, luv," she said. "Perhaps you could relieve me sometime when I take a break or go for lunch?"

"Sure," I said calmly, although inside I was squirming with excitement because now I had two part-time jobs, helping Richard with the press clippings and relieving Laurie at the switchboard.

A few days later I was working at the switchboard when Paul McCartney stuck his head into the tiny room. Of all the Beatles, Paul spent the most time at Apple, coming in almost every day and making the rounds of the offices, saying hello to everyone, and asking how we were doing.

"Hullo there!" he said, surprised to see me working the switchboard. "How's it going?"

Every time I saw Paul my heart jumped around a bit. I didn't think he was all that attached to Francie, and I was just waiting for him to be available again.

"Hi," I said, stumbling over the one-syllable word. Whenever a Beatle was nearby, my intelligence seemed to drop several percentage points along with my ability to communicate.

"Well, I see you've found a job," he said with a big smile. It seemed that every time I saw Paul he'd ask me if I was looking for a job. I always laughed but never answered with a yes or no. I didn't want to seem pushy.

"Just helping out." I smiled back. I adjusted my headset, took a deep breath, and figured what the hell. "But yes, I would like a job, something permanent," I said with more bravado than I felt.

"Stick around. You never know what's going to happen," Paul said. *Ooh*, I thought when he disappeared into the hallway, *that was encouraging*.

When Laurie returned a few minutes later, I wandered out into the hallway where Paul was talking to Mal Evans. Mal was the Beatles' road manager or, as Derek called him, "chief bodyguard." What that meant, I'd soon learn, was that you had to get through Mal—a burly guy who took his job seriously—to get anywhere near the Beatles. That worked out well for Mal because all the young women who threw themselves at the Beatles ended up bouncing off Mal, who was more than happy to entertain them.

"What's this?" Paul laughed when he saw me. "You out of a job already?"

"Back to the press clippings!" I said cheerfully, listening in a bit to their conversation. Mal was asking Paul about the recording session scheduled for that evening at Abbey Road Studios.

"Tricky business, this recording," Paul said, mostly for my benefit. He was being friendly and including me in the conversation.

I honestly don't know where I found the nerve to say what I said next although what went through my mind was, *Go ahead, take the leap!* I must have been hearing the voices of my mother and grandmother, both independent, outspoken women, reminding me that if I didn't ask for something, how was I ever going to get it? All he could say was no. What could I lose?"

"I'd love to come to a session sometime," I said. "Do you think I could come tonight?"

Paul looked at Mal, just a quick glance, and then turned back to me, an amused expression on his face.

"Why not?" he said. "Talk to Mal. He'll organize it for you."

Moments later Barbara, the head secretary who worked for Neil Aspinall and Peter Brown, pulled me aside. She'd overheard the conversation and was waiting for Paul and Mal to walk away.

"Chris, you can't do that," she said.

"Do what?"

"The recording sessions are closed. None of us is allowed to go into the studio."

"But Paul just told me it was okay." I was confused. "He said I should talk to Mal and Mal would arrange it."

"Paul had to say it was okay. You put him on the spot." Barbara fixed me with a look that said, "I've been here longer, so you need to listen to me."

Barbara's comment stunned me—Paul was a Beatle, after all. How could I put him on the spot when all he had to do was say no, and that was the end of that? I looked at Laurie, who had joined the conversation and was nodding her head in agreement with Barbara.

"She's right, Chris," Laurie said. "Brian never allowed anyone in the recording sessions. Why, when Brian was alive, we weren't even allowed to go to social events with the lads."

But Brian Epstein is dead, I thought. The Beatles themselves didn't seem to care about the old code of ethics as they sauntered through the Apple offices, socializing with everyone from the Tea Lady to the House Hippie. Times had changed, hadn't they? And it was a good thing, wasn't it? After all, the Beatles weren't Brian Epstein's "lads" anymore— they were the bosses of a whole new empire, not to mention the most famous people in the entire world.

I felt sorry for Barbara and Laurie—they seemed old-fashioned, stuck in the past. Those girls are never going to get anywhere, I found myself thinking. They're going to miss out on all the fun. All their talk about rules made no sense to me. Where were the rules and who enforced them? If someone like Derek or Neil or Peter Brown had said, "By the way, Chris, never ask the Beatles if you can go to their sessions, that's just not done," then I would have known there was a real rule, and I would have followed it. (Reluctantly, I have to admit.) But no one ever established that decree, and so it made perfect sense to me that I could at least ask if I could go to a session. Why not? That was the question: why not? How was I supposed to know what I could or couldn't do if I didn't go ahead and ask?

Still, I had to be careful not to alienate Barbara and Laurie, because they had been with the Beatles for ages. And I wanted them to like me; I don't like it when people don't like me. But even more important, and definitely more calculated, I knew that if the secretaries disapproved of me, I wouldn't last long at Apple.

"Thanks for the advice," I said. "I really appreciate knowing how things are done around here."

I escaped into the press clipping room. Richard was sitting on the floor, lost as usual in a world of his own. A loner in many ways, Richard had an admirable ability to remove himself from all the chaos and activity in the office; he knew, in other words, how to stay out of the shit. Richard looked like a hippie, talked like a hippie, and acted like a hippie, but here he was at Apple Corps Ltd., right smack in the center of everything. Smart hippie.

"Hi, what's up?" he said, looking up at me from his seat on the floor.

"You won't believe what just happened!" I sat down next to him and told him the story.

He laughed in his quiet, knowing way and glued a piece of paper into the scrapbook.

"Don't worry," he said, "they'll get used to you."

Later that afternoon I ran into Mal in the hallway.

"Paul said I needed to talk to you about coming to the session," I said. "Would it be okay if I stopped by?"

"No problem," he said, "just come by whenever you fancy."

I left Apple around eight that evening and took a taxi straight to EMI's Abbey Road studios. The uniformed guard at the reception desk smiled pleasantly. "Good evening," he said. "May I help you?"

"Yes, I hope so," I said, suddenly a little nervous about the whole adventure. I hadn't expected a guard. "I'm here to see Mal Evans."

The guard asked me to take a seat and disappeared down the hallway, returning a few moments later.

"He'll make his way here as soon as he's free, miss."

I waited. Half an hour later Mal appeared and sat down next to me. We chatted about all kinds of things—Apple goings-on, the weather, what he had for dinner—but he never once mentioned going into the studio. After a while I realized Mal was just passing the time and had no intention of taking me back with him. I was disappointed and a little miffed because just a few hours earlier he had led me to believe I could sit in on a session. I could have asked him straight out—can we go to the studio now?—but he knew why I was there, and I had some pride, after all. I was also afraid that if I asked, he'd explain the "rule" to me and then I'd never get in. So I just sat there, pretending to enjoy our conversation, all the while thinking that Barbara and Laurie were right about the "rule." It may not have been written down anywhere, but it sure was in force.

I also felt like Mal was coming on to me, which made me a little nervous because of the rumors I'd heard about Mal getting the girls the Beatles didn't want. I didn't want Mal to think I was hanging around Apple or the studio on the off chance that one of the Beatles might take a fancy to me (or slough me off to Mal). I wasn't there for social reasons; I wanted to know everything about Apple, to find my way into the thick of things, and make myself indispensable. But that night, it seemed, I wasn't going to get any farther than the reception area. I was thinking about going home and getting some sleep when a young man with curly, reddish-blond hair and a mustache sauntered into the reception area.

"Hey, Mal," he said, "the lads need you." Like Mal, he had an impenetrable accent that started out in the back of his throat, lifted up like song, and twanged like sheet metal.

"Thanks, Pete, I'll be right back," Mal said as he hurried off down the hall.

"I'm Pete Shotton," he said, taking Mal's seat and giving me a firm handshake.

"Hi, I'm Chris O'Dell," I said.

"So what are you doing here, Chris?"

Pete was a great listener, leaning toward me with his forearms on his knees, looking directly into my eyes as I told him about moving to London and hoping to get a job at Apple.

"And what about you? Why are you here?" I said, warming to him immediately. He had this little-boy way about him, with his curly hair and eyes that glinted with mirth and mischief when he smiled.

"I'm a friend of John's. I'm in London this week to do some work for him." I learned later that Pete was one of the original Quarrymen, the band John Lennon started when he was sixteen. Pete played the washboard. According to the story Pete told me, he often suffered from stage fright and one day when he was moaning and groaning about having to perform live, John took the washboard and hit him over the head. Pete quit the band, but he and John remained great friends.

"Well, I'm going back in the studio," Pete said, standing up and stretching. "Would you like to come with me?"

After all that waiting and hoping, I was suddenly unsure of myself. "I don't know if I should," I said. "Mal knew I was coming tonight, but he didn't invite me in."

"Well, I'm inviting you in," Pete said, reaching for my hand. "Don't worry. If you're with me, it's no problem."

And that's how I first entered the sacred Inner Sanctum. Pete led me through a basement door that opened directly into the vast, high-ceilinged room. A piano and various musical instruments were strewn about. The smell of stale cigarette smoke permeated the chilly air; when I shivered, Pete told me they always lowered the temperature in the studio to keep the instruments in tune. We were alone in the studio, but upstairs in the control room I could see people moving around.

"Let's sit over there," Pete said in a hushed, almost reverential voice, leading me to the piano bench. We sat down and waited in the dimly lit room. A cigarette in the ashtray was still smoking. Moments later the lights in the studio got brighter, the door to the control room opened, and John and Yoko walked down the stairs to the studio.

"Hey, Pete," John said, smiling and nodding at me. He picked up his guitar and sat down on a chair in the middle of the studio. Yoko sat next to John, pulling her chair close to his. She looked so small and fragile under the bright lights. She smiled at me, too, and then put her hands between her legs, as if to warm them.

"Okay, John, just add that bit after the bridge," a disembodied voice said over the intercom from the control room. The sound seemed suspended in the air above that vast, chilly space. I shivered again, partly from excitement and partly because the place was so damn cold.

John had headphones on and his foot was tap-tap-tapping on the floor, keeping time to the music, which only he could hear.

"We've got it," the voice upstairs said at the same time the control room door opened again and Paul, Ringo, and George came bounding down the stairs to the studio. Paul gave me a funny little smile, his head tilting slightly to the side as if to say, Hey, you actually made it! George winked at me, and Ringo, who I hadn't met yet, just gave me a perplexed look, clearly wondering who I was.

They stood around the microphone waiting for the people in the control room to start the tape.

"So what are we doing?" Ringo asked, looking around at the others like a little schoolboy who had fallen asleep during a lesson.

"We need some more background sound on the track," Paul said in his take-charge way.

"Pete, you can help us out," John said. "Actually, both of you can help."

Pete stood up and took hold of my arm, but I pulled back.

"No, I can't," I said. I was terrified.

"Why not?" Pete couldn't figure me out. John Lennon was asking me to help out on a Beatle track and I was hesitating?

"I can't sing," I said.

Pete laughed and pulled me to my feet. "You don't have to sing. Trust me. You'll be fine."

We joined Paul, Ringo, George, John, and Yoko at the microphone. Someone handed me a set of headphones. I was petrified and stuck close to Pete, depending on him to keep me from making a fool of myself.

"Testing one-two-three-," Paul said into the mic.

"Sounds good," said the voice from the control room. "We're just adding claps, right, John?"

"Yeah, and anything else that pops up." John laughed.

To my absolute and undying relief, nothing else popped up, and all I had to do was clap my hands. The red light over the control room went on, and I clapped as hard as I could. I never asked the name of the track they were working on because I was too caught up in the moment, but I think it was "Revolution 9."

Just as the song was ending, John scrunched up a piece of paper right in front of the microphone. I thought about all the strange sound effects on the *Sgt. Pepper* album and smiled to myself.

So, I thought, it's as simple as that.

7

THE LADY IS A CHAMP

Summer 1968

"You two look busy," Derek said one day, sticking his head in the office and making a face at the disorganized mess of newspapers, scissors, glue, and scrapbooks. "Look, Harry Nilsson is flying into town today to meet the Beatles. Would you be able to pick him up at the airport, Chris?"

"Sure!" I said. I was excited—this would be my first real assignment for Apple. I took the bus, hoping to save Apple money (only to realize later that no one else worried much about saving money, at least not at that time), but that was a huge mistake because the bus stopped about a hundred times before finally making it to the airport. Fifteen minutes late, I ran inside the terminal, searching everywhere for Harry and afraid that I had missed him and blown my first big responsibility. I knew who to look for because I'd met Harry once before, in LA at a private screening Derek organized to celebrate the release of *Magical Mystery Tour*. I scanned the baggage claim area looking for a tall, blond twenty-seven-year-old man with an aw-shucks manner and a killer smile. And there he was, following a limo driver who was carrying his bags and headed out the door.

"Harry!" I yelled out, running to catch up with them. "Derek sent me to pick you up. I'm Chris O'Dell. I met you once back in LA."

"Hi, Chris, sure, I remember you," Harry said, although I'm pretty sure he didn't. As I'd soon discover, Harry was one of the nicest, kindest, gentlest guys you'd ever want to meet, and the last thing he would do was make me uncomfortable.

"Hey, that was really thoughtful of you to pick me up," Harry said, "but it seems that Ringo has kindly left his limo for us. Apparently, he and his wife just left for Spain. Do you have a car here?"

"No, I took the bus," I said.

"Well, come with us in the limo." That was fine by me. By the time we arrived at his hotel on Park Lane, Harry and I were fast friends, and I spent the rest of the day with him, meeting up with Derek for lunch, and then hanging out with Harry at the hotel, having a few drinks, getting to know each other. When he left to spend the evening with John Lennon, I took a taxi home, put some coins in the meters, and cozied up on the couch with a hot cup of dark tea with milk, a proper English way to end the day.

A few days later Peter Brown called me into his office. Always prim and proper, a little standoffish, Peter Brown was even more serious than usual.

"This is a very special, private recording, Chris," he said, handing me a manila envelope. "It's incredibly valuable, one of a kind. I want you to take a minicab to the EMI pressing plant. They're expecting you. They'll press the tape onto vinyl. I want you to stay with them and with this tape throughout the recording process. Make sure no other copies are made. Then bring the master tape and the record immediately back to me."

Something big was going on. I felt extremely important and wondered if perhaps I had passed the "trust" test. Richard told me that gaining trust with the Beatles was the number one priority. If you weren't trusted, you'd be out, but you had to gain that trust and prove that you weren't going to be one of those people who blabbed to the press. You had to do a good job and get the right results. I took the package and held it tight. Peter Brown had given me strict orders, and I was not about to mess this up.

The EMI pressing plant was in Hayes, about twelve miles outside London. I thought it took an awfully long time to get there, but I managed to enjoy the scenery while holding the envelope on my lap, my hands folded over it as if in prayer. What was this tape I was holding? Why was it so valuable? Who besides Peter Brown thought it was so important? As we pulled up to the big gray building (everything seemed gray in London), the driver told me the structure had been used to develop radar equipment and guided missiles in World War II and later housed the first television transmitter for the BBC. I asked the driver to wait, then walked into the reception area where, just as Peter Brown had promised, someone was expecting me. An old wind-up phonograph was on display in the reception area, and I stopped for a moment to admire it. I'd never seen one before.

We took the elevator to an upper floor and immediately stepped into a brightly lit room filled from one end to the other with a bunch of hissing and sighing machines and employees intently focused on their jobs. We walked to one of the smaller machines, and the man who greeted me reached out for the package, which I had been holding tightly to my chest. My initial instinct was to pull the envelope closer to me, and only reluctantly did I hand it over.

"Peter Brown said only the one pressing," I reminded him.

"Yes, he made that perfectly clear," he said, rather grimly but with the hint of a reassuring smile. I loosened up a bit then and watched, fascinated, as a technician put the tape in a machine, pushed some buttons, and the process of transferring the tape to vinyl began. Seven or eight minutes later the technician played it back to check the sound. Frank Sinatra's voice filled the space around us. We stood there, aghast. I looked at the technician who looked at the manager-type man who looked at me, and we all couldn't believe what we were hearing. Frank Sinatra was singing to the tune of "The Lady Is a Tramp" except that the words were changed to "the lady is a champ," and it was all about Maureen Starkey, Ringo's wife. *There's no one like her / She married Ringo, but she could have had Paul / That's why the lady is a champ,"* Sinatra crooned.

They put a special printed Apple label on the record, packaged it up all neat and tidy, and sent me back to Wigmore Street. Back in Peter Brown's office, the 45 rpm record safely in his possession, he told me the story behind the tape. "Maureen is a big Sinatra fan," Peter Brown explained, "and for her twenty-second birthday, Ringo asked Frank Sinatra if he would record a song for her. Songwriter Sammy Cahn agreed to rewrite the lyrics to 'The Lady Is a Tramp' and Sinatra recorded the tape in Los Angeles. We'll make a few more copies of the record and then destroy the master tape."

Wow, I thought, as I walked down the hallway to Derek's office, *so this is what power looks like.* You pick up the phone, ask Frank Sinatra for a favor, and he's happy to oblige because you're a Beatle (or you're directly connected to a Beatle), word gets around and other people, famous people and factory workers, are thrilled to be involved because the Beatles are, well, the Beatles. My world seemed to stretch out a little bit at that moment. I saw the possibilities that this kind of power could create. No door would be closed to you. No person could—or would—refuse you. With that kind of power, you could do anything you wanted.

But I was still a long way from wielding any kind of power at Apple that summer of 1968. Even with my patchwork of part-time jobs—running errands, helping Richard with the press clippings, relieving Laurie at the switchboard, and filling in for secretaries when they went on breaks—I had a lot of free time on my hands. Every day I'd spend an hour or two roaming the hallways trying to make myself useful. I needed a purpose, a role in which I could prove that I was vital to the Apple enterprise. I wanted to be irreplaceable.

One day that summer, about a month after I'd arrived at Apple, I was leafing through a magazine in the reception area, waiting to relieve Laurie at the switchboard, when Neil Aspinall walked in.

"Anyone wanna get lunches?" Neil was a man of few words, and the secretaries were accustomed to being asked to run across the street to get sandwiches for the daily lunch meeting of the Apple brass in Neil's office.

That day I was in the right place at the right time.

"I'll go!" I said, jumping up out of my chair. I noticed a look of relief on the receptionist's face.

"Great!" Neil said, smiling broadly at my "I'll do anything" attitude. He gave me some money and instructions to buy a selection of sandwiches at the shop across the street.

The next day I volunteered to get the lunches again, but I had a bright idea. What if I brought them something a little fancier than plain old sandwiches? After all, these guys were running an important new company, and they deserved something better than egg salad or ham and cheese. I walked down the street to a cute little Italian place and ordered spaghetti, veal scaloppini, lasagna, and a few additional pasta dishes. As I waited for the order, I realized that the Apple execs couldn't eat Italian food with their fingers, so I asked the restaurant owner if we could borrow some dishes and utensils.

"I work at Apple Records for the Beatles," I said, "and I wondered if you might be willing to lend us plates and silverware for these fabulous lunches," I said, pouring on all my charm and promising to bring everything back later that day.

"*Si, si, grazie,*" he said with a big smile and a little bow. He was thanking *me!* But then again, why not? He could tell his friends and customers that he was making lunches for the Beatles—that had to be good for business!

When I walked into Neil's office with a large box that I could barely manage, Neil, Ron Kass, Peter Brown, Peter Asher, Derek, and Dennis O'Dell, the head of Apple Films, looked at me curiously. "What's all this?" Neil said as I pulled out the plates one by one, followed by the silverware, the napkins, and the steaming hot dishes, and placed them on the coffee table in front of the sofa.

"Well," I said, standing back, hands on my hips, a proud smile on my face, "I decided you should have something better than sandwiches." Of course, I didn't mention the fact that I knew I had to do something out of the ordinary in order for them to recognize that I was somewhat extraordinary.

"Thank you, luv!" Derek said, hungrily eyeing the food.

"Chris, you've outdone yourself!" Neil chimed in, eagerly uncovering each dish and releasing the delicious aromas into the room. They started heaping the food onto their plates.

Well, that was fun! I walked back into the reception area, picked up the same magazine I was reading an hour earlier, and thought about what I might do next. Then the idea hit me—if Apple had a Tea Lady, why not a Lunch Lady? And why not me, who had nothing else of importance to do?

The next morning I made a preemptive move.

"Do you want me to get the lunches today?" I asked Neil as I passed him in the hallway.

"Yeah, if you can match yesterday's lunch," Neil said, his eyebrow raised in a mock challenge.

"Of course I can. Any requests?"

"Let's have some more of that Italian," he said.

That day I ordered several different dishes at the Italian restaurant, and on my way back to the office I noticed a cute little Greek eatery. Hmmm. The wheels started spinning. This was Apple after all, and wouldn't it be nice if the lunches were varied every day? Why should the Apple execs lunch on just sandwiches and Italian food? So the next day I surprised them with a nice selection of Greek food, then Chinese, and spent many pleasant hours scouting the neighborhood for good food at fair prices. Every one of those restaurant owners was happy to lend us his best plates, silverware, and napkins.

And that's how I found myself steady part-time work at Apple, which soon enough, to my absolute delight, turned into a full-time job.

"Chris, can you come into my office?" Peter Asher asked one morning as he walked through the reception area.

"Sure!" I said. I have to admit that Peter intimidated me because he was always so serious and uptight, so matter-of-fact and businesslike. Unlike the other Apple executives who reported directly to the Beatles, Peter just seemed to go about his job, staying fairly isolated from the mainstream. I followed him into his office, just one door down from Derek's.

"Do you want to work for me?" Peter said, sitting down behind his desk and motioning for me to take a seat. "I'm looking for a personal assistant."

"Yes, I'd love to," I said, barely able to contain my excitement. Working for Peter Asher, head of A&R at Apple—what could be better than that?

"Good," he said in his quiet, understated way. He seemed a little embarrassed, as if he was wondering what to do next.

"What will I be doing?" I thought I'd better ask.

"Well, I've never had an assistant before, so I'm not certain how to get you started," he said. "But you'll help me look after the artists we sign, book studios, make sure everything is set up for the recording sessions, and, of course, do some typing, filing, answering telephone calls, that sort of thing. I've been using a studio called Trident. You might want to call them and introduce yourself. They're very good at giving us whatever we want."

"Great," I said. "I'll call right now."

Peter cleared his throat and looked at me directly for the first time during our conversation. Shyly, hesitantly, as if he feared I might say no, he said, "And would you still get me those lunches?"

8

IRELAND

August–September 1968

"Peter, my visa is going to expire in two weeks."

"Don't worry, we'll take care of it." Peter was distracted, as usual, listening to boxes of tapes from prospective artists while attending to the needs of James Taylor, Mary Hopkin, and the other new artists we'd signed. But I was nervous. Really, really nervous. My three-month visa was expiring in two weeks and no one at Apple seemed very concerned about it except me. I told Peter, I told Neil, I told Derek, I told Peter Brown, I told Richard. I told anyone who might be in a position to help me. Peter told me he'd take care of it. Neil said not to worry. Derek told me to keep bugging Peter Brown. Peter Brown shrugged it off; it wasn't his concern.

"It'll be cool," Richard said, giving me his stoned grin and telling me the story about how he got his work visa. Apparently Derek convinced an officer from the Home Office, who was rightfully wondering what it was that Richard did that an Englishman couldn't do, that Richard was indispensable because he was young, in touch with the current record scene, and understood the overseas market. Convinced by Derek's eloquent argument, the Home Office official wrote up the working papers and bestowed upon Richard the title of "Client Liaison Officer."

Which was all well and good, but where did that leave me?

Peter Asher finally spoke to Neil, who spoke to the Apple lawyers, who thought it would be best if I left the country while they applied for a work permit.

"You mean I have to go back to America?" I asked the Apple lawyer, unable to disguise my fear. I had this horror that once I was out of sight I would be forgotten.

"You could go to Paris, or perhaps Dublin. It's up to you," the lawyer replied.

Alistair Taylor, Apple's general manager, stepped in at that point to offer some advice. Alistair was here, there, and everywhere at Apple, arranging this and that and always involved, it seemed, in fixing one problem or another.

"Paris is very expensive," Alistair said. "You might want to consider Dublin instead."

"How long will it take?" I asked, trying hard not to seem too anxious.

"Well, luv, we're figuring it might take a week or two for the papers to be filed and accepted."

A week or two? "Do you think the Home Office will approve it, Alistair?"

"No problem, it's just paperwork."

After my conversation with Alistair, who had apparently been assigned the responsibility of seeing me through this little crisis, everything happened fast. I flew to Dublin the day after my conversation with the lawyer, with an advance from Apple of two weeks' salary, thirty-six pounds, or about one hundred dollars. Although it wasn't a lot of money, the advance made me feel good because it showed Apple's good intentions—after all, the Apple execs didn't have to go through the bother or the expense of keeping me. They could easily have left me to fend for myself, in which case I'd soon be on my way back to America. So I was deeply grateful for the salary advance and the plane ticket to Dublin, but at the same time I was all too aware that I was not in any sense Apple's highest priority.

A week passed while I waited in my Dublin hotel for the phone call from Apple. I used my precious shillings to call Barbara, who assured me everything was proceeding as planned. Another week passed with no word from Apple. That was when the paranoia set in. *Poor Chris,* I could imagine the secretaries saying, *she had to go back to America.* Richard might chime in about how much he would miss me as he sorted out press clippings. Peter would scramble for a while and then find someone else to book the studios and take care of the Apple artists. *She was a great help, wasn't she?* someone might say, just to wrap it all up, and the wheels would turn, the days would pass, and within a few months, no one would remember who I was.

I started writing letters home, working on an escape plan, hoping that my parents would be able to get the money together to buy me a ticket from Dublin to Tucson. Mom and Dad had always been so supportive of my dreams, encouraging me to believe that with a little hard work and faith in the process, anything might happen. And they'd been so excited about all my adventures, but now I'd be going back home in disgrace, my visa expired, my job ended, my short life with the Beatles a thing of the past.

Why didn't Peter call me? What was Alistair doing about the Home Office? Wasn't Derek worried about me? Was anybody even thinking about me all alone here in faraway Ireland? I felt abandoned, imagining that the circle had closed, and I was on the outside now, excluded and forgotten. In the months I'd been working at Apple I was always aware of how lucky I was to be there, and as an American, I knew I was doubly, triply, a million times blessed. Paul seemed to like having me around the office, George was always friendly and happy to see me, and John treated me as if I'd been around the place for years. I didn't know Ringo very well, but he never failed to give me a big smile and always called me by name. Derek, of course, would do anything for me. Peter Brown and Neil Aspinall had gotten used to my being around, and Peter Asher was always telling me what a good job I was doing and how much he depended on me. But everything happened so fast at Apple, it was like being part of a movie, the scenes kept changing, minor characters walked across the screen and then disappeared forever, and we all got swept up in the wild and crazy drama of it all. The Beatles would be the

Beatles forever, but the rest of us? In the end, we were all dispensable, replaceable, insignificant in the bigger scheme of things.

Besides, what was I doing that an English girl couldn't have done? Wasn't that the requirement for a work permit, after all, that I had some unusual skill or experience that gave me the right to this job? Sure, I was likable. I knew how to get along with all kinds of people, how to say the right thing, how to fade into the background, how to always be ready to do whatever was asked of me. But was I really all that special? Maybe I acted easygoing and confident, but perhaps they had seen through me to the insecurities lurking right under that bright and cheery surface. Maybe I worked more hours than the other office assistants, but who really cared? They all had lives outside of Apple, while I didn't.

Another week passed before I finally got an answer from Apple.

"Chris, luv, it's Alistair Taylor. Look, I'm afraid I've got some bad news for you."

Oh no, I thought, *this can't be true.*

"What's happened?" I managed to ask.

"Your working papers arrived today!" Alistair started to laugh. I wanted to kill him. "You've been given a year, longer than we had hoped. Usually it's six months."

"Alistair, you're horrible." I wanted to throttle him.

He chuckled.

"When can I come back?" I said.

"I booked a flight for this afternoon. I'll meet you at the airport."

I ran to my room and packed my bag, my hands shaking with excitement and relief. It was all over! I was going back to Apple and the Beatles! I was now legal to work in England and I had a whole year!

Alistair met me at Heathrow with all the necessary paperwork, the immigration man stamped my passport, customs waved me through, and I fell into the luxurious comfort of the limousine waiting just outside the door.

I smiled, all my troubles forgotten.

9

SAVOY TRUFFLE

October 1968

Life moved fast at Apple. In the three weeks I was in Ireland, Apple Records was officially launched; Ringo walked out of *The White Album* sessions and announced he was quitting the band; Cynthia Lennon filed for divorce; "Hey Jude" was released as a single; Ringo returned to the band ("I felt tired and discouraged," he explained, "took a week's holiday, and when I came back to work everything was all right again"); Paul officially broke off his relationship with Francie Schwartz, his American girlfriend, who flew back to New York never to be seen again at Apple; and Apple completed the move from Wigmore Street to Savile Row, a street in central London known as "the golden mile of tailoring." Now we were in the posh and elegant district, with eighteenth-century storefronts inhabited by high-class tailors with names like Grieves & Hawkes, Hardy Amies (Queen Elizabeth II's official dressmaker), Norton & Sons (once upon a time the tailor to Winston Churchill), and, soon after Apple moved in, Nutters of Savile Row, which catered to the likes of the Duke of Bedford, Mick and Bianca Jagger, and the Beatles. Tommy Nutter was Peter Brown's close friend. But our other snooty neighbors, I heard, weren't all that happy to have us in the area.

My new office, on the fifth floor, right next to Peter's much larger office, was a cozy gabled room set under the roof with a view out to the back sides of the adjacent buildings. Not much of a view, but I loved it. I settled in with a comfy cane rocking chair and my favorite possession of all time, a purple desk that I inherited from the Apple Boutique, which closed only a few months after its gala opening.

How can I even begin to describe how much that desk meant to me? It was mine, it was funky, it was part of Apple's history, no one else had a desk like it, and the light from my window turned the painted wood a beautiful deep purple that reminded me of Jimi Hendrix's purple haze. My little room with its slanted roof and gabled windows, tucked so sweetly under the eaves, filled with the sound of cooing pigeons perched on the gutters and the faint sound of cars passing on the streets below was the most wonderful place in the whole wide world.

Peter and I were returning from lunch one fine autumn day—now that Apple had hired two Cordon Bleu chefs, my lunches were history—when he suddenly picked up his pace. Parked at the curb right outside Apple's front door was a clunky flatbed truck with wood posts and a red canopy. Flowers and bells decorated the top of the canopy, and psychedelic prints of an Indian guru-type guy playing a flute and backlit by a halo were stapled on the wooden posts. Half a dozen men and women dressed in long, flowing saffron robes stood on the sidewalk smiling at passersby. Businessmen in their hats and fancy tailored suits walked in a wide circle around the unusual scene, casting wary glances backward as they continued down the street.

Peter pulled in his head, turtlelike, his chin fell to his chest, and he kept his eyes fastened to the sidewalk as he scurried right past the truck and into the safety of Apple. Now, to understand Peter's reaction you have to know a little bit about his background. Peter's father, Richard Asher, was a highly esteemed physician (he was the first to identify and name Munchausen syndrome), his mother was a senior professor at the Royal Academy of Music (she taught the Beatles' producer George Martin how to play the oboe), his sister Jane went to a private school called Miss Lambert's Academy for Young Ladies (and almost married Paul McCartney), and he grew up in the historic and prestigious Harley Street district of London. Peter had all the airs of an aristocrat but without the title. At Apple he always seemed to stay one rung above the madness—and, now that I think about it, having an office on the top floor of the Savile Row building was symbolic of both his elevated position at Apple and his privileged background.

My reaction to the carnival-like scene outside the Apple office was the complete opposite of Peter's. Fascinated by the colorful outfits, the white paint on their noses, the red dots on their foreheads, and the men's shaved heads—I was especially intrigued by the little ponytails at the back of their heads—I took my time walking past the truck, taking in all the vivid details and catching a big whiff of incense. I smiled at one of the women, who offered me a shy, friendly smile in return.

Peter was waiting for me by the reception desk.

"I hope they're not here to see me!" he said as we walked up the four flights of stairs to our offices. I could almost hear his sigh of relief as the office door closed behind him.

I'd just settled down at my desk when the phone rang. It was Debbie, Apple's receptionist.

"Hi, Chris, would you tell Peter that his one o'clock appointment is here?"

"Oh, Debbie," I said, stifling a nervous giggle, "please tell me it's not those people who were out in front of the building."

"Yes," she said, "that's right." I could tell by the polite tone of her voice that they were standing right there in front of her.

"Oh, dear. Okay. I'll call you right back."

I knocked lightly on Peter's open door and walked in. He looked up from his antique desk filled with papers, all set in neat little piles.

"Peter," I said in my this-is-not-necessarily-good-news tone of voice, "you know those people who we saw outside by the truck?"

"Yesssss," he said, dragging out the word, already dreading the bad news.

"They're your next appointment."

Squirming in his chair, Peter opened his appointment book. "Someone named Sam is to drop off an audition tape. Why do these people need to meet with me? Who *are* these people?"

"I guess we'll find out," I said, smiling to give him encouragement.

Peter started fidgeting with his pen, flipping it back and forth between his thumb and forefinger as if it were a metronome stuck on high speed. It went for a few seconds until he came to a point of acceptance and the pen came to rest.

"Ohhhhkaaay," Peter said, once again taking a deep breath and breathing into the word. "Bring them up."

"Hello," I said to the two men standing in the reception area, smiling at them as they did a little bow to acknowledge my presence. "I'm Chris O'Dell, Peter Asher's personal assistant."

"Hello," said the man with the little blond ponytail in a very polite, businesslike tone. "I'm Shyamasundar das."

"And I'm Mukunda das," said the man with the little black ponytail.

We took the elevator to the fifth floor and within minutes, they were having a very reasonable conversation with Peter, who seemed to relax after a while and even, it seemed, began to enjoy himself.

"Well, how did it go?" I asked Peter after I'd escorted them back down the stairs and out the door.

"They were actually quite pleasant. They want to make a record." For a moment Peter sat there, lost in thought, and then he picked up his pen. *Uh-oh,* I thought, *the metronome is going to start all over again.* But he just tapped it against the desk a few times as he gathered his thoughts.

"Well," he said, having made a decision, "I think I'll let George know about this meeting. He'll know what to do."

I got my steno pad. I never did learn proper shorthand, but I had developed my own method of note taking, simply spelling the words phonetically and leaving out vowels. Occasionally, I'd have a hard time deciphering my notes, but most of the time I could fake my way through it. I typed up the short memo and handed it to Peter, who signed it and handed it back to me.

"Would you mind taking this to George at the studio tonight?"

"Okay," I said, starting the word on a high note and singing it down, holding on to it for a few extra notes, smiling all the while.

Okay! That was my favorite word. I was a collector of experiences, and saying okay was the way I kept adding to the vault. The Beatles were recording the White Album; that night all four Beatles were scheduled to be in the studio, and Peter had just given me a real reason—a legitimate professional excuse—for being there, too.

It was close to 6:00 p.m. when I left Savile Row and took a taxi to Abbey Road. I walked past the guard, who smiled and waved me on. When I opened the heavy door to the control room, Mal immediately came striding toward me, a quizzical look on his face.

"Hi," I said calmly, smiling at him. I held up the envelope, reveling in the fact that I had a reason to be there. "I have a note for George from Peter Asher."

Mal visibly relaxed and moved away from the door. George was sitting on a sofa against the wall, smoking a cigarette and rummaging through a leather bag. Ringo was sitting in a chair, his head down, cigarette almost burned to the filter, listening to the playback. John and Yoko were cuddled up together against the opposite wall, heads touching as they whispered about something. Paul was standing behind George Martin at the console.

I walked over to the sofa where George was sitting and handed him the envelope.

"Peter asked me to bring this to you," I said.

"Have a seat, Chris," he said. I sat down on the sofa next to him and watched him read Peter's note. A big smile spread across his face.

"Did you meet them?" he asked.

"Just briefly. They seemed really nice."

"I'd like to meet them. Maybe we can set up an appointment in the next few weeks." George listened for a moment to the playback and then turned back to me. "Stay for a while if you like."

George offered me a paper cup of wine and after a few, I was feeling a little buzz. The hours—or were they minutes?—passed, the work for the night was done, and everyone except George left to go home.

"Look, if you want to stay, I'm just going to be putting the vocals on," George said.

"I'd love to," I said.

So I stayed. We drank a lot of wine that night and the more we drank, the closer I felt to George. I watched him getting a little drunk, and I realized that this was a new experience—I'd never gotten drunk with one of the Beatles before!

At first I stayed up in the control room, watching George singing into the microphones in the studio below. I sipped my wine, one foot tucked underneath me, the other foot swinging happily, and listened as George Martin isolated George's voice from the backing track. It was so pure, so melancholy. I'd never realized before how hauntingly beautiful George's voice could be.

"Not quite right, is it?" George said when he listened to the play-back. He was headed back down to the studio when he turned around and asked me to join him. "And why don't you bring the bottle of wine with you?"

I sat on a folding chair in the studio, a few feet away from George, listening to him sing and refilling our paper cups. That's how the night went on. George would sing and I'd listen, then we'd walk up the stairs to the control room, listen to the playbacks, and I'd grab another bottle of wine on our way back down to the studio. If I'm remembering right, at one point I think we did away with the paper cups and just drank from the bottle. I have no idea how long the singing and drinking and listening went on, but I do know that I was pretty drunk by the end of it. In fact, I started feeling not so good. I remember leaving the control room and walking down the hall to search for the ladies' room. It was a large room with a couch in a little anteroom, a big mirror, and a door leading into the restrooms.

I looked in the mirror and my image blurred. *Oh,* I thought, *I am not feeling good at all.* And then, with no warning at all, I was sick. I ran to the restroom and threw up, on my knees in front of the toilet. After a while I was able to stand up, using the toilet and the walls of the rest-room stall to balance myself, and I made my tortured way back to the couch. My head was spinning, so I lay down and that's all I remember until I woke up and daylight was shining through a window way up high on the wall near the ceiling. I had no idea where I was. I smelled awful. I was wearing a long maxi skirt and some kind of sweater and boots, and my clothes were all wrinkled. My hands were shaking. I looked in the mirror and drew back, horrified. My makeup was smeared all over my face, which was as white as the painted walls, my eyes were puffy and bloodshot, and my hair was matted down where I'd been sleeping and sticking out at odd angles everywhere else.

I sat on the couch with the light streaming in above me and tried to figure out how I had gotten there. I remembered being in the studio with George. I remembered going down the stairs with a full bottle of wine and coming back up the stairs with an empty bottle. Then what happened? Where was George? Had they just left me there? Were they still in the recording studio?

I used a wet paper towel, rubbing under my eyes to remove the makeup, fluffed up my hair a bit with my fingers and, trying to look somewhat dignified, walked down the hallway to the front desk.

"There you are!" the guard said, looking very relieved to see me. "Where have you been? They were all looking for you."

"Are they still here?" I asked.

"Oh no, they left hours ago."

"Okay, well, bye!" I said, acting as if this were absolutely normal, as if people walked out of the Abbey Road restroom at the break of dawn every day.

I jumped into a taxi and went back to my flat where I took a bath, changed my clothes, put on fresh makeup, and took another taxi straight to work, arriving right on time.

A few days later George stopped by my office. I was getting ready to do some filing, arranging folders into piles on my desk in alphabetical order.

"Hullo," he said. "Mind if I come in?"

"No, no, come in," I said, pushing the files off to the side of my desk.

"So what happened to you at the studio?" George said. "We were looking all over for you."

"I got tired and went home," I lied. *Please believe me, please believe me,* I kept chanting inside my head.

"You should have said something. We were worried about you."

"I'm sorry, George, I really am," I said, feeling grateful for the little scolding. It was so much better than the shame I would have felt if he'd known the truth.

10

HELLS ANGELS

December 1968

The Hells Angels' arrival at Savile Row in December 1968 was only the first takeover of Apple—Allen Klein, who was already lurking behind the scenes, waged the second and final battle for Apple's soul. So, in retrospect, maybe those three weeks when the Hells Angels took us hostage weren't really so bad. At least you knew, right from the start, exactly who they were. And it wasn't as if we weren't prepared.

On December 4, 1968, George Harrison sent out the following memo to all Apple staff members. I was sitting at my purple desk enjoying my morning cup of tea when I read about the motorcycle gang's imminent arrival.

> Hells Angels will be in London within the next week on their way to straighten out Czechoslovakia. There will be 12 in number, complete with black leather jackets and motorcycles. They will undoubtedly arrive at Apple's facilities. They may look as though they are going to do you in but are very straight and do good things; so don't fear them or uptight them. Try to assist them without neglecting your Apple business and without letting them take control of Savile Row.

Like everyone else at Apple I was a little nervous about twelve Hells Angels wandering the hallways looking as if they might do me in, but at the same time I thought a visit from the famous motorcycle gang might be kind of fun, another wild adventure to add to the experiences I'd had at Apple. The wording of George's memo made me laugh because it was so quintessentially Liverpudlian, with its downplaying of the potential drama. *Don't uptight them!* I loved that! In fact, I liked the memo so much that I made several dozen copies, added a little note in red and green, and sent them out as my Christmas cards that year.

Life was always unpredictable at Apple. Magic Alex, head of Apple Electronics, lurked in the basement of Savile Row looking like a mad scientist in a white coat as he worked like crazy on his futuristic twenty-four-track studio, planning to get it ready for the *Get Back* album. George peeked his head in the day before they were scheduled to start recording and was flabbergasted to see twenty-four individual speakers nailed up on the basement walls. George Martin saved the day, but the word around Apple was that Alex's state of the art recording studio was a major disaster.

The Beatles' personal lives were also in upheaval. In October 1968 John and Yoko were busted by the London Drugs Squad for possession of "cannabis resin" (hash). A month later Yoko had a miscarriage. The full-frontal nude photograph of John and Yoko on the *Two Virgins* album, released in late November, offended just about everyone—even Derek said the picture gave him "a terrible shock" and EMI and Capitol refused to distribute the album. And Paul met Linda, which put an end to any fantasies I might have had about a relationship with the only available Beatle.

Paul stopped by the offices almost every day, checking in on all of us in his friendly way but also, I was soon to learn, trying to get a handle on the financial mess at Apple. One day he called all the staff into the sparsely furnished "Beatle office" on the third floor. We all dutifully appeared at the appointed time and took seats at the large conference table or found places on the floor.

"First of all, you're doing a great job and we appreciate it," Paul said in his most diplomatic fashion. "But we're also losing a lot of money on things we don't need."

I listened half-heartedly as Paul talked about the need to cut unnecessary costs, such as taking minicabs home after work and charging the bill to Apple. And from now on, Paul continued, no more in-house Cordon Bleu lunches for anyone but the executives. But when Paul mentioned the amount of Scotch being consumed on a weekly basis, I realized that we'd all been taking Apple's generosity for granted, and it was time, as Paul warned, to cut back on our extravagant ways.

"We're going through cases of Scotch every week," Paul said. "We're the pub of choice and it has to stop."

Fat chance! I thought. Everyone went to the press office after work and we all kept Scotch in our offices to entertain guests (and each other). But little did I know that Scotch was only part of the problem—in a two-week period, according to a "drinks list" Richard showed me later, the press office consumed eight bottles of J&B Scotch, four bottles of Courvoisier, three bottles of vodka, four dozen lagers, eight dozen Cokes, two dozen ginger ales, two dozen bitter lemons, one dozen tonic waters, one dozen tomato juices, three bottles of lime juice, and six hundred cigarettes.

Apple's legendary hospitality wasn't reserved for just the famous guests who stopped by for a visit—Lauren Bacall, Duane Eddy, and Mick Jagger, for example. One day a hippie family walked into reception and announced their desire to peacefully kidnap John and Yoko and whisk them off to an island off Fiji. We let them stay, of course, and they set up camp on the fourth floor, ate our food, and walked our hallways as if they owned the place. If we couldn't say no to a peace-loving family with a breast-feeding mother who liked to walk around naked and her fifteen-year-old daughter who kept asking Derek if she could ball George, then how were we going to say no to the Hells Angels?

When the call came from customs that the Hells Angels had arrived at the airport—*Hello? Apple Corps Limited? Well, these people say they're in your care, and they've got motorcycles, are you going to take responsibility for them?*—the news traveled fast.

"Did you hear?" Barbara whispered to Laurie.

"Yeah. They're here." Laurie looked at Richard.

"Customs impounded their motorcycles," Richard told Chris.

"Uh-oh," Chris said to Derek.

"They won't release them until Apple pays the shipping costs," Derek said to no one in particular.

"Apple pays for the motorcycles?" Mal stuck his head in the room.

"Right."

"Shit," we all said in unison.

We were lucky. Only two Hells Angels showed up—Frisco Pete and Bill "Sweet William" Fritsch—but they brought along with them "the California Pleasure Crew," which included Grateful Dead manager Rock Scully, writer Ken Kesey, and San Francisco hippie Frankie Hart.

I was upstairs in my safe little haven under the roof when they walked into the press office and, according to Richard DiLello, sent "waves of fear" through the room. Peter Brown and Derek were speechless, or so I heard, but eventually Derek found his voice and his run-on sentences in this little welcoming speech, recounted by Richard DiLello in his book *The Longest Cocktail Party:*

> "Well!" Derek boomed. "You are here and so are we and this is Sally who has just joined us and that is Carol who has always been with us and Richard you know, and if you would like a cup of tea then a cup of tea it is, but if you would rather have a glass of beer or a bottle of wine or a Scotch and Coke or a gin and tonic or a vodka and lime, then that it is because it is all here and if it is not then we will come up with something, but have a seat or have a cigarette or have a joint, and I will be back in three minutes so please don't go away because there is a lot to talk about and more to find out and stranger days to come!"

"Beer!" they bellowed, and beer they got.

Sufficiently juiced, the Angels started casing the joint, peeking behind doors, opening closets, running up and down the stairs, playing with the elevator, and before long they found their way up to my office on the fifth floor. I was prepared, having decided that the best way to deal with them was to hide any anxiety I might be feeling and make friends with them. I didn't know much about the Hells Angels, but I intuitively understood that their barbarian bluster was intended primarily to cut through any extraneous bullshit. With their leather pants creaking, hips jutted out, eyes narrowed, and big steel-toed shoes tapping the floor, they looked right into your eyes, trying to figure out what kind of person you were. Were you afraid of them? Did you cower and cringe and say Yes, Sir, No, Sir? Or did you stand your ground, smile in a friendly but not sycophantic way, calmly invite them in for a cup of tea or another beer, and prepare to endure their feet on your desk for however long it took before they tired of you and went on to their next victim? If you were afraid, they lost all respect for you; if you were fearless, you might pass the first test. Or so I figured.

"Hi!" I said when they showed up at my office.

"I need a stapler," Pete said while Sweet William hung back at the door.

"Okay," I said, reaching for my stapler and pushing it across my purple desk. "Come on in."

"Hey, are you American?" Pete asked, taking a seat in the cane rocking chair and rocking slowly back and forth, checking me out.

"Yeah," I replied.

"Where ya from?" Sweet William finally muttered from the doorway.

"Tucson, Arizona." I replied.

"Cool." They both smiled, and kinship was established.

Later that day Frankie Hart, the only female in the entourage, showed up in my office and we became instant pals. Dressed in a long, flowing skirt and loose top, she regaled me with stories about the San Francisco hippie scene, Owsley's high-grade LSD, the Black Power movement, and the anti-Vietnam War student protests. I listened to her stories with something approaching awe. What a different world! Frankie was a ball of fire, always looking for the next adventure. Someone had let her loose in Wonderland, and Frankie wasn't going to waste a minute.

She was, I realize now, an awful lot like me.

I'd never taken acid, but I'd had some experience with amphetamines. Neil kept a stash of black bombers in the unlocked desk in his unlocked office and for several weeks that first summer, I'd come in on a Saturday or Sunday (I had my own key to the building), take a few bombers from the baggie in his desk, and get an amazing amount of work done. I knew the pills weren't for anyone to take, it wasn't like jelly beans (or Scotch, for that matter), but things were so loose around the office that I was sure Neil didn't keep track. And I figured that I was working on a weekend, so in a way I was entitled to an extra little something. I called them Magic Pills because I could work for hours without stopping, and when I ran out of work, I'd write letters back home describing my incredibly wonderful, amazing life in London. Eventually I realized that I was wearing myself down by taking too many amphetamines, not eating or sleeping enough, and drinking more than usual in an attempt to cut down the amphetamine buzz to a manageable drone. I decided to leave those black bombers in Neil's desk where they belonged.

I was always up for a new experience, though, and when Frankie suggested an acid trip, I figured it was about time I tried it. After all, the Beatles were going through an acid period, Derek had dropped LSD numerous times and raved about the experience ("there is nothing like a ride in a Rolls on a little acid on a Saturday afternoon in June in the lanes of Surrey," he wrote in one of his memoirs), and Frankie convinced me that she had some good shit (although it wasn't Owsley's acid that we took that night).

I was also hoping that an LSD trip might change me somehow, expand my horizons, and offer me a new perspective on life. I wanted to be more confident, more comfortable in my own skin. I believed in magic. My life in London was magical, Apple was magical, the Beatles were pure magic, amphetamines were, for a time, magical. I thought LSD might provide the magical lightning-bolt moment that would illuminate my inner strengths and light up the pathway to greater happiness.

So one snowy magical December night Frankie, Sweet William, Frisco Pete, and I dropped acid in my apartment. I waited. And waited. Nothing much happened. I watched the snow fall and it looked like snow falling. I had a few more drinks, figuring maybe the combination of alcohol and LSD would jump-start the process of awe and wonder. But not much happened, just a little tingling. Sitting there waiting, I thought about the first time I tried marijuana. I never got high, but I ate a whole loaf of white bread.

"Hey, Chris," Sweet William said, a big smile on his face. I think he was feeling it, but he probably took a lot more than I did. "Let's go for a ride in the snow."

"Yeah, that would be cool," I said. How could I say no to the opportunity to ride on a Harley with a Hells Angel—and not just any Hells Angel, but the famous Bill "Sweet William" Fritsch—on a snowy night in London, both of us high on acid? I couldn't. It was just so—well, so trippy.

The wind was whipping my hair, the snow stung my face, and I clung to Sweet William, my arms around his leather-jacketed waist as we traveled the Old Brompton Road to Knightsbridge. *Wow, there's Harrods,* I thought, gazing in awe at the holiday decorations in the huge glass windows flashing past. But at the traffic light, we made a U-turn, the back tire of the Harley spun out, and Sweet William fought for several terrible seconds to maintain control.

Oh shit, I thought, watching the world spin around me. *I'm going to die right here in front of Harrods just two days before Christmas, buried in the snow with a Hells Angel.*

We skidded to a stop, and Sweet William turned around to look at me. He looked like he also had watched his life pass before his eyes.

"Are you okay?" he said.

I couldn't speak. I just nodded my head.

When I woke up the next day, I was so disappointed. I was tired. I felt like shit. And I was the same person I had been the day before.

John and Yoko dressed up as Father and Mother Christmas for the Apple Christmas party on December 23, 1968, and all was going well until Sweet William and Frisco Pete showed up, drunk and stoned and high out of their minds. I was standing in the press office, drinking my third or fourth Scotch and laughing about something with Richard DiLello, when Frisco Pete walked in and demanded some fucking food.

"Let's have a little consideration here," one of the secretaries' husbands said, at which point Frisco Pete punched him full in the face. It was madness for a time in the press office, and I backed into a corner, staying as far away as I could, knowing that even though the Angels liked me, all hell could break loose at any moment.

Finally it was over, and several days after Christmas Sweet William and Frisco Pete left London and off they went to do whatever it was they were going to do in Czechoslovakia. I think it had to do with straightening out the political situation, probably by staring down some dictator or taking over a public square. Maybe they were just hoping to spread around some love and good cheer.

Peace be with them.

11

UP ON THE ROOF

January 30, 1969

I spent a lot of time that summer at Trident Studios, where I was book-ing sessions for Billy Preston, Mary Hopkin, James Taylor, the Iveys (who later changed their name to Badfinger), and other Apple artists. I'd sit on a sofa in front of the control board, watching the action through a big glass window overlooking the studio, listening through the speakers to the singing, playing, laughing, and chattering down below. I loved watching the song come alive as the backing track was laid down, the vocals and other solos were layered one by one on top, with bits and pieces expertly spliced together or cut away, and all the disparate parts slowly, amazingly, almost as if by magic became a whole. Watching from my perch up above, I felt as if I were part of the en-chanting mystery of it all and at times I literally forgot to breathe.

Recording studios are a world of their own. Time stands still. Hours pass and you don't know if you've been there for minutes or days. Day is night and night is day. There is sound and then there is silence, and the constant shifting between the two is lulling, almost hypnotic. Hear-ing is everything in the studio; all the other senses fade. Visually, it's a whiteout with the stark high walls and absence of natural light. The room always seemed to smell of incense, pot, cigarettes, and alcohol. I listened to the sounds coming out of the speakers, a cacophony of instruments and voices, like a freight train roaring down the track, all smoke and noise. But with a few pushes and pulls of the buttons and levers on the control board, the discordant sounds blended into a harmonious whole.

I was in the studio on August 1, 1968, the night the Beatles put the final touches on "Hey Jude." The master track had been recorded the day before, and they were adding overdubs, including backup vocals and the song's long refrain played by a thirty-six-piece orchestra. The studio was packed full of musicians with their violins, violas, cellos, bassoons, trumpets, trombones, drums, cymbals, you name it.

As usual I was sitting on a couch just in front of the control board, nursing a drink (it was going to be a long night) and watching all the activity below, when Paul came bounding up the stairs.

"How's it sound?" he asked George Martin, the producer. George always amazed me because he was twenty years older than most of us, classically trained, almost always dressed in a suit and tie. And yet no one understood the heart and soul of the Beatles music better than he did. I considered him a father figure, a patient, pragmatic, kind, and gentle man who was always ready with an endearing smile and a hearty chuckle.

"Yes, I really do think we've got what we were looking for here," George said as he leaned back in his chair behind the console, arms above his head in a stretch.

"Okay, let's get on with the vocals then," Paul said as he headed out the door. Suddenly he turned around and motioned to me.

"Come on, Chris, you can help," he said. "We need as many voices as we can get."

Sing on a Beatles track? The thought sent a little thrill of fear through me. I couldn't sing on key, or so I had convinced myself over the years, and the thought of being caught on tape and embarrassing myself in front of George Martin and all the Beatles unnerved me. I wanted to disappear into thin air and return a few hours later when it was all wrapped up and I could listen in peace to the playback. But I was caught. Paul had asked me to join in and he was the boss.

I stood at the microphones with the Beatles and perhaps thirty members of the orchestra, clapping my hands and singing along with the refrain.

Terrified that I'd sing out of tune and ruin the recording, I started off pretending to sing and just mouthing the words, but as we all clapped and swayed, our separate voices soon blending into one resounding chorus, my fears disappeared. With my eyes focused on Paul, the skilled conductor leading the troops, his hands swooping in circles, the look of joy on his face mirrored on the faces of all the rest of us, I sang my heart out.

In my time with the Beatles I had four major Magical Musical Moments (and many lesser, still awe-inspiring experiences). Singing in the chorus on "Hey Jude" was the first. The second—and the most magical—took place almost six months later on January 30, 1969.

"Are you going up?" Tony Richmond, the head cameraman, asked me that day as I was sitting in my office, despondent and depressed because, like all the other Apple staff members, I wasn't allowed up on the roof for the Beatles' final concert. The structure was too weak to hold all of us, we were told. I didn't take it personally, but I did take it hard because even though I'd be able to hear the Beatles play, I wouldn't *be* there. All week I'd had to endure the pounding and scraping in the hallways outside my office as workmen erected support poles to shore up the roof. With every nail that was hammered in, I was reminded that something huge and monumental was about to happen and I was going to miss it.

"I can't," I said miserably. "Only essential staff are allowed up there."

"Well," Tony smiled, walking over to my desk and reaching for my hand, "you're coming along as my assistant then."

"Are you serious? Do you think it will be okay?" I was afraid that someone—Mal? Peter Brown? one of the Beatles?—would realize I didn't belong there and tell me to leave. If I got that close and then had to turn around and go back to my office, head hanging in shame because I wasn't "essential," the disappointment would be more than I could bear.

Tony just laughed as he pulled me out of my seat. I reached for my coat—it was a bitter-cold January day and the wind was blowing like crazy—and followed him up the rickety steps to the roof.

As Tony set up his camera equipment, I sat on a bench next to him. We were right next to the building's chimney and just a few feet from the edge of the roof.

"Damn, it's cold up here," Ken Mansfield said as he sat next to me and pulled his thin white trench coat tight around him. Ken was the US manager of Apple Records and we'd become good friends, often partying together when he was in London. He gave me a big smile, but I noticed his teeth were chattering.

Paul was the first Beatle to appear, followed by Ringo and Maureen. Maureen took the seat next to Ken on the bench, huddling against the cold and keeping her eyes fixed on Ringo with barely a smile to acknowledge my presence. She was such an enigma to me because she always looked so tiny and vulnerable, yet she put up this protective wall that I felt I would never penetrate. John and Yoko arrived a few minutes later. Yoko sat on the far end of the bench next to Maureen, and within minutes, it seemed, the band started playing.

The chimney sheltered us slightly from the icy wind, but the Beatles weren't so lucky. The wind kept blowing their hair into their faces. John's nose was red, and Ringo looked plain miserable. George wore a red shirt, bright green pants, and a furry coat that he loved. Billy Preston, a musician loved by all the Beatles, sat on a chair by the roof door, playing keyboard, dressed in a black leather jacket, his shoulders hunched up into his neck as a defense against the cold. And Paul, unbelievably, wore nothing but a black suit jacket over a shirt. They all blew on their fingers and grumbled about how "bloody cold" it was. After every song, Maureen would clap and softly call out, "Yay!"

I can't remember any other details except for my favorite moment of all, just before the police came onto the roof and ended the concert. I was sitting on the bench, curious about what was happening on the streets below as people heard the music and wondered where it was coming from. I stood up and peeked over the edge of the roof, peering at the crowd gathered on the street below. The music rained down on them from the gray sky above and the look of wonder on their faces was something to behold.

When Joe Cocker recorded "She Came In through the Bathroom Window" at Olympic Studios in April 1969, I was there. Paul McCartney and recording engineer Glyn Johns were down the hall in a larger studio working on "Two of Us." That was my third Magical Moment.

I took a taxi to Olympic and slipped quietly into the control room, waving to my good friend Denny Cordell and taking a seat on the sofa. Denny was Joe's manager and producer. He had stopped by my office earlier in the day to invite me to the studio.

"You've got to hear Joe sing this song," Denny said. He didn't have to ask me twice.

Before long the band took a break and trudged into the control room. They did not seem like a happy group. Joe slumped down on a chair and closed his eyes. He looked exhausted and he was definitely grumpy.

"Does anyone have any fucking drugs?" he said, sinking even farther into his chair, his head hanging down, chin almost touching his chest.

"I wish," one of the band members sighed.

"Man, I can't fucking get it together," Joe said. "I gotta have a smoke."

"I have some hash," I said softly. I always kept a wad of hash wrapped in aluminum foil in my purse just in case someone (including me) wanted to get high. I always felt good whipping out my little silver packet and offering it up for a gigantic spliff.

Joe turned his head and looked at me, and I realized he was aware of my presence for the first time

"Joe, this is Chris O'Dell," Denny said.

"Well, hullo, luv, it's good to meet you," Joe said, his droopy face suddenly lifting up, as if a puppeteer had yanked on some strings. He jumped off his chair, full of energy now, plopped down right next to me on the sofa, and reached out to shake my hand.

"You're a savior," he said as I reached into my purse and handed him the hash, which he mixed with tobacco and expertly rolled into a fat joint.

I looked over at Denny, who gave me an appreciative smile and winked. Joe took several deep drags on the joint and passed it around. The energy in the room picked up. Later I listened to the playback of "She Came In Through the Bathroom Window," and I was blown away. Joe's rendition of Paul's song was so uniquely his own, so soulful and plaintive, that I knew Paul would want to hear it. After the playback ended, I ran down the hallway. Paul looked up as I walked into the studio and smiled at me in a welcoming way.

"Paul, can you take a break and listen to Joe Cocker's version of 'Bathroom Window'?" I said.

"Yeah, sure," Paul said, putting his cup of tea on the table and telling Glyn he'd be right back. We listened to the playback over the huge speakers in the control room. Joe was a little unnerved by Paul's presence, and we all sat there pensively, eyes downcast, waiting for Paul to voice his opinion about the recording. I watched Paul to see if I could read his reaction. He stood at the very back of the control room, foot tapping, head moving, a smile barely noticeable on his face. I knew by watching him that he approved.

"That's great, just amazing," Paul said, taking a few steps toward Joe and patting him on the back.

Well, Joe was "chuffed"—an English word I loved that conveys the sense of being puffed up with pleasure and pride—and after that night I was always welcome at his sessions. And I always brought hash, just in case.

In July 1969 my mother came to London for a two-week visit, and one afternoon I suggested that we go to a Hare Krishna session at Abbey Road Studios. Mom's eyes got big. Perhaps she knew that this would be the treasured moment of all the wonderful experiences she'd had on her trip, the event she would detail and embellish for my father, my sister, and all her friends back home.

"So this is Chris's mum," George said when he walked into the control room a few minutes after we arrived. "It's good to finally meet you."

"Nice to meet you," my mother said, very calmly. George introduced her to the Krishnas who had followed him into the control room, and I remember being impressed as my mother reached out to shake everyone's hand, answering their polite questions about her trip with a real sense of aplomb.

Moments later, from our chairs in the control room, we watched George pacing back and forth in the studio, casually chatting with one of the Krishnas as he waited for the microphones to be set up. Perhaps a dozen Krishnas were in the studio that day, sitting on the floor or wandering around the studio, prayer beads in hand, chanting softly to themselves. We watched in almost prayerful silence, for it was such a beautiful sight in that small studio (studio 2 down the hallway was much bigger) with all the Krishna oranges and yellows mixed with the red and purple flowers they were holding and an overall feeling of peace and tranquility. I felt strangely serene just looking at them.

"Which one is Harry?" my mother said, pointing to the cluster of saffron robes.

I looked at her, confused by her question, and then burst out laughing. "Mom, there's no one person called Harry. They all belong to what's called the Hare Krishna religious movement."

"Oooh," she said with a nod, as if she knew all about them. At that moment Shyamasundar walked through the door connecting the studio and the control room, his beads swinging back and forth on his neck.

"Chris! Why don't you come and sing with us, and bring your mother with you!" The Krishnas were always so inclusive, wanting everyone to join in and be part of whatever they were doing at the time.

I looked at my mother, who was shaking her head and waving her hands in front of her as if shooing him away.

"No no no no no, I can't sing, I don't know the words," she said, a slightly panicked look on her face.

I laughed. "There aren't that many words, Mom." The more she protested, the more determined I was to coax her into the studio. I wanted her to have the experience I'd had singing in the chorus on "Hey Jude." Imagine what everyone at home would say when Mom told the story about singing on a record that a Beatle produced—and singing with a crowd of Hare Krishnas, to top it off. This would be a story she could tell for the rest of her life.

"Mom," I said, putting my arm reassuringly around her shoulder, "even if you just mouth the words, it will be fun. Nobody expects you to have a great voice."

"Okay," she said, capitulating almost instantly. At that moment I realized how profoundly my mother had influenced my life. She had taught me that you can jump off a cliff with your eyes closed and, with enough trust and faith, land on your feet. Following her example growing up, I learned how to say "yes" to life.

One of the Krishnas wrote down the words to the chant so my mother could follow along, and that little act of grace gave her the confidence to step into the circle gathered around several microphones. We all swayed to the beat, absorbing the energy from the music, warming up inside. Within minutes, it seemed, all the separate voices joined together into one. I opened my eyes at one point to look at my mother, who was chanting intently, looking at the words, making sure she didn't mix them up. She smiled lovingly at me, and I felt a deep warmth and appreciation for her gentle but fiercely independent spirit. Young women don't often get to have that kind of experience with their mothers, so it was a special moment as I saw the world I lived in through her awestruck eyes.

I looked up at George in the control room, his hair pulled back behind his ears, listening intently to the music, smiling and nodding to the beat. *I get it,* I thought as the voices of my mother and all the Krishnas enfolded me, *this is why he chants.* It was a new kind of high, being in that recording studio with all the colors and smiles and my mother swaying next to me, and George nodding his head and smiling on the other side of the glass.

I felt so warm inside. It was a feeling of peace, and I wondered at the fact that you can feel physically and spiritually changed just by repeating certain words. Chanting the words over and over again was almost hypnotic, and once we got past the idea of not being able to sing, there was a point of freedom where there was no effort at all, no criticism or judgment, just the sound generated from deep inside, like a flame that warmed us from the inside out.

12

THE ISLE OF WIGHT

August 30–31, 1969

"Did you hear that Bob Dylan is singing at the Isle of Wight in August?" Bill Oakes said. Bill was Peter Brown's new personal assistant.

"Really?" I'd escaped to Peter Brown's office for a short break—that office was always good for the latest gossip. As I sat across from Bill at the table he used for a desk, I thought again how cute he was with his rosy cheeks, creamy English complexion, and little-boy look. As soon as he arrived at Apple earlier that summer, we started flirting and within a few weeks we were dating. It was so fun to have someone close to my age—he was twenty, a year younger than me, and he was easygoing and flexible, essential qualities for working in the crazy, chaotic world of Apple. We knew how lucky we were, working for the Beatles, and we'd share these great stories about our day at the office that always began with the words, "You won't believe what happened today!" Bill's stories were always fascinating because as Peter Brown's personal assistant he was privy to personal details about the Beatles and their wives. I loved having that little window, through my friendship with Bill, into the Beatles' private lives.

"It's his first live appearance in three years," Bill said with an eager look on his face.

"Let's go!" I said.

• • •

We had so much fun planning our trip to the Isle of Wight.

"Why don't we just take a couple of backpacks and jump on the train?" I said.

"That could be good fun," Bill said. "I'll organize the tickets."

"And what about staying in a bed and breakfast?" I said. I liked the sound of that—a bed and breakfast in the country. It seemed so quaint and sweet.

Bill laughed. He knew what I was thinking—we could pretend to be "normal" people for a weekend. I know this sounds sort of silly, not to mention snooty, but I'd been breathing the rarefied air of Apple for fifteen months, and I'd lost a sense of what "normal" meant. Every day when I showed up for work, the Apple Scruffs, the most loyal and loving of all the fans, would call out, "Hi, Chris!" I'd smile and wave, fully aware that the fairy dust of fame had settled all around me. There was something about being at Apple all the time that made me feel I was somehow different from everyone else. Even though I wasn't famous, I was rubbing up against fame every day. How could I not feel special? How could I not believe that I deserved to be treated well because I worked for the Beatles?

We were making dinner in Bill's kitchen, having a glass of wine and still working on our "normal people" plan, when the phone rang.

"Hello? Oh, hello, George." Bill stared out the kitchen window as he focused on the conversation. I could tell that he was being given an assignment of some kind, and I hoped it wouldn't interfere with our trip to the Isle of Wight. Bill motioned for paper and pencil, and I passed them to him. He scribbled away for a few minutes, then said good-bye.

"You're never going to believe this," he said. "Bob Dylan forgot his harmonicas."

"You're joking!" This was Dylan's first big concert in three years and he forgot to pack his harmonicas?

"No, it's true," Bill said, laughing. "George asked me to buy some at the music store in Soho tomorrow."

The idea of traveling as two of the normal folks with Bob Dylan's harmonicas stuffed into our backpacks appealed to both my love of adventure and sense of privilege. We might look like ordinary backpackers on their way to a rock concert, but inside those backpacks we held the key to the concert's success. The show wouldn't go on without us!

The next morning Bill called me at my flat to tell me that plans had changed once again.

"George called and said Dylan needs the harmonicas right away. He wants me to put them on a helicopter this morning."

"Okay," I said, thinking that then we could catch our train and everything would work out just as we'd planned.

"I was thinking that maybe we should just jump on the helicopter, too," Bill said. "It's going straight to the farmhouse where Dylan and his wife and George and Pattie are staying. George suggested the idea. What do you think?"

"Really?" That was all I could manage.

"Amazing, huh?" Bill laughed. "Okay, I'll get the harmonicas and meet you at the heliport in Battersea. We're scheduled to leave at ten-thirty. Can you make it?"

"You bet," I said, already moving my clothes from my backpack into a small suitcase.

We sat in the front of the helicopter, next to the pilot. A big, rounded glass window bubbled out and over us so that we looked right through the glass down to the ground, and as we flew over the city of London, I felt like I was going to free-fall right through the bubble to the earth hundreds of feet below. After about fifteen or so minutes the pilot turned to the right and we headed out over the English Channel. I didn't like flying over water.

"Where are we landing?" I yelled over the thunderous sound of the helicopter blades as the island came into view. "Is there an airport?"

"We're going to the south side of the island. We'll see a large stone farmhouse, and they said they'd lay out a sheet to mark our landing spot," Bill yelled back.

Several minutes later we spotted the farmhouse. But where was the landing spot? The helicopter flew in a circle around the farm, and on the second pass we saw several people holding a bedsheet and waving us toward the house.

"I think they want us to land over there," the pilot said, pointing toward the farmhouse.

"Next to the house?" Bill and I both looked at each other in amazement.

"Right behind the house." The pilot seemed rather amused.

We were hovering twenty or thirty feet above the ground, and dust was flying everywhere when I looked over at the farmhouse. Leaning out the second-floor window, a little grin on his face, was Bob Dylan. I nudged Bill in the ribs, pointed at Dylan, and we both burst out laughing.

"Nice landing," George said when we walked into the farmhouse a few minutes later. "You know Pattie, don't you?"

I'd had two face-to-face encounters with Pattie: fifteen months earlier at the Aretusa restaurant when I asked her if she might help me with my makeup someday, and then—this was the scene I'd just as soon forget—there was an embarrassing encounter in the hospital a few days after George had his tonsils removed. He called me from his hospital bed and asked me to bring in some paperwork. "And don't forget your grandmother's pajamas," he added, laughing. A week earlier, George had been in my office when I opened the package from my grandmother and he got a huge kick out of the lime green chiffon harem-style pajamas with the mostly see-through pants and the sequined brassiere. "Okay," I said, hesitating for just a moment before deciding it might be fun to walk into his room with my black maxi Biba coat covering the pajamas and flash him. Maybe that would cheer him up, and we could laugh about it for weeks. But when I entered the room with my hands tightly holding the coat closed, preparing to open my arms wide and give him a quick peek, I saw Pattie standing by his bed. George, greatly amused by the startled look on my face, introduced me again to Pattie, who said a gracious but somewhat cool hello. I mumbled a few words, pulling my coat even tighter around me, and minutes later, I was out the door of the hospital and safely hunkered down in a taxi headed home.

If Pattie remembered either of those incidents, she didn't let on when we met for the third time on the Isle of Wight. Instead, she smiled at me with such grace and good humor that I felt as if she were taking me by the arm and saying, "Come in, let's have some fun." Once again I felt a deep and intense longing to become her friend.

"Great entrance!" We all turned around at the sound of Bob Dylan's voice. Walking down the stairway with his wife, Sara, he looked as though he'd just rolled out of bed, with his hair tousled, his shirt un-tucked, and his face unshaven. Oddly enough, he seemed perfectly matched with Sara, who was elegant and soft featured, dressed in flow-ing clothes that gave her the look, as she floated down the stairs, of an angel descending from the heavens. He was the hoodlum to her choir girl, the knave to her queen, the beast to her beauty. And yet, when Sara stood close to me, I felt the intensity of her gaze and the keen intelli-gence that directed it. I learned later that she was of Russian descent, and I could imagine her as a czarina, full of mystery and mystique, wisdom and all-knowingness, earthiness and spirituality. To tell you the truth, she spooked me a little. I almost felt that she could read my mind.

"Thanks for bringing the harmonicas," Bob said, and with those few words, he turned around and walked back up the stairs, Sara following close behind him. Years later, when I toured with Bob and got to know him better, he'd remind me of a little long-beaked bird who would flit from one place to the next, staying put for only a brief time, all the while looking from side to side, ready to rise and take off if anyone came too close or talked too loud or somehow offended his sensibili-ties. He was a contradiction, for sure—a man of great presence who would absorb all the energy in the room and then suddenly disappear, leaving no trace behind except, perhaps, for the trailing smoke of his cigarette. I stood there looking at the legendary Bob Dylan and his enigmatic wife ascend the stairs, almost beside myself with excitement. This was one of those moments that I wanted to frame, a picture of me standing in the living room of a farmhouse on the Isle of Wight with

George Harrison, Bob Dylan, and their wives. Smiling to myself, I thought how much I loved my life.

"Are you two hungry?" Pattie asked, bringing me out of my reverie. Bill and I looked at each other—we hadn't had time to eat before we left London—and nodded our heads simultaneously. We were starving.

My favorite breakfast at the time was grilled tomatoes with eggs and bacon, which is exactly what the cook fixed for us that morning. Pattie and George sat down with us and drank tea, and after breakfast Pattie, Bill, and I walked over to the barn where Bob and the Band were rehearsing. We stood around talking to Mal for a while. Mal was there as George's bodyguard, but this wasn't George's show, so he didn't have a whole lot to do.

"Let's play tennis!" Pattie said suddenly. "Boys against girls!"

None of us had much skill, but I'd played some tennis in high school, and Pattie could get the ball across the net, so we beat the socks off Bill and Mal. Every time we scored a point Pattie would get this mischievous little grin on her face. She was so natural and good-natured, laughing and talking as if we'd known each other for years. I never once felt that day, or any day since, that I was with someone who considered herself "above" me in any way. In fact, in all the years I've known her, Pattie has never acted like a celebrity, even when she's directly in the spotlight with people fawning all over her. She is as unaffected and unassuming as anyone I have ever met.

George and Pattie asked us to go to the concert with them that night. We sat with John, Yoko, Maureen, and Ringo on folding chairs in a front stage area separated from the other concertgoers by a makeshift white picket fence. The concert, which lasted less than two hours, passed in a blur, but I remember standing up at one point and looking back at the vast sea of people in that huge circular concert area built to hold 150,000 people, seeing the tents up on the hill and the people sprawled out on the grass and thinking, *That's where Bill and I were supposed to be.* I looked up at Dylan on the stage, just twenty feet away from me, dressed all in white, and thought about the day—the helicopter ride, Dylan leaning out the second-floor window, Sara floating down the stairs holding Bob's hand, having breakfast in the farmhouse kitchen while George and Pattie drank tea, the barn, the tennis match, the limo ride, sitting next to Pattie in the front row with George, John, Yoko, Ringo, and Maureen—realizing how lucky I was. What an amazing day this had been.

It got better.

"How are you getting back to London?" John asked Bill after the concert.

"We're taking the train tomorrow," Bill said.

"Well, now," John said with a smile, "we've got a plane with extra seats, why don't you fly back with us tonight?"

John lit up a joint before the tiny prop plane even left the ground. After the second pass, I started to feel really, really paranoid. It was such a little plane, and there was a flimsy little curtain separating the four of us from the pilot. I imagined the smoke permeating that curtain, drifting around the top and the bottom and the sides. Was the pilot getting high, too?

I couldn't stop my thoughts from spiraling into panic. How could the pilot *not* be high? He was sitting in the same tiny plane with us, we were all breathing the same air that was saturated with hashish. High-quality hashish. If my eyes were burning, surely his were, too. If I couldn't think straight, how could he? If I could barely wrap my mouth around a few simple words, how was he flying the fucking plane?

I imagined the pilot, stoned out on hash, deciding to have a little fun with us. In my altered state, I visualized a scene in which he turned the nose of the plane to fly straight up into the sky. I swear I felt the plane tilting, rising, lifting. Just as I was fantasizing about how that scene might end, the plane hit some turbulence and started rocking up and down and from side to side. The four of us got big eyed. My hands were sweating, and I was taking shallow little breaths. The plane was bucking by that time and there were all these weird noises, like metal parts tearing and engines coming loose. John and Yoko started chanting "Hare Krishna," and then I knew we were in big trouble because I could tell by looking at their faces that they also thought we were going to crash and burn. I started chanting with them, Bill chimed in, and we were all chanting "Hare Krishna" for what seemed like hours but must have been only five or maybe ten minutes.

When we started chanting, I felt better. I reached a moment of acceptance. If we die, I thought, at least it will be on the front pages of all the newspapers in the world. I imagined the headlines, "John and Yoko Dead in Fiery Crash" and in smaller letters "Apple Employees Chris O'Dell and Bill Oakes Among the Dead" and in even smaller letters "Pilot Thought to Be Under the Influence of Hashish." Somehow imagining that newspaper headline (Derek would do a fabulous job with the press release) made me feel better, because if I died that day at least I wouldn't leave this world as an unknown.

We kept chanting after the plane landed, and we didn't stop until we took a few deep breaths of the sweet night air and knew for sure that our feet were firmly planted on good old solid ground.

13

LEON

September–October 1969

Three weeks later I was in the air again, flying to Ibiza for a holiday with my friend Leslie Cavendish, the Beatles' hairdresser (and mine, too). While Leslie worked on his tan and tried to recover from the end of a love affair with his girlfriend Susanna, I had a fling with a gorgeous, wealthy London aristocrat. His name was Ashley, and I swear he looked just like Ashley Wilkes in the movie *Gone with the Wind*. We danced all night, slept in a hammock under a full Spanish moon, drank piña coladas and tried to forget about the real world. But after two weeks of sun and sand, boats and booze, disco dancing, and daily, annoying hangovers, I was ready to get back to work.

In just two weeks everything had changed. Life at Apple hadn't been the same for months, of course, ever since May 8, 1969, when John, George, and Ringo signed a management contract with Allen Klein, a shrewd, abrasive, and some might say obnoxious New York businessman who promised to turn things around and make the Beatles lots of money. Paul refused to sign the contract, openly admitting that he didn't like Klein and wanted his father-in-law, Lee Eastman, to take over his business matters. Over the summer, the tension seemed to build. I'd heard the whispered rumors about the financial problems at Apple and the heated arguments between the band members (although

I'd never witnessed any quarrels or disagreements at work) and Derek kept muttering obscenities about the ABKCO (Allen B. Klein Company) takeover of our precious Apple.

I chose to ignore the warning signs, believing that the good times would continue forever, but when Klein fired Alistair Taylor, I was shocked. How could he do that? How could he sack Alistair, loyal side-kick to the Beatles for almost a decade, the beloved employee and friend who had earned the name "Mr. Fixit" because he could come up with solutions to just about any problem? When Klein fired Ron Kass, head of Apple Records, I was stunned. Ron was a fixture at Apple, a savvy businessman and a kind, thoughtful man. With Ron gone, it seemed as if nothing but paperwork and a few muffled screams stood between Allen Klein and total control of Apple.

When Peter Asher resigned in June to move to America and manage James Taylor's career, I felt as if I'd been cut adrift. Peter told the press that he joined Apple because "its policy was to help people and be generous," but now, under Klein, everything had changed and Apple had lost "its original feeling." As the days wore on, I realized how much I missed Peter—he was the best boss I'd ever had, and a good friend. Without Peter's steady guidance and support, I felt sad and lonely on the nearly deserted fifth floor, with only my purple desk to keep me company. I decided to move down to the press office to be closer to Derek and Richard.

What a zoo! I'd been up in the rafters for so long that I'd forgotten the frenzied energy and excitement of friends and strangers wandering in and out, phones ringing literally all the time, news flashes flooding the wires, and questions constantly shouted across the room: *How's the album doing? Who's doing that interview tomorrow? What do we say to these "Paul Is Dead" rumors?* For those first few weeks, work was much more fun, more like the early days at Wigmore Street. Something was always happening in the press office, supporting my well-tended illusion that everything would calm down and life would soon return to the normal Apple crazy chaos. Derek was still around, the Beatles continued to stop by to say hello, records were selling, and I was able to fill a good part of the day booking the Iveys, Jackie Lomax, and the Beatles at Tri-dent Studios, finding studio musicians to fill in whenever needed, and helping out in the press office by answering phones, running errands, filing papers, typing, and, of course, catching up on all the gossip. I wanted to believe that all would be well, that everything would be like it had always been. I was in denial. I could not imagine being any place other than at Apple, in London, with the Beatles.

"O'Dell!" Denny Cordell came striding into the press office, walked over to my desk, and gave me a huge hug. I snuggled into him. Oh, it was so good to see him. Denny was a bearlike man who didn't seem to consider his appearance a priority. His jeans were expensive but worn and his shirts, though neatly pressed, appeared to have been thrown on, with the cuffs unbuttoned or rolled up. His curly brown hair was tousled, even though he undoubtedly had it cut at one of the more expensive and trendy salons. With his "take things as they come" atti-tude, he was one of the most fascinating people I'd ever met, a fabu-lously successful British record producer who at age twenty-four produced "A Whiter Shade of Pale" for Procol Harum. That one song earned him five million pounds, or "five cool and funky big ones," as he liked to put it. Now twenty-six years old with a huge appetite for life, Denny seemed to me, at age twenty-one, a very wise, experienced, much older man.

"I want you to meet someone," Denny said, turning toward the door. Standing there, staring at me, was a man with long salt-and-pepper hair, dark mustache and beard, and deep-set eyes that seemed to look right through my clothes, my skin, even my bones, deep into my heart, maybe even my soul. He kept his chin tucked low and fixed those eyes on me. I felt my knees begin to buckle.

I knew that face, the long salt-and-pepper hair, those piercing eyes. I'd seen a photograph of him, almost a year earlier, when I was sitting with Frankie, the hippie from San Francisco, in my fifth-floor office looking at a Delaney and Bonnie Bramlett album.

"Whoa, look at this guy," I said, pointing to Leon's picture on the back of the album.

"That's Leon Russell. He's probably one of the greatest piano players in rock and roll. He lives with Rita Coolidge."

I looked at his image for a few seconds and pretended to shiver. "Can you imagine living with this guy? He's way too intense for me."

"Chris O'Dell, meet Leon Russell," Denny was saying. I couldn't find my voice and Leon didn't seem to want to talk. He just kept staring at me.

"Leon is here to work on his first album," Denny said, breaking the silence.

"Oh good, hi," I stammered, struggling to decide what to do next. My mind was spinning.

"Let's sit down," I finally managed. Denny and Leon sat together on the couch and I pulled up a chair.

"I wanted Leon to meet Derek," Denny said. "Is he here?"

"No, he's out today," I responded as I looked around the room, hoping that Derek would appear from out of nowhere and rescue me.

"Okay." Denny smiled, settling back into the cushions. "So what's new at Apple?"

"Well, it's getting weird here," I said. "People being fired and quitting. Peter left for LA, Ron Kass is gone, and I haven't seen Paul in weeks."

"Big changes," Denny said.

"Yeah," I sighed. "So how was LA?"

"Well, Joe Cocker and I finished the album, which went very well. And Leon and I are thinking about starting a company together."

"Really? Does that mean you're moving to America?" I asked, hoping that it wasn't true. I liked having Denny around.

"Very possibly," he responded without offering any other information. That was Denny, divulging just enough to get you interested but not enough to satisfy your curiosity. He loved mystery—or perhaps he just loved being mysterious. But at least Denny was a good conversationalist. Not Leon. He just watched as Denny and I chatted away, and I was so flustered by his silence and his dark, brooding way that I stumbled all over myself. What was it about him that intimidated me? I felt like I was on display. I was conscious of every move I made, every word I said, and the more nervous I got, the more the words kept tumbling out. He'd turn his head and look at me with this weird, knowing smile, and I felt like I amused him somehow. What was he thinking?

I wanted him to go away and leave me alone. I wanted Derek to walk in, take over the conversation, tell a few jokes, offer them a drink, and give me an excuse to fade back into the shadows. I had no idea, not a clue, that my uneasiness around Leon might be related to his sexual energy. I didn't think he was sexy, or at least that thought didn't register; I just thought he was slightly terrifying.

"Can we show Leon the studio?" Denny asked.

"Yes, sure, absolutely," I said, grateful for the opportunity to escape from Leon's intense stare. We walked down the stairs to the basement, and I showed them around the studio. I knew the Beatles were disappointed with the way the studio had turned out. Magic Alex, the engineer who was hired to create a state-of-the-art studio right in the basement of Savile Row, turned out not to be so magical. I'd heard rumors floating around about a promised seventy-two-track tape deck that never materialized, a mixing console that was scrapped after one session, and a complete lack of soundproofing, but none of it made any sense to me. It turned out that Magic Alex's only electronic experience was as a TV repairman. Klein would soon fire him, too.

Denny and Leon spent some time looking at the studio—they were clearly not very impressed—and then we returned to the press office. Denny drifted off to talk to someone, leaving me alone with Leon. I couldn't think of anything to say, and I grasped at the first thought that came into my mind.

"You know, you look just like your picture," I said. If he hadn't thought I was an idiot before, he certainly would now.

He fixed those intense dark eyes on me and said, "What picture?"

"The one on the back of the Delaney and Bonnie album," I said. He laughed. *Oh,* I thought with relief, *he isn't nearly as scary when he laughs.*

When they finally left, Mavis walked over to my desk. Mavis was

Derek's assistant. She looked over her shoulder, just to make sure they were gone. "Who was that?" she said, stretching out the word *that*.

"Leon Russell," I said, laughing at the look on her face. It felt good to laugh.

"I think he's rather weird," she said, wincing a bit at the thought of him.

"I agree," I said.

The rest of the day passed quickly. Around 5:00 p.m. word got round the office that George was downstairs. Word always traveled fast when one of the Beatles was in the building. I ran down the stairs to Peter Brown's office, hoping to catch George before he got too embroiled in meetings with Peter or Neil. I'd encountered a few problems lining up musicians for the Jackie Lomax sessions that George was producing.

"Well, hullo there," George said, giving me that sly, sexy smile that always unnerved me a little, even later, after we'd known each other for years.

"Hi, George," I said, shyly responding to his flirtatiousness and moving quickly on to business. "I've booked the studio and everything is set for Jackie's session this Saturday, but there's a problem. Nicky Hopkins just called to let me know that he's in America and won't be back in England for some time. So we don't have a keyboard player. What do you want me to do?"

"That's a drag," George said, his eyebrows pushed together in a frown. I just loved the way George hit the "g" notes at the end of a word. "Drag" became *drag-uh*. "Thing" became *thing-uh*. "Strong" became *strong-uh*.

"Piano is really important to this track," he said. "Let me think about it and I'll get back to you."

Right then I had a little *aha!* moment. Leon Russell was supposed to be a great piano player. Maybe he could fill in for Nicky. I approached that possibility from an oblique angle.

"Leon Russell was here today," I said. "I showed him the studio."

"Leon was here? Really? What's he doing in London?"

"He came in with Denny Cordell," I said. I hesitated for a second, as though the thought had just occurred to me. "Maybe he would help out with the session. Should I ask him?"

"That would be great," George said with a big smile. "But look, even if he has something else to do, let him know that I'd like to see him while he's here."

I ran back upstairs to the press office and called Denny.

"Do you think Leon might be interested in doing a Jackie Lomax session on Saturday? George is producing the album." I had my fingers crossed.

"Why don't you ask him yourself?" Denny said. "He's right here."

"Hello?" Leon said. His Southern drawl was even more pronounced over the phone and his voice sounded so soft and smooth, which surprised me because it didn't match his gruff exterior.

"George wondered if you might be available to play on a Jackie Lomax session he's doing on Saturday night." I took a deep breath. My heart was beating faster for some reason.

"Sure, I'd be happy to." I smiled to myself, then, uncrossing my fingers and remembering the power of the Beatles. Even one of the best piano players in the world wouldn't turn down a chance to play with the Beatles.

"Great. I'll tell George. And I'll phone you Friday with the details."

I hung up the phone and headed downstairs to tell George the good news.

"We have to cancel the Jackie Lomax session," Peter Brown told me Friday morning. "George's mother is very ill and he left this morning for Liverpool."

I canceled the studio and called the musicians, then Derek walked in with a press office crisis—probably something related to the "Paul Is Dead" rumors that were driving us all crazy—and before I knew it, the day was almost over.

"Chris, the second line is for you," Mavis said with a knowing smile and a raising of the eyebrows. "It's Leon Russell."

Shit. I'd forgotten to call and tell him the session was canceled. I cringed as I picked up the phone.

"I hadn't heard from you about the session, so I thought I'd better call," he said. Once again I was struck by how gentle Leon sounded on the phone.

"I'm so sorry, Leon, I should have called you earlier, but George had to go to Liverpool. His mother is ill, and I'm canceling sessions for the next week. I hope this hasn't messed things up for you." I took a deep breath and sat there, horrified by my oversight and waiting for him to get angry with me for not calling sooner.

"I'm sorry to hear about George's mom," he said. "I hope everything's okay. Well, if he reschedules the session and still needs me, let me know."

I let out my breath. "That's great of you, thanks," I said. And then, to be friendly, "How long are you planning to be in London?"

"Well, Denny and I are starting my album next week, so I'll probably be here for a few weeks." I smiled to myself, aware that we were having something that more or less resembled a conversation.

"That's wonderful," I said. "Well, listen, I'll phone you when we get things sorted out here."

"Okay," he said, with a little hesitation in his voice. "But look, I'm wondering, since I left tomorrow night free, would you like to have dinner with me?"

Though completely unprepared for that invitation, I gathered my composure, reminding myself that this was a professional relationship that needed to be nurtured for George's sake.

"Sure," I said, keeping my tone casual, "I'd like that."

After I hung up the phone, I stared at it for a few minutes. What was going on? Was he interested in me? Well, I wasn't the least bit interested in him, but I had to be nice to him because he was a musician and the Beatles admired his work. That was a big part of my job, after all—being nice to musicians.

Why, then, were my emotions all roiled up? I was kind of attracted to him, I had to admit, even though he scared me. And if I went out with him, I could make up for the fact that I forgot to call him about the canceled session. So it all made sense. Sort of. The biggest question on my mind was how I was going to keep up a conversation with him for an entire evening.

Leon showed up that night right on time. That surprised me. Musicians are notoriously unreliable. I figured maybe he'd forget and actually found myself hoping he would. But there he was, big as life.

I invited him into my flat—my fourth address in eighteen months—while I grabbed my purse and keys. We walked to a Chinese restaurant down the street, and the whole way I kept asking myself, "What the hell am I doing?" I didn't want to get involved with anyone, especially not an American. I liked my little English flings, nothing serious, but here I was going out on a traditional date with a man who at some level terrified me. As the night continued, however, I became more comfortable with his silences, and we actually had an interesting and surprisingly easy conversation. At one point I asked him where he was from.

"Oklahoma. Tulsa."

"That's funny," I said. "I grew up in Oklahoma."

"Where in Oklahoma?"

"I lived in Keota until I was nine, and then my family moved to Owasso for a few years before we settled in Tucson."

"I played in a church in Owasso once," Leon said.

"Maybe it was my church!" (It was, I discovered later.)

I felt myself warming to him at the same time that I wanted to push him away. I didn't want to be reminded of Oklahoma—or Tucson or LA or even America, for that matter. I was happy right where I was.

I had it all. And then along comes this guy who grew up twenty miles away from me but who epitomized the word "different" (definitely not the boy next door). I felt a terrible tension. I wanted to spend time with him because he was so warm and familiar, but I was afraid that having a relationship with him would somehow be like going back to Oklahoma and would expose the vulnerable, insecure girl I used to be. If I allowed myself to fall in love with him—and I knew all too well how easily I could fall in love and how desperately I wanted to find someone who truly loved me—that would mean giving up everything that I had built for myself in the last year and a half.

These fragmented, half-formed thoughts raced through my mind, coalescing into a one-word alarm: *Danger!*

"Would you like to go to a movie next week?" he asked me at the door to my apartment.

I tried to act calm, cool. "Sure, I'd like that. Why don't you call me at Apple?"

He leaned down toward me and kissed me gently on the lips. Then he stared into my eyes, and I felt this thrilling shudder run from the top of my head all the way to the tips of my toes.

"I think I'm falling in love," he said.

"With who?" I said.

I seem to always say the most ridiculous things in awkward intimate moments. But this was definitely too much too soon. I wasn't ready for love.

14

PISCES APPLE LADY

October 1969

"Hi, Leon," I said, a little coolly. I wished he hadn't called. Four days had passed since he kissed me good night. In those few days I'd convinced myself that this relationship was not meant to be. I couldn't get sidetracked by some twenty-seven-year-old guy from Oklahoma, even if he was a great musician and even if he did make my heart beat faster.

"Eric Clapton invited me to come out to his home in Surrey for the evening." Leon sounded excited by the idea. "Would you like to drive out there with me later this afternoon?"

I'd heard about Eric Clapton, of course. I'd seen the graffiti ("Clapton Is God") on the wall outside the Pheasantry, across from the Aretusa restaurant, and I knew that Eric was good friends with the Beatles, especially George. I'd always wanted to meet him, but things were moving too fast with Leon. I needed to stay focused on my job and my future at Apple—my whole life centered on the Beatles, not on Leon Russell or Eric Clapton. I'd just been promoted to the strangest position ever created at Apple; officially, I was the new Apple promotion person and, unofficially, I was the first un-promotion promotion person ever to be hired anywhere.

"Your most important responsibility is to make sure that no one—absolutely no one—gets a copy of *Abbey Road* before it's released," Tony

Bramwell told me when he promoted me. A childhood friend of the Beatles, Tony was head of the one-person promotion department. Now it was a two-person promotion department.

"Okay," I said. I moved my purple desk to the large back office on the ground floor, near Tony's desk, and spent my days pretending to be busy, pushing papers around, all the while trying to figure out what the hell I was supposed to be doing. Mission Impossible, if you asked me. But it did give me an excuse to turn down Leon.

"I'm not sure how long I'll have to work today. We've got some little crises going on," I lied. "Why don't I call you later and I'll let you know."

The day flew by even though I didn't do much of anything. Somewhere around five o'clock that evening Leon called again. *Oh shit,* I thought when I heard his voice on the line.

"Leon, I'm so sorry, I didn't call you back," I said. "I'm still working and things are a little crazy here. I think you probably should go on without me."

I thought I sounded very convincing, but I could hear the disappointment in Leon's voice. That night I went out with Ashley, the English aristocrat I'd met in Ibiza, and I didn't think once about Leon. In fact, I didn't think about him all week, not until my conscience started to bother me. I really should call him, I thought, just to keep the relationship peaceful in case George needed him for the Jackie Lomax sessions. And it wasn't very nice of me to keep him waiting that day when he invited me to Eric Clapton's house. I was feeling a little guilty.

I called Denny Cordell, who told me Leon was still at Eric's. "I think he's coming back tonight," Denny said. "Shall I have him phone you?"

"That would be great," I said. I had this gnawing feeling of guilt in my stomach. And something else that I couldn't really identify.

Leon called the next day.

"I'm leaving for Los Angeles on Saturday," he said.

"Oh," I said. I hadn't expected him to leave so soon. "I'd like to see you before you go. Maybe we could have dinner."

"Well, I'm going to be at Olympic Studios tonight," he said. "Why don't you come by if you get a chance?"

"Okay, I'll stop by after work," I said. I could tell he didn't think I'd show up.

Around ten that night I tiptoed into the control room. I smiled at Denny and Glyn Johns, who were busy at the control board—I'd spent a lot of time with Glyn in the control room when he was remixing "Let It Be"—and sat on the sofa, looking through the large glass window into the dimly lit studio. Leon was playing the piano, his eyes closed, his long, thick hair falling like a curtain over his face. Suddenly he straightened up, tossed back his hair, and began to sing, his voice rough and raw, the intensity of his emotions—love, longing, loss—etched into the very lines of his face. As his hands flew across the keyboard, I knew that I was witnessing a baring of the soul, a confession of the heart as profound as anything I'd ever seen or heard before. His music was like an aphrodisiac, drawing me in, pulling me toward him, bringing to the surface my own buried yearnings.

As I looked through the glass, Leon glanced up at me, nodded, and smiled. I smiled back, noticing for the first time that Eric Clapton was also in the studio. I was struck by how thin and fragile Eric looked. I'd always imagined him as the strong, silent type, a dynamic presence that would pull all the energy of the room around him, but any power he had seemed to come from the guitar—almost as if the guitar were playing him rather than the other way around. I shifted my attention back to the control room, and that's when I became aware that someone else was watching the men in the studio. Delicate and frail, almost ghostly, a beautiful young woman was sitting on a chair in the corner of the room. When she saw me looking at her, she pulled her head into her shoulders and stared at the floor as if she wished she could disappear. This is just the kind of girl that musicians fall for, I found myself thinking, the Sara Dylan ethereal type with the long hair, the wide, intense eyes, the high cheekbones, and that intoxicating aura of mystery, stillness, and silence

So I sat up straighter, lifted my chin, and pulled my emotions back where they belonged. Leon must have a new girlfriend. I hadn't seen him for a week, and he'd obviously found someone else to fall in love with. I had turned him down and he had moved on. I had waited too long. That's the way it was in rock and roll, a revolving door.

I concentrated on the music, trying to focus my mind on something more soothing and dependable than my emotions and reminding myself once again that I had never really wanted a relationship with Leon. What did it matter if he had a girlfriend? Everything always worked out just as it should. Besides, I continued with my rationalizations, I was in the studio that night to listen to the music. I shut my eyes and let myself drift with the melody. That was odd, because I'd always been a lyrics person, but there was just too much going on in my head to focus on anything but the pulsating rhythm of the song.

The word "Apple" brought me out of my daze, and I began to pay more attention. Leon sang the word "Pisces." Pisces? I listened more carefully and the lyrics began to tell a story. Leon was singing about coming to England to forget his Delta girl and meeting the Pisces Apple Lady who got his heart going *"like English leaps and pounds."*

I felt a chill run through me. This song was about me! "What's your sign?" Leon asked me that first night at the Chinese restaurant. "Pisces," I said. "Pisces," he repeated. *Pisces. Apple. The Pisces Apple Lady who took him by surprise.* I crossed my arms over my chest and sank deeper into the couch, feeling completely exposed. Leon was singing to me! If I could have run out of the studio at that very moment without making a spectacle of myself, I would have. But I was paralyzed. Like the girl in the corner, I wanted to disappear.

From the other side of the room I heard Glyn ask Denny, "What's the title? 'Piece of Apple, Lady'?"

" 'Pisces Apple Lady,' " Denny replied. He looked at me and smiled. He knew. Leon wrote that song for me.

What was I supposed to do? I looked away and stared at the floor, confused thoughts tumbling all over themselves. This was a love song. Leon was telling me, through his music, that he loved me. What a feeling that is—to have a song written about you and to hear it for the first time in the studio as it evolves from words and notes on a page to a real thing, a recorded song, part of an album, something that can never be pulled apart but will always be a whole, forever and ever, heard by thousands, maybe even millions of people.

But what about that girl in the corner? Who was she? If Leon had these feelings for me, why was she there? Did he write the song after we kissed and then, in the next week, did he fall in love with this girl? Was he trying to make me jealous by bringing her into the studio? The words in the song kept going through my mind, especially the part about how he "fell into a hundred pieces" right before my eyes. If Leon fell into pieces after meeting me, had it taken him only a few days to pull himself back together again?

The door to the control room opened and Eric and Leon walked in. Leon sat down next to me while Eric walked over to the girl in the corner. They talked in soft voices. *Oh,* I thought, feeling a little confused by all the conflicting thoughts and emotions. *She's not with Leon at all, she's with Eric.* I'd heard rumors that Eric was dating a seventeen-year-old girl, Alice Ormsby-Gore, apparently a real English blueblood who was descended from William the Conqueror and Mary Tudor, Queen of France.

"Hi," Leon said, giving me a little kiss on the lips. "You made it."

"Hi," I said softly. I could barely speak. If I had a year and a hundred pens and a thousand pieces of paper, I couldn't begin to describe what it felt like to listen to a song written about me.

"How'd you like your song?"

"Is it really for me?"

He nodded. His eyes, formerly so dark and penetrating, now looked warm and gentle. I could melt into those eyes. My face flushed. What was happening to me?

"It was wonderful." We looked at each other, both of us feeling slightly uncomfortable, wondering where we would go from here.

"I didn't think I was going to see you again," he said, taking hold of my hand. "I wrote it hoping that one day you might hear it and know what I was feeling for you."

Leon held my hand while we listened to the playback. My emotions were rocketing all over the place. He really had written this song for me. It was like receiving an honorary degree or being knighted or winning the Oscar or the Nobel Prize. I felt honored. I felt immortalized. I felt—oh, I don't even know what I felt, but I guess it came down to the fact that I felt loved. He cared enough to write a song about me, a song that would last forever. Nobody could ever take that away from me.

"Why don't you stay around for the weekend?" I said. My voice was trembling. "I could show you some of the sights." I knew what I was doing and it terrified me, but my feelings for him were suddenly stronger than my fear. In an hour I had fallen in love. And I was going to follow it. I was going to say yes to it.

He looked long and hard at me, and my emotions must have been written all over my face.

"Why, Miss O'Dell," he said, his eyes laughing.

One week later Leon broke my heart.

"It's time for me to go back to Los Angeles," he said.

"Why?" I asked. I felt crushed. I was head over heels in love with him.

"I can't find the kind of drummer I need," he said, "and I need to finish the album."

"What kind of drummer do you need?" I asked.

"Well, someone like Ringo," he said. That comment raised a red flag. Was he using his relationship with me to get close to the Beatles? *No,* I thought, *he really does love me. And I love him.*

"Why not Ringo?" I said.

"I just don't think Ringo would play for me," he said.

"Why?" I asked.

"Well, he's a Beatle and he probably doesn't even know who I am," Leon said in all honesty.

I didn't want Leon to leave. I worked for the Beatles, which meant I worked for Ringo, and I thought I might be able to talk him into helping out Leon. If I could get Ringo to play on his album, Leon would stay longer. That was my chief motivation, but it also felt good to have a purpose and a goal. Connecting people was part of my job. I liked the idea of knowing that I might be responsible for helping Leon's career— this was, after all, his first album—but I wasn't sure how to make it

happen because Ringo rarely came into the Apple offices. I didn't know
him as well as I knew the other Beatles.

The next day George showed up at my old office on the fifth floor. I
was still retreating upstairs to my purple desk whenever I booked studios. He'd just returned from visiting his ailing mother in Liverpool,
and he wanted to get back on schedule with the Jackie Lomax sessions.

"Is Leon Russell still here?" he asked.

"As a matter of fact, he is," I said.

"Do you think he'd be willing to come into the studio next week to
help out with Jackie's album?"

And right then, at that moment, my plan came together.

"You know, George, Leon was actually going to go back to LA this
week because he can't find a good drummer," I said. "But if we could
help him out and find a drummer for him, I think he'd probably stay
for another week or two and help out with Jackie's sessions."

"What kind of drummer does he need?"

I figured, *Oh what the heck,* and jumped right in and said it. "He told
me Ringo would be really good for the tracks he's working on." George
didn't seem fazed at all, so I just pushed on. "Do you think you might
be able to organize that?"

"I'll get hold of Ringo," George said, looking at me with a little playful smile, "but only if I can play, too."

My mouth dropped open. I'd only been trying to get one Beatle for
Leon, and I got two. "Really?" I managed to say.

"Sure," he said, grinning widely. I thought about something Derek
always loved to say—"The Beatles are generous with the fun"—and at
that moment I knew exactly what he meant.

"Great," I said, trying not to sound too excited. "Why don't I phone
Leon now and you can talk to him about it."

I was in the control room a few days later when Leon, Ringo, and
George rerecorded the entire "Pisces Apple Lady" track, scrapping the
original version with Eric Clapton. In the middle of the session John
and Yoko stopped by the studio. They sat together on the sofa holding
hands, and after a few minutes John started tapping his foot and getting

into the music. Feeling flush from my part in bringing George and Ringo into the session, I decided it might not be too late to invite John, too.

"Why don't you go in and play with them?" I said.

"Because Leon didn't ask me," he said in a low voice. I looked at him, then, hearing something in his tone that surprised me. He's disappointed, I realized, because Leon neglected to invite him.

"John, I'm sure if you just tell them, they'd love to have you in there," I said.

"No, Chris, it's fine. They're into it now. I'll just watch." I actually felt sorry for him, but there wasn't anything I could do because Leon was in the studio and it never occurred to me to interfere once the session had started.

After the session, Leon and I went back to my apartment and I told him about my conversation with John.

"I think he really wanted to play with you," I said.

"Really?" Leon looked stunned.

I described my conversation with John, and Leon's surprise turned quickly to disappointment.

"I was afraid to ask him," Leon moaned. "I thought about it, but I didn't think he'd be interested. Wouldn't that have been something to have three Beatles playing with me on the album?"

I think I was even more distressed than Leon, because I knew I could have arranged it if I'd only thought to ask John. Seeing the look on my face, Leon leaned forward to give me a kiss.

"Imagine having two Beatles on your song," he said. "And another Beatle sitting in the studio, listening."

"Yes," I said with a big smile. "Imagine that."

15

HUMMINGBIRD

November 1969–March 1970

Four weeks after I met Leon, we flew back to Los Angeles to start a new life together. I've never regretted that decision, even though life didn't turn out the way I had imagined. If I had stayed in London that autumn and winter of 1969–1970, I'm almost certain I would have been fired. Allen Klein and his accountants, seeking absolute control and autonomy, were on a rampage during those months, and only a few select people survived. Jobless, penniless, Appleless, I would have had no choice but to leave England and return to America. Who knows what would have happened then. Life follows its own convoluted pathways, and only when we look back from the vantage point of time and distance can we see that the twists and turns along the way make some sense, after all.

As the plane lifted off from Heathrow Airport, I stared out the window and blinked back tears, thinking about all the bizarre coincidences that had brought me to this point in time. I was leaving my job, which I loved, and Derek and Richard, whom I adored, and the Beatles, whom I would have followed to the ends of the earth, to fly back to America with a man I had just met but who, in a few short weeks, had become the love of my life. Leon knew I was struggling with my emotions and in an effort to make the journey easier for me ("I want to take you back to LA in style"), he tried to get us seats in first class. But they were all taken—by the Rolling Stones. Looking out the tiny airplane window, I smiled, comforted by the idea of the Stones sitting up front. At least I wasn't leaving everything behind all at once; some of the glamour and excitement of London was coming along with me. I felt even better when Bill Wyman and Charlie Watts came back to coach to chat with Leon.

On that long, long trip back to LA, I tried to imagine what Leon's house might look like. I pictured a little place in the hills with a white picket fence, taffeta curtains, a kitchen with pies in the oven and a dog in the yard, but the house wasn't quite as I had pictured it. Oh, it was nice enough from the outside, a two-story tract home on the valley side of the Hollywood Hills, but the inside was something else again. I walked in the front door to find a living room stuffed full of studio equipment and musical instruments and only one piece of furniture—a sofa that you could reach by stepping over or crawling across the amps and instrument cases. The kitchen reminded me of a recording studio kitchen with only the bare essentials—coffee cups on the counter and traces of sugar and powdered creamer that would build up until someone got sick of the mess and cleaned it up. I opened the oven door, took one look at the black-crusted surfaces, and never opened it again. A small bedroom on the main floor housed the control board, and Leon had converted the garage into a studio. Basically, the entire main floor of the house was a recording studio.

Upstairs there were three bedrooms. One bedroom was occupied by a couple, both musicians and old friends of Leon's, who sensed right away that I was a threat to their continued presence in the house. They basically pretended I didn't exist. Another couple, a bass player and his wife who were also Leon's good friends, lived in the second bedroom. They were much nicer to me, probably figuring they might be able to hang around for a while if we got along. Jimmy, a drummer friend of Leon's, lived in the walk-in hall closet and hardly ever came out, or at least I rarely saw him. I'm sure they all took one look at me and thought, *Oh, shit, there go our free digs,* although Jimmy didn't seem all that concerned. After all, he was only taking up an empty closet.

That first night, in our bedroom—the only private place we had in a four-bedroom house—Leon and I talked about his love affair with Rita Coolidge and how she broke his heart when she left him for drummer Jim Gordon. He didn't want to go through that pain again, he said, so he started off our live-in relationship with a little "rule" that would turn out to be the end of us.

"If either one of us should ever sleep with someone else," Leon said, holding my hand and looking deep into my eyes, "we have to promise to tell each other."

That shook me. I had this uneasy sense that Leon was predicting the future. Either he thought I was going to cheat on him—like Rita did—or he was warning me that someday he would cheat on me. He framed the whole discussion so that it seemed he was trying to protect himself after getting his heart broken by Rita, but it felt like there was more to it than that. Maybe he knew the relationship was doomed from the start. I don't know. It hurts now just to think about it because from that moment on, even though we were still so much in love and so hopeful it would work out, I was waiting for something bad to happen. I was afraid—afraid to trust him, afraid of being hurt, afraid that he would cheat on me, afraid of Rita, afraid of all the people in the house, and, soon enough, afraid of everything.

"I feel like we're living in a fishbowl," I complained after a few days.

"It's your house, Chris, do what you need to do," he said.

That didn't feel quite right. Why was he leaving the dirty work to me? Well, maybe this is my job now, I thought, the role of the "old lady." So I went to work. I got rid of everyone except Jimmy the drummer because he was sweet and only took up a closet, and I moved furniture around in an effort to make the house more like a home. In Leon's bedroom, the largest in the house, I created a living room space where we could relax and watch television. I found out who owned the motorcycle parked in the upstairs hallway and told him to move it out to the yard, and then I enlisted Leon's help painting the hallway where the motorcycle had scuffed up the walls. I bought several cans of fire engine red paint, we put shower caps on our heads, rented a machine to spray paint the walls, and blasted away. Leon's face and beard were covered in paint, which dripped like blood from the end of his beard.

In the end, of course, I created more chaos. I talked Leon into getting a dog and after an impromptu trip to the pet store, we came home with two blond cocker spaniels that we named Sam and Dave. They ran around the house, pooping and peeing wherever they went, and as I walked around cleaning up after them, I realized that I wasn't very good at this domestic bliss thing. I couldn't cook and I hated to clean. I wanted to be with Leon and I didn't have anything else to do, so I spent virtually every hour of every day with him at home or in the studio. I loved Leon—that much I knew for sure—and I was determined to make the relationship work. I could forget about everything else, I kept telling myself.

"Come to the studio with me tonight," Leon said one evening when I was watching television in the sitting area I'd created just off our bedroom.

"Sure," I said, lifting up my voice to sound excited about the idea, "that would be fun." Inside, my heart was pounding. I loved being in the studio, but that night I knew Rita, Leon's Delta Lady, would be there working on her new album. The words to the song Leon wrote for her, especially the part about him whispering sighs to satisfy her longing, cycled endlessly through my mind at times—I couldn't stop them—and I'd just get crazy with jealousy.

I wasn't in the same league as Rita. She was tall, dark, and exotic looking with thick black hair and full-moon eyes. Along with Leon, Bobby Whitlock, and Carl Radle, she was one of Delaney and Bonnie's "friends," singing backup vocals with the rock-soul group while Leon played the piano and guitar. She had a career, a following, a life that she could call her own. How could I compare? She was dark while I was fair, she was famous and I was a nobody, she was Leon's Delta Lady (a big hit) while I was his Pisces Apple Lady (which never became a hit). Who was I, really? I had no role, no job, no identity. I lived in a house with Leon and two puppies that I couldn't control and that was filled with musicians jamming downstairs at all hours of the day and night, and no friends and no family close by, and

London and Derek and Apple and the Beatles eight thousand miles away, on the other side of the earth.

That night in the studio as I watched Leon working with Rita, I felt somewhat reassured that he was no longer in love with her. During the breaks, he would come straight to the control room, smile down at me, touch my arm, kiss me. He was trying to let me know that I had nothing to fear. I wish I could have absorbed his adoration and allowed it to fill me up. Instead, I fretted, doubted, and questioned everything. Sitting on the sofa in front of the console watching Rita sing, her eyes closed, her body movements so graceful and fluid, I felt awkward and childlike, acutely aware that I was allowed into the studio only because I was Leon Russell's old lady. I remembered, with fondness and longing, the days when I hung out at Trident, Olympic, and Abbey Road studios and the Beatles, George Martin, and Glyn Johns would smile and welcome me into the inner sanctum. Back then I had something to do. I was a member of the team. I had earned my right to be there.

But now that I was with Leon, I reminded myself of poor Alice Ormsby-Gore, the waiflike girl-child sitting in the corner, not saying a word, not having a damn thing to do, just waiting for her man to finish his work so they could go home and be together. No wonder the Beatles' wives so rarely came to the studio. It wasn't that they were banned, I suddenly realized—they just didn't want to sit around watching, waiting, and as Maureen would put it years later, acting like just another "nodding appendage."

Well, that's what I was becoming, just another nodding appendage. I was losing myself, bit by bit, piece by piece, and I had no idea how to put myself back together again.

I took up painting by numbers. I wanted to do something creative but didn't have the talent to paint freehand, so I painted landscapes. By number.

Leon laughed at me. Not in a cruel way, but he thought it was pretty funny that I'd sit around the house with my white numbered canvases, concentrating on staying within the lines and putting the right colors in the right spots. I laughed with him, but I didn't think it was funny at all. Something was happening to me that I didn't understand. I was searching for structure and meaning, even if I had to find it in a silly paint-by-number kit. Leon was busy with his first album, *Leon Russell,* and Shelter Records, the new record company he and Denny Cordell had started, and he spent more and more time away from me during the day. I was lonely. And scared. And so so so so sad. So horribly desperately hopelessly sad. I realize now that I was depressed, but at the time I had no idea that the fear and despair that threatened to engulf me came with a label, a diagnosis. I could not move out of the gloom that settled around me. I couldn't shake it. I was smoking a lot of marijuana and drinking a lot; cocaine was my new favorite drug. The hopelessness would lift for a bit, then settle in even thicker. I had no idea the drugs were making things worse.

I kept thinking back to a few months earlier when I was working at Apple, nine, ten, twelve hours a day, always at the center of the activity, loving each and every moment of my life. Now I had one role—Leon's girlfriend—and I was spending all my time at home (which didn't feel at all like my home) with the bedroom door shut, painting by numbers, ironing Leon's shirts and my jeans (anything, believe me, that needed ironing), watching mindless television programs, and leafing through movie magazines.

I was waiting for something to happen. I knew it would be bad. I knew that from my first night in Leon's house when he made me promise that if I ever cheated on him I would have to tell him. I wasn't going to cheat on Leon, but I knew, deep down, that eventually he would cheat on me. He was out in the world, in the studio, downstairs jamming and recording with his musician friends, in meetings with record producers and studio executives, surrounded by famous people, almost-famous people, or people who wanted to be with famous people. Especially girls. Girls could smell the early stages of fame. They were hanging around Leon, enchanted by his moody, intense masculinity. And his sexuality. Leon was a very sexy man.

One night I got really drunk, sitting around the kitchen with guitarist Jesse Ed Davis and horn player Jim Price. They had stopped by to see

Leon and maybe sit in on a session. I pulled out the Scotch and Coke and we sat around the kitchen table drinking and talking. I have no memory of going to bed. The next morning when Leon and I woke up, he leaned up on one elbow and looked at me with loving concern.

"Are you okay?"

"Ooooh, I don't think so," I moaned, feeling sick and shaky. I had only brief flashing memories of the night before. "Oh God, what did I do last night? Did I do something stupid?"

"No," he said, putting his arms around me and holding me close. "You just kept coming into the studio while we were trying to record and telling me that you had to go back to London."

"I'm sorry," I said softly. I was so ashamed.

"I want you to hear something." Leon got out of bed, walked over to the bookcase, and returned with a tape recorder. "I wrote a song for you last night."

He hit the play button and his voice filled the room as he sang about the woman he loved who was more than he deserved, repeating the words "Hummingbird, don't fly away" over and over again.

"It's beautiful," I whispered, struck by the haunting melody and the lyrics that seemed so full of love and longing. Leon smiled, and I wondered what it would be like to create something so beautiful, almost out of thin air, with no lines or boundaries to keep you fettered and chained. "Last night I watched you sleeping so sweetly and thought how much I love you," he said. "The song just came to me."

"What's the title?" I asked, my heart full of love for this strange, beautiful man who had become my whole life.

" 'Hummingbird,' " he whispered, leaning down to kiss me.

He flew first. It happened one night when I was feeling even sadder than usual and took some amphetamines to make myself feel better. I was sitting in front of the television, my arms folded tight across my chest (holding myself together), staring straight ahead. I was way too high, so high that my jaw was locked tight and I literally couldn't speak. Leon sat with me for a while.

"Remember, no matter what happens, I love you," he said as he stood up. He stopped at the door and watched me for a moment, then softly closed the door behind him. I don't know how long I sat there, but after a while I started to think about his words. What did they mean? *No matter what happens.* No matter *what* happens? What was *what*? My heart was pounding out a drumbeat that made my head pound and sent the room spinning. I stood up, my legs wobbly underneath me, and went looking for Leon. He wasn't in the upstairs bedrooms or bathroom. I walked downstairs. He wasn't in the studio or the kitchen. I patted the puppies on the head, and they squirmed and wiggled with the attention. Every time I looked at those beautiful puppies, I felt guilty.

I found Leon in the living room, up against the wall, kissing one of the Oklahoma girls who was always hanging around. Her knees were bent, her back against the wall, and he was leaning into her, his arms wrapped tightly around her, his mouth pressed hard against hers. I don't know how long I stood there before they sensed my presence. They both turned and looked at me. No one said a word. I went back upstairs and shut the door. Minutes later Leon came in and stood by the bed, looking down at me.

"It was nothing," he said.

Nothing? I thought. It was over. I knew that. I'd figured it out, at long last. While I'd been losing myself, Leon was finding himself. His confidence was rising fast while mine was falling even faster. We couldn't survive that. We didn't have enough of a foundation to endure the disconnect between my self-pity and Leon's soaring ego. And he had predicted it, after all.

I moved in with my new friend Eileen Basich, Denny Cordell's secretary at Shelter Records, and stayed with her for a week. I knew it was over between me and Leon, but I was desperate to see him again. Every day I'd wait for Eileen to come home from the office so we could talk about Leon. He didn't call me. I wouldn't call him. I couldn't sleep. I remember being in an elevator one day and not being able to figure out the buttons. I kept going up and down, stopping at floors to pick people up or let them off, and just continuing on, pushing buttons that were taking me nowhere.

I waited. Something would happen. I trusted that. Something always happened.

A week passed. I was asleep when the phone rang.

"Hello," I whispered.

"Chris? Is that you?"

"Oh, Derek," I said. I started to cry.

"How are you, luv? I've been thinking about you a lot this week and wondering if you were okay. I called you at the other number, but a man there gave me this number. Is everything all right?"

"No," I said, trying to hold back my tears. "Leon and I have broken up. Everything is falling apart here."

"Why don't you come back?" Derek said. "Allen Klein is still in charge of things here, but I feel sure he'd give you your job back. I'll help you in any way I can, you know that."

I hadn't even considered returning to England. But now it seemed like the only thing to do. If I was ever going to get back together with Leon, I'd have to find myself again. I'd have to go back and become that Pisces Apple Lady who had it all together.

"Okay," I said.

A week later I was back in London. So much for white picket fences.

16

FLYING AWAY

February 1970

So I fled. I flew back to London, back to the place where I belonged and felt safe. I arrived at Heathrow exhausted and in desperate need of a bath, but I had nowhere to stay so I jumped in a taxi and headed straight for Apple. I couldn't wait to see my old friends, especially Derek and Richard.

The moment I stepped out of the taxi parked in front of 3 Savile Row, I felt that I'd come home again. The Apple Scruffs weren't hanging around outside, so I knew there were no Beatles in the house, and Jimmy the Doorman wasn't around that day for some reason, but everything else seemed to be just as I'd left it four months ago. I dragged my suitcases into the front reception room, leaned them up against the wall, and turned to greet Debbie at the reception desk.

"Chris! It's so lovely you're back!" Debbie said, jumping up and coming around the desk to hug me. I was so happy to be at Apple again! Everything looked so familiar, the stapler on Debbie's desk, the photographs on the wall, the green carpets and white walls. After Debbie assured me it was okay to leave my suitcases in the reception area, I took the stairs to Derek's office. That's when I began to feel a strange kind of tension in the air—and an eerie silence. The place seemed empty and silent. It was the silence that affected me most. That deep

stillness, an unspoken hush where you wait for something to happen—
you're not sure what—and you hold your breath, waiting, wondering,
and knowing somehow that whatever it is, it's not going to be good.

Derek was still enthroned in his white high-backed wicker chair,
and when I walked into his office, he stood up, put out his arms, and
gave me a huge hug.

"Welcome back, Chris," he said. Richard looked up from his desk,
smiled, and sauntered across the room to greet me. *Ahhh,* I thought, *I'm
home.*

"Do you have a place to stay?" Richard asked.

"Well, no, I'm planning to stay in a hotel until I can find a flat."

"Stay in my place," Richard said. "I have an extra bed in my flat, and
you can stay until you get yourself situated."

"Okay!" I said gratefully. Leon had paid for my plane ticket and had
given me one hundred dollars, but that was all the money I had left.

"Would you like a cup of tea?" Derek said.

"I'd give anything for a cup of tea."

"Could you get us a cuppa, please?" Derek asked Richard.

"Sure, man," Richard said as he walked over to the tea kettle on a
table near the door. We hadn't had a tea lady in a long time, but I suddenly flashed back to those wonderful early days at the Wigmore Street
office. Those were the best days ever, when Apple was young and innocent, and the Beatles and every single person who worked for them
still believed their ideas and ideals could change the world.

"Well," Derek said, as he took a cigarette from a packet lying on the
table and struck a match. "I guess we had better get you working
again."

"If Allen Klein will agree," I laughed. Derek laughed, too, even
though we both knew there was nothing funny about it. Then I got
serious.

"What's happening, Derek?"

"Well now," Derek said, settling back into the sofa with an air of
resignation. "The Apple we once knew and loved is gone, replaced by
ABKCO—Allen B. Klein and Company. Somewhere around two dozen
people have either been fired or quit in disgust. All the fat, so to speak,

is being trimmed from the bone: the free drinks, the hired cars, the lunches. No more waste, no more laughter, no more creative fun. Our fresh and lovely Apple is all chewed up."

Was it really that bad? I was still in denial. I could hear the resignation in Derek's voice, the echo of things to come, but I was so happy to be back and so relieved to be away from the pain of Leon that I couldn't bear to think that Apple might not last forever. Yet how could I ignore the despair in Derek's voice, seeing the sadness in his eyes, feeling the oppressive hush of the press office? Why was it so quiet? Surely, there were still things going on. Weren't the Beatles still around? What about the Iveys, Jackie Lomax, Mary Hopkin, Doris Troy, Billy Preston? Why weren't the phones ringing? Where were the media people clamoring for interviews and the visitors relaxing on the sofa with a Scotch and Coke and blowing smoke rings?

Even after Allen Klein arrived on the scene in the winter of 1969, the old Apple spirit lived on. We were quieter, that's true, and there was a sadness lingering over us all, a yearning for the old days. But we had convinced ourselves that Apple would come back.

Now it was different. As Derek put it, the circus had left town, but the Beatles still owned the place. Only the sawdust and peanut shells reminded us of what used to be.

The next morning I went to work as usual, arriving with Richard about 9:00 a.m., and acting as if my four months in Los Angeles were just a weekend fling. I was home, even if the place felt like a graveyard. Somehow we'd bring it back to life. I really believed that.

I was walking up the stairs to Derek's office, hoping to find something to do, when Dee stopped me in the stairwell. One of the few secretaries who was still employed at Apple, Dee worked for Jack Oliver, head of Apple Records.

"Chris," she whispered, looking up and down the stairs to make sure no one could overhear her. "I just heard Allen Klein's secretary telling someone that Allen didn't want you working here."

"Why?" I asked in disbelief. I'd just arrived back; what had I done? I was hopelessly naïve, of course—I had no idea of the power Klein wielded—but I couldn't imagine that he would fire me if Derek was still at Apple. I always felt safe and protected as long as Derek was around, and I figured that even Klein, as ruthless as he was reputed to be, wouldn't mess with the legendary Derek Taylor.

"I don't know," Dee said, her hand already on the banister as she prepared to retreat to her office. "But I thought you ought to know. Don't mention that I said anything." She practically flew down the stairs to her office.

I walked into Derek's office, sat down on the sofa, and groaned.

"What's the problem, luv?" Derek said.

"Allen Klein doesn't want me here," I said.

Derek looked up at me, pen in one hand, cigarette in the other, cup of tea steaming on his desk. I could see in his eyes that he already knew.

"Don't worry, we'll work something out," Derek said. "He's just an obstacle that we have to climb over occasionally these days."

He leaned back and tapped his cigarette in the ashtray as I tried to imagine what to do next. Would I have to go back to LA? My work permit had been extended, but it was good only if I worked for Apple. If Klein fired me, I wouldn't be able to work anywhere else in London, and I'd have no choice but to fly back to the States.

Derek, who had been talking on the phone, suddenly interrupted my despairing thoughts. "George is down in Peter Brown's office," he said with a little hint of the old merriment. "Why don't you go and say hello?"

I ran down the stairs and stuck my head in Peter's office. George was standing in front of Peter Brown's desk, looking at some papers that Peter had handed him.

"Hi, can I come in?" I said as I pushed the door open a little wider.

"Chris O'Dell!" George said, surprised to see me. He gave me a big hug. "What are you doing here? Is Leon with you?"

"No, things didn't work out for us," I said. I was embarrassed, remembering the night that Leon played on the Jackie Lomax session. "I'm so happy for you," George had said before I left. "You and Leon are a great couple. You deserve this." George admired Leon, and I felt as if I had let him down somehow.

"I'm really sorry," George said. "I thought it was great, the two of you together." A moment passed. I didn't know what to say. "So what are you going to do now?" he asked. "Are you working here again?"

"No," I said, hesitating for a moment before deciding to tell him that my future at Apple was in jeopardy. I didn't want to burden him, yet I knew that Derek had a reason for sending me to see George. "It seems Allen Klein feels that there isn't a job for me here."

"What do you mean there isn't a job for you here?" George glanced sideways at Peter Brown, a look that conveyed his dislike and his distrust of Klein. For one brief second, a frown crossed Peter Brown's face. That was unusual. Peter Brown was really good at hiding his emotions.

At that moment Neil Aspinall walked through the door that connected his office to Peter Brown's. Neil looked surprised—and, thank heavens, happy—to see me, smiling widely and giving me a quick kiss on the cheek.

"It seems Klein doesn't have a job for Chris," George informed Neil.

"Oh, really," Neil said, still smiling. He crossed his arms over his chest and leaned against the fireplace mantel.

"Well," Neil said, "I think I can find something for you to do. Would you like to be my assistant?"

"Your assistant? Really?" I was stunned.

"I'm putting together a film with all the old Beatles footage. You could help me sort that out. In fact, you can start right now if you like." He gave me a rather smug smile. "Fuck Allen Klein" is the way I read that smirk.

I looked at George, who was also grinning.

"I'd love to work for you, Neil," I said. I must have thanked them both a dozen times.

When I told Derek the good news, he laughed. I knew then that Allen Klein didn't have total control of Apple and, even better, there was still some of the old fun lurking around the building.

• • •

Working for Neil Aspinall was like putting my desk in the locked vault in the center of a bank. This was the true core of Apple Corps Ltd. and, along with Peter Brown's office, the beating heart of Beatle activity. All the Beatles' personal business was conducted in the shelter of their offices, and this was the one place where Klein had no power at all. Klein couldn't touch Neil or Peter Brown because the Beatles wouldn't have stood for it. Peter Brown had been with the Beatles since the early 1960s, first as assistant to Brian Epstein and, after Brian's death, taking over many of his day-to-day management duties. Neil grew up with Paul and George and worked as the Beatles' first road manager. When the Beatles were inducted into the Rock and Roll Hall of Fame, George Harrison named Neil as one of the two "fifth Beatles"—Derek Taylor was the other one. As long as the Beatles were around and had any say at all over their business dealings, Neil, Peter, and Derek were untouchable. And as long as I was safely installed in Neil's office, Klein couldn't touch me either.

I loved working for Neil. He had a dry, somewhat sarcastic, and, at times, cynical sense of humor, but he was never mean-spirited. He was honest, a man of his word, and he told it like he saw it. Somehow Neil was able to stay above the fray and refused to get caught up in the Klein shenanigans. He was a true professional who could work with anyone and everyone, a mediator who could make friends of bitter enemies. I believe Neil was able to keep a perspective on the whole Klein takeover of Apple, and it was almost a spiritual point of view. Sure, Allen Klein is bad news, Neil seemed to convey, but there are worse things in life and, since we don't have any control over this situation, let's learn to live with it. Neil would not—could not—be swayed by the winds of fame, fortune, or greed. He was steady as a rock, solid as the earth, trustworthy, loyal, full of integrity, and those are just a few of the qualities that the Beatles—and the rest of us—loved about him.

Sometimes in the evenings—perhaps timing their visits with the hope that Klein and his accountants had gone home for the day—George or Ringo would drop by Neil's office for a chat. Paul, who had always been the most visible Beatle at Apple, rarely came by anymore.

I knew he was spending a lot of time at his farm in Scotland with Linda, her daughter, Heather, and their new baby, Mary. I also suspected that Paul didn't want to deal with Allen Klein, nor did he need to because his father-in-law, Lee Eastman, had taken over all his business matters. I figured the tensions between the band members had increased to the point that Paul felt more comfortable staying away. I missed him; he was such an energetic, positive presence at Apple, always checking in with the office staff to make sure that we were having a good day, making everyone feel good about themselves and important to the company.

But Ringo started showing up more than he ever had before, and he often brought Maureen with him. They were always holding hands. Every time she picked up a cigarette, Ringo would suddenly appear next to her with his silver lighter. He'd look at her adoringly, she'd look at him lovingly, and when she exhaled, she'd lower her eyes as if the moment was too intimate even for a man and woman who had been married for four years. They were crazy about each other, no doubt about that, and although I sometimes felt envious, I also felt soothed and consoled. They took my mind off Leon. Rather than reminding me of what I didn't have, their casual intimacy assured me that it is possible to keep a love story going even after several years of marriage.

True love really is possible, I found myself thinking. The thought comforted me.

17

FRIAR PARK

March 1970

"Chris, baby! What the hell are you doing here?" Doris Troy's deep, powerful voice resonated through the large office I shared with Neil on the second floor. Doris, known to her adoring fans as "Mama Soul," was a force of nature. Discovered by James Brown when she was working as an usherette at the Apollo Theater in New York, Doris cowrote and recorded the 1963 Top 10 hit "Just One Look" and was signed by Apple in 1969. We became good friends and spent many memorable evenings together, drinking, listening to music, and telling stories about our lives. Mostly I listened because when Doris was anywhere within shouting distance, she commanded all the attention. A large, sturdy woman with a booming voice, she lavished laughter and love on everyone. I loved watching her with Billy Preston as they hooted and howled, using black street talk and humor that I often couldn't understand, always ending a conversation with the conviction that God would make everything work out in the end or, as Billy wrote, "That's the Way God Planned It."

"Baby, baby, baby," she said, when I told her about my failed romance with Leon and my return to Apple, "I just gotta see you, spend some time with you. Come on over after work. I wanna hear all about LA. I missed ya."

Neil was surrounded by celluloid when I walked into the small windowless room that he used for screening the hundreds of reels of film scattered all around him. On a table in the middle of the room sat a projector facing a makeshift screen on the wall. For weeks he'd been going through those reels, watching every frame, looking for the pieces he deemed most valuable. He'd stay in that dark room for hours, while I sat in his office typing lists with dates, places, names, and other essential details for each reel of film.

"Neil, I'm leaving, see you tomorrow," I said.

"Okay, kiddo," he said, barely looking up from the screen. "You going to Doris's place?"

"Yeah, I'm spending the evening with her," I said, smiling to myself. I could never quite figure out what Neil thought about Doris. She could be hard to take because she craved control and wanted to be in the know about every decision involving her career, unlike Billy Preston, who trusted the Beatles and the Apple brass to do whatever was right and never worried about the details. Whenever she stopped by the office, she'd hound Neil, Peter Brown, or, if she was lucky, one of the Beatles, asking questions nonstop about why they had or hadn't done this or that. Her intensity could wear people down after a while. George had a great way with Doris. "Relax, Doris, it'll all be okay," he'd communicate to her in his soft, soothing voice, and she'd heave a big sigh, trusting him for the moment to take care of everything.

"Okay, see you tomorrow," Neil said as he reeled the film onto the projector. I shut the door softly behind me.

Doris lived in a cute little mews house in the West End. I loved hanging out with her because people were always stopping by to talk about music, smoke some hashish, have a few drinks, sing (Doris and Billy Preston once talked me into belting out a James Brown song and even had me believing I had some soul), laugh, tell stories. But on this night we were all alone.

"Oh, baby, I'm sorry you had to go through that shit with Leon and get your heart broken."

"Well, now I'm back where I belong," I said, blinking back tears and changing the subject. "I'm so grateful to Neil for coming to my rescue before Klein got rid of me."

"That Allen Klein is trouble, baby, mark my words," she said. "Things have really changed around Apple since he came in. It breaks my heart to see what's happening there. I can't get anyone to tell me what's going on with my contract. I'm getting pretty upset."

"Well, maybe I can find something out," I said as I reached for my Scotch and Coke.

"Ooohh, baby, I'm glad you're back," Doris said, reaching across the table to pat my hand. "You belong here, just like I belong here. Did you know I've been singing with Marsha Hunt and Madeline Bell? There's a lot going on here. I'm gonna stay even if the Apple deal falls apart."

When the phone rang we were halfway out the door, on the way to dinner. "Now who could that be?" she said with a big smile. Doris loved phone calls, drop-in visitors, and spontaneous parties. She threw her purse on a chair and balanced her hand on her hip as she picked up the phone.

"Hey, baby, how ya doing?" Doris said, throwing me a huge smile. "You in the studio? Oh good. Uh huh. Sure, yeah, she's here, hold on, baby." She handed the phone to me with both eyebrows raised. "It's for you, darlin', it's George."

I looked at her, my eyes wide, and mouthed, "George?" Why would George call me at Doris's place? She handed me the phone, picked up her half-finished drink, and lit another cigarette.

"Chris, look, I was wondering how things were going with Neil," George said. "Is the job working out?"

"Neil is great, we get along really well," I said, smiling at Doris, who was watching my face, trying to pick up clues about the conversation. "And the job is great, too. Thanks for your help with everything, George."

"Well, listen, I talked to Neil a few minutes ago and told him that I'd like to offer you a job working for me. Are you interested?"

"You want me to work for you?" Totally flabbergasted, I looked at Doris, who was shaking her hips at me in a little celebration dance.

"Pattie and I moved into this new house and it needs a lot of work.

Terry Doran is staying with us at the moment, but I thought perhaps you could be of some help, too. You'd have to live there for a while."

I was still camping out at Richard's, so I needed a place to stay—and how much fun would it be to move in with Pattie and George and pal around with Terry, fixing up the house, moving furniture, shopping, partying? Spring in the country—I imagined it would be absolutely beautiful. Oh, but what about Neil? I owed him a huge debt. How could I just up and leave him after he'd been so good to me?

"What did Neil say?" I asked George.

"He said it's up to you."

Up to me? Was there a choice? George Harrison was asking me to work directly for him. Then I'd really be out of Klein's reach. But just as enticing, George was giving me the opportunity to live with him and Pattie. Ever since I sat across from Pattie at the Aretusa restaurant, just four days after I arrived in London, I'd had fantasies about some-day becoming her friend. Playing tennis with her and sitting next to her at the Isle of Wight concert fueled my fanciful flights of imagination. I had no doubt that I could live with her. I could live with anybody (ex-cept, I thought with a painful twinge, Leon), but would she be able to live with me? I found myself wondering if she was aware that George was inviting me to work for him and stay with them at the house. Was I being hired as her companion? George had Terry and now Pattie would have someone to keep her company and to help her around the house. But did she really want me there, a constant presence in her home?

And I worried about disappointing Neil. He had stuck his neck out for me. I didn't want him to think I was ungrateful, nor did I want to let him down. Would he think that I was just selling out somehow, that I'd been bought out by a Beatle? But then again, weren't we all, in one way or another, "bought out" by the Beatles? They were our employers. They paid our salaries. I'd be crazy not to take this chance to get to know George better and work with him directly. Neil would under-stand, wouldn't he?

I had all these thoughts in two or three seconds, and then I made one of the most important decisions I have ever made.

"I'd love to come and work for you," I said.

"Good," he said, sounding really pleased about my decision. "Look, I'm at Trident Studios and I'll be here for a few more hours tonight. If you can get some things together and meet me here before midnight, you can drive back to the house with me."

"Okay, I'll be there," I said, hanging up the phone. Doris was staring at me, hand still on her hip, smile even wider, eagerly waiting for the details.

"George wants me to come to his new house and work for him. I'm supposed to pack some things and meet him at Trident tonight." I was totally dumbfounded.

"Hey, baby, that's great!" She threw her arms toward heaven and then bundled me up in a huge smothering hug.

"I'm wondering what Neil will say," I said after we'd both calmed down a little. "I feel like I'm letting him down. But this will be a lot more fun, won't it? I'll have a place to stay and I won't have to go into the office every day. As much as I love Apple, I always feel like I'm trying to avoid Klein and all his henchmen by hiding out in Neil or Peter Brown's offices."

"That's right, baby," Doris said, "it makes all the sense in the world to go with George. Now look, just call Neil, he'll understand, and then hurry along. You've got to get yourself packed!"

Neil picked up on the second ring, almost as if he'd been expecting my call.

"Well, I figured you'd take it," he said when I explained my decision. "It's a lot more glamorous working for a Beatle, isn't it?"

For a moment there I feared that Neil would consider me a traitor, but he wasn't angry with me. I could almost hear him shrugging his shoulders as if to say, "Oh well, it is what it is." I even wondered if he might have been relieved that I had safely escaped Savile Row and still had a job—with Apple paying my salary but having no control over my destiny, Klein couldn't touch me. That wouldn't turn out to be completely true, but at that point I couldn't imagine a safer place to be than in George Harrison's home.

I took a taxi to Richard's flat and spent an hour or so trying to figure out what to pack. Should I take all three of my bags, or just one? It was early March, almost spring. Would it be cold in the country? Should I pack my winter clothes or leave them behind? I finally decided to take just one bag and wait until I was settled to pick up the rest of my things. I could only imagine what George and Pattie might think if I showed up at Friar Park with three suitcases, moving in with all my possessions, as if I were going to stay forever.

I arrived at the studio before midnight, but George was head to head with the engineer, working out some problem with the vocals. I made myself a Scotch and Coke and sat down in my usual place on the sofa in front of the control board. A few minutes later Eric Clapton walked into the control room.

"Hello," he said, sitting down next to me. I turned to look at him, he looked at me, and in his eyes at that moment I saw a depth of emotion that I was not expecting. I saw pain, vulnerability, fear. And longing. I didn't interpret that longing as a sexual hunger so much as a spiritual craving for connection with another human being. He seemed unbearably lonely. And then, in an instant, as if realizing his vulnerability, he seemed to pull back.

"Hi," I said. God, he was handsome. I don't think I'd ever noticed that before.

He stared at me for a moment, his eyes narrowing. "Have we met before?"

"We met in Los Angeles. I was with Leon Russell," I said, deciding not to mention the "Pisces Apple Lady" session when he seemed so out of it and huddled in the corner with Alice.

"Oh." He obviously didn't remember that meeting either. "Are you still with him?"

"Not really," I replied. I wondered later why I didn't just say, "No." I was definitely attracted to Eric, and that spiritual longing I thought I'd detected now seemed much more sexually oriented.

George walked around the control board toward us, looking relaxed now that the problem with the vocals was resolved. "Eric, have you met Chris O'Dell?" he said, sitting on the sofa next to me. "She's a friend."

"We're just meeting," Eric said, smiling at me.

I found myself hoping we'd meet again.

It was after 2:00 a.m. when George and I drove through the village of Henley-on-Thames, which seemed quaint and charming even in the dead of night. At the edge of town George took a right turn through an ornately decorated wrought-iron gate and there to my left, surrounded by stately trees and sculptured bushes, was a fairy-tale gingerbread house with dark-and-light-patterned brickwork, multiple chimneys, stained-glass windows, and a gabled roof. The house was all lit up, and I was excited because it looked like Pattie had waited up for us.

"It's beautiful," I said in a hushed tone, awed by the old-world charm of the place.

George looked at me with an odd expression and then burst out laughing. "That's just the front lodge," he said. "The main house is a little farther along."

We continued down the long, narrow, curving drive, passing the middle lodge, and when we came around a bend, the full moon beamed down on a huge Victorian Gothic mansion. I gasped. I had never seen such a magnificent sight. The house posed regally in the dark, cold English night. Soft, dim lights reflected through stained-glass windows and the mansion's high turrets threw long shadows on the sweeping lawn. I felt as though I'd been transported into another time, the era of Jane Eyre and the ghosts of Ferndean Manor and of Heathcliff and Catherine wandering the moors at Wuthering Heights. This castlelike mansion was Friar Park—my new home.

Terry Doran was waiting for us when we arrived. A former car salesman in Liverpool—he once sold Brian Epstein a Maserati—Terry eventually joined the publishing division of Apple. The story goes that John hired him as his personal assistant, promising to keep him on as long as he made him laugh—Terry was a genius at making people laugh—but after John married Yoko, Terry went to work for George and moved into Friar Park to help with gardening and all the myriad tasks that needed to be done every day.

We gathered a few things—Terry said he'd bring in my suitcase and the rest of George's belongings—and walked through the massive carved wooden doors. A marble entrance hall led to another set of doors which opened on to the double-height main hall. The entire room was oak paneled in both light and dark wood, and a gorgeous wood staircase rose elegantly to a minstrel's gallery. A chest-high fireplace was set right into the paneling and a fire was blazing. Above the fireplace a stained-glass window reached all the way to the ceiling. Aside from a wrought-iron bench with a padded leather seat in front of the fireplace, the main hall was completely bare of furniture.

I was standing there, head tilted upward, gaping at the magnificence of it all, when Pattie suddenly emerged from what looked like a panel in the wall. *Geez,* I thought, *there are even secret doors here.*

"Hello," she said, softly, even a little shyly. She wore deep red velvet trousers, a big bulky sweater, and furry boots that reached up to her knees. Her hair was pulled back in a casual, somewhat messy look, with blond tendrils framing her face. Although she was gracious and friendly that night, I'd later learn that she was a little "miffed" with George for asking me to come stay and work at the house. She later told me she saw me as a threat, because almost every girl she knew made a pass at George—and far too often he responded to their advances or initiated the romantic liaisons on his own. She thought George had brought me into her home because he intended to sleep with me.

"Your house is amazing," I said, almost as much in awe of her as I was of her new home.

"It's wonderful, isn't it." Pattie smiled at me. "Would you like a drink?"

"I'd love a drink," I said.

"Tea for me," George said.

Terry came in with my suitcase, and I could see right away that Pattie adored him.

"Teddy, just leave the bags here, we'll get them later," she said. Teddy was his childhood nickname and Pattie's favorite pet name for him. They laughed and talked, obviously very close friends, and I have to admit that right from the beginning I was a little jealous of Terry's intimate friendship with both George and Pattie. I became good friends with Terry, too, but I often felt that I was competing with him for Pattie's and George's attention.

George and Terry wandered off down the hallway, disappearing into one of the rooms, while Pattie and I sat down on the bench with our glasses of wine. We leaned up close to the fire, our shoulders pulled up to our ears, and I found myself shivering. I still had my coat on; in fact, I don't think I took my coat off for the first two weeks I lived at Friar Park. It was just unbelievably bone-chillingly cold in that magnificent, massive, drafty house.

She shivered. "It's cold in here, isn't it? We don't have central heating. George wants to put it in, but it will take time. All the rooms have little gas heaters, though, so you should be all right at night." She took a sip of her wine. "Oh, and just wait until tomorrow, Chris. You'll be able to see everything then. We'll take a tour of the house."

George and Terry returned, and George told Pattie how I had mistaken the front lodge for the main house. We all had a good laugh about that, and then George suggested we all go to bed.

"Where shall I sleep?" I asked.

"Anywhere you like," George said. "There's plenty of space."

"We change rooms quite frequently," Pattie explained. "It gives us a feeling for the house."

"Do all the rooms have beds?" I asked.

"Beds?" George laughed. "There aren't any beds. Pattie and I sleep on a mattress on the floor. Terry will give you a sleeping bag."

I smiled to myself. So this is how the other half lives!

I chose a small room just off the main hall, explaining that I wanted to stay close to the fireplace, the main source of heat in the house. What I was really trying to do was hide the fact that I was a little frightened of sleeping alone in some far-off room in this gargantuan Gothic mansion.

"By the way," Terry said as we stood up and said good night, "the first person to get up in the morning has to bring the tea around."

What if I woke up first? The thought of wandering down the upstairs hallways trying to find out where they had camped out for the night scared me. Would I just knock on all the doors until someone answered?

"But how do you know where people are sleeping?" I asked.

"That's the fun of it," he replied.

George was standing on the stairs, hand on the banister, looking down at me and smiling. "Welcome to Friar Park, Chris."

18

PATTIE'S BIRTHDAY PARTY

March 1970

I woke up the next morning shivering. During the night I must have inched up right next to the gas heater, trying to stay warm. I pulled the sleeping bag close around my shoulders and leaned up on one arm, looking around the room. Daylight flooded in through the large French windows that looked out onto a sweeping lawn with stone steps leading down to a magnificent fountain. From there the lawn stretched to a forest of trees that surrounded the property. Dark clouds thickened the sky, and a cold wind blew through the still-leafless trees, but that view made me forget all about the weather.

There was a knock on the door. Terry came into the room, all smiles, holding a mug of tea. The steam rose from the cup and hovered, ghostlike, in the chill air.

"Good morning!" he said cheerfully. Then he stopped, looking at me in horror. "Fucking hell, Chris, you didn't sleep that close to the heater, did you? It's lucky you didn't catch on fucking fire."

I scooched back several inches, still wrapped up in my sleeping bag.

"Is everyone awake?" I asked, reaching gratefully for my cup of tea.

"I just took tea to George and Pattie," Terry said with a big smile. He sure was cheerful in the morning. "When you're ready, come to the kitchen for breakfast."

"Where is the kitchen?" I asked, feeling a little frantic and trying to untangle myself from the sleeping bag. On our drive the night before George told me there were 120 rooms in the house. I could just imagine wandering around all day, getting lost in a maze of dusty, cobwebby, cold, and drafty rooms.

"Put your coat on and follow me," Terry said, heading out the door.

We walked across the main hall to a door that led into a long tiled corridor, which I guessed was a servants' hallway. At the end of the hallway and after a right turn (*shit,* I thought, *I never would have found this on my own*), Terry opened a door that led into an enormous tiled kitchen with an old stove, a hutch used to store dishes, and a long wooden table with benches on either side. A series of tall, lead-paned windows filled the wall behind the kitchen table, looking out past the driveway to the gardens and greenhouse. The sink, refrigerator, washing machine, and dryer were in a connecting room, another large, tiled, empty space with windows on two sides and a gigantic cutting board in the center.

Pattie was standing in front of the stove stirring porridge while George sat at the long table with a steaming cup of tea, blowing softly on it while turning the pages of the morning newspapers. That was the normal routine—tea, porridge, and three or four newspapers spread around the kitchen table.

"Good morning," I said as I entered the kitchen. They both looked at me and smiled a good morning back.

"Hey, Chris," George said, "how'd you sleep?"

"Amazingly well," I said. I didn't feel it was right to complain this early on about the bitter cold or the sunburn I got from sleeping too close to the heater.

"Would you like some porridge?" Pattie said, spooning oatmeal into a big white bowl.

"That'd be great, thanks," I said as I walked across the vast kitchen to take the bowl.

That was such a strange and indescribable experience, waking up in that enormous house and finding myself having breakfast with George and Pattie Harrison. It was a dream, almost exactly like the dream I used to play out in front of my mirror.

"I have a lot to show you today, Chris," Pattie said, spooning out her own bowl of hot cereal. "We have the whole house to explore, and I thought we'd also do a little shopping in Henley."

And so my life at Friar Park had begun. After breakfast—usually porridge or boiled eggs and tea—George spent the day in the garden, dressed in an old shirt and pants and, when it was raining or the ground was soggy, knee-high wellies. During the day but more often at night he'd play his guitar in the kitchen or retire to the music room alone. When Pattie, George, Terry, and I gathered in the kitchen for drinks or meals, most of our conversations focused on Friar Park. It was as if there were no world outside Friar Park, and as time went by, the walls seemed to close in, shielding us from all outside influences.

Sometimes we'd all watch a movie in the office next to the kitchen, another large room with big windows, furnished with a heavy wood desk, sofas, chairs, and audio and video equipment. George loved Monty Python, and his favorite movie was the Mel Brooks film *The Producers,* with Zero Mostel and Gene Wilder. We must have watched that movie a dozen times, and he'd always howl with laughter during the "Springtime for Hitler" scene, especially when the woman with the pretzels on her breasts came flouncing down the stairs.

In those first few days of March 1970, while George and Terry puttered around the property—ten acres of formal gardens and an additional twenty acres of land—Pattie and I toured the sprawling mansion. There were so many rooms leading off so many hallways in so many wings that I always got a little spooked. We must have set out to explore the place, hoping to see everything, at least a dozen times, but we always got distracted—a hidden door, a sudden creak in the floor, the feeling that someone was following us—and we'd walk or sometimes run as fast as we could back to the main hall, giggling all the way.

As we explored the different wings and peeked into the dusty rooms, Pattie told me a little about the history of the place. In 1898 Sir Frank Crisp, a wealthy London lawyer, built the Gothic mansion on the site of an old monastery. With its towers and turrets, gargoyles and gardens, stained-glass windows, and underground caves filled with stalagmites and stalactites, Friar Park was both regal and fanciful. Sir Frank must have had a wonderful sense of humor and a childlike love of play. On a high spot of the grounds he built a massive sandstone replica of the Matterhorn, and the three small lakes on the property were connected with tunnels large enough to row a boat through. Engraved into the mansion's stonework were numerous pithy sayings ("Eton boys are a Harrowing sight"). George's favorite dictum, carved into a monument on the grounds was "Don't keep off the grass." I loved the little scene, carved into the front of the house, titled "Two Holy Friars," showing a monk holding a frying pan with holes in it. Giant mushrooms and little red gnomes greeted you in the underground caves, and all the light switches in the house were monks' faces that you switched on and off by the nose.

After Sir Frank's death, Pattie told me, an English lord bought Friar Park for his bride. He died soon thereafter and she moved to the stables, eventually selling everything but the area around the stables to the Catholic Church to run as a school (and during World War II, as a shelter for children).

"For the children's safety, the nuns sealed the doors to the underground caves and filled in the lakes." Pattie pointed up at the cherubs on the ballroom ceiling, her eyes bright with amusement. "And for the sake of the children's souls," she said, "the nuns painted diapers on the cherubs' naked bottoms. The school closed eventually, but when we bought the house, there were still six nuns and a monk living here."

I'm not sure if it was the nuns, the dead lord, the ghost of Sir Frank, or the labyrinthine tunnels underneath the house, but as much as I loved living at Friar Park, I never felt completely at ease there. It was too big to be homey and at times felt more like a mausoleum than a place where people actually lived. At night, especially, I'd feel the cold draft in those high-ceilinged rooms and feel a chill running down my spine. Terry didn't help things. He was convinced the house was haunted. One night he came tearing down the hallway into the kitchen, his face drained of color, breathing hard.

"I . . . just . . . saw . . . a . . . bloody . . . fucking . . . ghost."

Pattie quickly poured him a glass of wine—and filled ours to the brims—as we listened intently to his story.

"I was walking along the minstrels' gallery," he said, "and suddenly there was this man standing there. I asked him what he was doing. And then he just—he just disappeared into thin air!"

I don't know if Terry actually saw something that night, but his terror was real enough. It took several glasses of wine and a lot of comforting words for him to settle down and start breathing normally again.

The kitchen always felt like the safest room in the whole house, and we spent most of our time there. It was certainly the warmest room, with the light streaming in through the windows, the gas heaters faithfully pumping out warm air, and the oven and stove, which always seemed to be in use as Pattie experimented daily with new vegetarian recipes. I never ceased to be amazed by her energy and creativity. She wanted to grow vegetables, so she bought books on gardening, studied them, dug out the space, planted seeds, and harvested the vegetables for her fabulous meals. And she was also a gifted interior decorator, careful to buy lamps, tables, rugs, bed frames, and bureaus that matched the style of the old house.

As the weeks passed and spring settled in with the seeds sprouting and the trees leafing, I began to feel that Friar Park was my home, too. Pattie, George, Terry, and I became a little family, eating most of our meals together, watching movies, listening to music, puttering around in the garden, even predicting each other's moods. The dinners were the most fun of all. I was Pattie's sous-chef. I'd wash and chop vegetables; she'd use whatever was growing in the garden to make the most fabulous sauces and pasta dishes. She was always trying something new. We sipped wine while we cooked, and due to the elaborate recipes, the vastness of the kitchen, and the time-outs for conversation, we were usually quite tipsy by dinnertime. Pattie would give me directions ("gently pull the lettuce leaves and wash each one individually, chop the eggplant sideways rather than straight up and down, add a liberal amount of basil to the tomatoes"), which I would follow diligently.

Although I wolfed down those vegetarian meals, after a few weeks I began to crave meat. It got worse as time went on. When Pattie and I went food shopping in Henley, I would stare longingly at the meat hanging in the butcher's window, wondering how I could possibly smuggle a nice little steak into the kitchen. I couldn't tell Pattie about my cravings, because I knew she would "tsk-tsk" me and with laughing eyes tell me to "behave myself." But whenever I could, I'd slip away from her on our grocery trips into Henley and stand for a minute or two outside the butcher's window, staring at the forbidden red meat.

I loved talking about the goings-on at Apple, chatting about family news such as Pattie's sister Jenny's marriage to Mick Fleetwood or her sister Paula's involvement with Eric Clapton, and all the other tidbits of information that found their way to our peaceful, secluded hideaway.

I hated those days, though, when George was moody and intense, because he'd quickly tire of the gossip and lash out at us with short, quick, sarcastic little jabs. "What a load of rubbish!" he'd say with a tinge of disgust. We would immediately feel ashamed of ourselves, and the conversation would stop dead in its tracks.

I began to realize that there were three Georges in the house. When I heard him striding down the long hallway toward the kitchen, always with a little bounce in his step, I'd find myself silently saying, *George, please be in a good mood.* The first George was great fun and loved to gossip, drink, smoke a little pot, and even, on rare occasions, snort a line or two of cocaine. This was my favorite George, the one I first got to know and love at Apple, and whenever he'd hang out with us, we were all happy. The second George was intense, sarcastic, and detached; he'd morph into this George when things were bothering him at Apple or with the other Beatles, or when something wasn't going quite right with the garden or the remodeling efforts. Little things would set him off at these times, and we'd all have to watch our step. The third George was the spiritual seeker, the one who would walk around with his hand inside his prayer bag and chant silently to himself. At these times he was peaceful and serene, totally absorbed in otherworldly thoughts. I had many amazing discussions with this third George and learned a lot from him, but truthfully, he wasn't a whole lot of fun for the rest of us who really preferred drinking, talking, laughing, and having fun.

When George was in a good mood, we'd often sit in the kitchen after dinner and talk, smoke cigarettes, have a few drinks, and listen to him strum his guitar while singing the new songs he was working on. George's voice was so much warmer when he was in the same room with you. Something rich and vital was lost when his voice was surrounded by guitars and drums, overdubbed several times, mixed way down under the instruments, and then pressed onto vinyl. When he sang for us in the kitchen, the library, or by the big fireplace in the main hall, we heard his true, naked voice with no control board, engineers, musicians, instruments, or microphones to dilute its purity or its power. I would watch and listen, knowing how incredibly lucky I was to be there, literally "framing" those moments and locking them away in my memory.

When he wasn't drinking or doing drugs, George became the spiritually minded George, and the transformation could be instantaneous. On those evenings, George and I often ended up in the kitchen alone. Pattie was wearying of George's obsessive meditating and chanting and had begun to resent the way he disappeared for hours into his music room or the makeshift temple he'd constructed upstairs. Her grand plans for an exciting, people-filled life at Friar Park—summer parties on the grounds, private dinner gatherings for friends, musical events for charity, family reunions—did not align with George's increasing need for space and privacy. Pattie loved to have fun, and she always found a way to focus on the joy in life, while George was wrestling more and more often with issues of karma and the meaning of life. As time went on, the separation between them grew wider and deeper. I saw it happening but, like Pattie, chose to believe that the George who loved to play and laugh would make his way back to us. Whenever

George started in on one of his spiritual rants, Pattie and Terry would yawn somewhat dramatically and excuse themselves to go off to bed.

I was always a willing listener. I wanted to know more about Eastern religious beliefs. I'd tried meditation but never experienced the serenity that George talked about. So I figured I'd sit at the foot of a master, or at least the closest thing to a master I was ever going to encounter. And George always smelled so good; the fragrance of sandalwood oil followed him wherever he went. It was in his clothes, his hair, his skin, and in every room of the house. Just sitting near him made me feel at peace.

"We must always be thinking about karma," he said one night as he took a drag from his ciggie.

I nodded. I knew what karma was because I'd read about it. Bad actions or thoughts generate more bad actions or thoughts, while good calls forth good. Karma was like a giant fan in the cosmic universe that blows back at you whatever you happen to throw out. Everything we do, big or small, good or evil, happy or sad, compassionate or cruel, has consequences in this life or the next.

"I don't want to have to come back to this earth again," George said, almost ruefully. "All I can do is the best I can do in this lifetime."

"Are you talking about reincarnation?" I asked him, having also read about that.

"Yes." He got quiet and thoughtful for a moment. "There is no place like Nirvana!" he said, making a little joke of it as if he were Dorothy in *The Wizard of Oz* announcing, "There's no place like home."

"But what *is* Nirvana?" I asked, truly interested in his answer

"Nirvana is the release of the soul from the endless cycle of rebirth. The final destination." A look of peace spread across his face. I sat there contentedly, wide eyed, attempting to take in every word he was saying, finding comfort in his soothing voice, being consoled by the idea that there was a great "plan" for all of us and that a God of some sort was watching over us. Every so often I nodded my head or muttered a soft, "wow" or "really?"

"You have to deal with the karma of your past lives, Chris, that's the purpose for being here," he said. "Say the Hare Krishna chant over and over and you will feel closer to God."

"I believe that," I said, remembering the plane flight from the Isle of Wight with John and Yoko.

"If you keep chanting, after a while you realize that God is with you, God is right there with you, sitting next to you, inside you."

"Wow," I said. I wasn't faking the *wow* part. When George talked to me about his spiritual beliefs, I felt there really must be a higher plane, a safer place.

When I told Pattie about my conversation with George the next morning, she smiled as she put down her gardening book, her hand resting on the open page, marking her place. Pattie had a gift for listening, gently pausing, repeating back what I said just to make sure she understood my thoughts and feelings, allowing me to say everything I needed to say before she offered her perspective. But I could tell she was feeling threatened by George's intense focus on his spiritual practice and the ongoing, seemingly never-ending renovations of Friar Park. He seemed to have lost sight of her needs. Although she didn't express her feelings in these exact words to me, I think she was wondering, how can someone get more "spiritual" and at the same time pull away from the people he loves most in the world? What sort of spirituality is it if it comes between relationships? More than a decade later in an interview with his old Hare Krishna friend Mukunda, George admitted that there was one problem with chanting. "I start beginning to relate less and less to the people I know," George said. "I suddenly find myself on such a different level where it's really hard to relate. It feels as though I'm at a point where I should slow down or pull back toward those people in order to take them with me . . . There's a point where I can't relate to anyone anymore."

"Let's have a party!" Pattie said. Pattie, George, and I were sitting in the kitchen, reading the morning newspapers and sipping our tea while Pattie leafed through one of her cookbooks. George kept his head down as he took a screwdriver to one of his garden tools. George was always working on garden things.

"George?" she repeated. He seemed not to have heard her. "Don't you think we should have a party? A combination birthday and St. Patrick's Day party!" Pattie's birthday fell on March 17, St. Patrick's Day.

"Where would people sit?" he said. There was still no furniture in the house except the bench by the fire.

"We could bring in a few chairs and sit on the rugs on the floor," Pattie said, her hands gesturing happily as she made plans. "It would be great fun. Everyone is so anxious to see the house."

"I'm sure they are," George mumbled. Pattie's smile quickly turned to a frown when she saw the expression on George's face. Friar Park was his kingdom, and he clearly did not want to have a party. He'd finally found a way to get away from all the fans and reporters, not to mention the bickering that had gone on among the Beatles, and he didn't want his tranquility disturbed.

"George, listen to me." Pattie folded her arms in front of her chest, straightened her back, and set her jaw. "None of our friends has seen Friar Park. And besides, it's my birthday."

Terry walked into the kitchen at precisely that moment.

"Teddy!" Pattie said. "Don't you think it would be wonderful to have a party?"

I was impressed by Pattie's strategy. Terry was always up for a party and George didn't stand a chance between the two of them.

"Fucking brilliant," Terry said as he grabbed an imaginary partner and danced across the room. "It would be fucking great to have some people around."

I sat on the sidelines watching the whole thing unfold, completely entertained. I knew George would give in eventually. Who could possibly say no to Pattie?

"It wouldn't have to be large, George, just our closest friends."

"Who would we invite?" George put down the screwdriver and looked up at her for the first time. Ah-ha. He was softening.

"Well, I was thinking we'd invite Ringo and Maureen, John and Yoko, Paul and Linda, Neil and Susie, Derek and Joan, Peter Brown, and maybe a few others. Fewer than twenty all together, just a few good friends so they can see the house and the gardens."

"Hmmmm," George said again, but this time he put a little more oomph into it. A small party wouldn't be so bad, he seemed to be thinking, and it might be fun to show off the house and the gardens.

"It is my birthday, after all," Pattie said with her prettiest pout.

"Okay," he said with a little "I give up" sort of smile. He stood up from the table, picked up his tools, and walked down the hallway and out the back door to the garden. Terry followed close behind.

Pattie leaned across the pine table, a big victory smile on her face. "Oooh," she said, "we're going to have so much fun!"

The party was a great success. Ringo and Maureen, Paul and Linda, John and Yoko, Derek and Joan, Neil and Susie Aspinall, Klaus and Christine Voormann, and Peter Brown were all there. I think Mary and Peter Frampton were there, too, along with several other people I can't remember. Pattie and George gave tours through the house, and I took on the job of making sure that everybody's glasses were full and the food trays were constantly replenished. As I flitted around the room, taking part in bits and pieces of conversation, I couldn't help thinking that I had reached a new high. I was on the inside now, George and Pattie's friend, living with them at Friar Park, and one of the invited guests at their private party.

Part of the night's plan was to take everyone through the caves. Sir Frank Crisp had created a dark and fascinating world under Friar Park. We had only a few flashlights, so the group stuck close together, oohing and ahhing our way through the tunnels. We found a dwarf at every turn, little mushroom chairs in the corners, and a chest with fake jewels spilling out the top. We felt like little kids on a treasure hunt at Disneyland.

"This is a real magical mystery tour," someone laughed, but just a few minutes later Susie Aspinall started crying, freaked out by the darkness and weirdness of it all. The group split up, with a few people accompanying Susie back to the main hall and the rest of us making our way to the end of the tunnel, emerging at the Matterhorn and then walking back across the grounds to the house. People gathered around the fireplace, comforted by the light and the warmth. I was sitting on the floor talking to Neil and Susie, who was still a little shaken up. Neil had his arm around her, smiling and comforting her, when Ringo sat down next to me.

"Hey, Chris," he said, smiling at me. "So you're living at Friar Park, working for George now, are you? Good gig."

"Yeah, it's been a lot of fun. I loved working with Neil, but this has been great."

He hesitated, looking at me for a moment as if deciding whether or not to bring up the subject. "Didn't you go to Los Angeles with Leon Russell?"

"Yeah, I was there for a while, but it didn't work out." I felt the expected flush of embarrassment, but I was also surprised to discover that it felt really good to talk with Ringo about Leon. I'd been trying to forget about him, but that was impossible because people kept talking about the wildly successful Mad Dogs and Englishmen tour he was doing with Joe Cocker. My longing for Leon and my misery over the end of the relationship hadn't ebbed. Sometimes I'd talk to Pattie about him, my heart feeling as if it would break at the mention of his name, but I didn't want to risk boring her too much with my loneliness and longing. I couldn't get over the breakup, not realizing yet that I was less troubled about losing Leon than I was about feeling rejected and unworthy.

"I like Leon," Ringo said. "He's a good musician."

"Yeah, he is a good musician," I said.

"Sorry it didn't work out for you. I really liked playing on that session with him."

I brightened up a little at the memory of George and Ringo in the session with Leon. "That's right, you played on 'Pisces Apple Lady,' the song he wrote for me," I said. "Leon was going back to America because he didn't have a drummer and I mentioned that you might be available. Did you know that part of the story?"

"No, I hadn't heard about that. But that's great," he said, tilting his head to the side and regarding me with more interest.

We were chatting on about this and that when suddenly I felt a shadow. I looked up and saw Maureen staring down at us. I smiled, thinking she might want to join the conversation.

"Richie," she said, her lips pulled tight, "I think it's time we leave."

Ringo patted the floor next to him. "Come sit with us," he said. "You've met Chris O'Dell before, right? She works for us."

"Yes. Hello," she said, cold as ice.

"We were just talking about Leon Russell," Ringo said. "Chris lived with him in LA for a while."

"That's nice." She shifted from one foot to the next. She wasn't smiling. "We need to go, Richie."

Brrrrr, I thought, actually shivering a little.

"Okay, good talking to you, Chris," Ringo said. Maureen walked over to Pattie and George, Ringo following close behind, and they said good night.

The party broke up soon after they left, and we all went happily to bed.

The next day I went up to Pattie's sewing room where she was sorting through some fabrics that she had picked up on her travels. I could tell that she was more absorbed in the beauty of the materials than she was in the project she was working on. Pattie loved beautiful things. We talked about the party, who was there, what people said about the house, how Susie and the others reacted to the tunnels, just going over all the details to share our experiences and fix the night in our memories.

"You know, it was kind of weird with Maureen last night," I said, describing my conversation with Ringo and what I perceived as Maureen's icy behavior. "I don't think she was happy to see me talking to Ringo."

"Well, you know Maureen is very protective of her marriage," Pattie said. She looked at me for a moment, her brow furrowed, as if trying to decide how much to tell me. Then she relaxed and smiled, having made up her mind.

"Maureen phoned this morning to thank me for the party. And she asked who you were."

"Really?" I said. Had Maureen misinterpreted my conversation with Ringo? Did she think I was coming on to him? I'd heard stories from Pattie about the fans who literally threw themselves at the Beatles and how they often said and did hateful things to their wives and girlfriends. A fan had even clawed at sixteen-year-old Maureen's face soon after she started dating Ringo.

"Do you have a lot of close friends, Pattie?"

"I've never really had many girlfriends before," Pattie said. "I feel safest with my sisters and a few old friends. It seems that just when I've begun to really trust someone and let them into my life, they start after George. When you're married to a Beatle, it's very difficult to trust women."

Pattie was quiet for a few moments, and I could see that she was gathering her thoughts. Over the years, as our friendship deepened, I'd learn that when she would stare at me in the middle of a conversation, she was simply thinking about what words to choose. You could almost see the wheels spinning and the thoughts being processed. Pattie was very careful with her words, knowing how they could be misinterpreted, and was always hesitant about saying something that might hurt someone's feelings.

"You know, Chris, you're actually one of the first girls I've allowed myself to get close to." Again, she hesitated, but this time I could tell she was really struggling with what she had to say. Many years later she told me that she thought George had brought me to Friar Park to sleep with him.

"I'm sorry, I've never said this to anyone before," she said, "but you will only be my friend as long as you don't let George have you."

I didn't have to think for one moment about my response. "Okay, that's a deal," I said. "I'd rather be your friend."

Later as I thought about that conversation, I felt a little confused. On the one hand, I was so happy and grateful that Pattie considered me a close friend and I had no doubt that I could keep my promise to her about George. She was right; he was a terrible flirt, and once or twice at Apple and again at Friar Park he had tried to come on to me. "Stop that, George!" I'd say, raising my eyebrow as if I were scolding a little boy for naughty behavior, and we'd have a good laugh.

But the situation with Maureen unnerved me a little. Maybe I had been flirting with Ringo, which was interesting because I'd never thought of him in a romantic or sexual way. He just seemed so nice— that was the word that came to mind. A really nice guy who was devoted to his wife and children.

I just couldn't imagine that a Beatle wife would ever see me as a threat.

19

HARE KRISHNA

April–May 1970

One glorious spring morning Pattie and I, yearning for a day in the big city, shed our country pants and boots for dresses and fancy shoes and drove in her cherry red Mercedes to London. We shopped on Bond Street, stopped by Apple to see Peter Brown, had a massage at a fashionable spa right off Berkeley Square, and met actor John Hurt for dinner at a French restaurant. By the time we headed back to the country, it was after midnight, but the hour drive flew by as we recounted all the details of our fun-packed day.

As we approached the house, we noticed that most of the lights were out and concluded that George and Terry must have already gone to bed. We parked the car in the back of the house near the garage and the kitchen entrance. Pattie turned the back door handle, but it wouldn't open. She tried again.

"Chris, something is terribly wrong," she said in a low voice, trying not to sound panicked.

"What?" I asked.

"I don't have any keys and they've locked the doors. What shall we do?"

"It can't be locked, it never is," I said. "Try again."

She tried once more, but the door was firmly locked.

"Let's try the front door," I suggested. "Maybe they thought we'd come in that way."

We walked around the side of the large mansion to the front, holding on to each other and being careful not to wander off the driveway. It was very dark that night and an eerie wind whistled through the surrounding trees and shrubs. I was terrified, and I could tell from the way Pattie was squeezing my arm that she was, too.

The front door was firmly bolted from the inside.

"What shall we do?" I asked in a low whisper. We clung more tightly to each other as the night closed around us.

"We could always sleep in the car, I guess."

"Pattie, don't be silly!" I said, giggling nervously. Her car wasn't big enough for one person to sleep in.

"Well, I guess we'll have to wake George."

We looked at the suddenly unfamiliar house, a towering and frightening stone edifice. It looked so huge and massive in the dark night that I couldn't help wondering what was behind the doors of all the rooms I'd never explored. The walls and windows were thick, and the wind, which seemed to be howling, would make it almost impossible to wake George, who was probably sound asleep by now.

Still holding on to each other and staying as close to the house as we could without tromping through George's beloved flower beds, we walked to the south side of the house and looked up at the second-floor bedroom window. We both began calling George's name, hoping that somehow he would awaken and rescue us. At first we kept our voices low, but as the minutes went by we started yelling as loud as we could. Shivering and scared, horrified by the idea that someone might be watching us from behind one of the trees or bushes on the property, we called out George's name for what seemed like hours.

Eventually the window opened and George's silhouette appeared.

"Who's out there? Pattie, is that you?"

"George, the back door is locked!" Pattie cried out. "Can you let us in?"

"The back door isn't locked."

"Yes, it is," she said. "Please, let us in. It's freezing out here."

ᴀʙᴏᴠᴇ: It was a freezing January day when the Beatles performed their last concert on the roof of Apple. In front of
the chimney (*left to right*) are Yoko Ono, Maureen Starkey,
Ken Mansfield, a friend from LA, and me.

ʟᴇꜰᴛ: The door to Apple Records on Savile Row in London.
There was usually a group of Beatle fans outside, but the
sidewalk was deserted on the day that I took this, which
meant there were no Beatles inside.

(Tom Hanley)

(Author's private collection)

CING PAGE, TOP: I took this picture of erek Taylor sitting in his white cane air in the press office of Apple. Notice e Sgt. Derek Taylor desk sign.

CING PAGE, BELOW: My mom came to visit e in the summer of 1969, and I took r to a recording session at Abbey Road udios where George was producing e Hare Krishna mantra record. One of e Krishnas took this photo of me with eorge and my mom, Barbara.

IS PAGE, TOP: This picture of George and e appeared in the Dublin Evening Her- d in 1969. I'm not sure exactly where was taken but I assume at Apple. I ved my shag haircut.

IS PAGE, BELOW: After I heard "Pisces pple Lady," the song that Leon wrote r me, we began spending all our time gether. I took this picture of him with nny Cordell's son, Tarka, at Denny's t in Chelsea.

Richard DiLello took this photo of Pattie's sister Jenny Boyd, Pattie, and me in front of the fireplace in the Main Hall of Friar Park. I have no idea who the dog belonged to.

One day during the summer before Bangladesh, Pattie, Harry Harrison, and I decided to spend a quiet d at the beach. I loved Harry and spent a lot of time with him over the next few years. We asked a stranger take this photo of us.

I took this photo of George in 1970 during my Christmas stay. The kitchen had moved to the room that I slept in my first night at Friar Park.

I took this picture of Pattie that same night. She always seemed to be in the kitchen. Check out the sign over the stove.

ABOVE: Pattie and I wrote to each other ofte[n] and in one letter she enclosed this photo [of] her and George in the south garden at Fria[r] Park.

LEFT: Pattie took this photo of George and Do[n] Nix, a musician from Memphis, on a boat the[y] chartered to Catalina Island. During this tr[ip] Don agreed to help get background singers f[or] the Bangladesh concert.

(Photo courtesy of Pattie Boyd)

LEFT: This photo of me and Mick Jagger was taken during the *Exile On Main Street* sessions at Sunset Sound Recorders in spring 1972. I am sure I dialed the number for Mick's phone call.

BELOW: I finally found my place at the back of the Stones plane during the '72 tour near Mick and Keith. Notice the cigarette hanging out of my mouth and the map of the tour behind me.

I don't remember this photo being taken but it looks like a familiar pose Mick and I would strike when camping around. It was taken during the '72 tour backstage in a dressing room.

This is one of my favorite photos. It was taken backstage in Nashville just before the week break when I decided to leave the tour. I love the way it captures the sweetness of Keith Richards.

Ringo and I were in his bedroom at the Santa Monica beach house that John Lennon had rented from Peter Lawford while they recorded Harry Nilsson's *Pussy Cats* album.

Hilary Gerrard, Ringo's financial adviser and one of my best friends, was in Japan with Ringo and Nancy Andrews when she took this photo.

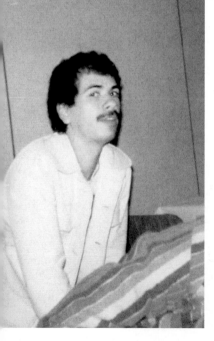

I took this photo of Carlos during a sound check in Paris on the Santana/Earth, Wind & Fire European tour of 1975. Carlos is one of the most considerate musicians I've ever worked with.

LEFT: Pattie and Eric at their wedding reception in Tucson, Arizona, right before the food fight. I was a bridesmaid, although I chose to sit the pews, as I was afraid Eric would make some snide remark about me in front of everyone.

BELOW: Bob Dylan, Louie Kemp, and Sam Shepard during the Rolling Thunder Revue tour. This was taken on a New England summer day and Bob looks as relaxed as I'd ever seen him. Sam and I were involved during this time.

(Photo courtesy of Pattie Boyd)

(Photo © Ken Regan/Camera)

ABOVE: On the Rolling Thunder Revue band bus with band members Rob Stoner (*left*) and David Mansfield (*right*) both playing guitars. Ava Megna, who also worked on the tour, is standing next to me and I sadly can't remember the other two people's names.

LEFT: T-Bone Burnett was a very good friend during that tour and we kidded around a lot. Here we are backstage at one of the Rolling Thunder gigs.

ABOVE: My dear friend Neal Preston took this photo of r
backstage in Munich at a Queen concert. He had flown ov
to Europe to photograph Queen and captured this dark m
ment. Brian May, the lead guitarist in Queen, is behind r
with his back turned.

LEFT: My cigarette holder is a remnant of my years with Ma
reen, who used one just like it. The arrogance in my expr
sion belies the pain of alcoholism and drug addiction duri
these lost years.

RIGHT: I spent time with Astrid Lundstrom in the South of France after leaving Germany. She and Bill Wyman had broken up, and she was packing up all her possessions from their house. It was during this time that I met Anthony, my future husband.

BELOW: During the years that I was living in Germany I flew home to see my family. I went to New York first, and May Pang and I decided to drive to Los Angeles, stopping in New Mexico to spend Christmas with my sister and parents.

Pattie took this 1983 photo of Maureen in Maureen's kitchen on the evening we interviewed her for c proposed book. She was divorced from Ringo and not yet married to Isaac Tigrett.

Anthony and I decided to get married at his family home, Leeds Castle, on June 21, 1985. My dad, John; my sister, Vicki; and Pattie escorted me to the chapel in the castle. We had to wait until all the tourists had left for the day.

We had our reception in a marquee between the Maiden's Tower (Anthony's mother's home) and the castle. Two hundred people were invited for a sit down dinner and dancing to a live band. Anthony and I are having our first dance.

(...thor's private collection)

(Author's private collection)

...is has to be my favorite picture in ...e whole world. We were living in Los ...geles and we didn't like the preschool ...oto taken of three-year-old Will, so ...e photographer agreed to retake it at a ...rk in Santa Monica. What luck.

Ringo came to Tucson in 1992 for the Ringo Starr Invitational Golf Tournament at Loews Ventana hotel. We went to visit him and Barbara and I took this picture of him and Will.

Kathy Ketcham took this photo of Will and me in Tucson in 2007. He has become quite a wonderful young man of whom I am very proud.

We ran back down the driveway all the way around the massive house and waited for the sweet sound of a key turning in the lock. The door opened and George stood there, clad in his dressing gown, hair tousled.

"This is really weird," he said, running his hand through his hair. "We knew you didn't have a key, so we purposely left the door unlocked. How strange."

A week or two later Richard DiLello arrived at Friar Park to deliver some publicity photos for George to okay. He took a spin around the property on one of the dirt bikes, fell off, broke his arm, and ended up staying for two weeks. Pattie and I loved having him around the house and got a big kick out of his reaction to life at Friar Park. The longer people stayed at Friar Park, the more out of touch they felt with the real world. Richard gradually got wrapped up in the web of that self-contained, self-absorbed place. Yet we still yearned for news of the outside world, and whenever George was out of earshot, we grilled Richard with questions. Mostly we wanted to know about Apple. Allen Klein, Richard told us, seemed hell-bent on removing every vestige of fun and frivolity from Savile Row. The phones had stopped ringing. Neil was still working on his cinematic Beatles chronicle, spending all his time in his office surrounded by reels of film. Music producer Phil Spector, always difficult and often volatile, was finishing up the remix of the *Let It Be* album and had managed to annoy just about everyone with his eccentric and often temperamental behavior. Derek was still holding on, but just barely. "It's a deathwatch," Richard said, admitting that he was just waiting for the ax to fall.

One evening George and Terry went to London, most likely for a recording session, and Richard, Pattie, and I took our customary positions, sitting on pillows on the floor in front of the blazing fire in the main hall, drinking wine and chatting. Richard went upstairs to fetch something from his room, which was off the second-floor landing and tucked back into the darker, scarier part of the house. As he walked around the minstrels' gallery that surrounded three sides of the main hall, he spotted someone climbing in a window in the upstairs hallway.

"Hey, man what are you doing?" he asked in a steady but surprised voice.

The guy was so shocked that he bolted back out of the window and disappeared. Richard returned to the minstrels' gallery and shouted down at us.

"Some guy was just trying to climb in the window." Calm Richard was uncharacteristically shaken.

"What? Is he still there?"

"No," Richard said as he looked fearfully over his shoulder. "I think I scared him away."

The local police searched the grounds with flashlights, finding a ladder pushed up against the outside wall of the house but no other sign of the intruder.

We never felt totally safe after that.

And then the Krishnas came to live at Friar Park.

At first we thought it would be a great adventure, and we were happy for George because now he'd have people to chant with whenever he felt like it, and they'd be a big help with the gardens. I was a little in awe of the Krishnas. From the moment they moved in, a saffron glow seemed to permeate the entire house. They created a temple in the formal dining room, filling the entire room with candles and incense burners. I often went there to meditate. Shyamasundar and Mukunda would often join us in the kitchen for a cup of tea, thanking us with little prayerful bows, their orange robes flowing softly around them, before leaving to join George in the garden. The women sometimes cooked delicious spicy vegetarian dishes for us in their kitchen upstairs. Every morning we'd awake to find a prayer or spiritual reminder on the kitchen blackboard, reminding us of our earthly bondage and our essential spiritual nature.

"That's cool," I'd say.

Pattie would nod her head in agreement as she prepared the morning tea. "Isn't it nice to wake up to those little sayings?"

We just hadn't figured on the children. In the beginning, the patter of their little feet above us brought smiles to our faces. But then they started playing in the fountain on the south side of the house. The first time one of the children almost drowned, Pattie frantically called the doctor—the child, just three or four years old, was choking and struggling to breathe. We honestly thought he wouldn't make it. As the doctor tended to him, patting his back and calming him down, the Krishna women stood around with no visible concern on their serene faces. And no remorse, either. Weren't they a little ashamed of themselves for losing sight of their children and allowing one of them to climb into a fountain and nearly drown? Pattie and I looked at each other, perplexed.

But the kids continued to run loose on the grounds, climb into the fountain, play in the water, and sure enough, one of them almost drowned again. When the doctor arrived the second time, he was very upset. With a stern look on his face and speaking through clenched teeth, he delivered a little lecture.

"Mrs. Harrison, I'm sorry, but I am not prepared to come out a third time," he said. "These people really need to take care of their children."

When the doctor left and the Krishnas disappeared back upstairs, Pattie and I tried to figure out what to do.

"Oh God," I said, looking at Pattie in dismay. "I hope he doesn't think we're the irresponsible ones."

"Me too," she said grimly. Later she had a talk with the Krishna women, but they were upset about the doctor's critical remarks and told her that they trusted Krishna to take care of the children who were, after all, only on loan to them in this lifetime.

"What is wrong with them? They can't even take care of their own children!" Pattie was thoroughly exasperated and ready to kick them out right then and there, but George wanted them to stay. So they stayed—and stayed and stayed and stayed. The washing machines were always full of diapers and kids' clothing. Even the cleaning ladies complained about the fact that the machines were never available. The cleaning ladies also grumbled about the mess upstairs in the wing the Krishnas occupied—clothes strewn all over the place, candles leaving piles of wax, dishes piled up in the sink. The sickly sweet odor of saffron permeated everything, even our clothes and our skin; in the morning I could smell it in my hair. The little sayings on the blackboard, often taken directly from the *Bhagavad Gita,* the sacred Hindu scriptures, began to piss us off. We interpreted them as preachy little quotes intended to chide us for our profligate ways or undisguised attempts to convert us.

What made it even worse was that George was spending more and more time with them. He was disappearing into spiritual bliss while Pattie, Terry, and I continued to gather in the kitchen for our nightly ritual of wine, marijuana, gossip, and belly laughs, telling stories about the Krishnas' latest antics and trying not to worry too much about George. After a while, though, the laughter was forced, and we drank too much wine and smoked too many cigarettes and stayed up too late talking because we were all trying to find a way to cope with the realization that George would rather be with the Krishnas than with us. He was slipping away from all of us, and while Terry and I felt the despondency of losing a dear friend, Pattie was in despair, fearing she was losing her husband. She never once complained but every so often, in the saddest tone of voice, she'd say, "Where's George?"

George walked around all day with his hand in his prayer bag, quietly repeating the words, "Hare Krishna, Hare Krishna, Krishna Krishna, Hare Hare." Friends didn't stop by as much, except for occasional visits from Eric Clapton, who enjoyed sitting with Pattie and me in the kitchen. We kept our voices low and tried to contain our laughter. The house was so quiet—that's what I remember more than anything, how quiet it was. Whenever we felt like we couldn't take it anymore, we escaped to the pub in the village.

Then, one day, they were gone. I don't know why they left, but they packed their children and all their belongings in their wood-paneled truck and drove off, waving and chanting all the way down the driveway until they disappeared around the first bend.

That night as we fixed dinner, Pattie and I clicked our wineglasses together and in unison, with great joy and relief, said, "Hare Krishna!"

• • •

"Good morning!" I sang out to Pattie as I walked into the kitchen for breakfast.

"Oh, Chris!" Pattie cried out. "You won't believe what's happening!"

"What?" I said. From the look on her face I thought someone close to us must have died. "What's happened?"

"Paul did an interview for the papers. He said he is no longer with the Beatles. He says they are finished."

"Finished?" I couldn't put my mind around it. How could they be finished? They were the Beatles. Wouldn't there always be the Beatles?

"It's on the front page of all the newspapers. Terry went to get them this morning." Pattie pointed to the kitchen table, and for the first time I noticed the newspapers strewn around the table next to a half-empty cup of tea. All I could think about at that moment was George, sitting there reading about the demise of the Beatles at the very same moment as the rest of the world.

"Where's George?" I asked.

"He's in the garden," Pattie said. "He's beside himself! After all, when Ringo and then John and then George quit, Paul talked them into coming back. Now he just up and leaves, without telling anyone except the newspapers?"

Later that day John Lennon stopped by to talk to George. We watched them wander off by themselves, heads bent low. It struck me, then, that this was the first time I'd seen John without Yoko.

"George, why don't you start working on your album?" Pattie said one night at dinner. We'd all been tiptoeing around George for days, trying to think of ways to help him out of his funk. He was always off by himself, tending to his vegetables, chanting in his top-floor sanctuary, or locked up in the music room playing the guitar and writing new songs.

"Yeah," George said thoughtfully. Then he smiled, lifting all the hearts around the table. George had talked about a solo album, but as long as the Beatles were together, it never seemed the right time. Terry looked at Pattie, who looked at me, and we all looked at George with more hope than we'd thought possible just a few hours earlier. "I guess I have enough material now, with the new songs and the old ones that never got on Beatle albums. Why not?"

"I could help you," I said. "I could type up the lyrics."

"That would be great," he said.

And so began the work on George's first solo album, *All Things Must Pass*.

I set up my workplace in the kitchen, using a brand-new IBM Selectric typewriter, complete with a correction key that magically erased the mistakes. I typed the lyrics that George had written in pen or pencil on pieces of paper torn from notebooks, Apple stationery, and the backs of envelopes. Some of the lyrics were neatly printed while others were hastily scrawled, and he drew thick lines to separate the verses. Sometimes he'd read the lyrics to me and I'd type them as he dictated. We started with his old songs, the ones that had never been included in a Beatles album. He'd come into the kitchen every so often and hand me a piece of paper with scribbled lyrics to a new song, sipping his tea as he looked over my shoulder. Then I'd hand him the typed lyrics, he'd change a word here and there, and give me the handwritten draft to retype.

Sometimes he'd walk in with his guitar, sit down at the table, and sing the songs I'd just typed. Listening to George play his twelve-string guitar in that huge kitchen with daylight streaming in the windows, his feet moving back and forth in a little shuffle that was uniquely his own, was magic. It was such fun for me to be involved, even in a small way, in the creative musical process. In the studio I'd seen the music grow and change as the musicians recorded the songs, and the producer and engineer worked together mixing and editing the songs to shape the final product, but now I was witnessing the real birth of a song, from the very moment it was conceived and penned onto paper.

I didn't know then that Pattie felt excluded from the process as George and I worked so intently together, but I wonder now how I could have been so insensitive to her feelings. I just assumed she was overjoyed, as I was, about George's shift in mood and the positive energy that seemed to spread light throughout the house. The garden was in full bloom, the windows were thrown open to the light breeze that even contained a hint of approaching summer, and the meals Pattie cooked seemed lighter and brighter, full of spring vegetables—yellows, greens, oranges—and fragrant herbs.

I must have been in a different world, because I also had no idea that Eric Clapton was writing love notes to Pattie or that they were secretly meeting for romantic trysts. Eric would stop by now and then and spend a few hours hanging out with us in the kitchen. I assumed he wanted to see me as much as he wanted to be with George and Pattie. We'd become good friends and I had set my sights on him. I knew he liked me, and now that he had broken up with Paula, Pattie's sister, I hoped something might develop out of our friendship. I even called him one day and asked if he would pick me up so I could spend some time at Hurtwood Edge. When he drove up in his Ferrari, I didn't notice the look on Pattie's face nor did I pick up on the way he gazed longingly at her.

I was just clueless.

"Chris! Guess what? I'm going to Los Angeles next week," Pattie literally bounced into my bedroom, waking me from a little nap. "MGM is having a huge sale in their props department—lamps, chandeliers, furniture, all sorts of things that would be perfect for the house!"

My face must have registered both excitement and disappointment. I wanted to go with her. I couldn't stand the thought of being at Friar Park without her.

"I wish you could go," she said, reading my mind. "We'd have so much fun together in LA! Maybe George would get you a ticket, too—I'll ask him."

Later that day Pattie told me she'd talked to George. "He thinks I should go alone," she said with a pout. I knew she was disappointed and nervous about hurting my feelings, so I told her not to worry, reassuring her that I had lots to do and the week would fly by. But I was crushed. I felt rejected—by George. Why didn't George want me to accompany Pattie? I wondered if the thought of Pattie and me cavorting around LA by ourselves made him jealous. Sometimes he could be weird like that. Or maybe it was the money. Renovating Friar Park was expensive and the government taxes were taking something like 95 percent of his income. But a ticket to LA wasn't all that expensive, and I'd be keeping Pattie company, which was one of the reasons he brought me to Friar Park after all, wasn't it? My whole life, I realized a little glumly, depended on his moods and whims. I had no power. I was a lady-in-waiting, an employee who was being paid to live someone else's life and not my own.

Pattie left and I was all alone in that huge house with George and Terry off doing their thing and no one to laugh with or drink with or cook meals with. Once again, for maybe the fifth time in three months, I polished all the doorknobs in the house (but not in the far-off rooms of the distant wings, which still terrified me), but let me tell you, that is one boring job. After two days I was beside myself. When George and Terry announced one morning that they would be gone all day, I figured it was a perfect opportunity to escape for a few hours. I decided to drive to London—Pattie told me I could use her little red Mercedes while she was gone—and it was such a lovely day that I put the top down and turned the radio up full blast. Freedom! I realized then what I'd been missing—my life! George and Pattie had been wonderful to me, and I loved being in the fantasy world at Friar Park, but it wasn't real and it wasn't mine.

I stopped in at Apple to see everyone. Derek, Richard, Peter Brown, Neil, Mavis, and Carol were all there that day, and I had a great time visiting with them. I had lunch with my friend Leslie Cavendish, and then I just drove around London for a while, enjoying the feeling of being behind the wheel again and choosing where I wanted to go. I returned to Friar Park just before dark.

I came in the back door, as usual, and headed down the long tiled corridor to the kitchen. Terry confronted me in the hallway.

"George is very upset that you took Pattie's car," he said.

"Well, she told me I could use it," I said, staying calm on the outside but inside thinking, *Oh, shit, George is upset with me?* That did not feel good.

"He said you're not insured," Terry said.

That conversation threw me. I wondered why George didn't speak to me himself rather than send Terry to convey his displeasure. That thought led to others, each a little more paranoid than the one before. Was I falling out of George's favor? First, he didn't want me to go to LA with Pattie, and then he was upset that I'd used Pattie's car when she was gone. Maybe he thought I wasn't paying enough attention to the work that needed to be done in the house. Maybe he believed I had become too comfortable at Friar Park, shedding my role as companion and helpmate and daring to imagine that I was part of the family. Perhaps he was trying to put me in my place and remind me that I was just a visitor at Friar Park and my stay there was coming to an end. But at the same time, I knew George was fond of me and enjoyed my company. He sought me out, confided in me, asked for my help, respected my opinions. Why, then, was he so angry with me, and so ungenerous?

Pattie came back from Los Angeles, gushing about the wonderful time she'd had and all the quirky and amazing items she'd bought at the auction—lamps, mostly, and a chandelier, but all unique and perfect, she said, for Friar Park.

"Oh, Chris, you should have been there!"

"Was it wonderful? Tell me about it, Pattie," I said. "I'm soooo jealous."

After listening to her stories, I told her what had happened with her car.

"But I said you could use it," she said, giving me one of those blank looks that meant she was thinking and trying to figure out how to respond. When Pattie is deep in thought, her face gives nothing away.

After a moment, she pursed her lips in disapproval. "Oooh that George," she said.

A few weeks later my doubts and fears were confirmed. I'd slept in late that morning and was feeling a little guilty about it.

"Good morning," Pattie said when I walked into the kitchen. "Would you like some tea?"

Something was wrong. I'd spent nearly every day of the last three months with her and I'd gotten pretty good at reading her moods.

"Chris, look, I have to tell you something," she said, setting a teacup on the pine table. "George is going to tell you that he thinks you should go back to Apple."

I knew what that meant, of course. I had lost favor; George had tired of me. I also knew that Pattie didn't have the power to stop him. First Leon, now George. Those awful feelings of rejection washed over me.

"Shit," I said. I sat down at the table and took a sip of tea, trying to pull my thoughts together. "What's this all about? Do you know?"

"No, I really don't. You know how George is. He just said this morning that he thought you should go back to Apple and that he was going to talk to you. I wanted you to know beforehand."

"Okay." I felt a great sadness. I loved George and couldn't understand why he wanted me to leave. I tried to comfort myself with the thought that he had picked up on the fact that I was bored and missing the city. Maybe he thought I'd be better off at Apple. But still, this was pretty much a directive, not a discussion.

"I don't want you to go," Pattie reassured me. I looked at her and for one moment I wondered if she might be the one who wanted me to leave. Maybe she was bored with having me around, tired of my always being underfoot. I was so hurt and felt so rejected, an outsider now, no longer part of the family.

Somehow I had to save myself. The only way to do that, I realized, was to beat George to the punch. I might even be able to salvage our friendship if I brought up the idea of leaving before he did.

George walked into the kitchen a few minutes later and said a cheery hello, an absolutely normal sort of greeting. I stood up and walked toward him, meeting him halfway across the vast kitchen. I got right to the point.

"George, I really need to talk to you," I said, drawing on every ounce of courage I had. "Listen, I've been thinking about it, and now that I've finished typing up the lyrics, there's really not much for me to do here. I think it would be a good idea if I went back to work at Apple. What do you think?"

I saw the relief on his face. "Well, yeah, sure, if that's what you want to do, Chris," he said. I nodded my head and after a moment's silence, he gave me a big hug.

I saved face that day, but much more important, I salvaged my friendship—and my future—with the two people who meant the most to me in the world.

20

BACK TO APPLE

June 1970

I wasn't really sure there was a job waiting for me at Apple. I didn't have a place to live. I had some cash, several hundred pounds, but no savings. George, my friend and spiritual mentor, was getting tired of me—and I was worried that Pattie, the best friend I had ever had, might be wearying of me, too. I missed Leon, who had also rejected me. I felt lonely and friendless, lost and alone.

Still, I've always been resilient when things don't go my way. I'd been lost and lonely before, and things had worked out. Technically, I was still on the payroll at Apple, since they had paid my salary the whole time I was at Friar Park. I hoped I could just pick up where I left off three months earlier and go back to work with Neil on his film project. And that's how it worked out. Neil welcomed me back, so I had a job (although I didn't have much of anything to do). Richard let me stay at his flat for several nights and then Diane, one of John and Yoko's secretaries, offered to let me rent an extra room in her flat, so I had a place to live. And although I missed Friar Park, it felt good to be back in London with the honking horns, crowds of people, and restaurants with meat on the menu.

For the next few weeks I spent my days at Apple helping Neil with his film and hanging out with Richard in the press office. Derek never came to the office anymore because he was working on a book, and Mavis had resigned, so Richard was responsible for all press matters. Since nothing was really happening press-wise, we had a lot of time to sit around and talk about what it all meant. What had happened to the great dream of Apple? We knew it was all over, even the shouting part, because the Beatles were all broken up, Klein had taken Savile Row and dumped it upside down, spilling all the laughter and fun and creativity out of the place, and we were basically sitting in an empty shell waiting for someone to grab us by the necks and toss us out, too.

"What does it all mean?" I asked Richard.

"Well," he said, letting out a big sigh, "maybe we need to write a book."

"A book?" *What a great idea!* I thought. I'd love to write a book.

"Sure, why not?" Richard said. "We've been in a pretty unique position, two Americans in the thick of things for the last two years. Maybe that's what this has been all about, huh?"

Well, that immediately perked us up. Now we had a project to fill the hours of those long, uneventful days, something besides standing next to Neil watching those endless and often boring film clips. Richard suggested we go through all the file cabinets in the press office to establish time lines and verify dates and events. I helped him out a bit, but he had the energy and the vision for the book and did 99 percent of the work. Well, okay, he did all the work.

We also spent a good part of our day avoiding an overweight, straight-assed office manager who we called Peter Something. We didn't know his last name nor did we care to know anything more about him than the fact that he was Allen Klein's clone and personal henchman, the underling who would fire us someday, and soon, too. The press office still felt safe, it was Derek's place after all (even when he wasn't there), and Derek stood for everything that was good and honest and funny and bright about Apple. But aside from going through the files and dodging Peter Something (I literally peeked around corners when I went from one office to the next), I really didn't know why I was coming to work anymore. All the joy had gone out of it, and with little or nothing to do most of the day, I was bored out of my mind.

There was a little social bright spot in those first few weeks after leaving Friar Park. My friend Janice Kenner, who was going out with Denny Cordell when I was living with Leon in LA, called one day.

"Chris! I just moved to London and got a job with Mick Jagger!" she said.

"Wow," I said. "That's a lot better than cleaning Leon's house, isn't it?" One day when both Denny and Leon were at the studio, Janice stopped by for a visit. I was cleaning, vacuum in one hand, dust rag in the other. Janice offered to help and after a while we got so hot and sweaty that we took off all our clothes. Denny and Leon were pleasantly surprised when they returned and found us in the bedroom in our undies, cleaning away.

"A lot better." Janice laughed. "I love working for Mick. I'm living at his house, doing the cooking and cleaning, and generally running his home life. Stop by soon, and we'll catch up on everything."

A few days later I grabbed a taxi to Mick Jagger's house on Chenye Walk on the River Thames in Chelsea, a high-priced residential district of London. I was hoping I might run into Mick that afternoon—I'd seen him several times at Apple and at sessions and concerts I'd attended in LA with Leon, but I'd never talked to him. Janice and I were having a glass of wine in the kitchen when, sure enough, Mick walked in, pulled up a chair, and poured himself some wine.

"Hello," he said. "So what's going on here, heh?"

"Hi, Mick, this is my friend Chris O'Dell," Janice said, her cheeks flushing pink. *She's got a crush on him!* I thought.

"Are you American, too?" he asked offhandedly, looking at Janice with a sly, teasing grin. He was flirting with her.

"Yes," I said, feeling a little overwhelmed by his presence. He was awfully cute close up, which surprised me. I especially liked his smile, so sly and innocent at the same time. "I met Janice when I was living in Los Angeles."

"She was living with Leon Russell," Janice said, trying to give me a little credibility in Mick's eyes.

"Really?" he said, not overly impressed. But Mick, I would learn, always seemed a little blasé about things.

"Actually, I met you once in LA," I said, figuring I'd play all my cards, "in the studio when Leon was playing on one of your tracks. You were recording 'Live with Me.'"

He raised his eyebrows, trying to capture the memory. Then he got it, and his whole face lit up. That was the wonderful thing about Mick's face, all the different parts seemed to be connected so that even the hint of a smile lifted his cheeks, which squinched his eyes, which lowered his eyebrows, everything moving all at once. He was just like a little kid that way. "Oh yeah," he said. "I remember that day. Leon's great."

Mick spent the rest of the evening with us in the kitchen. As Janice prepared dinner, I found myself envying her job. Over the next few months I spent a lot of time at Mick's house and I picked up a lot of tips from Janice about how to take care of a rock star's home. That information would definitely come in handy.

I was beginning to settle into my life in London, even though I knew my tenure at Apple was uncertain. Something would work out, somehow; I never doubted that.

One night the phone rang in the apartment I shared with Diane.

"Hello?" I said.

"Who is this?" I immediately recognized the voice but wondered at her tone.

"Oh, hi, Yoko," I said. "This is Chris O'Dell."

"Chris O'Dell." The words came out slowly, one by one, like ice cubes dropping out of a freezer dispenser. "What are you doing there?"

"Well, I live here."

"Oh."

Silence.

"Have Diane call me when she gets back," Yoko said, hanging up.

I stood with the phone in my hand for a few moments, my head cocked to the side, finger pushed into my cheek, wondering what that was all about. She certainly wasn't very friendly. In fact, she sounded downright distrustful. Maybe I should have let the damn phone keep ringing.

I gave Diane the message when she returned. An hour or so later, she came into my room and sat on my bed, a miserable look on her face.

"Chris, I just got off the phone with Yoko," she said, her voice shaking slightly. "She's not very happy that you're living in the flat with us."

Diane had just started working for John and Yoko, and she didn't want to lose her job. She was telling me, without actually saying the words, that I needed to find a new place to live.

"Why is Yoko unhappy?" I had no idea what was going on.

Diane looked uncomfortable and started to pick specks of lint off the bedspread. "Well, she said that you're part of George's camp. And I guess she doesn't want you involved in any way with her and John's business."

"Okay," I said, "that's fine, don't worry." I knew this was a difficult situation for Diane and I didn't want to make it any worse for her. But my mind was spinning. The Beatles had broken into camps, apparently, and I didn't even know it. Yoko didn't have anything against me personally; at least I didn't take it that way. But I realized at that moment that relationships between John, Paul, George, and Ringo were much worse than I had imagined. I always believed that if you loved one Beatle, you loved them all—they were indivisible, inseparable.

The next day I was telling Richard about my woes, and we were trying to figure out what the word "camps" meant when the phone rang. Richard answered it.

"Hi, George, yeah, sure, she's right here."

"Hullo. It's George." His voice sounded particularly gentle on the phone that day and I remember feeling relieved; he was my friend again. "Look, I just want to let you know that Allen Klein is going to fire you. I don't want you to be surprised by it. But I also want you to know that I'll support you in any way I can. If you need anything, you can call me. Okay?"

"Okay," I said, thinking that when bad things happen, they happen all at once.

His voice was soothing. "Look. It may not seem like it right now, but this is the best thing that could happen."

It didn't take long for the ax to fall, although when you know it's going to happen, the waiting period can be excruciating. I even called Peter Something at one point to try to hurry things along, but he put me off for a while, telling me that he'd call me soon to make an appointment. In the meantime, I needed to find another place to live, and the first idea that came to mind was staying with Eric Clapton at Hurtwood Edge. In the three months I'd lived at Friar Park, I developed a major crush on Eric. We'd go to a movie or have dinner now and then and sometimes I'd sit in on his recording sessions, but the relationship never developed beyond friendship. I couldn't quite figure out why he never made a move, but I was content just to be his friend. Like I said, I had absolutely no clue that he and Pattie were meeting in secret or that Pattie was falling in love with him.

I called Eric one day and told him I needed to get away from London and Apple for a while. "I wondered if I could stay with you for a few days," I said.

"Sure." Eric laughed. "Join the crowd. Some of the Delaney and Bonnie musicians are here." Jim Gordon, Carl Radle, Jim Price, and Bobby Whitlock were all staying with Eric at the time. I was excited to see Carl, a friend from my Leon days, but I was really intrigued by the idea of meeting Jim Gordon, the man who stole Rita Coolidge from Leon. It didn't take long before I fell for Jim, a baby-faced, shy, always smiling guy who exuded an aura of naïve vulnerability. Of course, it helped that he was tall, well built, and good looking in a little-boy way, but I have to admit that a big part of my attraction to Jim was his connection to Leon. Rita left Leon for Jim, and then she rejected Jim; on the rebound from Rita, Leon hooked up with me, and then he rejected me. So in the deep and confusing way that some people who are not meant for each other end up together, Jim and I sort of fell into each other's arms. I don't think we ever really developed any kind of intimate feelings for each other. It was more that we comforted each other in trying to get over the pain Leon and Rita had put us through.

Hanging out at Hurtwood Edge and pursuing my little fling with Jim took my mind off Apple. But since I was still on the payroll, I'd drive into London with Eric once or twice a week and spend the day at work, looking for something to do with myself. Neil, like everyone else at Apple, knew I was going to be fired, and he didn't have any work for me to do. I was just biding my time.

On one of those days I was sitting in reception talking to Debbie when the phone rang.

"Yes, she's here, Peter." Debbie handed me the phone with an *oh shit* expression on her face.

"Chris, can you come up to my office?" Peter Something said in his smooth, smarmy hatchet man's voice. "We need to meet."

Well, finally, I thought. Walking up the stairs I was surprised to find that I was apprehensive about this meeting. I think it was finally hitting me that the whole Apple dream was coming to this sad, sorry end. I sat down in the chair facing Peter Something's desk. He was a pudgy guy with strawberry blond hair, and there wasn't one thing about him, not one, that looked remotely like it belonged in the world of rock and roll—no sense of humor, no sly grin, no edgy energy, no sarcastic put-downs, no sexy come-ons. Just blah. I looked around the office and remembered what it used to be like at Savile Row, and before then at Wigmore Street, when Derek was liberally pouring Scotch in the press office, Richard pasted newspaper clippings into scrapbooks, the Hells Angels roamed the hallways, one of the Beatles dropped by to make all our hearts beat a little faster, and Apple was a lively, special place. Now it was a funeral parlor, and Peter was the spitting image of an under-taker.

He was genuinely trying to look sad, with his head turned slightly to the side and his dry red eyes attempting to convey how terribly difficult this meeting was for him.

"Look," he said, "I'm really sorry to have to tell you this, but I'm going to have to let you go."

I sat there with my eyebrows raised slightly, mouth open in a little gesture of shock, trying to act as if it were a big surprise. He knew I was acting and I knew he was acting, but we had to play this whole thing out. Even though our hearts weren't really in it, we gave it all we had.

"Wow, this is unexpected," I said, and that was about all the emotion

I could muster. He knew that I knew that this had been a long time coming and so without anything more to say to each other, I walked back down the stairs, down the hall and into the press office, gave Richard a hug, and walked out of the door of 3 Savile Row for the last time.

21

ERIC AND THE DOMINOS

Summer 1970

Eric found a job for me.

"Do you want to find a place in London for the band?" he asked one day when we were sitting in the den at Hurtwood Edge. He was watching television and I was reading the new bestseller *The Godfather.* Everyone else was down the road, drinking at the local pub.

"They're going bonkers here," he said. "I'm thinking something in central London."

"I'll look for a place," I said, already getting excited about the idea. Maybe I should have been a real estate agent because I loved finding houses for people. When I was living with Leon in LA, Leon and Denny Cordell asked me to find a house for Shelter Records and I was so proud of myself when I found a funky old Hollywood house in the "less desirable" part of Hollywood Boulevard, definitely in need of repairs but charming on the inside with built-in cabinets, gorgeous wood floors, and a screened sunporch. It had a "down home" feel, which Denny and Leon loved, and we all agreed that I'd discovered the absolute perfect home for Shelter.

For the Dominos, I found a two-story flat directly above a real estate office and across the street from the South Kensington tube station. Ah, I thought, when I first set eyes on it, this is ideal—beautifully furnished, with a huge living room featuring an upright piano, a gorgeous crystal chandelier, and a cabinet filled with expensive china and stemware; a small but serviceable galley kitchen with all the needed utensils; and three upstairs bedrooms, one for Carl, one for Bobby, and one for Jim Gordon. Best of all, the real estate people on the ground floor left work precisely at 5:00 p.m. so they wouldn't be bothered at all by the blasting record player, the people constantly coming and going, or the wild late-night parties. While the real world went about its business, we slept, only to come alive in the evening when everyone else started winding down.

The move-in date was still a week away when I asked the question I'd been rehearsing ever since I first set eyes on the flat. We were all sitting around the kitchen table at Hurtwood Edge, eating bangers and mash (sausages and mashed potatoes) prepared by Eric's housekeeper.

"I have an idea," I said casually. "When you move into the flat next week, why don't I stay and be your housekeeper, buy groceries, clean up, help you organize things, keep the place together?"

"Sure, great idea," said Bobby Whitlock, in his Southern drawl, "we can always use a little help."

"Fine with me," Carl said, shrugging his shoulders in his quiet, laid-back way. Jim Gordon was all for it, since we were having our little fling and getting along fairly well at the time, and Eric thought it was a fine idea to have someone around to keep the guys organized. For the two months we lived there, I answered the phone and took messages, arranged for a weekly cleaning lady, washed the dishes, bought groceries, and did little errands around town. For the most part, the guys were pretty clean and they weren't at all demanding. None of us liked to cook, so we kept the grocery shopping pretty simple: cheese, bread, eggs, beans, easy stuff like that. Basically the only meals I could cook were shepherd's pie, tuna casserole, spaghetti, and beans and eggs on toast, their favorite meal of all.

Most of the time, though, I just hung out with them, staying up all hours of the night and sleeping late into the morning or early afternoon. When they took a minicab to Hurtwood Edge to jam in Eric's basement studio, I'd go with them. They had developed their own unique sound, loud, strong, and to my ears, a little heavy, maybe even a bit depressing. But then again I had a hard time separating the music from the band, and the band was starting to get all fucked up. As Eric put it in his memoir, "drugs were the beginning and the end of the band."

One night Eric stopped by the flat, and they all asked me to cook up their favorite meal—beans and eggs on toast. I was happy to escape to the kitchen because Eric was drunk and getting moodier all the time, moaning and groaning about how he couldn't have the woman he loved. I knew by this time that he was mad about Pattie. Pattie was all he would talk about. Sometimes she would drive down to London and anybody with half a brain could tell that she was in love with Eric, too. I'd watch them sitting on the couch in the Kensington flat, looking into each other's eyes, their knees touching, and all kinds of feelings would flood through me. I was pissed at Eric, realizing that he had used his friendship with me to get close to Pattie. When he'd drop by Friar Park, ostensibly to see me, he was only interested in Pattie. His phone calls were just excuses to chat with Pattie (who he knew would answer the phone, as she always did). I was the unwitting go-between, the dense dupe, and while I felt impossibly naïve wondering how I could have missed all the clues, I also felt intensely guilty about my part in further-ing their relationship. I felt complicit in this love triangle, as if I had somehow helped it take shape and gain momentum.

But on this particular night Pattie wasn't around and Eric was in a foul mood. He just went on and on about this terrible situation with Pattie, and why did it have to happen to him, why was he in love with a married woman, why was she married to one of his best friends, why oh why oh why. Bobby, Carl, and Jim all seemed to commiserate with him, nodding their heads sympathetically, listening to him go on about how much he loved Pattie and how he would never be able to get her and how tragic it all was.

With no warning at all, Eric picked up his glass and threw it against the wall where it shattered into pieces. I remember ducking my head and putting my hand over my eyes to avoid the flying glass. When I looked up, everyone was frozen in place. No one said a word. I don't think anyone took a breath. Seconds passed and then Jim, a crazy, wild look in his eyes, picked up his half-finished plate of beans and eggs, and threw it straight up at the ceiling. The plate came crashing down to earth, but the eggs and beans got caught up in the chandelier and little chunks of yellow and brown goo began to fall to the floor. Eric burst into hysterical laughter, and the rest of us joined in, literally laughing so hard that we were bent over double with tears streaming down our cheeks as we watched Jim's dinner dripping off the chandelier. Eric picked up another glass and threw it against the wall, which sent us off into another round of hysterical laughter. Now that we were all in a good mood, Eric included, we settled back to drink and talk and snort a few lines of cocaine.

Only later did it hit me that I'd be the one to clean up the bloody mess.

My relationship with Jim Gordon did not come to a good end. On the day the Dominos returned from recording the *Layla* album in Miami, Florida, Jim took a white packet out of his pocket, emptied the powder onto the piano, and chopped it into lines.

"Go ahead," he said, smiling at me, "have a line."

I snorted a big fat line of the cocaine, and seconds later I began to feel sick.

"Are you okay?" Jim asked. I was holding my stomach, feeling waves of nausea rising from my gut into my throat.

"What was that?" I knew it wasn't cocaine.

"Heroin," Jim said, looking at me with concern. He had no idea I'd react that way to a drug that he'd been using regularly for weeks. I spent the entire night throwing up.

The nights at the flat got crazier and crazier in the weeks before the Dominos left for their American tour. We were all drinking heavily, doing a lot of coke, and using Mandrax to increase the intensity of the high. Also known as methaqualone or Quaalude, Mandrax is a downer, similar in effect to barbiturates, but I liked its soothing, hypnotic effect, especially when I'd been doing cocaine all night and needed to come down a bit and take the edge off the high. Mandrax seemed like such a great drug. We all loved it, in large part because it allowed us to keep on snorting cocaine long past the time we should have stopped. We used alcohol in much the same way; alcohol took the edge off the cocaine high, but if you'd had too much to drink, cocaine could give you just enough energy to keep on going. It was all about adjusting, fine-tuning, finding just the perfect mixture. We were trying to discover happiness, relief, euphoria, bliss, and when we found it, we wanted to stay there. The drugs were spiritual supports, little bits of heaven in pill, powder, or liquid form, and we knew we could count on one or two or three to take us to a good place. We also knew that we might eventually slip or fall or crash into a bad place, but if we could just figure out the perfect mixture—and sometimes it really worked—we could keep the high going and successfully avoid that painful plunge. We were on a quest to find that perfect place of balance, and in those days we thought we were smart enough to figure it all out.

Heroin really threw things off. The whole heroin thing began in earnest when the guys were in Miami and by the time they got back to London, they were deep into it. Things started to fall apart, slowly at first and then it was like a bloody train wreck of twisted minds and sick souls. Jim's behavior got weirder and weirder. He withdrew inside himself. His shyness morphed into paranoia. He didn't trust anyone, including me, and he was convinced the band was trying to get rid of him because he wasn't a good enough drummer. Jim's drug use was out of control, I knew that much, but I didn't know he had serious mental health problems; in fact, more than a decade would pass before Jim was diagnosed with paranoid schizophrenia.

I would try to console him, but we were both in a lot of emotional pain from our failed relationships with Rita and Leon and we didn't have much to give each other. We couldn't create the intimacy that we both craved. We just kept hoping that it would appear one day, pick us up, and carry us along, but it never did.

One night Jim and I started arguing. I honestly have no idea what started the whole thing except that we'd been drinking all day and snorting a lot of cocaine. Eric and the others were off somewhere, so

Jim and I were alone in the flat. We'd had our share of arguments and even a few shouting matches, but that night, as we sat on the bed upstairs, something in Jim snapped. He yelled at me. I yelled back. He got angry. I got even angrier. Yelling turned to screaming, anger turned to fury. His face, which always seemed so angelic to me, a little boy's face surrounded by this mass of reddish-blond curls, twisted into a grotesque caricature of itself. His eyes were crazy, crazy mad. He suddenly jumped up and tried to grab me and hold me down on the bed. Jim was a big guy—lean, big boned, well over six feet tall—and I weighed about one hundred pounds, but adrenaline was surging through me and somehow I managed to escape.

I bolted down the stairs and he came tearing after me. As I ran to the kitchen door (the only door to the flat), he ran after me, so I kept running, into the living room. When I turned around, he was coming after me, a butcher knife in his hand. I used the sofa as a barricade, but Jim kept lunging at me, his face crimson red, his mouth pulled back in a satanic grimace, his fingers clenched white on the knife.

"Jim!" I shouted. "Stop it! Leave me alone!"

"I'm going to get you," he snarled.

My mind flashed back to that scene in *Psycho* when Anthony Perkins stabs Janet Leigh in the shower. I don't know why I didn't scream. I'm not sure I could have screamed at that moment because I was paralyzed with fright. And who would have heard me? The real estate office on the ground floor was closed for the day. All the windows in the flat were shut. Music was playing on the stereo and the volume was up.

"Jim, stop!" I yelled again.

"Shut up," he said, swinging wildly with the knife, "or I'll shut you up!"

When he came around the sofa, I decided my only hope was to run back up the stairs and try to lock myself in one of the bedrooms. I was almost at the top of the stairs but he was right behind me, and I knew I wasn't going to make it because he was taking those steps two at a time, when someone called out hello. It was Robert Stigwood, Eric's manager. He had a key, thank God, to the flat.

"Is anyone here? Hullo?"

Just like that, Jim snapped back into himself. A blank look crossed his face as he walked down the stairs, put the knife on the piano— gently, as if he feared it might scratch the polished surface—and disappeared into the kitchen. Seconds later, Robert and a friend, followed by Jim, walked into the living room. What did Robert think when he saw me standing there on the steps, frozen in place, a look of horror on my face?

"Oh, hello, Chris, sorry, I hope we didn't interrupt anything," Robert said. He introduced me to his friend. "We were just in the area and thought we'd stop by and see how everyone is doing."

I looked at Jim, who smiled sweetly at me. Whatever had come over him was gone now. I quickly pulled myself together.

"Robert! It's good to see you," I said. *You're an angel sent from God,* I was thinking, *you saved my life!* I never mentioned a word to Robert or anyone else about what happened that night. Jim apologized later, although he didn't remember the knife, and I chalked it all up to stress about the upcoming tour and all the hard drinking and drugging he was doing. I hadn't heard, then, about the night he argued with Rita Coolidge at the Warwick Hotel when they were both on Joe Cocker's Mad Dogs and Englishmen tour. They stepped out of the room, or so the story goes, and he hauled off and punched her in the face, sending her sprawling and giving her a black eye that lasted for the rest of the tour. But even if I'd known about that incident, I'm sure I would have dismissed it as a drug-induced event rather than evidence that Jim was mentally ill. I knew a lot of people who got weird on drugs.

We never talked about that night again, but thirteen years later Jim Gordon killed his mother by smashing her head with a hammer and plunging a butcher's knife into her chest three times. He told the police that the murder had just "happened," in a sort of dream. "I had no interest in killing her," he said. "I wanted to stay away from her. It was so matter-of-fact, like I was being guided like a zombie. She wanted me to kill her, and good riddance to her." When I read those words in *Rolling Stone,* I felt a chill go through me. When Jim came after me that night in the Dominos' flat, he looked like a zombie, guided by something beyond his control. If Robert hadn't shown up, would Jim have killed me? I prefer not to think about that.

The end was near. The Dominos were leaving in a few days for their American tour, and the lease on the flat was about to expire. On our last night in the flat, Eric, Jim, Carl, and I had dinner at an Indian restaurant. We drank. And drank and drank and drank. By the time we got back to the flat, we were all completely and thoroughly wasted but having a great time sitting around, talking, laughing, getting excited about their upcoming tour, and reminiscing about some of the great times we'd had together that summer.

"Hey, Eric," Carl said, "remember that night when you threw the glass and it shattered all over the place?"

"Yeah, I remember that," Eric said. "That felt really good."

"What a crazy-ass thing to do," Carl said.

We all sat there looking at each other for a few seconds and then Carl, a gleeful smile on his face, picked up his wineglass and threw it against the wall. Everybody cracked up—the sudden explosion of glass, the red wine streaks on the wall, the intake of breath and startled looks immediately followed by the uncontrollable belly laugher was so typical of the crazy life we'd lived together that summer that it seemed a fitting sort of ending. But then Jim hurled his glass at the opposite wall, and Eric did a sort of cricket pitcher's wind-up and flung a heavy glass ashtray filled with cigarette butts at the wall. Jim, not to be bested, strode to the kitchen and emptied out the glassware while Eric walked over to the wine cabinet in the corner of the living room near the front window and began smashing the crystal stemware on the floor. As fast as he could reach in and throw a glass, he'd pick up another.

I sat on the piano bench with my mouth dropped open. Part of me was thinking, *Wow, this is really wild and sort of fun, a crazy rich person's version of a food fight.* The release of all that pent-up energy felt good, the way a thunderstorm clears the air of impurities. At the same time another part of me, the side that still had some semblance of rational thought, was looking at the scene and thinking, *Shit. This is not good.*

They're all leaving tomorrow and guess who has to face the real estate people?

Then came the coup de grâce. I didn't see it coming. Someone—I don't remember who—threw a glass at the television and the screen just exploded in tiny shards of opaque glass, leaving a jagged black hole in the center. A moment of stunned silence was followed by more hysterical laughter.

The next morning they all drove away, leaving me in the flat to face the rental agent, who was arriving later that day to do the inspection.

"Hello, how are you?" she said very sweetly, with that big, cheerful, cheesy, superficial smile that salespeople have perfected. She sort of peeked over my shoulder, already beginning her inspection.

"I'm great," I said, matching her smile. I let her into the flat and held my breath. She took a few steps into the living room and stopped. Gasped. Her hand went to her throat.

"Oh," she said, a horrified look on her face. "Oh my God."

I was embarrassed, perhaps even a little ashamed. I couldn't wait to walk out of that room and never see it again, but I had to act as if all that broken glass and the shattered television were just what one would expect from a group of rowdy musicians.

"Don't worry," I reassured her.

She swiveled around and looked at me as if I were mad. I waved my hand around the room and put on a big smile.

"They'll pay for everything."

22

MISS O'DELL

1971

Eric offered to let me stay at Hurtwood Edge while the Dominos went on tour. So there I was alone in the country, without a car, without a job, and without any idea of what to do next. I took up crocheting to pass the time, and then I got the bright idea to paint Eric's dark and dingy kitchen. I chose the colors yellow and orange, hoping to bring some light back into my life. I didn't really care what Eric might think about my color scheme; he probably wouldn't even notice.

Sometime in mid-November 1970, I was standing on the kitchen counter, finishing the orange trim on one of the cabinets when the phone rang. Paintbrush in hand, I turned to look at the black telephone sitting on the counter across the room. Should I answer it? Probably, I thought. It might be Eric who checked in with me every few days to see how things were going at the house. Maybe it was Pattie—we talked almost every day—or Richard DiLello, who was still in England even though Klein had fired him in the beginning of August. When I saw the announcement in the August 4, 1970, *Evening Standard,* I cut it out and kept it as a memento of my Apple days:

Earlier this week the Apple Press Office was closed down and the two remaining employees dismissed. Since the breakup of the Beatles their

Apple empire has diminished to little more than a center for collecting their royalties and dealing with their private affairs.

Good for Richard, I thought, he hung on until the very end.

The phone kept ringing. Who else could it be? Eric might be calling to see how things were going. Or maybe it was Stephen Stills. Stephen lived nearby in a fifteenth-century mansion that he bought from Ringo (who bought it from Peter Sellers) when Ringo and his family moved back to London to be closer to the studio. Stephen's first album had just been released to rave reviews (it eventually went platinum), and he was taking it easy for a while during a hiatus from touring with Crosby, Stills, Nash, and Young. I liked Stephen a lot, and we had a lot of fun together. Every now and then I'd have a fantasy about getting into a serious relationship with a musician, but I didn't have any illusions about our little fling because Stephen wasn't really my type.

I placed the brush on the lid of the paint can, careful not to get the handle sticky with paint, and jumped off the counter to answer the phone.

"Chris!" I couldn't immediately place the English accent. "Hello, it's Peet-ah, Peet-ah Ash-ah."

"Peter!" I felt a rush of nostalgia flooding over me. Oh, how I missed Peter. I missed his black-framed Buddy Holly glasses, shy smile, and quirky sense of humor. Just thinking about Peter brought back memories of the Apple of the old days.

"Where are you? How did you get my number?" I asked.

Phone numbers were always a very big deal. George, John, Ringo, Paul, Eric, Stephen Stills, the Dominos, the Stones—every musician I'd ever met—had private phone numbers, and if you were one of the insiders who knew the number, you sure as hell better not tell anyone. I'll never forget when I was visiting Pattie and George at Friar Park in the late seventies, and I gave Astrid Lundstrom, Bill Wyman's longtime girlfriend, their phone number. She was working on the Jerry Lewis telethon, and she called one day to ask George if he would appear on the show. He was furious. He didn't like anyone intruding on his world.

"I'm in London on business," Peter said, ignoring my question. "I was wondering if you had any plans for work or if you are looking for something."

I smiled. I loved the way Peter hurried through sentences, always racing to get to the main point, unwilling to waste words along the way.

"I'm just taking care of Eric's house right now," I said, looking at the kitchen cabinets. Damn, those orange and yellow colors really did brighten my mood. "I'm not really looking for anything, but I guess I'll need a job soon enough."

"Would you like to come to work for me in Los Angeles?"

"LA? Really?" I was stalling because my emotions were suddenly flip-flopping all over the place. Hearing Peter's voice brought back all the happy memories of working with him at Apple in our top-floor office with the dormer windows and my purple desk and George or Paul stopping by for a chat. And now Peter was in LA, and Leon was in LA, and I was still in love with Leon. Maybe if I were back in LA and had a real job, we could get back together again and make the relationship work.

But what about leaving England? I was sort of comfortably adrift and hadn't really thought about moving. I'd also been having recurring nightmares about returning to LA and concluded that my bad dreams were warning me never to leave England. But I was definitely ready for some sunshine and if I moved back to the States I wouldn't have to worry about visas or work permits.

"I'd like you to come and work in my office," Peter was saying.

"Hmmm," I said. "I'll have to organize a lot of things before I leave here. I need a place to live, for one thing."

"You can stay with Betsy and me until you get settled," Peter said.

"When would you want me to start?"

"As soon as possible. I'll organize a plane ticket for you." He hesitated a moment. "Chris, it would be wonderful to work with you again."

A plane ticket, a free place to live, a job with a man I adored and admired, the chance to work with James Taylor again, and the possibility of reconnecting with Leon—what else could I do?

I said yes.

• • •

Two weeks later I moved in with Peter and Betsy and started my new job. I loved my room with its own bath in the front corner of the house. Betsy was a meticulous housekeeper, and the house was charming and comfortable, an older home in an established neighborhood. The only drawback was its location on the corner of a major street. Every time a bus went by, the whole house seemed to shake. You got used to it after a while.

I settled right into the work routine, putting in long hours for Peter, just as I had when I worked for him at Apple. I helped organize his office, located in the guesthouse behind the main house, answered the phones, typed correspondence, created a filing system, made appointments, booked studios, organized itineraries, and took care of the musicians he represented, arranging transportation, helping them with personal problems, and generally watching over them, letting them know I was right there if any problems arose.

James Taylor was Peter's most famous client—James's second album *Sweet Baby James* was released in February 1970 and hit #3 on the Billboard Album chart; the song "Fire and Rain" reached #3 on the Billboard Hot 100. During the time I worked with Peter, he also represented Tony Joe White, Cat Stevens, and Kate Taylor, James's sister, and he worked with dozens of other musicians in the LA area including drummer Russ Kunkel, guitarist Danny Kortchmar, bass guitarist Lee Sklar, singer/songwriter Carole King, and singer Linda Ronstadt and her current boyfriend, songwriter J. D. Souther. So there were always people coming and going in the house and office, and Betsy's hospitality was legendary. She loved to give dinner parties and acted a little like a mother hen, treating Peter's clients like her own children.

I'd been living with Peter and Betsy for two months when I began to realize that I had overstayed my welcome. Putting up with my late hours and wild ways had to take a lot of patience on Betsy's part. I was footloose and fancy free, as my mother might have put it, definitely not the kind of person to disappear into my room at the end of the workday. Looking back from this distance of decades, I cringe when I think about what Betsy must have gone through with me living in her house. I was doing a lot of drugs and feeling the effects—mood swings, crushing headaches, depression, loneliness, and anxiety attacks. I worked hard and I was always available, seven days a week; my work, at that point, was my life. But I wasn't Betsy's idea of a professional woman. She was sophisticated, skilled at public relations, neat, organized, and a newly married woman, while I was single, and, as she told Peter, too chatty, too quick to make friends with their friends, too informal with Peter's clients, and too forthcoming with my ideas. I lacked the reticence and reserve Betsy deemed proper for either a secretary or a houseguest.

I felt her coolness toward me and tried to ignore it, but it hurt my feelings when Betsy would have a dinner party and not invite me. There I was upstairs in my bedroom with nothing to do, my stomach grumbling, listening to Carole King, James Taylor, Linda Ronstadt, and J. D. Souther chatting and laughing in the dining room below. I have to admit I got a little jealous watching Betsy fawning over Linda, but then again, I didn't know anyone who could resist smart, adorable, bouncy, big-eyed Linda who, we all knew, would someday be a big star.

Once again, I was being put in my place. I was part of the inner circle, well liked, even loved, privy to all the private details and inner workings of Peter's business, but I never did earn a place at the dinner table.

After three months of living with Peter and Betsy, I moved in with my friend Eileen Basich and her two children, twelve-year-old Juli and nine-year-old Nick. I'd been talking on the phone with Eileen almost every day; she was still working as Leon and Denny's secretary at Shelter Records, and she patiently endured my lovesick longings and neverending questions about Leon, how he was doing, who he was seeing, was he happy, what album was he working on, where was he touring next. I couldn't seem to get away from Leon—as he became more famous, I heard his name all the time—but the truth is, I didn't want to escape him. Leon was the first musician I ever dated, the first man I ever lived with, and the first true love of my life, who rejected me before I had the good sense to leave. For a long time, just the thought of Leon with another woman was too much for me to bear. I wanted to exert some kind of magical control and change the ending of that sad story and, at twenty-four, I was still naïve enough to believe I could.

Eileen never judged me or tried to change me, wise woman that she was (and is). She always gave me good advice that I tried my hardest to follow. We found a four-bedroom house in Laurel Canyon with a semi-finished basement for her kids and a bricked-in patio that overlooked the hills and was perfect for sunbathing. I settled into a routine, getting up about the time the kids went to school, driving to Peter's house, working all day, coming home, listening to music, watching television or working on the scarf I was crocheting for my father. My parents and my sister Vicki were still living in Tucson and after I moved back to LA, we talked once or twice a month.

On the weekends I'd sleep in until noon or later, sunbathe on the patio, do some cocaine or amphetamines, and talk endlessly with Eileen. The simple life, I told myself—boring but really not so bad. I put a smile on my face and tried to look on the bright side. But in the darker moments, when I was alone with my thoughts, I couldn't deny the fact that I was depressed, unfocused, directionless, bored with my job in LA, homesick for London, and still in love with Leon, who was not in love with me. I was living with a single mother with two preteens, I had a water bed with no frame, and I hated it. It was always cold, and it was stupid. Stupid—that's the word that always came to mind when I looked at that big bag of water sitting on the floor. I thought maybe having a dog would lift my spirits, but within a few weeks it ran away. Even the dog didn't like being with me.

Drugs helped me cope. By that time in my life I had my favorite and not-so-favorite drugs. I loved alcohol, the whole idea of it, a nice cold drink, that warm flush of good feelings, the conviviality of drinking with friends, that lovely freeing sense of being able to come out of your shell for a while. As much as I hated the way I felt the next day (because I rarely if ever had only a few drinks), I did the same thing, starting to drink in the late afternoon and not stopping until bedtime.

I didn't like pot. The drug made me paranoid and did nothing for my sense of confidence. I smoked it because it was always around, but it was never my drug of choice. There was really just one thing I liked about pot: I always felt so aware of the present moment when I was high. But along with that awareness came paranoia, so that under the influence of marijuana I always felt paranoically present, not my favorite feeling in the world.

Cocaine followed alcohol in order of preference, and amphetamines were in third place. I started using cocaine regularly when I moved to LA with Leon in 1970, and I just loved that drug. It made me feel instantly alive, supremely confident, amazingly productive, and deeply intelligent, but there was a downside, of course. Like amphetamines (and marijuana), cocaine made me feel paranoid and edgy, which is why I always had a drink or two when I snorted a line. Cocaine took me up, fast, while alcohol took the edge off that jittery high and at the same time made it last longer. Alcohol and cocaine, I had discovered, were the perfect combination cocktail.

So, cocaine was my newfound friend, and I spent hours sitting in the living room, listening to music, snorting a line, and crocheting. Crocheting! It was an obsession—I snorted coke, crocheted, snorted more coke, crocheted a little faster. What started off as a scarf that I was making for my father for Christmas became a twin bedspread, and then a double bedspread, and finally a king-size bedspread. I just couldn't stop.

One night I was sitting in the living room listening to Van Morrison's new album, *Tupelo Honey,* when the phone rang. I put down the bedspread of many colors (I changed yarn color according to the season, and I was currently in spring) and picked up the phone, reaching for the pack of Marlboros and my lighter as I said hello. Eileen was in her bedroom, where she often hibernated, and her kids were in the basement watching television.

"Chris?" I immediately recognized George's voice, and my heart skipped a beat. I hadn't heard from him in months, and I hadn't let myself think about how much I missed him. George and Pattie were my lifelines to the world I had left behind, a world I had loved and hadn't wanted to leave.

"George! Oh my God, where are you? Are you here in LA?"

"Yeah," he said, and I could almost see him smiling on the other end of the line, pleased by my reaction. "I'm in Malibu. I just got here today for some meetings with Capitol Records. Hey, why don't you come out and see me?" I smiled to myself, surprised and happy that he called me the day he arrived in town.

"It's kinda late, and I'm sure you're tired from the trip," I said. "How about if I drive over sometime this weekend?"

He gave me the telephone number at the house and before we hung up, I promised to call him within the next few days.

But I didn't. Every time I'd think about driving down the canyon roads to the beach house, something would stop me. I told myself I couldn't deal with all the "yes" people who were always hanging around George whenever he was in LA, the record producers, managers, sycophants, and general hangers-on who sat around swapping stories, drinking, smoking, reaching into their pockets to pull out some high-grade cocaine, and generally trying to outcompete one another for George's attention. I just wanted to be with George like in the old days at Friar Park. I couldn't cope with the LA crowd of people who floated around him like a cloud and were so obnoxious in their efforts to be cool and control the conversation as they spread gossip and talked about all the rich and important people they knew.

And then there was the matter of the drugs. In addition to my almost-daily cocaine habit, I'd recently purchased a bag of Seconals, a barbiturate that I loved because it cut through that shaky, anxious coked-up feeling and helped me sleep. I didn't think I had a problem with the drug because I was only taking two, maybe three Seconals a day, usually at night, and I thought I knew how to manage my cocaine use. Besides, I showed up for work almost every day, so the drugs weren't affecting my work ethic, and Peter never complained about my performance. But underneath all my little rationalizations, I knew I should stop or cut down, and I was afraid that George might be able to see through my defenses. Also, I didn't want to say or do something stupid that I'd regret later.

A few days later, George called again. "Are you coming out to see me?" he said. He sounded lonely.

"I'll try to drive over this evening," I said. But I didn't. Who can explain the irony of this? I loved George and I was dying to see him. After I moved out of Friar Park and stopped working for Apple, we'd become even closer friends. But the drugs made me—what? Lazy? Unmotivated? Dull, indifferent, inattentive, careless, apathetic? I wouldn't have put those labels on myself, but there was no avoiding the truth that I had no energy and absolutely no motivation. Somehow just the idea of trying to pretend to be my old cheerful self and hold a reasonable conversation, even with my old friend George, was too much to deal with. So I took a pill and went to bed.

I came home from work the next day to find a message on my answering machine.

"Chris, what's happened to you? I thought you were coming out here. Give me a call."

I stared at the phone. Why was I putting this off? For some reason, I didn't think I could muster the energy that it would take to drive to the beach, put up with the crowd of hangers-on, and, to be absolutely truthful, deal with George's intensity. Over the years, and especially during the months I lived at Friar Park, I'd had some deep conversations with George, and he would get so intense and so present—so intently focused—that it was almost unnerving. His deep brown, penetrating eyes stirred feelings inside me that were both intimate and chilling; it was almost as if he could see inside my soul. It was scary to go into that deep internal place with him, or with anyone for that matter, and talk about the things that meant the most to me, thoughts and emotions that touched the very truth of who I was and what I believed in. I'd find myself pulling back, afraid of the depths, and backpedaling to safer ground. But then, all of a sudden, he'd switch into his fun, flirty side and everything would be light and we'd all be laughing and having a good time. With George the hard part was not knowing which side you were going to encounter.

I looked at the phone then and laughed. What was I scared of anyway? I dialed his number.

"Hi, it's me," I said.

"Chris? Hey, are you avoiding me?" he asked, only half-kidding.

"I'm sorry, George, things just keep happening. What are you doing now?"

"Just hanging about, looking at the ocean. It's a bit lonely out here."

"Okay," I said, making up my mind in a second, "I'm coming out now. I'll be there in an hour or two." I changed into my jeans, struggling to put them on because, as usual, I'd sewed up the seams to make them really tight, grabbed my jean jacket, jumped into my yellow-orange Corolla, and headed out on Sunset Boulevard to the beach.

It was a beautiful spring day, the sun glistening on the water, almost blinding me as I drove along the Pacific Coast Highway. I couldn't deny the fact that I was nervous. I hadn't taken my drugs because I didn't want to act weird or out of control in front of George. He never was much of a druggie, although at times he drank plenty of alcohol. He'd go through these "clean" phases when he'd stop using any kind of drug but then, without warning, he'd join in and start drinking or using with us. Pattie and I used to joke that we didn't know if his hand was in the prayer bag or the coke bag.

The house stood on stilts right on the beach, a few miles past Malibu on a quiet back road that ran parallel to the Pacific Coast Highway. George answered the door with a welcoming smile on his face and gave me a big hug and cheek kisses. Dressed in green, straight-leg pants and a long-sleeved, striped shirt rolled up to his elbows with a black vest hanging loosely over the shirt, he had a beard and his hair was long and parted in the middle. I always loved George's hair, it was so thick and coarse, with a gentle wave to it. He led me into the combination living room–dining room.

"Wow," I said, looking past him to the view. "This place is fabulous!" The whole back wall was glass, and the sliding door was open to a balcony that stretched along the back of the house. Seagulls swooped across the waves that rolled in one right after the other, reaching right up to the stilts that supported the house. Music played softly in the background, and the smell of incense filled the room. I sighed, suddenly filled with a sense of peace and serenity that had eluded me for a long time. Being with George, I realized, was like being home.

We sat down to a meal of rice and veggies and talked about the success of his first solo album, *All Things Must Pass.* He seemed surprised that it was a hit. He'd always lacked confidence in his songwriting skills (hard to be around John Lennon and Paul McCartney and not question your talent), and I have to admit his occasional insecurities were nice to see; they made him human.

"I thought there would be a lot of people out here," I said. I was feeling a little shy. I hadn't expected to be alone with him.

"It's been really quiet," he said. "Allen Pariser came out one day. Benny, my driver, stops by to bring me things or drive me into town. Other than that, it's been pretty lonely."

I asked about Pattie, and he told me about the recent renovations at Friar Park, friends and fellow musicians who had been out to visit, and general gossip about people we both knew. When George was in the right kind of mood, he loved gossip—not the rumor-spreading, scandal-creating, whispered stuff but just general chitchatting about who he'd seen around town lately, what John and Ringo were doing (he rarely mentioned Paul in those days), how Pattie kept herself busy, why he was in town, the different meetings he had to attend, that kind of thing.

But that night at the beach he wasn't all that interested in small talk; instead he wanted to talk about the situation in Bangladesh and how Ravi Shankar was asking for his help to bring attention to the starving people and the terrible suffering in that country caused by military upheavals and a disastrous cyclone. He talked for a long time, educating me about what was happening there politically and how the Bangladeshi people were affected. I didn't know much at all about the situation and listened in amazement as he detailed the horrors that had befallen the country.

He suddenly looked at me, his eyebrows raised, as though he had just remembered something.

"I have something for you," he said. He jumped up from the couch and headed for the bedroom. I felt my heart beat faster. *Uh-oh,* I thought. What if he comes back with a negligee and asks me to try it on? You just never knew with George.

He returned half a minute later with his acoustic guitar and sat down next to me on the couch. Pushing his hair back behind both ears, holding the pick in his right hand between his forefinger and thumb, he looked at me, his head tilted, and said, "I'm going to make you famous."

I had no idea what to expect. He began singing, looking straight at me. It was such a fun song. So light and folksy.

> *I can tell you nothing new*
> *has happened*
> *since I last saw you . . .*

As George sang I tried to cling to every word, hoping to remember them. He sang about the rice that never made it to Bombay, the smog polluting the shores, and how he couldn't care less about the broken record player on the floor.

> *Won't you call me Miss O'Dell?*
> *Why don't you call me Miss O'Dell?*

I was dumbstruck. I didn't know what to say. I felt—awkward. That was the word. Totally awkward. I had no idea how to react.

He played the last chord, hands still on the guitar, and laughed. He knew full well what it meant to have a Beatle write a song about you, and he was getting a big kick out of my stupefied reaction.

"So what do you think?" he asked, finally breaking the silence. And it was then that I said the absolutely most stupid, ridiculous, asinine thing I ever could have said.

"I feel like a switchboard operator." Where did that come from? Okay, so I'd had a few jobs as a switchboard operator, like at Apple and Dot Records, but nothing in the song reminded me of switchboards. I was just blabbering, because I couldn't believe George had written a song for me, and he'd even used my name as the title of the song! I was embarrassed and I was overwhelmed. I didn't know what to say or how to act. The song was a gift and it was too big, too much.

George looked at me with an odd expression on his face. What was he thinking after that stupid switchboard remark? That was one of those horrible, embarrassing, confusing, "I wish I could take it back" moments. But I recovered quickly.

"I just can't believe it," I said, finding my voice and trying hard to sound like the confident girl I wanted to be. "You actually wrote that for me? When did you write it?"

"A few nights ago, when you said you were coming out," George said. "I was sitting here alone waiting and I ended up writing the song."

"I just can't believe it, George," I said. "Thank you. I really like it."

I heard George sing "Miss O'Dell" many times in the years to come, but it would never sound as good as it did that night with the waves breaking and the breeze blowing through the room providing the only background music. We talked for a while longer and then I left because it was late and dark and I had a long drive ahead. We hugged good-bye, and I waved out the window as I drove away. All the way home I hummed the tune, trying to remember the words, excited about telling Eileen that George had written a song, just for me.

23

BANGLADESH

Summer 1971

That summer Pattie and George rented a house in Nichols Canyon and George's father, Harry, joined them for several weeks. I spent every weekend and most weekday nights at their place, often showing up for work at Peter Asher's office several hours late. Every so often I'd take Mondays or Fridays off, too, sometimes both at once, creating a long weekend to hang out with Pattie by the pool, go with Harry to the beach, or explore the trendy shops in Beverly Hills. Pattie and I discovered a new food market called the Chalet Gourmet with all kinds of exotic cheeses, patés, teas, coffees, vegetables, and fruits. Cherry cheese and kiwis (I'd never seen them before) were my favorites. Just like at Friar Park, Pattie loved to experiment with different recipes, cooking up tasty vegetarian dishes while I chopped the veggies, making sure the conversation never flagged, and keeping everyone's glass filled to the brim.

One evening after dinner we were all gathered in the living room by the fireplace when George picked up his guitar, gave me an impish little grin, and began to sing "Miss O'Dell." He seemed to get a real kick out of my reaction. I sank down into the sofa cushions, feeling embarrassed and uncomfortable being the center of attention. I was also worried about Pattie's reaction. When George told her that he'd written a song for me, how did she feel? Did she think something might have happened between us when he was living in the house by the beach all by himself? I instantly felt protective toward her, knowing how deeply she had been hurt by George's flirtations and affairs. Pattie always came first, no matter what, and I didn't want bad feelings to come between us. I couldn't bear the thought of her being upset with me.

When George finished, Pattie gave me a big smile.

"It's wonderful!" she said. She looked so sincere, and I believed her, but I always had a nagging little worry that she might have been a little jealous that George had written a song for me. I recently asked her how she felt about the song. "Oh, Chris," she said, "I really loved it! You were always such a good, loyal friend. I thought it was wonderful that George would write a song about you." That finally set my mind at rest.

My relationship with Pattie and George was so different now that I wasn't working for them. They were no longer the King and Queen of Friar Park, and I didn't have to play the role of the lady-in-waiting. The whole aura of the Beatles had faded a little, and we were in laid-back LA, where the sun was shining, the beach was beckoning, and we could all just hang out together. George was so relaxed and happy, perhaps even relieved after the phenomenal success of *All Things Must Pass,* Pattie was glowing because George was attentive and affectionate, and I was content just to be near them. Whatever had happened between Pattie and Eric seemed to be over and forgotten, part of a crazy period in all our lives had ended, and I think we all breathed a sigh of relief.

Relaxing was easy that summer. I had a big stash of Seconals (we called them "reds"), and Pattie and I would sit by the pool, take a red, and drift away. We'd lie there for hours, turning over, drifting off, turning over again, all the while getting fabulous tans. I loved the dreamy feeling of the Seconal slowing everything down to a pleasant hum while the bright sun painted a pinkish haze inside my eyelids.

Leon was beginning to hit the peak of his fame as a solo artist, and one day that summer I talked Pattie and George into attending one of his concerts in Long Beach. George had great respect for Leon, so I didn't really have to twist arms. After the concert Leon invited us to a party on the *Queen Mary,* which was now permanently docked in Long Beach. George, Pattie, and I sat and talked at one of the dozens of tables in a gigantic room with hundreds of people mingling around. I kept looking around for Leon, hoping he'd come over to the table and pay some attention to me. Meanwhile, an attractive brunette sat down next to George, batting her eyelashes at him, and moving her chair so close that their shoulders touched. He didn't mind at all, of course; George always loved attention from pretty women.

"Who is she?" Pattie whispered. I could see the vulnerability in her eyes, but even in the most stressful times, Pattie somehow seemed unruffled and unaffected.

"I have no clue, but she sure is all over George." I was mad at George for flirting with the beautiful brunette and pissed at Leon for ignoring me.

That's it! I thought. *I've had enough.* I looked under the table, getting the aim just right, and then I kicked her shin as hard as I could.

"Ouch!" she cried out, looking first at Pattie and then at me. Pattie gave me a confused look while I smiled sweetly at the girl. She pushed back her chair and left the table.

"What happened?" Pattie asked.

"I kicked her under the table."

Pattie burst into laughter. "Oh, Chris, I love you!"

George was completely oblivious to the whole thing.

I was in a bad state with work. When I did bother to show up, I couldn't stay focused and I actually began to resent my job because it got in the way of my social life. All I cared about was hanging out with George and Pattie, where all the fun and excitement were.

I don't know why Peter put up with me, especially since Betsy's attitude clearly conveyed that she was tiring of my work ethic. She'd give me these little disapproving looks and Peter would have little chats with me that confirmed my suspicions. "Betsy thinks you should . . ." he'd say, or "Betsy says that you're not . . ." I think that was Peter's way of trying to keep me in line without having to come right out and express his own opinion. He hated conflict and would avoid it any way that he could, but he was also an extraordinarily patient man who didn't like changes in his routine. I was unpredictable, but at least I was reliably unpredictable—he could count on my showing up sometime during the week and being a cheerful presence around the office. He once joked that I was the only person he knew who could be a week late for work; he was referring to the time I flew to Memphis for the weekend to visit Don Nix, a musician friend of Leon's (trying, unsuccessfully, to make Leon jealous). I ended up staying a week and forgot to let Peter know about my change in plans. Betsy was right: he should have fired me on the spot.

Pattie and I were in the living room searching through recipes in a new cookbook when George came bouncing into the room, smiling from ear to ear. George always bounced when he walked, almost as if he had little springs in his shoes.

"I've just been on the phone with Ravi," George said. "We're thinking about getting some friends together to do a concert for Bangladesh. All the proceeds would go toward helping the people there."

"What a brilliant idea!" Pattie said as we both leaned forward, anxious to hear his ideas. He seemed so excited about the phone call. "Who would you have?"

"Well, Ravi of course, and Ringo, and John if he could make it. Maybe Eric could play." George never mentioned Paul. Lawsuits were flying, and I think all the other Beatles were mad at Paul for the way he'd broken up the band. But why Eric? Pattie and I stole a look at each other. We knew that Eric had gone back to heroin and locked himself up at Hurtwood Edge with his former girlfriend Alice Ormsley-Gore. They were apparently in pretty bad shape.

Whenever Eric's name was mentioned, Pattie would sigh and shake her head. "Poor Eric," she'd say. Years would pass before Pattie told me that sometime after the Dominos tour, Eric asked her to leave George and move in with him. When Pattie refused, Eric threatened to use heroin full time. Pattie told Eric not to be stupid, but he followed through with his threat. I heard that Alice, just twenty-one years old, was drinking two bottles of vodka a day.

Pattie quickly changed the subject. "Who else?"

"What about Leon?" I said, as if I had no investment in that idea.

"Leon would be great," George said. "And Jim Keltner."

"And Klaus Voormann," Pattie said.

"And, of course, Billy Preston!" I added.

"And Badfinger!" George said. In 1969, while still at Apple, the Iveys had changed their name to Badfinger.

"Let me help, George," I said. "I can get phone numbers through Denny Cordell and Eileen, and I can call Don Nix to arrange for backup singers."

We kept throwing names around that night, and George wrote them all down. From that very first day when we talked about the possibility of a Bangladesh concert, we knew what a big deal it was for George. Except for a few appearances with Delaney and Bonnie when the spotlight was on them, not him, George hadn't done a live public concert since the Beatles appeared at San Francisco's Candlestick Park in August 1966. And this would be the first concert where he'd be on his own, not as a Beatle but as solo artist George Harrison. The concert was his brainchild, which raised the ante even higher. He'd be gathering the musicians together, organizing the concert (the first benefit concert ever), and taking care of all the little details necessary to make it work. Because *All Things Must Pass* was such a huge commercial success, he felt the pressure of getting it right. Pattie and I promised to do everything we could to help him, and that's how it started and ended, as a team effort with lots of ideas and creative effort from dozens of people who loved music and, even more important, who admired and respected George.

Within a few days, musicians—Bobby Keyes, Jim Keltner, Carl Radle, Klaus Voormann, and Jesse Ed Davis are the ones I remember—started dropping by the Nichols Canyon house to offer their help and discuss plans for the concert. The date was set for August 1 at Madison Square Garden. George spent hours on the phone those days, sitting in his office-bedroom making calls, receiving calls, setting up the details.

Leon told George he'd be there as long as he could bring his band with him, since they'd be on tour at the time. Don Nix came into town and after the four of us spent a day sailing to Catalina Island, he agreed to organize the backup singers. Billy Preston didn't even have to be asked; he'd do anything for George.

"I can't believe this is all coming together," George kept saying. The whole thing just grew right before our eyes.

I flew into New York City two days before the concert and went straight to the Park Lane Hotel on Central Park South. I was rooming with Eileen—George paid for both our plane tickets to thank us for our help organizing the musicians—but she was visiting an old friend (and later spent most of her time with Leon and Denny), so I unpacked my bags and headed straight to Pattie and George's two-bedroom suite overlooking Central Park. For the next two days that's where I camped out, spending almost all my time with Pattie hanging out in the hotel room, chattering on like two teenage girls, or venturing out to shop at Bergdorf Goodman, strolling through Tiffany's trying on diamonds and pretending we were going to buy something, or stopping for a drink in the hotel bar where everyone seemed to gather in the late afternoon. George was on a different wavelength, of course, edgy, distracted, and intently focused on the last-minute details.

The night before the concert, George, Pattie, and I took a limo to Madison Square Garden for the rehearsal. I knew I'd see Leon, but I was prepared, having taken extra time with my hair and makeup (Pattie helped me with my eye shadow) and wearing the jeans that I stitched up along the seams so they were tight, tight, tight. My stomach was in knots and my hands were ice cold, but I put on my confident face and treated everyone I met as if they were my personal best friend. I was upbeat, cool, calm, and collected on the outside, although my insides were in a frenzy of adrenaline rushes.

Pattie and I wandered around the enormous hall, all lit up with nobody there, and imagined what it would look like the next day when both the afternoon and evening shows were completely sold out. Roadies were swarming the stage, checking wires, lights, and equipment, and the musicians were tuning up their instruments onstage, playing bits and pieces of songs, trying to get the sound right. Ringo, Billy Preston, Klaus Voormann, Jim Keltner, Carl Radle, Jesse Ed Davis, and the four members of Badfinger were all hanging around the stage— my memory is a little vague on the details, but those are the faces I remember—but the two musicians George was most concerned about hadn't shown up yet.

Earlier that afternoon in the suite, when Pattie and I were sorting through some shopping we'd done, George sat down with us, his eyebrows knitted together in a deep frown.

"I'm not sure Eric is going to make it," he said.

"Is he okay?" Pattie said. We were all terribly concerned about Eric. Pattie couldn't understand why George had asked him to join the concert when he was so desperately ill with his addiction. I think she was afraid he might go into withdrawal and die right there on the stage, although we had talked about the need to get drugs for him to make sure he could make it through the concert safely and get back on the plane without going into full-blown withdrawal. But I believe she was at least as concerned that if Eric was in bad shape, he might somehow distract attention from the concert and undermine all George's hard work and the efforts of the other musicians.

"I heard that he's on the plane," George said, "but I don't know if he'll be in shape to play. He's pretty messed up. Somebody is finding some heroin to give him as soon as he arrives."

We all looked at each other and at that moment I wondered what George must be feeling. Eric was one of George's best friends. But Eric was in love with Pattie. George knew that because Eric told him straight out. "I have to tell you, man, that I'm in love with your wife," Eric said. (Pattie told me at that moment she wanted to die.) I never really knew how George felt about Eric's confession, but I do know there was a history between George, Pattie, and Eric that had started a long time before that and involved cheating and flirting on all sides. But it was clear from the troubled look on George's face that all those entanglements were in the past, forgiven and forgotten for the time being at least, as he focused on the concert and his concern about Eric.

Bob Dylan was the other unknown. "God, I hope he shows up," George said in the limo on the way to the rehearsal. Eric might not make it because he was so sick and out of control with his addiction to heroin, but if Bob didn't show up, it would be perceived as, well—a snub. George had already been deeply disappointed when John Lennon called just a week before the concert, bowing out because of something to do with Yoko, a heated argument, a vacation in the Virgin Islands, or a gallery opening in upstate New York, I can't remember. But after John's disheartening phone call, Pattie and I were terrified that the elusive Bob Dylan might let down George, too.

So we were all at the rehearsal, on edge, waiting to see if Dylan would show up. Pattie and I spent a few minutes talking to Al Aronowitz, the music columnist for the *New York Post* and the man who first introduced the Beatles to Bob Dylan back in 1964. He was standing by the side of the stage, watching the goings-on, when we joined him.

"Do you think Bob will show up?" Pattie asked, obviously worried about the possibility he might not.

"Sure he will," Al said with great confidence. "Bob wouldn't let George down."

A few minutes later Pattie tugged at my arm. "There he is," she said.

It was as if the Lord Himself had floated down from the heavens. The lights seemed to brighten momentarily, the musicians froze in position, and we all held our breaths as we watched George walk across the stage to give Bob a hug. That was a moment, I'll tell you. When Eric showed up sometime later, the energy in the hall was almost static with electricity as we all realized that this event was going to be seriously huge. Eric looked like shit—he'd lost a lot of weight, his face was gaunt and his skin ashen, he walked with a shuffle and had trouble looking anyone in the eye—but he was there, after all, and that's all I cared about. George had pulled it off. The audience was definitely going to get their money's worth.

The next morning Eileen and I dilly-dallied around in our room, talking about what to wear and our schedule that day. She didn't know

George or the other English musicians very well, so she was sticking close to Leon and his band. After breakfast we went our separate ways; she was going to both shows, but Pattie and I had decided to attend only the evening show so we could spend the afternoon together. After George left for the afternoon concert, Pattie and I lazed around the suite, ordering lunch from room service, taking baths, watching a soap opera, worrying a little about how the concert was going, and figuring out what we were going to wear that night. I finally decided on my super-tight jeans with a nice blouse and jacket. We were in the bedroom leaning up against the pillows and trying to find something to watch on television when the door opened and in walked George, still dressed in his stage outfit, a big bright smile on his face. Bob Dylan was right behind him.

Pattie jumped off the bed and gave Bob a big hug.

"Hey, Bob, this is Chris O'Dell," George said, obviously forgetting about the day Bill Oakes and I delivered the harmonicas to Dylan at the farmhouse before the Isle of Wight concert. But then again, why would he remember it? Dylan clearly didn't.

Bob and I shook hands, Pattie called room service and ordered some tea, and we listened to George's summary of the afternoon concert.

"The audience was just fantastic," he said, the words practically tripping over each other, he was so pumped up. "They loved Ravi and his band. Everybody played great and the order of the show seems to work. It was really great."

Dylan hung back, thumbs tucked into his jean pockets, smiling that enigmatic smile of his, nodding his head now and then and mumbling, "yeah, really good." After a while they moved into the living room to talk about the evening show, while Pattie and I continued our long, drawn-out preparations.

When we arrived at Madison Square Garden, fans were lined up at the entrance to the ramp that led into the building and up several floors to the backstage area. They cried out, "Hi, George!" "Good luck, George!" and "Georgeeee!" as they waved and stuck their faces up against the windows of the limo. George was beaming. Backstage Pattie and I mingled with the musicians, their wives, girlfriends, and guests. I said hello to Maureen, but she barely acknowledged my presence and immediately started talking to Pattie. I shrugged it off, figuring that she still saw me as a threat for some reason and found it safer to ignore me.

Leon walked by and said hello, without any real warmth or interest in having a conversation. As I watched him walk away from me and greet other people in the same way, it finally started to dawn on me that he wasn't going to sweep me up in his arms and beg me to come back to him. I was beginning to let him go. It was about time.

When Ravi Shankar opened the show, we stayed backstage chatting, drinking, and taking hits now and then off a joint somebody was passing around. After Ravi left the stage, Pattie and I made our way to our center-stage seats in the second row. We loved being in the thick of the crowd, feeling the surging energy and excitement as we sat on the hard foldout chairs looking up at the stage, which seemed to tower above us with the stage lights changing from blue to green to red, creating a different mood for each song. When Billy Preston started dancing across the stage, we knew there was no turning back—this concert was going to be a huge success. With every new performer—Leon, Ringo, Eric Clapton, Badfinger—the audience's excitement and enthusiasm ratcheted up a notch as people jumped out of their seats, whistling, clapping, and hollering for more. But Bob Dylan hushed the crowd, like a preacher mesmerizing his congregation, half-singing, half-speaking his stories about stumbling along on the misty mountains and crawling on crooked highways in "A Hard Rain's A-Gonna Fall," ending his five-song set with "Just Like a Woman" and my favorite line of any Dylan song, "but you break just like a little girl." Something about Bob Dylan's voice had changed—the tone was deeper, more soulful, as if he were reaching deeper and singing from his heart rather than his head.

When George sang "Bangladesh," Pattie and I leaped to our feet with the rest of the audience, our hands raised above our heads, clapping as hard as we could. We were so proud of George. His dream had become a reality. He had pulled it off, focusing the world's attention on the tragedy in Bangladesh by assembling a group of his friends, all rock and roll superstars, in the first benefit concert ever. That concert would be the model for all the big-name benefit concerts to follow.

With shining eyes we looked up at George standing in the spotlight, humbly acknowledging the thunderous applause while gathering the other musicians close around him. Up until that moment I had been proud to know George, but now I was proud *of* him. Many times over the years I'd known him, he'd expressed his insecurities about his songwriting talents, his intense dislike of public performances, and even his fear that he wouldn't be able to draw a crowd.

I looked at Pattie and saw tears welling up in her eyes. "Wasn't that wonderful, Pattie?" I shouted above the noise of the crowd.

"It was so exciting," she shouted back, giving me a big hug. "Didn't you just love Billy?"

"And what about Dylan?" I said. "Wasn't he amazing?" We were talking so fast we hardly had time to take a breath.

"And George," she said in a softer tone of voice. "George was magnificent."

From the expression on her face, I knew there was a bond between them that could never be broken, no matter what happened.

"Let's go back to the dressing rooms so we can be there when they come off stage," Pattie said as George and the other musicians prepared for an encore.

She grabbed my arm, holding tight, and we headed backstage.

After the show we took a limo from Madison Square Garden to an "invited guests only" party at a small club in the basement of a brownstone. I remember dancing with a lot of people, including Billy Preston and Andy Williams. Andy Williams! I could tell he was interested in me, and he was a famous guy and good-looking, but more than twice my age and about as far removed from a rock star as you could get in the music world. After a few dances I made some lame excuse about needing to catch my breath and went looking for Billy Preston. Now, Billy could dance!

When I returned to the table where I'd left my drink, Ringo and Maureen had joined the group. I smiled at Maureen, and she leaned across the table toward me. "You look great in jeans," she said.

I nearly fell off my chair. It wasn't because of the compliment, although it felt good and actually kept me in tight jeans for years to come, but because Maureen was actually being nice to me. *Finally*, I thought. I'd always hated feeling uncomfortable around her, and I really wanted to be friends with Ringo. If Maureen was willing to give me a chance, maybe I could be friends with both of them.

After the concert, I spent two extra days in New York with Pattie and George. I moved out of my room and slept in the extra bedroom in their suite. While George took care of business, Pattie and I walked and shopped and ate and drank. When they flew back to Friar Park, I returned to a dismal world of boring nothingness in LA, driving my Corolla to work, watching television, crocheting in the evenings, and resuming my daily habit of snorting coke, swallowing Seconals, and drinking alcohol to even everything out.

After all the excitement of the past few months, life was suddenly dull and predictable, and I was not happy. *Thank God for the drugs*, I thought, as I opened the ziplock bag containing my stash of Seconals. Where would I be without them?

24

THE ROLLING STONES

November 1971–February 1972

"Hey, Chris, it's Sid!"

I was sitting at my desk in Peter's office, typing a letter and ignoring a big stack of papers that needed to be filed.

"Hi, Sid, what's up? I was going to come by after work, is that okay?" Sid was my new best friend, a high-class drug dealer who sold to the "in" crowd in the Hollywood motion picture and record industries. He looked a lot like Santa Claus, big and round with a short white beard and collar-length white hair. And he always gave me free cocaine.

"Yeah, sure, that's great, but look, I'm calling because I spoke to Marshall Chess last night," Sid said. "Marshall is Leonard Chess's son, he's running Rolling Stones Records now, and he's looking for an assistant. Are you interested in another job?"

"The Rolling Stones?" I said. I felt a rush of adrenaline and, God, did that feel good. How cool would it be to get back in the action and work for an English group again—and not just any group but, in my opinion, the second-greatest band in the world.

"I think it might be a good change for you," Sid said, giving me Marshall's number. I stared at that number for a long time, trying to think, the adrenaline still pumping. How could I leave Peter? We'd been working together since the Apple days, he'd paid for my plane ticket to LA and let me live in his house, and he was always so patient with me, so good and kind, putting up with my erratic schedule, long weekends, and periodic hangovers. But how could I turn down a chance to work for the Rolling Stones?

"Look, this is not going to be easy," Marshall said as we talked in the office of his house set high above the Pacific Coast Highway. Very carefully, very strategically, he put the emphasis in that sentence on *not*. Thin, small, dark-haired, with nice eyes, a prominent but not unattractive nose, and a smile that made his eyes crinkle, Marshall was definitely an attractive, even sexy man, but his intensity scared me. I was accustomed to gentle, sensitive, tactful Peter with his polite English manners. Marshall was high energy and hard edged, his gaze unwavering, eyes narrowing as I detailed my work experience. His fingers tapped the table as if to hurry the conversation along.

"Mick and Keith will be living here for the next six or seven months, along with Bianca and Anita, and Mick Taylor and his wife, Rose. You'll need to find nice houses for them, take care of daily business, book the recording sessions, attend to their personal needs, and then there's the album to worry about: getting the cover designed, lining up photographers, the whole fucking thing. Charlie and Bill will be in town now and then, too, and they'll need hotel rooms, limos, cash, dry cleaning, that kind of stuff. I'm hiring you as my personal assistant, so you'll also be helping with the contracts, secretarial work, phone calls, and all the rest of it. Can you handle all that?" Marshall leaned back in his chair and actually took a breath.

"I can handle it," I said. I'd had plenty of experience at Apple balancing the demands of the office, the studio scheduling, and various needs of the Apple artists, and I trusted my ability to handle the egos and demands of the Stones.

"I can offer you two hundred and fifty dollars a week," he said. Well, now. Peter was paying me three hundred dollars a week, which wasn't all that much money, even back then. But I weighed in the extra excitement of working for the Stones, along with the chance to add the experience to my résumé (and not being stuck in the office all day—freedom!), and took the job. Peter was sad to lose me, but he certainly understood the allure of the Rolling Stones. I found a replacement, Gloria, who ended up staying with him for many years, and as soon as I stopped working for Peter, Betsy and I became close friends, so it all worked out in the end, as things always seem to do.

My first responsibility as the Stones' personal assistant was to find rental houses for Mick and Keith. I spent the next few weeks searching out the real estate listings and hoping to find the perfect house for each of them. Marshall was the opposite of a micromanager and seemed to trust that I knew what I was doing. I loved the freedom of waking up in the morning whenever I wanted, hitting the road in my trusty Toyota Corolla, and driving through the tree-lined streets of Beverly Hills. I was on my own, free to set my own schedule, and as I drove through the curving streets in the sunshine, the thick, salty presence of the ocean nearby—feeling the energy that always seemed to be hanging in the air—I fell back in love with LA. The smog wasn't so bad back then and the trees didn't droop the way they do now. LA was my town then and I loved it.

Finally, I found what I hoped would be the perfect house for Keith, a dark cottage-style home, on Stone Canyon Road in Bel Air, tucked away from the street and surrounded by big trees with a huge, sweeping front yard. I'd never met Keith Richard (who had dropped the "s" from his name at the time but would add it back on in 1978), but I'd certainly heard about his drug habits and outrageous ways, and I was guessing that his rough edges might need a comfortable place to rest and even, perhaps, soften, in this luxurious, elegant home. I went along with my instincts, and, thank God, Keith and Anita loved the house.

But still no house for Mick Jagger. I was having a hard time, to tell the truth, because I was worried about Bianca. I'd had only one encounter with Bianca, back in 1970 when I was spending a weekend at Mick's country house in England. She was sitting on a kitchen stool, swinging her long, brown legs and looking seductively at Mick, when one of the houseguests came tearing down the stairs to announce that the upstairs bath was overflowing, and water was all over the place.

Bianca swiveled on the stool and said in a low, cool voice, "Oh, I must have forgotten." She was completely nonplussed by the whole thing, and I got the distinct feeling that she had taken control of the house and of Mick. I looked at Mick as he looked at her, entranced, and I thought, *Boy, is he hooked.*

Bianca was accustomed to luxury, and I knew I'd better find the right house or I'd never hear the end of it. After weeks of scouring all the exclusive areas of Beverly Hills, I found the perfect house at 414 St. Pierre Road in Bel Air, just a five-minute drive from Keith's house. A grand old mansion built in 1927 on a 6.5-acre estate, its best features were a large ballroom on the lower floor, a wood-paneled library, and a gargantuan bedroom suite, all decorated in heavy velvets and brocades.

The grounds were equally extravagant, with a swimming pool the size of a football field, another pool made to look like a river and big enough for a rowboat, tennis courts, four pink stucco guesthouses, and stately old trees with overarching branches and dense foliage. Newspaper tycoon William Randolph Hearst had bought the house for his mistress, actress Marion Davies; Howard Hughes had been a guest there in the grand old days of Hollywood, and John and Jackie Kennedy had honeymooned there in 1953. At least that's what I was told, and I believed it.

Mick and Bianca loved it.

When I think back to those days, it seems so bizarre that we didn't give any thought at all to security. None of the houses had walls or gates. The press wasn't so pushy back then and fans, for the most part, were relatively well behaved. A few years earlier, when I was living with Leon, I remember a conversation he had with another musician. "Someday," he said, "we'll all live in gated houses."

How paranoid, I thought at the time. *Leon is so pessimistic.* But of course he was right.

"C'mon, Chris, let's go over to Keith's."

Mick and I were sitting on the floor of the wood-paneled study of the grand old Bel Air mansion I had rented for him. Bianca was out for dinner with friends, and their infant daughter, Jade, and her nanny, Sally, were upstairs in the nursery. The study was filled with deep-cushioned furniture and floor-to-ceiling bookcases. Heavy gold curtains lined the windows. Despite its elegance, though, the room had a musty, heavy, even slightly depressing feel.

I yawned and stretched. I was exhausted. I'd been working all day on the song lyrics for the Stones album *Exile on Main Street,* and now the typed sheets were spread out in front of us on the floor as we listened to the acetates and checked them for accuracy. Mick had a pen in hand and was correcting the words I had typed in preparation to send them to the record company for the final go-through on the album. For the past week or so, it seemed that all I did was sit in front of the stereo, straining to decipher the lyrics—Mick's words weren't always easy to understand—writing them down and playing the same song over and over again to make sure I got it right. Then I'd type them, double and triple checking the finished version as Mick looked over my shoulder.

I looked at my watch—it was almost 10:00 p.m.—then gathered up the sheets of paper and grabbed my purse. I wasn't all that excited to go to Keith and Anita's place because I found it dark and depressing. I often stopped by there to do errands for Keith—deliver laundry from the dry cleaner, pick up a check to be cashed, get his signature on a legal document —but I rarely stayed for long. I wasn't crazy about the hard-drug crowd that was always hanging around, and I wasn't comfortable with Anita, who had a way of dismissing people with a flick of her hand and a few well-chosen words delivered in her heavy German-Italian accent. I didn't take her bad manners or drugged-out behavior personally because I felt absolutely no connection to her. She was a man's woman, not a woman's woman like Pattie, and we pretty much ignored each other.

I liked Keith a lot. He had such a gentle way about him, and he was always kind to me and quick to express his gratitude for any little errand I would run for him. I worked for both Keith and Mick, but unlike Mick, Keith didn't need much. He'd sign a bunch of blank checks, hand them over to me, and when he needed something—cigarettes, magazines, or cash for drugs—he'd call me. "Hey, Chris, would you have time to stop by the bank today?" he'd ask. I'd fill out the check for however much he needed and bring him the cash, the cigarettes, or the magazines.

"Thanks, Chris," he'd always say with a smile and a little nod of gratitude. "Wanna hang out for a while?"

"Not today, Keith, sorry," I'd say, making some excuse about having to get back to work at Mick's place, where my office was set up.

Like Keith, Mick was a great boss, fun to be around and always telling me how much he appreciated my help. I'd type letters or lyrics, book studio time, hang out in the studio in case Mick or Keith needed anything, contact photographers for the album cover or the PR people to work on publicity, stuff like that. I also helped Mick with his personal life, responding to invitations to parties, returning calls to the Stones entourage of PR and businesspeople, making appointments for Bianca to get her hair done or her nails polished, or dealing with issues that affected Jade, such as finding a new nanny when Sally left suddenly.

I was the Stones' go-to person, and I liked being right in the thick of things. With Mick, something exciting was always happening, and I was always included. Once again, I was part of the inner circle, a member of the elite club. There was no end of activities to keep me occupied, day and night. Working was part of the fun—how difficult is it to listen to rock music all day, type a letter here and there, organize studio sessions, call record executives, and sit in recording sessions half the night? That doesn't mean there weren't days when I wasn't tired or angry or fed up with some or all of them, but most of the time I had so much fun it didn't feel like work at all. I could show up at two or three in the afternoon, and if there was nothing pressing to do, I'd spend half the day lying out by the pool. There was no water in the pool, but still, it was a pool, the sun was shining, and I was working for the Rolling Stones. Life couldn't get much better than that.

November and December passed quickly, and we were beginning a new year when Mick asked me if I wanted to go to a Chuck Berry concert.

"Sure!" I said, my standard response. I knew Mick had a lot of respect for Chuck Berry, one of the great pioneers of rock and roll music, and Keith idolized him. I was standing backstage watching the show with Mick and Keith when Chuck invited Keith to join him onstage. The sparks began to fly from the moment Keith swaggered out and the audience went wild. Chuck Berry put up with it for a while, but when he realized he was being upstaged and outshined, he didn't look happy about it. From my position at the side of the stage it seemed as if Chuck pumped up the volume on his amp trying to outdo Keith (as if that were possible).

Mick was furious. "What the fuck?" he kept saying over and over again, his jaw tensed, brow furrowed, cheeks sucked in. I don't know how long we stood there watching, but suddenly Mick was out on the stage with Chuck and Keith, dancing around in his sexy Mick dance, clapping his hands, knees bouncing together, pelvis thrusting, bottom wriggling. The crowd went berserk, which really pissed off Chuck Berry. Knowing that he'd made his point, Mick danced off the stage with Keith following right behind him. Minutes later we were in the limos, cracking up over the fact that Chuck Berry tried to screw around with Keith and got fucked royally.

It was sort of sad, actually. Chuck Berry had been one of their heroes, and they'd just seen his worst side. That happens in rock and roll, just as it does everywhere else in life. You idolize someone, put them on a pedestal, sing their praises, and wish you could be just like them, and then they do something that reveals their own insecurity or meanness of heart and you end up crushed. Even as we laughed about the whole thing, I felt bad for Mick and Keith. I felt especially bad for Keith, knowing that he wouldn't be able to laugh it off and forget about it like Mick. Four years later, when Keith organized the *Hail! Hail! Rock 'n' Roll* concert and film as a tribute to Chuck Berry, the two men apparently got into a heated argument over the song "Carol." Later Keith said that Berry gave him "more headaches than Mick Jagger, but I still can't dislike him."

In spite of his rough, I-don't-give-a-shit exterior, Keith Richards was a softie at heart. I adored him.

• • •

The *Exile on Main Street* photo shoot is absolutely clear in my memory.
Bill Wyman and Charlie Watts were in LA for it, and we lined up Robert
Frank, a well-known photographer and filmmaker, to take the pictures.
Robert had already taken a Polaroid of me at Marshall Chess's new
place on Mulholland Drive. I love that picture, with my hair blowing
away from my face; it appears on the lower-left corner on the back of
the album cover and, I've learned, I'm sometimes referred to as "the
mystery woman."

We took limos down to LA's squalid Main Street, where Robert
had decided to take the photos. We followed him down the barren
streets, glancing every now and then at the lost souls—the homeless,
the drunk, and the destitute—peering at us from windows and doorways. At first they ignored us, but after a while people started following
us down the streets.

"Hey, you Mick Jagger?" someone shouted.

Mick looked back, smiled, and did a small wave.

"You *are*, man, you are fucking Mick Jagger."

"What are you doin' here, man?" someone else shouted out. "Damn!
This your band? Damn! It's the fuckin' Rolling Stones. We got the
fuckin' Rolling Stones here, walking down the damn fuckin' street."

As I watched the people following the Stones down Main Street, I
flashed back to a conversation Pattie and I had at Friar Park one day.
"You know, Chris, musicians are like Pied Pipers," Pattie said. "They
walk through the village playing their instruments and people just follow them to wherever they may be going."

Men and women, young, old, black, brown, white, came out of the
doorways and joined the little parade. As Robert snapped away and we
led the group through the dirty and deserted streets of downtown LA,
I had this amazing feeling of togetherness and unity with the Stones
leading the way and the people of the street following along behind.
Everything seemed connected—super-famous, super-rich superstars
walking the streets with the impoverished citizens of Main Street, Los
Angeles, seemingly breaking down the doors of difference, smiling in
the warm winter sunshine, laughing, feeling good, happy to be alive.

Of course, I was high on pot, along with everyone else, including the Stones, Robert Frank, Marshall Chess, and, from all appearances, the people we'd picked up along the way.

"Hey, you got anything to smoke?" I heard more than once, and we just laughed, because they knew we did, and we knew they did, and no drugs changed hands that day because there was no need.

As the sun descended in the west, sinking beneath the tall empty buildings and vacant parking lots, we drove back in the golden light to Beverly Hills, back to the big mansions and the expensive drugs and the quiet streets, looking forward to an evening of good food and wine. We were no longer thinking about the disconnect between us and them, the street people who were returning to their dark doorways and boarded-up windows, content to have had their brief but unforgettable experience of brushing up against fame.

One night in mid-February, three or four weeks before the Stones left Los Angeles for a break before their tour, Keith, Mick, Anita, and I were at Keith's place drinking and passing a joint around. I went to the bathroom, just off the living room, and sitting right on the bathroom sink next to the toilet was a silver spoon. The middle of the spoon was all black, burned from cooking heroin. I stared at it, fascinated. I'd tried heroin once or twice, but I'd never injected the drug—shooting up was too risky, too crazy, too far-out. I'd seen what the drug had done to the Dominos, but as I stared at that black spoon I couldn't help wondering what it would feel like to shoot up heroin.

I had a sudden, terrible thought. *Shit—I hope that's not the silver that came with the house. Because if it is,* the thoughts kept spinning, *then guess who is going to get stuck, once again, cleaning up after them and making things right with the real estate company.* Memories of the Dominos breaking every bit of glass in their rented flat in London flooded over me. Breaking glass was one thing, but using the sterling silver spoons to mix up heroin was something altogether different.

I walked out of that bathroom feeling really depressed. Maybe it was the fact that I wasn't getting enough sleep. Maybe it was all the coke I'd been snorting. Maybe it was the damn spoon. I don't know what it was, but all I wanted to do right then was go home and sleep for three days.

Keith was sitting on the sofa, a cigarette dangling from his mouth, reading the *Rolling Stone* magazine I'd bought for him a few days earlier. Anita was fiddling with one of Marlon's toys; just two and a half years old, Marlon was asleep in the back bedroom. Mick was smoking a joint, smiling in his cocky way.

"Listen to this fucking article in *Rolling Stone* about Harrison's Bangladesh concert," Keith said. He started reading from the article.

" 'The Concert for Bangladesh is rock reaching for its manhood.' " Keith raised an eyebrow. " 'Under the leadership of George Harrison, a group of rock musicians recognized, in a deliberate, self-conscious, and professional way, that they have responsibilities, and went about dealing with them seriously.' "

Keith looked at Mick and then at me. "Do you believe that shit? But wait, it gets better. Harrison is 'a man with a sense of his own worth, his own role in the place of things . . . with few parallels among his peers.' "

"Bollocks." Keith laughed, tossing the magazine on the coffee table. "What a fucking load of shit."

I knew that Keith wasn't really amused. He could be terribly insecure. A few weeks earlier he had asked me to listen to his song "Happy." "Do you think it's okay?" he asked me, clearly nervous about my reaction. "Yeah, it's great," I said. "It's really a great song, I love it," I added because he still looked like he wasn't convinced it was any good. He seemed to relax a little, but I knew he'd be asking the same question again. "Is it okay? Is it any good?" What a paradox Keith was—a sweet, sensitive soul who wrote songs about needing love to be happy and yet he lived his life as if he couldn't give a shit about anything.

But at that moment I wasn't too interested in Keith's feelings. I sat at the far end of the sofa, my legs and arms crossed, smoking a cigarette and drinking my Scotch and Coke as if it were straight Coke. I was pissed. Sure, I knew they were just being competitive, but I couldn't stand listening to them make fun of George. I wanted to jump into the conversation and tell them to leave him alone. But what could I do? I worked for the Stones now, not the Beatles. This is weird, I know, and particularly strange in the context of the Stones' remarkable longevity, but at that moment I had a sinking feeling that I was beginning my climb *down* the ladder. I'd started at the very top with the Beatles and now I was on the rung below. I found myself thinking at that moment that the Stones were sometimes a little too raw, too raunchy, too nega- tive. I liked their music, and I liked each of them individually, but if I had to choose, the Beatles would win.

"You know," I said, trying to smile but having a hard time of it, "George is my friend."

Mick looked over at me as if he had forgotten I was there. "Oh yeah, Chris, you're a Beatle person, aren't you? Sorry about that."

We let it go, then, but after I dropped Mick at his house and headed home through the dark canyons, I felt a sudden, intense longing to see Pattie and George. Mick was right. When it came right down to it, I was a Beatle person.

25

THE STONES TOUR

June–July 1972

"Marshall told me there isn't a place for me on the tour." I was pouting as I stretched out on the chaise longue. Mick and I were sitting by the pool at the new house I'd rented for him and Keith. He'd been gone for a few months, jetting from San Francisco to New York before taking Bianca and Jade on a three-week holiday to Bali. Keith and Anita had left LA, too, entering a Swiss drug clinic together. Keith told me later that the staff put him to sleep for three days and "changed" his blood— to get rid of the heroin—in exchange for nice, clean, fresh blood. It sounded like Dracula's clinic to me, but when I met him at the LA airport in May, he looked fabulous—his face was bright, skin clear, hair spiky with a cool bleach-blond streak. He wore a fitted black suit jacket with clean, pressed jeans, and his swagger was gone, replaced with an aristocratic stroll, embellished by the use of a cane. *Whoa,* I thought, *he's kind of cute.* That thought had never occurred to me before. Keith really wasn't my type.

"Don't worry, Chris," Mick said as he ate a spoonful of yogurt with honey swirled on top. He'd been taking really good care of himself in the weeks before the tour, eating healthy food, exercising, getting more sleep.

I sighed, sinking deeper into the comfy chaise longue.

Mick took another spoonful of yogurt and looked at me with

understanding eyes. "You never know when you'll be needed," he said. "Trust me."

"Chris! It's Mick."

"Mick! How's the tour? How was the show? Are you okay?" I had so many questions to ask. It just killed me to think of the Stones touring around America and I was all alone, stuck in Los Angeles by myself. I had plenty of little odds and ends to clean up: phone calls to return, bills to pay, getting Mick and Keith's rental house in shape to be returned to its owner. But while the Stones were happily gallivanting all over the country, I felt like the unwanted child left at home to take care of the thankless jobs, sweeping up the memories of all the good times we'd had.

"Yeah, everything's great," Mick said, brushing aside my questions and getting right down to business. "Look, Ossie Clark is sending a package from London. He's designed some more stage outfits for me. The package is addressed to you and it's scheduled to arrive tomorrow at the Los Angeles airport. I want you to collect it at customs."

"Okay!" I said, already reaching for my purse. "Where do you want me to send them?"

"I don't want you to send them. I want you to *bring* them to Chicago."

"Really?" My heart was beating like crazy.

"You wanted to come on tour, didn't you?" he said, with that sly hint of mischief in his voice. I knew what he was thinking. *See Chris? I found a way to get you here.*

I flew into O'Hare airport the next day, June 19, 1972, and took a taxi to the International Amphitheater. With my precious all-access backstage pass, which Mick had given me during the Southern California part of the tour, and the even more valuable box of costumes tucked under my arm, I went straight to Mick's dressing room. Steve, the makeup artist, was fussing over Mick, applying eye shadow and mascara.

"Hey, Chris, you made it!" Mick said, standing up to give me a big hug. I proudly held out the box, happy that Mick was glad to see me, happy to be in Chicago, happy to feel part of the gang again.

"Any problems?" Mick asked as he opened the box and took out each of the soft one-piece jumpsuits, looking them over to make sure they were perfect. They were all basically the same cut, designed to be skin tight, made from velveteen, velour, and satin in shades of purple, lavender, pink, blue, white, turquoise, and dark blue, some studded with sequins, others framed with fringe, all stunning, all utterly and completely Mick Jagger. Holding each costume in front of him, he checked his image in the mirror as he turned this way and that, looking at me to see if I approved. Mick loved the way those suits stretched across his abdomen, clung to his little butt, and accentuated the bulge in his crotch. He was "definable"—that's how I'd put it—with every muscle and tendon, every crack and indentation, every protrusion and protuberance showing, leaving little to the imagination.

"What d'ya think?" he asked as he handed the jumpsuits to Steve to hang up.

"They're fabulous," I gushed, knowing that's what he wanted to hear, but to tell the truth, I thought Mick should mix it up a little bit with his stage clothes. Why not a great pair of pants and a frilly top or even a funky suit?

I left Mick to finish his makeup and walked around the backstage area, searching for Astrid and Bill. Astrid and I got to know each other when she arrived with Bill for the *Exile on Main Street* recording sessions. At first I was wary of her, having heard that she could be demanding, but when she realized that I would do everything I could to make her and Bill comfortable—including moving them from a three-star hotel to the swanky Beverly Wilshire, a real feat because the hotel was overbooked—she warmed up to me. By the time the tour began several months later, we'd become close friends.

When I walked into the hospitality room of Chicago's International Amphitheater, Astrid broke off her conversation with one of the road crew and walked over to give me a kiss on both cheeks.

"Chris. You made it. I was glad when Mick told us you were coming." Astrid was not one to show her emotions, and her Swedish accent drew even more attention to her cool demeanor. "Come, let's go and get a drink before the show starts." Although Astrid seemed somewhat aloof and standoffish, once I got used to her, I knew how to read her moods. I told her once that when I first met her, I thought she was stuck up.

"Yes, everyone thinks that, I guess," she said, pouting a little. "Even knowing that, it's very hard for me to change. I grew up feeling as if I were in a glass house and my emotions were there for everybody to see. It became an obsession of mine not to show any emotion. I was so afraid—afraid to be alone and afraid of people. But I can't express that, and so I hide my insecurities."

Like a lot of us, I thought.

Moments before the band went on stage, Bill came into the hospitality room and gave me a big hug. Charlie Watts walked in right behind him.

"Welcome back, Chris," Charlie said with a big grin. Charlie was the quiet one, a chiseled, craggy-faced jazz musician who formed, or so I imagined, the granite foundation underneath the rocky cliffs of the Rolling Stones. While I was chatting with Charlie, Keith walked past and gave me a little kiss on the cheek. Minutes later they all left to go onstage and Astrid went to her usual place at the sound mixing board in the middle of the audience. I was sitting at a table in the hospitality room, just about to go into the ladies' room for another big hit of cocaine before the show, when Robert Frank took a Polaroid of me. I still have that photograph and although it's badly faded, every time I look at it I remember how I felt at that moment, just a few hours after arriving in Chicago. Exhilarated. Ecstatic.

When the Stones started the show with "Brown Sugar," a song Mick had written about African American model and singer Marsha Hunt (who bore his first and her only child, Karis), I joined Astrid at the sound mixing board where we listened to the whole set from beginning to end. One of my favorite songs was "Midnight Rambler"; I got such a kick out of the way Mick snapped his belt at the floor, and the stage lights flashed brighter with each crack of the belt. Raunchy, raw, rude— no wonder the Stones have so often been called the greatest rock band ever. I closed my eyes and felt the vibrations, the boom-boom-booming of the bass and the drums almost like a second heart beating inside me. I felt—*alive*. God, it was good to be back with the music.

After the show I jumped into Bill and Astrid's limo and drove with them to the Playboy mansion, where they were staying along with the rest of the band. We spent two sleepless nights there, hanging out most of the time in Keith's room drinking and snorting coke. I remember laughing hysterically when Bobby Keyes snapped an amyl nitrate under a waiter's nose, and he started spinning like a top, trying like mad to keep the crystal glasses full of red wine, Tequila Sunrises, and straight whiskey from crashing to the ground. The tray and the waiter toppled over, and Keith immediately rushed over to help the poor guy to his feet.

"Sorry, man," Keith said, gently putting his hand on the waiter's shoulder in an attempt to make him feel like he was part of the fun and not just the butt of the joke. That's one of the reasons I loved Keith: he looked like he'd bite your head off but, paradoxically, he was extraordinarily sensitive to other people's feelings. Within minutes, it seemed, the mess was cleaned up, and the drinks redelivered.

Every so often I'd wander down to the lower level of the house where the swimming pool and game rooms were located. Mick and I played Pac-Man and watched, just barely stifling our giggles, as Hugh Hefner floated around in the indoor pool with his bunnies surrounding him on all sides.

Stevie Wonder and his band—the opening act for the tour—arrived sometime later that first night, and we all sat around in the main room listening to him play—Mick, Keith, Charlie, Bill, Hugh Hefner, the bunnies, Astrid, and me.

By the second day in Chicago, I found a job on the tour. I was standing near the stairs that led to the stage, waiting for the band to go on, when Alan Dunn, the tour manager and one of the Stones' most trusted employees, approached me.

"I want you to collect all the old ladies at the beginning of 'Jumpin' Jack Flash,' " Alan said, "and get them to the limousines so we can leave as soon as the band comes off the stage."

"Okay," I said, happy to have something legitimate to do. From that night on, my main responsibility at the shows was to round up the women—Astrid, varied and assorted girlfriends, and, sometimes, Bianca, Anita, Shirley Watts, and Rose Taylor—from their various places in the audience, at the sound board, in the dressing rooms, or the hospitality room, and get them into the limos before the show was over. "Jumpin' Jack Flash" was the second to last song (third to last if the Stones did an encore, which was rare), giving us plenty of time to get backstage and into the waiting limos. Even today, that song makes me want to jump up and head for the door.

Totally exhausted from those two raucous days in Chicago, we flew to Kansas City for a more subdued show and a few good hours of sleep, then off to Texas, with an overnight in Dallas, two shows in Fort Worth, and a show in Houston.

"You're coming with us, Chris," Mick announced in Chicago, and that was all it took to get me a seat on the Stones' chartered jet, a commercial-sized plane reconfigured for comfort, with seats arranged to face each other and plenty of space to walk around. I thought it was the height of luxury until a year later when the Starship appeared, a plush tour plane with a TV, video library, electronic organ, full bar, bedroom, and shower.

That first day I wasn't sure where to sit. I didn't want to take anyone's favorite seat, so I waited until Astrid and Bill called me over to a seat toward the front. For the first few days, I sat in the front with Astrid and Bill, Gary Stromberg the public relations guy (who always had a prophylactic filled to bursting with cocaine, making him the ideal seat mate), Larry the Doctor, Peter Rudge the tour manager, Alan Dunn the Stones' right-hand man, Jo Bergman, manager of the Stones' London office, and two bodyguards who had once been FBI agents. Soon enough, though, I discovered another great seat next to Keith and Mick at the very back of the plane next to the US map that showed all the cities we'd be visiting on the tour. That map was a well-used resource, giving us all a reference point for where we'd been, where we were, and where we were going.

Keith, Mick, and Bobby Keyes liked the back of the plane and Bobby (like Gary Stromberg up front) always had plenty of drugs to share. No matter where I was sitting, though, as soon as the plane took off, I'd wander around visiting with people. I spent hardly any time in my seat on those flights.

Dallas. I was resting in my hotel room in Dallas when the phone rang.

"Hey, Chris, it's Keith." Keith always spoke in a monotone, never giving away his emotional state. "Can you come down to my room for a few minutes?"

"Sure." Keith didn't ask for much, so when he did, I jumped. Being on tour meant always being ready and willing to "do something" for Mick or Keith—collect their dirty laundry after the show and deliver it to their room the next morning, search out phone numbers for long-lost friends, fly from St. Louis to New York City to get Mick's favorite camera fixed, call room service ("and tell them to hurry up with my dinner"), or, most commonly, "Come down to my room and hang out with me for a while, okay?"

Keith's hotel rooms always had the same look—scarves thrown over the lamps, imparting a red, pink, creamy, or tie-dyed glow, a layer of smoke like fog hanging overhead, ashtrays overflowing with cigarettes, whiskey bottles on the dressers and empties in the wastebaskets, television on with the sound turned down, shades drawn.

"Come on in," he said. I sat in a chair and he flopped down on the sofa.

"Hey, look, I need you to go to LA today and get some supplies." I knew what he meant by "supplies." He handed me a scrap of paper with a phone number.

"I called the guy, so he knows you're coming. Meet with him tonight and then bring the package back tomorrow. I'll give you money for taxis and expenses, and somebody will get your plane tickets organized."

Keith looked at me, his head tilted sideways. "Okay?" Like—okay, I'm asking you to run drugs, you okay with that?

It never occurred to me to say no.

When I got on the plane, I felt immediate culture shock. There I was sitting with men in business suits and mothers with babies in a crowded commercial airplane in an assigned seat, allowed to get up only when the seat belt sign was off, having to listen to people walking up and down the aisle telling me what I could and couldn't do. I got haughty with the stewardess, which actually surprised me a little. I'd spent only five days on a private plane and I already had an attitude.

I called the drug dealer from my LA apartment. He gave me an address and told me to meet him at 9:00 p.m. I decided to drive my car rather than risk taking a taxi to a drug dealer's house, but the farther away I got from my comfort zone of the West Hollywood–Beverly Hills area into an unknown part of LA, the more anxious I felt. It was dark. I was alone with what I assumed was a lot of money (I never looked in that envelope), meeting a drug dealer on his turf. What the hell was I doing?

The house was dark. I knocked on the door and the porch light went on. I was under the spotlight and someone, I knew, was looking at me. The door opened. "Come in," he said.

"Hi," I said with a big smile. "I'm Chris." I sure was out of my league.

"Have you got the money?"

I gave him the envelope and he gave me a package the size of a paperback book. I wasn't sure exactly what it was—hash, cocaine, heroin?—but I hoped it was coke. I knew it had to be good stuff or Keith wouldn't have sent me all the way to LA to get it. I have no idea how much money I handed over, figuring that if I didn't look, I didn't know, and if I didn't know, I'd be okay.

I wanted to push my foot down on the accelerator and get the hell out of there, but I drove back to my apartment very slowly, very carefully, looking maybe a hundred times in the rearview mirror. The next day I arrived at the LA airport with the drugs in my purse—there was no security check back then—got on the plane to Houston where somebody was waiting for me at the airport, and went straight back to the hotel. The Stones were getting into the camper that was transporting them to the show at Hofheinz Pavilion, and Keith waved me over.

"Hey, Chris, come with us!" he shouted. I got special treatment that day—hardly anyone ever got to ride with the Stones to the shows. I felt safe; nobody could touch me now that I was back in the thick of things with the Stones.

Somewhere around Dallas I started sleeping with Mick. It was no big deal. We were good friends and we trusted each other, so it seemed like the natural thing to do. For all those months we spent together in LA, Mick always treated me like a sister, someone he trusted and felt comfortable confiding in. We acted more like two children rollicking around and acting silly than two grown-ups who were sexually attracted to each other.

Given Mick's appetite for women, I really don't know why he didn't come on to me before the tour began. Maybe it was because I was in a live-in relationship with Jon Taplin, who I met through Pattie and George at the Bangladesh concert and who was working in LA with the Band and Bob Dylan. Or maybe Mick didn't make a move because he didn't want to ruin our friendship, although that hadn't stopped him in other cases.

One sultry evening in Dallas, when we all had a day off, I was in my hotel room getting ready to go to a downtown club with photographer Annie Leibovitz and a few other people from the tour. The phone rang just as I was headed out the door.

"Chris. What are you doing?" Mick asked.

I told him about the plans for the evening and asked if he wanted to come along.

"No," he said, very matter-of-factly, "but why don't you come up to my suite?" I heard something in the tone of his voice that made me realize he had sex on his mind.

"Okay," I said, feeling a little anxious. I was definitely attracted to Mick, and he'd always treated me with respect. I'd even call him "gentlemanly." But did I want to mess things up by sleeping with him? Oh, what the hell, I thought. Why not? It just seemed like the natural thing to do.

Sleeping with Mick didn't really change our relationship at all. I never ever thought there was anything more to it than sex. Every so often he'd call me in my room or grab me after a show, and we'd go back to his room, but I don't think I ever spent the night. It just was what it was, for that moment and that period of time. Mostly we laughed. I didn't have any romantic fantasies about the future, and I never once, not ever, thought, Boy, I'd sure like to be Mick's girlfriend. No, being Mick's girlfriend would have been too much work. He was just too unpredictable, too unfaithful, too—well, just *too much*.

It was a simple relationship. Mick liked to spend time with me, I loved the attention, and sleeping with him strengthened the trust between us. I'd bet that most of the women who worked for Mick had slept with him. If there had been a job description for being employed by the Stones back then, I'm pretty sure it would have included a proviso that went something like this: *Sleep with Mick whenever he asks.*

Mobile. Tuscaloosa. Nashville. By the time we got to Nashville, we were dead tired. The Stones had played to over 240,000 people in seventeen cities in less than three weeks. We were all, it seemed, losing weight from the drugs and lack of sleep. Gary Stromberg had lost over thirty pounds and Marshall more than twenty pounds. I was down to about ninety pounds. The drugs had a lot to do with it. Most of the time we'd skip meals without even realizing it, snacking on carrots and celery sticks before or after the show. The constant squabbling was also a calorie burner. The tour managers and organizers—Peter Rudge, Alan Dunn, and Jo Bergman—were fed up with all the Stones' "friends" hanging around and getting in the way. Running a tour is a difficult business because you're always moving, always packing, always changing cities and hotel rooms. Extra people—"friends" with no reason for being there and no work responsibilities—are extra weight. It's expensive to cart people around from one city to the next, and the tour staff knew it was way beyond time to trim the fat.

And, of course, there was jealousy. There's always jealousy around famous people because everyone wants to be close to the inner circle, and that circle means something only if it's tight and closed. When people get pushed out of the circle, they get pissed off. When someone with a legitimate job is working fifteen hours a day doing all the logistical work and a "friend" like me is hanging around the hospitality room munching on celery sticks, joking with the roadies, and getting high on alcohol, coke, pot, or pills, patience begins to wear thin.

After Nashville we had a six-day break before the next show in Washington, DC, but I was done, finished, kaput. I spent several days with Bill and Astrid in Memphis at the home of Duck Dunn, bass player for Booker T. and the MG's, and it seemed like the first time since Chicago that we were able to take a deep breath. I knew I was part of the "fat" that needed to be trimmed, and even though Mick and Keith came to my defense on several occasions, I didn't have a good reason for staying on the tour. I hated having no set purpose or routine, and with all the in-fighting and gossiping, not to mention all the drugs I was doing, I was getting really depressed. *Better to quit now*, I thought, *before I'm kicked out*—my usual pattern of flight before fight. I packed my bags—trying Bill Wyman's strategy of packing clothes flat with tissue in between—and, much to Astrid's dismay, flew back home to LA.

I'd just been home one day—July 4, Independence Day—when Keith called from Washington, DC.

"Why aren't you here?" he asked.

I had to think about that for a few seconds, and then I stumbled my way through an explanation. "Well, I really don't think I need to be there," I said. "I don't have anything essential to do, and it's pretty obvious that certain people don't want me around anymore."

"Fuck them. It's our tour. Fuck what they think—I think you need to be here. I'll give you things to do. Fuck them."

I didn't know what to say.

"I want you to come back," Keith said. And I thought, *Shit. If Keith wants me there, maybe I should go.* Keith once gave me what I thought at the time was the greatest of all compliments. He told me that I could drink like one of the guys. It was hard to keep up with Keith, and he seemed to appreciate those of us who didn't know when to call it a night. Still, a lot of people fell by the wayside trying to match Keith drink for drink and drug for drug. I watched Bobby Keyes hanging in there with Keith, getting more and more fucked up, and there were lots of others, including myself, who thought we could handle the drugs and who ended up in bad shape or dead.

"All right," I said after a moment.

"Don't worry about anything," he said, "we'll cover all your costs." Later I found out that Keith, Mick, and Bill and Astrid paid for all my expenses for the rest of the tour.

Norfolk. Charlotte. Knoxville. St. Louis. Akron. Indianapolis. Detroit.

In Detroit all hell broke loose again after one of Keith's friends got in a fight with one of the bodyguards, prompting a closed-door meeting about who needed to go and who could stay. After the meeting Astrid told me that when my name came up as someone who should go, Keith refused to back down. "Chris isn't even a question," he said. "The tour isn't paying for her, we are."

So I got to stay to the bitter end.

Toronto, Montreal, Boston. Logan Airport was fogged in, and riots had broken out in Boston's Puerto Rican ghetto, with looting and firebombing and rock flinging, so we ended up landing in Warwick, Rhode Island. The airport was tiny, with a makeshift customs counter outside a hangar. A few policemen, whom we assumed were there for our protection, were nearby. We couldn't leave the airport until we cleared customs, and as we were waiting for the paperwork to be completed, a photographer wandered among us, shooting pictures. Mick asked him to leave, very politely, I thought, and when the guy refused, Peter Rudge approached the police and asked for their assistance in removing the photographer. But the cops weren't listening.

Keith was already in a bad mood because we'd had to sit on the tarmac in Montreal earlier that day while mechanics worked on some engine problem, and then we got diverted from Logan Airport to Bumfuck, Rhode Island, and we still had thirty miles to go before we could unload all our shit at Boston Garden and start the show. When the photographer kept taking pictures after Mick asked him in such a nice way to stop, Keith got upset. When he walked over to Keith and stood directly in front of him, his camera raised to shoot, Keith lost it. He swung at the guy, who started screaming in a high-pitched voice, "He hit me, he hit me," and in seconds police were swarming all over the place.

As the cops marched toward Keith, he very calmly handed me his brown leather bag. I knew what was in that worn old leather bag. It was filled with drugs. Keith carried it with him everywhere he went.

"Take this," he said, his lips barely moving. I took the bag and tried to play it cool, moving a few steps away from Keith. My heart was pounding, thinking that maybe the police had seen the handoff, or that the fucking photographer would suddenly yell out, "She's got his drugs!" And that would be the end of me.

When the police grabbed Keith, Mick got really pissed off. "What the fuck are you doing, man," Mick yelled, his neck jutting forward, veins throbbing. "He hasn't done anything. What the *fuck* is going on here?" So Mick was arrested. Bobby Keyes got all riled up about the cops hauling off Mick and Keith, so they arrested him. Realizing that he couldn't let Keith and Mick go to jail by themselves, Peter Rudge started shouting at the cops so they would arrest him, and he got taken away, too.

Meanwhile, the rest of us stood around wondering what the hell had just happened. We finally got through customs and climbed into a school bus that took us to the arena, where the promoter told us the crowd was getting uneasy, and if the Stones didn't get out of jail soon, he was afraid there would be a riot. With Boston's entire police force occupied by the firebombings in the city, that was bad news. The promoter called the mayor, who came to the arena and assured the audience that the Stones would be there soon, and public transportation would be available to everyone who needed it. All the while I held on tight to Keith's bag.

When Mick, Keith, and the rest of them finally showed up for the concert, it was 12:45 in the morning, more than three hours after Stevie Wonder had finished his opening act. Keith had some kind of radar thing going, because he homed in on me within seconds after the limos dropped them off backstage. I had the bag in my hand, waiting for him.

"Are you okay?" I said.

"Yeah," he said, reaching for the bag with a huge shit-eating grin. "I'm fine now, just fine."

"There's going to be some kind of sex thing on the plane," Astrid whispered. We were in the backseat of the limo on the way to the Philadelphia airport for a short flight to Pittsburgh. Then on to the final three shows in New York City.

"What kind of sex thing?" I said. Bill's twelve-year-old son Stephen was traveling with us.

"I don't know, but rumors are flying," Astrid said, tight lipped. "I heard they're going to film it."

The orgy in the back of the plane on the ninety-minute flight from Philadelphia to Pittsburgh was—what's the word? "Debauched" comes to mind, but I think "sad" sums it up best. Just before we left Philadelphia, three young women boarded the plane and disappeared into the back section with Willie the Luggage Man and Larry the Doctor. The curtain dividing the airplane into two sections was drawn, but from the sound of things we all knew exactly what was going on. People were laughing hysterically, hooting and hollering, and somebody was using bongos to slap out a jungle beat.

I was sitting up front with Astrid, Bill, Stephen, and several others who couldn't stomach the idea of it all. Maybe twenty minutes after we left Philadelphia, Gary Stromberg came through the curtain and sat down next to me. He looked like he hadn't slept in a week, which might have been true.

"Man, they're all screwing back there," he said.

"Who?"

"The doc and the baggage guy and the three girls." Gary shook his head as if to dislodge the memory. "Man, this is too weird. Twisted. They're staging the whole thing for the film." Robert Frank was shooting a documentary of the tour, later titled *Cocksucker Blues*. It was never officially released by the Stones.

We all sat there, waiting for it to end. Bill kept pointing out the window, trying to distract Stephen. Astrid chattered away, talking about absolutely nothing. She'd seen a lot of outrageous behavior being around the Stones, but her dismayed expression told me this was way beyond anything she'd witnessed in the past. I felt tense and angry. I had watched girls throw themselves at the Stones and other musicians many times before, but this felt different. They were using the girls, treating them with absolute disregard. My anger turned to tears that welled up in my eyes. Gary pretended to sleep, his shoulders hunched up around his ears as if he could drown out the sudden peals of laughter, the clapping and whooping, and the constant beat of the bongo drum.

The plane finally landed, and people came spilling through the curtain. I concentrated on putting all my stuff in my bag, checking my seat to make sure I'd left nothing behind, my head bowed down, waiting for the plane to clear out.

"I hope you don't think bad of me." I looked up to see a young woman with a tear-streaked face. I remembered talking to her right before the show. She had that dazed look shared by so many of the girls who hung out at the backstage door—a blurry-eyed stare filled with loneliness and a longing for connection.

I didn't know what to say. Her makeup was smudged, her lower lip was trembling, and her eyes searched mine for understanding. Before I could respond, she was running down the aisle and out the door. I heard that the Stones paid for the girls' plane fare back to Philadelphia.

New York was awful. Mick, Keith, and Charlie were staying at the Carlyle, Bill and Astrid were at the St. Regis, I can't remember where Mick Taylor stayed, but the rest of us were holed up at a cheap hotel opposite Madison Square Garden. Stevie Wonder and his band and most of the roadies were staying there, too. My room was dark and smelled like musty old carpet.

For the first time since I had joined the tour in Chicago, I was separated from my friends. I knew that the Stones couldn't afford to pay for all of us to stay at the expensive hotels, and it made sense that they'd put us up right across from the Garden, but I couldn't bear being cut off from the band. The fact that Mick, Keith, or Bill and Astrid didn't offer to pay for my room at one of their hotels made sense, I guess, since it was their money, after all, but it still hurt my feelings and bruised my fragile ego. Separated from my friends and in the same hotel as the tour staff, I felt as if I had been abandoned again. But I was all messed up on drugs and not thinking straight at all.

I hung out at the hotel with some of the musicians in Stevie's band and a cameraman named Danny. Danny was about my age, stick thin, with a long mustache and a great personality.

On our night off before the final four shows at the Garden, I visited Danny in his room. The TV was on with the sound turned down. He was lying on his bed, staring up at the ceiling. Danny liked heroin, and he was always high. Everybody on the tour worried about him. He was one of those people who tried to keep up with Keith and eventually failed. I heard he went sailing and died at sea.

"What's it like to shoot up?" I asked him. For some reason, I was enthralled with the idea of shooting up. It was kind of like climbing Mt. Everest after you'd conquered all the lesser mountains. As the tour wore on, and I spent more time with Keith and Bobby Keyes, who were shooting up heroin, I began to romanticize the whole idea of having track marks. It was the ritual that intrigued me, the flame, the tying off, the needle in the vein, watching the red blood mix with the brownish liquid. It wasn't so much about getting high but more the mystery and death-defying adventure of the whole routine that fascinated me.

Keith was my role model. I saw him as a true rebel who didn't seem to have a care in the world and didn't give a fuck what anybody thought about him. That rebelliousness, that "fuck you" attitude enthralled me.

I wanted to be like that, too. I was tired, depressed, and worn out from all the emotional entanglements of the tour, the backbiting, the competition for attention, the need to always prove that I was "necessary." I had spent my whole life doing what people wanted me to do, thinking about their needs before my own, putting everyone else first. I was sick of always following the rules. I wanted on some deep level to tell the world to fuck off. Maybe it was the fact that Keith had shown me, through his reckless, even foolhardy behavior, how to be my own person, go with my needs, wants, and desires, and not give a shit what anyone else thought.

"What's it like to shoot up?" Danny repeated my question. "It's fantastic. The most fantastic feeling in the world."

"I want to shoot up," I said.

"No way. You don't want to do that, Chris."

"Why not? You do."

Danny was totally coherent. Somehow he always stayed in control. "Look at me. I'm totally addicted to this drug, I can't live without it. I'm not going to help you get like that."

"I just want to know what it's like. I just want the experience of shooting up. Just once." He tried to talk me out of it. Most drug addicts would say, "Cool, let's get high." But not Danny.

I kept after him. Finally, he made a deal with me.

"First, you have to go up and get clean syringes from Dr. Larry," he said. "Second, you have to promise me that if you really like it, you'll never do it again. And I mean that."

"I promise."

Larry agreed to give me some syringes; he thought they were for Danny.

"So, Chris," Danny said with a sigh, "do you want to shoot up heroin or coke?"

I thought about that for a moment. "Coke," I said.

"Okay, Chris." Another sigh. I knew Danny was afraid that I'd get hooked like he did, but I reassured him again that it was just this once, I just wanted to try it, and then I'd never do it again. I lay down on one of the double beds and put my feet up against the wall. Somehow that seemed to steady me.

"Give me your arm," he said, gently. He tied my arm off with a scarf, right above the elbow, to make the veins protrude.

"Squeeze your hand," he said. *Oh, this is just like giving blood,* I thought. I have really good veins. I've always been proud of them.

He put the needle in, pulled out the back of the syringe to draw in some blood, waited while the cocaine mixed with the blood, pushed the mixture back into my vein, and flipped off the tubing.

Comfort. Calm. Happiness. Bliss. It all swept over me.

"Whoa," I whispered.

"Are you okay?"

"Amazing," I said.

Later he asked me if I liked it.

I nodded my head and smiled. "Yeah, I liked it. It was amazing." A moment passed. "But I'll never do it again."

"Promise?"

"I promise." And I never did. But I felt initiated, having put another notch in my belt of rock-and-roll experiences. I had a track mark on my arm. I'd taken it all the way and now I was free. Like Keith, I could tell the rest of the world to fuck off.

26

TOO MANY SUNRISES

July 1972–February 1973

I'd been flying east for the last two months, so without much thought I just kept going. After the tour ended, all the Stones went east—Mick went to Ireland, Keith went to Switzerland, and Bill and Astrid went to the south of France—and so I sort of followed along and went home. Home to Friar Park. Dead tired and strung out, I knew Pattie and George would take care of me.

From the moment I arrived, though, I pulled them into my drugged-out craziness. On my second day, still jet-lagged and exhausted, I knew I needed some cocaine. I didn't just *want* the drug—I *needed* it. My body was screaming for it. "I'd love to get some coke, wouldn't you?" I asked Pattie, trying to be casual about it. We were having our morning tea in the kitchen.

"Mmmm. That's sounds good," she said, looking up at me from the shopping list she was making. I couldn't quite read her expression.

"Do you know where we can get it?" I asked, holding my breath. This wasn't a drug that Pattie and I had done a lot of together, and I couldn't remember many times that we'd actually brought it to Friar Park.

"Well, I could call someone," she said.

"Do you think George would mind?" I asked.

"Probably not," she said with a little smile. "He might be up for a bit of fun."

Pattie knew exactly who to call—someone at Apple, I remember that much—and we drove into London that afternoon. It was after dark when we arrived at the new Apple offices, housed in a modern three- or four-story building on St. James's Street. We walked into the large office on the second floor and who should be there but Ringo and Harry Nilsson, straight from the set of *Son of Dracula,* relaxing with a drink and some cocaine of their own.

"Look who's here!" Harry said when we walked in the door.

"Ah, well, if it isn't the magnificent duo," Ringo chimed in. "Come in. Join us." He motioned to two chairs by the desk.

Music was playing, the lamps were lit, and the coke was laid out in lines on the desk. It felt so warm and cozy there, and it was so good to see them both after what seemed like a long time. They told us how much fun they were having filming *Son of Dracula* and encouraged us to visit the set later that week. The four of us sat around, snorting coke and chatting happily for an hour or so before Pattie and I headed back to Friar Park with our little packet of cocaine.

That night George, Pattie, and I drank Scotch, snorted coke, and played pool in the game room off the main hall. George and I stayed up long after Pattie had gone to bed, drinking and reminiscing. I told him stories about the Stones' tour, focusing mostly on Keith Richard's insane capacity for drugs and his ability to stay up for days without sleep, and George talked about the new songs he was writing. I remember thinking that this was the old George, the fun, light, mischievous George I remembered from my first days at Apple, almost as if the Bangladesh concert had released him from the cares and woes of the past. He seemed—happy.

Just as we'd promised, Pattie and I visited the *Son of Dracula* set. Ringo was dressed up as Merlin the Magician in a black robe with stars all over it, pointed hat, long gray hair, and a full beard (my heart lurched inside me because with all that gray hair he reminded me of Leon). Harry, handsome as ever, wore a black coat with a high collar, black suit and tie, and white shirt. I laughed as I watched Ringo and Harry joking around on the set, mugging for Pattie as she took photographs. Their play seemed so childlike and innocent, especially in contrast to the Stones, who always seemed to be precariously balanced on the edge of destruction with the drugs, the sex, and their "who gives a fuck" attitude. I felt safe and somehow reconnected with a more innocent world.

During a break in the filming Ringo introduced me to Hilary Gerrard, his financial adviser, a stick-thin man who wore his thinning hair tied back in a little ponytail and was dressed impeccably and expensively in a silk shirt, vest, and pinstripe trousers, a scarf casually tied around his neck, and spats. Though just eleven or perhaps twelve years older than I was, it felt like he belonged to another generation with his slight bows and "with all due respects."

Hilary carried a strand of amber beads in his right hand, each the size of a large marble, and when he wandered off, a slight frown creasing his forehead, I asked Ringo if the beads had some kind of meaning or significance. I felt close to Ringo that day, almost as if we were old friends, in part because we'd had so much fun sharing cocaine a few days earlier but also, I'm sure, because he reminded me of Leon with his long silver hair. With that gray beard and pointed hat, Ringo looked very handsome, even regal. "Oh, they're Hilary's worry beads," Ringo chuckled, obviously very fond of this rather eccentric man. "He must be very worried today because he's clutching his largest beads."

Worry beads! I loved that. And in all sizes! From the moment I met him, I felt a strong connection to Hilary. In many ways, he reminded me of Derek, who was so protective of me and concerned about my well-being, but while Derek was lighthearted and witty, Hilary tended to fret and fuss over little details. At the same time, once he made up his mind, he didn't hesitate to express his opinion, always in a very civilized way of course. "With all due respect, sir, you are being fucking boring," I heard him say more than once. I'd soon discover that Hilary would always tell me the truth. Sometimes it hurt, but I knew I could trust it. "No matter what role you have played in the rock-and-roll world, my dear," he once told me, "at heart you will always be a small-town girl."

Worry beads, Merlin, *Son of Dracula*, Friar Park—part of me wished I could stay with Pattie and George forever, but I knew I didn't belong there anymore. My life was somewhere to be found in between the fantastical extremes of the Beatles and the Stones, although I had no idea where to start looking for it. But I did know one thing for certain: I couldn't bring George and Pattie into my cocaine-craving world. It was too dark, too dreary, and besides, I needed to find someone with a steady supply of coke.

I flew back to LA and reality struck. Coming off a tour is miserable business. You're part of a tight little community that exists only for itself and then BAM! it's over and everyone goes their separate ways. I didn't love everything about the Stones tour, that's for sure, but I hated not having Mick, Keith, Charlie, Bill, and Astrid around anymore. I looked for them in every face that I saw, confused by the sudden change of reality. They had been my family, dysfunctional as it was, and I felt as if a part of me were missing. I needed to rest and recuperate from the tour, but I missed all my friends and the loneliness was, at times, unbearable.

I remember reading something that Keith said about coming off the road and having to adjust to a whole new way of life. "The one thing I can't handle is that sudden change in pace of living. I can handle it through slowing down or speeding up; that's easy. But I just haven't got any brakes."

I didn't have any brakes either. The drugs had just shredded the shit out of my brake pads.

I settled back into my apartment and developed a routine of sorts. I'd sleep late in the morning, often until noon, when I'd stumble out of bed and make a pot of strong coffee. An hour or so later I'd have my first snort of coke. That worked to take the pain away from the night before. I'd wait a bit, snort some more coke, and when I started feeling too edgy from the coke, I'd take a Quaalude. Around four or five in the afternoon I'd start drinking. Every once in a while I'd smoke a joint, and once I tried angel dust (PCP). It was horrible. I hated hallucinogens.

Long before I realized it, a vicious cycle had set in. Cocaine made me anxious, Quaaludes took the edge off, alcohol made it possible to do more coke, which required more Quaaludes and more alcohol, and on and on it went. I was always looking for that perfect balance.

For the first few weeks after I returned to LA, I hung out with Eileen, Denny Cordell, and Gary Stromberg, but things got bad in a hurry. The tipping point was the day I met Marshall Chess for lunch in the Polo Lounge at the Beverly Hills Hotel. I was still getting a weekly paycheck from the Stones, but I didn't have anything to do. Marshall wasn't paying much attention to me because he was struggling with his own demons. Heroin was his drug of choice.

We sat at a small table for two out on the patio, surrounded by lush plants and flowering trees. Marshall was really twitchy. He played with his silverware, ran his hand through his hair (which seemed to me too long and a little greasy) while we talked for a while about the tour and what the Stones were doing now that they were back in Europe. Suddenly, he leaned across the table with a serious look in his eyes. I knew what was coming.

"Chris, there really isn't a job for you now." Marshall wasn't the type to beat around the bush, but I remember feeling grateful because he was letting me down softly by taking me to the exclusive Polo Lounge, buying me an expensive lunch, and speaking in a sympathetic tone of voice, even as he went about the business of firing me.

"Yeah, I figured as much," I said. I noticed that my hands were shaking, probably from cocaine and alcohol withdrawal, but at the time I figured it was nervousness about losing my weekly paycheck. The thought of being unemployed scared me. I ordered a salad and glass of wine, although I wasn't hungry. After lunch we hugged good-bye and I drove home, locked the door, poured a drink, and chopped up a line of cocaine. I always wondered if Marshall knew I was in trouble with drugs. He was a heroin addict, true, but addicts are pretty good at identifying each other, even if they can't recognize themselves.

So now I didn't have the pretense of a job, let alone a job, and my life started spinning out of control. I continued to hang out with Gary, spend time in the evenings with Eileen, and with Denny Cordell at his beach house or the large suite he rented at the Chateau Marmont, a famous old hotel on the Sunset Strip. I was getting messed up more often than not, and the drugs began to affect my emotional and mental state. What was I going to do? Who would I work for next? If I'd descended the ladder, as I'd imagined when I stepped down from the heights of the Beatles to work for the Stones, what rung was I on now? The only way left, it seemed, was down, down, down. Maybe my future in rock and roll was over.

I was going crazy thinking about it. Sometimes I'd drive around town, looking at the houses I had rented for Mick and Keith, remembering all the great times we'd had together. Now the only thrill in my life was getting high. Drugs were my best friends; when I got sad or scared, when I needed something to make me feel better, they never let me down.

I began to hole up in my apartment. When Eileen or Gary called, I made up excuses to stay home. I was thinner than ever, my skin was a pale shade of gray and all broken out with pimples (I hated looking in the mirror), and the perm I got just before the Stones tour was turning to frizz. I'd sit and pull at the split ends for hours. I wasn't aware of what day it was or even when the day began or ended because I was doing the same thing at almost every hour of every day—going up, coming down, going back up again. It got to the point where my only outside connection was the phone, but the phone hardly ever rang, and the only person I felt safe calling was Eileen. She knew I was taking too many drugs, but she never judged me or lectured me. Maybe she should have, because I was out of my skull.

One morning I tried to get out of bed and fell, hitting my head on the side of the end table and knocking myself out. I woke up lying on the floor with a walloping bump on my forehead. That week—or the next or the previous week, who knows—someone from the bank called and said they were repossessing my car if I didn't make a payment. "How dare you call me at my house?" I said in the most indignant tone I could muster. *They had invaded my private space*, I thought, slamming the phone back into the receiver.

I had no trouble getting drugs. One of the backup singers I knew had introduced me to an inner-city dealer who supplied me with anything I wanted. He wasn't one of those Hollywood types, the sleazy, slick guy who will get anything for you because he wants to be "in" with Mick or Keith or John or George or whoever. This was the real deal, a guy from the "hood" who wasn't impressed by anyone or anything. He just sold drugs.

One time he stayed the night.

"I'm too stoned to go home, baby, I gotta stay," he said after we'd snorted a bunch of coke. That was the night he brought out the PCP and encouraged me to try it. We were both in bad shape, and he crashed on the sofa.

In the middle of the night his girlfriend called. He must have given her my phone number.

"Let me talk to my old man," she said.

"He's sleeping," I said, hanging up the phone. I was so out of it. I'd taken a few Quaaludes to calm down from the PCP, and nothing was registering in my brain. The next morning, sometime around noon, the drug dealer stumbled into the kitchen where I was making coffee.

"Hey, your old lady called this morning," I said.

"What! What the fuck did you tell her?"

"I told her you were asleep." I yawned, wanting him to leave. Immediately. Now. I felt sick with the guilt and shame of getting so out of it and letting this lowlife stay in my place.

"Why the fuck did you do that? Why didn't you wake me up?" He was yelling at me. His old lady was going to give him hell.

"Look, I'm not responsible for you. Why don't you just leave." I was standing in the kitchen in my bathrobe, eyes bloodshot, head pounding, stomach heaving. All I wanted to do was take a bath and wash away the whole experience.

"You stupid bitch," he said, slapping me hard across the face.

I was so stunned I didn't even feel the sting. He left, slamming the door and yelling "bitch" at me one more time.

I sat on the sofa, my head in my hands, in the depths of despair. I was a fucked-up chick getting slapped around by a drug dealer. How could I get any lower than that?

But drug bottoms are bizarre things. You think you've hit the bottom, and then there's a trapdoor that opens and you fall through another floor. Those trapdoors just keep opening. As low as you think you can go, there is always something waiting down below, something much worse, much darker, blacker than night. It's shame so intense you can taste it, smell it, feel it on your hands, on your body, like grease or paint. And the pain is physical, in the belly and the soul, an aching despair created by the things you've done that you never thought you were capable of doing.

I met a guy outside of the cleaner's on Santa Monica Boulevard one day and invited him to my house. He was young and cute. He started coming over every day, and we'd snort coke and take Quaaludes. I thought we were developing a relationship. One day he came over with a video camera and asked me to pose nude. At first I agreed. I knew it was wrong, but I wanted him to like me. But then he told me he had a different kind of videotape in mind: he wanted me to have sex with his brother so he could film it.

I couldn't do it. Maybe there was still some innocence left, something good inside me that wouldn't let me cross that line. I closed the door behind him and never saw him again.

I needed help. But where could I go, who could I trust? I didn't know where to turn. I couldn't face my parents or my sister. I knew they loved me and would do anything for me, but they had no idea that I had gotten into drugs. I just couldn't tell them the truth. I couldn't turn to my friends, either. What would they think of me if I told them a drug dealer had slapped me around, or that a guy I'd met on the street tried to talk me into doing a nude video?

I was too ashamed to ask anyone I loved for help. I couldn't even look at myself in the mirror. I'd made such bad choices. That's what I figured was wrong with me: I'd made these terrible, irresponsible, self-destructive choices. I knew I wasn't an alcoholic—I'd seen Jack Lemmon and Lee Remick in *The Days of Wine and Roses,* and I wasn't anywhere near that bad. Drug addicts live in deserted buildings and sleep on filthy mattresses. I had a nice apartment, a car, rich and famous friends. I'd made bad decisions, I'd lost my self-respect, I was filled with shame and self-loathing, but I believed I still had some control.

I picked up the phone and made an appointment with John Kappas, a hypnotherapist who had helped me through some rough times in the past. John would figure out what was wrong with me. He'd help me understand what I needed to do to get back on my feet again. And sure enough, John offered me hope and direction, explaining that our subconscious mind sometimes gets programmed in ways that lead to harmful, self-destructive behavior. Hypnosis, he reassured me, can change that subconscious programming to create more desirable behavior. I wasn't sure exactly how it worked, but I trusted John completely and I always felt so much more relaxed and focused after a hypnotherapy session.

One more trapdoor, though, was waiting to open up beneath me. The day of my hypnotherapy appointment, I was feeling shaky and out of control and took two, three, four, I don't know how many Quaaludes to calm myself down from the coke. I started to walk down the stairs of my apartment to my car, but my legs were rubbery, my eyes wouldn't focus, and the stairs seemed to change shape before me. I sat down on the top stair, looked down at the floor below me, and knew I wouldn't be able to walk down those stairs. They were too steep. Somehow I stumbled back to my apartment. I dialed Eileen's number, but she didn't answer. I called John's office.

"This is Chris O'Dell," I told the receptionist. Her name was Chris, too. "I'm having a hard time getting there."

"Are you okay?" she asked. I was slurring my words.

"No, I'm not," I said. "I've taken too many drugs and I can't drive. But I have to see John. Please don't give my appointment away. I'll find a way there."

Making it to that appointment felt to me like a life-or-death situation. Maybe it was. I called Eileen again and then I tried Gary, but neither of them answered. I didn't have any other friends in LA that I trusted. Who could help me?

"Wait a minute," I said out loud. I could call the limo company that the Stones used when they were in LA. I'd become friends with Walter, the manager of the company, and I knew most of the drivers. They liked me there.

I looked in my phone book and found the number.

"Hey, Chris, how's it goin'?" Walter said.

"It's okay," I lied. "Listen, remember when you told me that if I ever needed a limo for myself to call and you'd do it for free for me?" I have no idea what those words sounded like to him, but that's what I intended to say.

"Sure," he said. "I remember."

"Well, I need a limo to take me to the Valley."

"Sure, just say when and I'll have one there for you."

"Now," I said.

"Now? I'm not sure I can get one that quick, Chris."

"You have to, Walter. Please. I have an appointment. I have to get there. I'm desperate. Please."

I sat in my apartment, waiting. I was already hours late for my scheduled appointment, but Chris had agreed to hold it for me. I just had to get there. That's what I kept repeating to myself. *I have to get there, I have to get there, I have to get there.* That was all I had to hold on to as I slowly made my way down the stairs to the front door of the apartment building.

At last the driver appeared. I sat slumped in the backseat barely able to keep my eyes open.

"Are you okay?" the driver asked, looking at me in the rearview mirror.

"Yeah, I'm okay," I said, slurring those three simple words together. I was trying so hard to stay focused.

"Listen, I can take you to a hospital," he said with real concern. I think he was afraid I might die in his backseat.

"No!" I actually shouted the word at him. "Just take me to the address I gave you."

He shrugged his shoulders and kept driving. Half an hour later I felt the limo come to a stop.

"We're here," the driver said, turning around in his seat. "I'll help you in." He walked me to the door of John's office and seemed a little spooked when he read the sign on the door, "Hypnosis Motivation Institute." I told him I could make it the rest of the way, and he sped off in the limo.

I opened the black door leading into the reception room with its familiar black furniture and red carpet. Chris smiled up at me with no hint of annoyance that I was several hours late. She took my arm, gently, lovingly, and led me straight into John's office.

I sat down on the recliner and minutes later John came into the room.

"So, what's going on with you?" he asked, a look of concern on his face.

"I took too many pills, I think," I said, closing my eyes and drifting off to sleep.

"Okay, well let's put you into hypnosis," he said soothingly. That was all I remembered.

"Zero, one, two, three, four, and five, and wide awake." With those familiar words, slowly, with a little bit of a struggle, I opened my eyes. I was amazed how good I felt—no more nausea, no more drowsiness, no more shaking.

"I feel so much better," I told John. He was so compassionate, so caring and empathic, that I found myself wanting to be like him.

"John," I said, braving the question in my mind, "do you think I'd make a good therapist?"

"Why not?" he said with a deep and rare kindness. "You've experienced it all."

Maybe that will be my future, I thought. Maybe someday I will have a stable job with a meaningful purpose, helping other people get over their problems. It was a dream, a glimmer of light in a dark, dark place.

Then reality hit. How could I ever hope to dedicate my life to helping others when I couldn't even help myself?

"I think I have to quit using drugs and alcohol," I said in that moment of self-revelation. "I think I have a problem."

There. I finally said the words. If I wanted a future, I had to give up the drugs.

"That sounds like a very good idea," John said.

27

MAUREEN

Spring 1973

When I got sober, I started writing in a journal. I inscribed my journal with three words, written in big block letters that summarized what I considered the most important elements of my new life: EAT, THINK, FAITH. One entry in particular sums up a lot of what happened in the year I tried to stay sober.

> *March 16, 1973.* Depressed. Need money. Going to bed at 9:30 a.m. and sleeping til 4 p.m. I guess I really want to be with a man again. I thought I could accept being alone, but I can't. Try to live life as it happens.

I was depressed, broke, and bored. I often slept most of the day away. I wanted to have a man in my life because I didn't like being alone. And although I was trying really hard to live in the present, I couldn't help wishing that I was somewhere else—either in the adventurous past or an equally exciting future.

I didn't tell any of my close friends—except for my hairdresser and my hypnotherapist—that I was trying to stay sober. Instead, I told people I had decided to cut down for a while. Most people just didn't get it and they'd either get angry with me ("What a load of bullshit," one acquaintance said) or they'd try to goad me into using with them. One night my friend Gary Stromberg, whom I love to this day and who would eventually get into recovery himself, kept pestering me when I turned down some coke. "Oh, come on, lighten up, O'Dell, don't you want to have fun?"

No one knew about the drug dealer or the guy who wanted to videotape me having sex with his brother, the day I fell out of bed, or the time I collapsed on the stairs, nor did they understand the anguish of my fear, guilt, and shame. But all that was in the past. I was trying to focus on the present by going to hypnotherapy twice a week, getting a lot of sleep, watching television shows featuring clean-cut kids and happy families (*The Partridge Family* was my favorite), eating good food, thinking about what I wanted to do with my life, and hoping that somehow it would all come together into something resembling happiness.

"Hello, Chris! Mal here."

"Mal! Are you in town?" I was so excited to hear from one of the old Apple gang. And I just loved Mal's rich, thick Liverpudlian accent.

"I'm here with Ringo; we're starting sessions for his new album. Just a minute." Mal covered the phone, talking to someone in the background. "Okay, look, luv, can you come by the coffee shop at the Beverly Hills Hotel in half an hour or so? Great. See you then."

When I walked into the coffee shop, Mal was sitting on a stool next to Maureen Starkey. My first reaction was, *Oh shit, this is going to be awkward.* Ever since our first encounter at Pattie's birthday party at Friar Park, Maureen seemed to keep her distance from me—although she did tell me I looked good in jeans at the party following the Bangladesh concert. Maybe this time she'd be nice to me, too.

"Chris!" Mal said as he stood up to give me a cheek kiss and nice, comfy hug. "You know Maureen, don't you?"

Maureen looked smaller and darker than I remembered her. She'd dyed her hair dark brown (she was a blonde when I first met her, although brown was her natural hair color) and painted on heavy eyeliner to create a Cleopatra look. She used no blush at all, so her face seemed even paler than I remembered. But what really hit me that day was her perfume—Tabu, I found out later. I swear she must have bathed in it.

We were both a little shy with each other at first, but with Mal there to ease the tension and carry on the conversation, we were soon laughing at his jokes and carrying on like old friends.

"Ringo's album is going to be smashing," Mal said proudly. "Everyone's helping."

"Everyone" included George Harrison, John Lennon, Harry Nilsson, Billy Preston, Klaus Voormann, Nicky Hopkins, Jim Keltner, Marc Bolan, and members of the Band. Richard Perry, a big name in the music industry, was producing the album.

"That's an all-star cast," I said, impressed.

"It is indeed, the closest thing to a Beatle reunion we're likely to get for a while," Mal said. He looked at his watch. "In fact, I need to get Ringo and head for the studio."

Maureen invited me to come up with them to the suite, and I was happy to tag along and get the chance to say hello to Ringo. He was watching television when we walked into the suite.

"Chris O'Dell!" he said, jumping off the sofa and giving me a cheek kiss. "It's good to see you."

"We've gotta go," Mal said, faithfully carrying out his role as the shepherd guiding one of his precious flock of sheep.

Ringo went into the bedroom, reappearing with a jacket in one hand and a black bag in the other. "See ya later," he said, giving Maureen a kiss and heading out the door.

"Do you want to stay for a bit?" Maureen asked me.

"Sure!" I said.

I was still there when Ringo returned late that night, and that's how my friendship with Maureen began. Whenever Ringo was in the studio, Maureen would call me. We spent almost every day together.

"I'm going apeshit here," she'd say. "Can you come over and keep me company?" After a while she didn't even need to call because we both just assumed we'd spend the days and evenings together. She liked to drink, although she wasn't a particularly heavy drinker at the time, so I never felt like it was a big deal when I didn't drink myself and instead had a club soda with a twist of lime or a cup of tea. Every now and then I'd have just one drink, or maybe two, but I wasn't worried about a small amount of alcohol, figuring that "sober" meant staying away from cocaine and pills. Moderation was the key, after all. I just needed to stay in control. I never would have identified alcohol as a drug, of course, and nobody ever told me then that part of staying sober is letting go of control. But even if they had, I wouldn't have had the slightest clue what they were talking about.

Our days generally started late, around three or four in the afternoon when Ringo left for the studio, and I'd often still be there when he came back late at night. The three of us would sit around talking, sometimes until dawn. When Ringo was at the studio, Maureen and I would go shopping and have lunch or dinner together. We spent hundreds of dollars on room service. I didn't have any money—I was collecting unemployment—and Maureen would always pay for everything, sometimes even slipping a hundred-dollar bill in my pocket. When I protested, she'd say, "Not to worry, just a little gift." But my favorite times of all were when Maureen and I relaxed on the sofas in the suite. She'd tell me stories about her life with Ringo, who she always called Richie. They met when she was sixteen and he was twenty-two. I'd curl up on the sofa, my legs underneath me, my back propped against the pillows while Mo (I'd started calling her by her nickname) leaned forward, her elbows on her knees, an intent expression on her face.

"How did you meet him?" I asked.

"Outside the Cavern. He'd just that week joined the Beatles. I put me hand on the car and told him to stop. I wanted an autograph."

"So you knew who he was?"

"Yeah. It was blasted all over everywhere. They'd just got a new drummer. And I had all the other autographs." She laughed. "The first real date we had was after the gig. He probably asked me to dance. Usually we danced. Then I'd have a Coca-Cola or whatever and then he'd take me home, but I'd take me girlfriend with me. He'd have to drop her off first. I was terrified. Absolutely petrified."

"Because you were with him alone?" I said.

"Yeah," she said, nodding her head, "and because he was older than me. Guys that I knew before were all my age. This is what is known as an older man."

I asked her about the rumors I'd heard about fans coming after her.

"Once the word started goin' round it got a bit vicious," she said, lighting up a cigarette and blowing the smoke at the ceiling. "I used to get phone calls at work saying if I didn't stop seeing him, their brothers were going to beat me up or throw acid in me face. It should have been a wonderful thing that was happening, I should have been so happy—but the fear!"

Maureen was working at the time as an apprentice hairdresser. "I used to do chicks' hair, and they'd never say a word to me until they were leaving," she told me. "There would be lines like, 'You know when you leave here tonight? Just watch that corner 'fore you get to the bottom.' I was getting punchy with it. One chick whipped me down the side of the face with her hand. So Richie said it was time for me to give up work. It was actually getting dangerous. There were a lot of threatening phone calls."

Maureen paused for a moment, and I could tell that the memory still bothered her. "It's strange when chicks come in and you're doing their hair, I mean, when you're taking the bloody rollers out, that look they give you," she said. "Not nice. And when you're bloody sixteen, it's not a happy situation."

I could have listened to Maureen telling stories all night. One of my very favorite Maureen stories took place in India when the Beatles visited the Maharishi. The flies almost drove her crazy.

"We were in this tiny room with a table with a Formica top," Maureen recalled. "I said to him, 'Maharishi, I can't cope with this. It's freaking me out. I don't like flies. I'm not happy with them. They terrify me.' 'Oh my dear, don't worry,' he said. He climbed on the table and he's swatting the buggers. I couldn't cope. Swat swat, with the end of his whatchacallit, the thing you wrap around you that goes through your legs, he's up on the bloody table swatting those things. I said, 'I've gotta go home.'"

I loved Maureen's fabulous collection of Liverpudlian colloquialisms. "Bloody hell!" or "sodden hellfire!" she'd say when she was frustrated or angry. "It's breakin' me brain," she'd say when she felt overwhelmed. "They've got more front than Selfridges," she'd say when someone was brazen or belligerent. But my favorite Mo expression, which I heard her say just once or twice, and only after she'd had a good amount to drink, was a simple reflection on her life. "I haven't done badly, but never mind," she'd say with a little shrug, "I'll do better."

There wasn't an ounce of bullshit in Maureen. She was authentically, wholly herself. "I really like Maureen," I wrote in my diary. "She's so positive. She makes me think. I must watch her though, because she's a stirrer." That was the truth; she was always stirring something up.

One night when Ringo was in the studio, Maureen and I ordered room service and I mentioned that David Bowie was playing in town next week.

"And?" Maureen said, lowering her chin to fix me with a look. "Is that supposed to change the world?"

I laughed. "No, but I'd sure like to meet Mick Ronson," I said. I'd seen David Bowie in concert for the first time in Santa Monica a year or so earlier, and I couldn't keep my eyes off of the shaggy-haired, craggy-faced, hard-strutting guitarist who appeared to be Bowie's right-hand man.

"Don't be daft," Maureen said, teasing me. "Why would you want to meet a guitar player!"

"Okay, okay. Forget I ever mentioned it." I reached over and picked up the new cigarette holder I had just purchased at the smoke shop on Sunset Boulevard. It was just like Maureen's.

The next day we went shopping in Beverly Hills. "Okay, missy, do I ever have a surprise for you," she said.

"What?" I asked.

"We're going to the Bowie concert." She had on her I'm-the-cat-who-just-ate-the-canary look. "But better yet—I arranged it so we're meeting up with everyone afterward for dinner."

"You're kidding!"

"It's the God's honest truth," she said.

"Mick Ronson, too?" I asked. She rolled her eyes.

The show was fabulous. At one point Maureen leaned over and whispered to me, "What do you see in him?"

"He's so cute!" I actually giggled.

"Cute!" Maureen sniffed. More than once she told me that she didn't understand the word *cute*. "It's so—*American*," she said, with just a slight tinge of condescension.

After the show the limo dropped us at Lost on Larrabee, a tiny hidden restaurant just off Santa Monica Boulevard in West Hollywood. The dining room contained one long wooden table, all set up with crystal and linen, and the entire room was lit only by candles. I drank wine that night and, as was becoming my habit, I didn't worry too much about it. I was with my good friend Maureen in a safe situation and it was only wine. No big deal.

David and his wife Angie arrived, along with the rest of the band and David's manager Tony DeFries, and half an hour later Ringo and Mal Evans showed up. I'd seen it happen a hundred times, but it never ceased to amaze me—as soon as a Beatle entered a room, the atmosphere changed completely. Ringo was in a fabulous mood after a productive day at the studio, and, believe me, when Ringo was in a good mood, we were assured of a fun evening. My only complaint was that he kept teasing me about my crush on Mick Ronson, who showed up that evening with some woman on his arm. Funny, even though I did have a big crush on Mick Ronson, I wasn't the least bit bothered by the fact that he had a date. After all, I was with Ringo and the gang.

As we were leaving the restaurant that night, David Bowie put his hand around my waist and pulled me close. "Can I have your phone number?" he whispered. "I'd love to see you again."

"David! Come along! Enough for tonight!" That loud, brash voice belonged to Angie Bowie.

"I'm at the Beverly Hilton, call me," David whispered as he followed her into the waiting limo.

Well, I never called him and it's a darn good thing, too. In the mid-1980s I interviewed Angie Bowie for a book Pattie and I were working on about the women behind the scenes in the rock-and-roll world, and she talked about her difficult relationship with David. "Every time I'd actually sit down and organize something serious, moneymaking, a project, he'd go, 'No, no, dear here's some money, go spend this, what about a limo, would you like a limo, why don't you come to LA, come and see me in LA, I miss you.' So I'd go to LA and we'd have a fight after three days and he'd have six black whores on a string and I'd think fuck this. I'm going back to New York where I can speak to some sensible people."

Angie looked me straight in the eye, and I swear it was some sort of time-warped warning.

"If I ever got my nose out of joint, my revenge was always short and sweet, but it was very effective. It's real simple, isn't it? You don't mess with me."

I'm sure glad I didn't.

I kept messing with my hair. I thought it might be fun to put henna streaks in my naturally blond hair, but I ended up looking like a red-headed skunk with big, thick, orange-red blobs from front to back and top to bottom. Then I dyed the whole thing red and chopped it short, so I looked like David Bowie's space alien Ziggy Stardust.

When Maureen saw my new haircut, she announced that I needed a makeover. She put all her makeup—eyeliners, eye shadows, mascaras, lipsticks, concealers, foundations—on the coffee table and I sat down on the sofa as she stood in front of me, brush in one hand, cigarette holder in the other, turning her head this way and that as she evaluated what she'd done and what she needed to do next.

Around midnight the door to the suite opened, and Ringo walked in. Maureen put the brush down and walked over to give him a kiss.

"How'd things go?" she asked with real interest.

"We got a lot done," Ringo said, his mood already lifting. "George was there. The session was great. This album is going to be fantastic."

He sat down on the chair next to the sofa and lit a cigarette while Maureen fixed him a drink before returning to fuss over me again.

"I like the hair, Chris," he said.

"You like the hair?" I asked incredulously. I wasn't at all sure that I looked good with red hair.

"It brings out color in your face and eyes," Maureen said, agreeing with Ringo.

Ringo stood up and moved closer to the sofa, leaning down to study me. I watched him as he pursed his lips together in concentration and turned his head from one side to the other, taking in my hair, my eyes, my lips. I felt myself redden with embarrassment. I'd never seen this side of him before—who would have thought he'd care about makeup?—but then I remembered a story Maureen had told me.

"One day Richie just turned to me and said, 'You look terrible.' " Maureen's face fell, just remembering that awful moment, and then she shrugged her shoulders. "I mean, what a bloody drag. Here I was with two small children, fans climbing in our bedroom window, and he tells me I look like shit. Well, I'll tell you what I did, 'cause I didn't want to lose my husband, I sat in front of the mirror in my dressing room for hours, trying to get it right. Finally, with a little of this and a little of that, and a lot of whatever, I re-created meself."

A little of this and a little of that and a lot of whatever—is that what it would take to re-create myself, too? I smiled, remembering Maureen's story, and looked up to see Ringo staring at me, a thoughtful expression on his face.

"Soft," he said. "That's the look for you."

I blushed.

28

CHRISTMAS IN ENGLAND

December 1973–January 1974

"Maureen! It's Chris. I'm coming to London for Christmas."

"Fan-tas-tic! You can stay with us. We've got lots of room!"

"Well, actually, I just talked to Pattie and I'll be staying with her and George at Friar Park."

"But I want to spend time with you," Maureen said and her matter-of-fact tone left no doubt that it wouldn't do me any good to argue with her. You will stay here, she was saying, discussion over.

Uh-oh, I thought. Now I've got a problem. I immediately felt guilty, caught between my old friend and my new friend. I didn't want to upset Maureen, but my first loyalty was to Pattie and I always stayed at Friar Park. I felt pulled in two directions, as if I had to choose between them.

"And you have to be here for the New Year's Eve party." Maureen had a way of stating things as absolute fact—that was that, final, done deal, no need discussing it further—and of course I wouldn't have missed that party for the world. I remembered hearing about Ringo's annual New Year's Eve parties when I worked at Apple, and I imagined a fantastic bash with all the rock-and-roll elite jamming together and celebrating the new year with delicious food, expensive wine and liqueurs, and dazzling fireworks. I'd never imagined that one day I'd be invited, too.

"I know, Mo," I said, thinking on my feet. "What if I stay with Pattie and George for Christmas and then come and stay with you and Ringo for New Year's?"

"Brilliant!" she said. And that was that. Problem solved.

When I hung up the phone, though, I realized that while I'd solved one predicament I still had another one. How was Pattie going to react when I told her I wouldn't be staying the entire time at Friar Park? Maureen and Pattie were always cordial with each other, and they'd been through a lot as fellow Beatle wives, but they weren't really great friends. They respected each other and liked each other, but I couldn't imagine that this would be a fabulous threesome.

Pattie answered the phone in her usual chipper way. "Chris! Hello, dear. I'm in the kitchen just starting dinner."

"I wish I were there with you," I said dreamily as I thought of the fun we always had cooking up mischief in the kitchen. We'd be filling our glasses to the brim and laughing uproariously over nothing, just for the joy of being together. I was drinking again, of course, but I'd cut way down, which was my goal, after all.

"Listen, Pat, I just got off the phone with Maureen, and she wants me to stay at her house. I want to stay with you, but I don't want to hurt her or upset her. So what would you think if I stayed with you and George over Christmas and then stayed with Maureen and Ringo for New Year's?"

"Okay," she said in a hurt, little-girl voice. *Uh-oh,* I thought again, *now I've upset Pattie.* Although I was nervous about the phone call, I expected Pattie to give me a little fight, playfully telling me how much she wanted me to be with her at Friar Park and oh, couldn't I just visit with Maureen and Ringo, or at the very least just stay there for a day or two? But she just gave in and then retreated, withdrawn and reserved. I knew something wasn't right and, looking back, I realize I should have paid more attention to what Pattie *didn't* say. But I was too preoccupied with thoughts of how much fun it would be to spend time at both Friar Park and Tittenhurst, and I figured it would all work out because Pattie and George would be at the New Year's Eve party and I'd go back to Friar Park for the rest of my vacation. So I'd only be with Maureen and Ringo for a couple days.

We talked for a few minutes more and I asked if she'd be able to pick me up at the airport.

"Of course, darling," she said.

I was so excited. What a Christmas this would be!

On December 22, 1973, I walked out of customs and immigration looking for Pattie, and there was Maureen. I was caught between two emotions. *Oh, good!* I thought when I saw her walking toward me, because I loved her and because I've always had this terrible fear of arriving at an airport and having no one there to pick me up.

I walked over to Maureen with my little trolley, carrying two big suitcases (I always pack too much, trying to be prepared for everything), a big smile on my face but a lot of questions in my mind. Had Maureen called Pattie to tell her she would pick me up? Did Pattie get confused and think I was staying at Tittenhurst first?

"I'm so glad to see you!" I said, giving Maureen a big hug and then looking around the terminal, confused by the change of plans. "Where's Pattie?"

"Pattie is coming, but I wanted to be here when you arrived," Maureen said. Tittenhurst wasn't too far from Heathrow, but I was still surprised that she would drive all the way to the airport to see me when we'd be getting together in a few days. I must admit I felt pretty special, especially when I saw George walking toward me. He threw his arms wide and gave me a huge hug. Looking over his shoulder, I saw Pattie beaming at me, and right behind her was Ronnie Wood, lead guitarist for the band Faces (he'd later join the Stones). What a welcoming committee!

As we walked out of the terminal, Maureen waved good-bye as she started off in a different direction.

"I'll see you all later this week," she called out.

"Hey, Mo, don't you want to come back to the house?" George called after her. At the time it seemed like such an innocent question.

"Oh," she said offhandedly, as if she hadn't even considered the idea before. "All right."

Well, I should have figured it all out then, but I was too exhausted to think very clearly, especially now that I was caught in the middle again. I wanted to drive with Pattie, George, and Ronnie—they had come all that way to pick me up, and I'd hardly gotten a chance to say hello—but Maureen was all alone in her Mini Cooper. So I walked with Maureen to her car and we drove to Friar Park.

That was the strangest night. After George fixed me a Scotch and Coke, I followed Pattie and Ronnie into the library, assuming we would all gather there. After a few minutes I wondered where George and Maureen were, so I excused myself for a second and went looking for them. They were sitting on a sofa in the Main Hall.

"Why don't you guys come join us in the library?" I asked.

"No, we're all right," George said. Maureen just smiled at me. I sat down with them and chatted for a while and then made up an excuse about leaving my cigarettes in the other room. I left my drink with George and Maureen, though, so I would have a reason to go back and forth between the two rooms. Cigarettes in one room, drink in the other, and all sorts of confusion in between.

And that's how I spent that first night of my Christmas vacation at Friar Park, going back and forth between the library and the Main Hall, stopping off at the kitchen now and then to fill up my drink, all the while trying to figure out what the heck was going on. Pattie and Ronnie were like brother and sister, childlike and playful, while Maureen and George were private and intense, sitting close together, obviously having an intimate conversation. I split my time between the intense twosome and the laughing twosome, trying to act as if everything was absolutely normal.

But what the hell was going on? I'd heard a rumor about Pattie and Ronnie having a fling and now I wondered if that might be true. Maureen and George were just old friends, right? I'd also heard rumors about Ringo using a lot of cocaine, and George was definitely in a flirtatious mood. Well, I thought, it's the holidays, everyone is excited to be together, and I'm jet-lagged. Everything will be back to normal in the morning.

"Good night, everyone, I'm going to bed," I said, grabbing my cigarettes and my drink, giving Pattie and Ronnie a kiss in the library and then giving Mo and George a kiss in the Main Hall, and walking up the staircase and down the long hallway to my room.

George was in a good mood the next morning when he bounded into my room with a steaming cup of tea and a big smile on his face. I sat up in bed, fluffing up the pillows behind me, thinking that it was just like old times.

"How are you feeling?" he said, sitting on the edge of the bed.

"I'm exhausted!" I said, managing a smile. I'd woken up probably fifteen times during the night. I figured it was jet lag, but wondered if it might also be the four or five Scotch and Cokes I'd had the night before. Still, I was so proud of myself for giving up marijuana, Quaaludes, and cocaine, and I didn't really even think about alcohol and nicotine as drugs. They just seemed so safe in comparison. And even though I cut back on my drinking and even stopped for a while, I never really considered giving up alcohol forever. Everybody drank. How would I ever stay away from alcohol in this crowd?

"You should jump into something warm and walk around the grounds," George said, staring out my bedroom window, which overlooked Friar Park's sweeping formal gardens. "Things have changed a lot since you were here. We've cleaned all the dirt and debris out of the lakes, and I've planted quite a few trees and shrubs. And flowers. Lots of flowers." I smiled, sipping my tea. George so loved his gardens.

He stood up and moved to the window, then turned to look at me, a serious expression on his face.

"You know I'm in love with Maureen."

I held tight to my cup of tea. "Wow," I said. That was all I could manage. I just stared at him. Just like that, all the events of the night before fell into place. Now I understood why Pattie was upset on the phone when I told her I'd be staying with Maureen for a few days. Now it made sense that Maureen had shown up at the airport and driven back with us to Friar Park. Now I understood why Pattie and Ronnie stayed in the library, and George and Maureen spent the entire evening on a sofa in the Main Hall. Everything suddenly made sense. They weren't fighting over me at all.

Something happens inside when you realize that you're not the center of the universe, some little painful twinge at the center of your being. It hurts. But what hurt even more was the realization that everything I knew and loved might change. Pattie and George were my family, and Friar Park was the place where I felt safe and at home. I depended on them, I *needed* them. If George was truly in love with Maureen, if this wasn't just another one of his little flings, then what did that mean? What would that do to Pattie, to me, to all of us? It was just a fleeting thought at the time; not until later, after I'd talked to Pattie, would it all sink in.

"Does Pattie know?" I asked.

"I suppose she's figured it out," he said. I realized then that George knew Pattie would tell me about this eventually, and he wanted me to hear it from him first. Maybe he wanted me to help Pattie, to make things better for her somehow. Maybe he wanted me to understand and even, perhaps, give him my approval. Maybe he just needed to confess the truth to someone.

"This is really complicated," I said. It was such a silly thing to say, such a superficial synopsis of all the complexities of the situation, but I had no idea what George wanted from me or even what I was prepared to give him. I couldn't put it all together.

George looked out the window. For a few minutes he didn't say a word but just stared out at his garden, all the greenery of the previous summer buried under a layer of frost.

"Look, Chris," he said, walking over to the bed and sitting down next to me again, looking me straight in the eye. When George spoke from the soul, his eyes darkened and his words felt as if they were almost drilled into you.

"You may think we're lucky because of all this," he waved his hand around, taking in the room, the gardens, the floors above and below us. "But in the end you're the lucky one."

He was telling me that things weren't all that great being George Harrison. He knew I would love to be in a position where I didn't have to worry about money. He knew I adored him and considered Pattie my best friend. He knew, too, that I hoped someday to have a stable, loving relationship with someone and have a home I could call my own. Yet he envied what he regarded as my simple life. His life was complicated by the very realities that seemed to be blessings—the money that needed to be safeguarded, the house that required constant repairs, the relationships that needed tending, the spiritual yearnings that could not wholly be fulfilled.

I was the lucky one, George was trying to tell me, because I could go where I wanted to go, do what I wanted to do, love who I wanted to love. He didn't have that sort of freedom. His fame bound him even as it released him, and his passions entangled him in all sorts of webs of guilt and shame, even as he tried to free himself through chanting and asceticism. George Harrison was a paradox, a man caught between his earthly and spiritual yearnings. All George ever wanted, after he had more than he had ever dreamed of having, was a simple, uncomplicated, meaningful life with no dishonesty or bullshit to muddy the clear waters.

Like Chance, the main character in *Being There* (one of George's favorite books), he wanted to just "be there" in his garden, in his solitude, with his hands in the dirt. He didn't want to "be" anything but a man who loved music, the earth, women, and God. Listening to George, watching the tea steaming into the space between us, I wondered if I might find, someday, the serenity that fame and fortune had denied George. I experienced a shiver of recognition, a thrill of gratitude for all the gifts in my life that I had forgotten or ignored. I was, for a moment, outside of time. I don't know if I can explain it, but it was a treasured moment of understanding and sudden insight. What was happening with George, Maureen, and Pattie was inside of time, but George was offering me a perspective that was outside the events taking place. He was lifting me above and beyond, allowing me to look down from above at what I had only been able to imagine from below.

Many years later I read the following passage in Derek Taylor's book

*Fifty Years Adrift,** and I thought about that morning with George in my
room at Friar Park.

> The famous, the rich, they are just people, like the rest of us . . . the
> great and the ungreat are all One People under God, only some are on
> television and others aren't . . . though I knew the Beatles were human,
> I looked at them as leaders and together with everyone else who had
> grown to love them, I began to build the legend of invincibility . . . I
> looked to the Beatles to show the way and the poor devils were them-
> selves crying out in pain and in vain that they were looking for a Way,
> a Truth and a Life, and not finding it. John through Yoko and Peace,
> Paul and Ringo through familial cosiness, George through Krishna, all
> searching . . . all of them just like the next man . . . and when I discov-
> ered that, I was, again, alone. You, too?

Yes, Derek. Me, too.

After George left, I finished my tea and knocked on Pattie's bedroom
door. George had brought her a cup of tea, too. She was sitting at her
dressing table, putting on her makeup.

"Hello, sweetie, did you sleep well, did you get some tea?" she said,
looking at me in the mirror.

"Yes, George brought me some tea, and did I ever need it this morning!" I said, standing behind her and leaning down to give her a little
hug. We looked at each other in the mirror.

"Pattie," I said, softly. "What's going on?"

She was holding the mascara wand, her chin tilted up, gently sweeping the ends of her lashes. Just her eyes moved and she stared at me as
if frozen in the mirror.

"What do you mean?" she said.

---

*"The title was to have been *Fifty Years Adrift in an Open-Necked Shirt*," Derek wrote
in the book's author's note, "but somehow someone beat us to the printing presses with the
phrase 'open-necked shirt'; and so (not wishing to run the old Liverpool joke into the
ground) . . . we decided to settle for just plain *Fifty Years Adrift*, which of course I have
been."

"What's going on with you and George? It was weird last night with Ronnie and Maureen. What's happening?"

"Oh, Chris," she said with a deep sigh. "Maureen comes over all the time. She stays here."

Pattie's tone changed. Now I could hear the anger. "She stays here!" she repeated. "She and George go into a room and shut the door. The other day I knocked on the door, and they told me to go away. They had locked the door! When they finally opened it, I asked Maureen when she was leaving, and she just looked at me and smiled. Oh!"

That little word "oh" was invested with so much sadness and pain, I thought it would break my heart. I tried to put myself in her place, and I couldn't. I didn't know what that would feel like, to have an old friend, almost a member of your family, come into your house and lock herself up with your husband. I just couldn't imagine it. How did she put up with it?

"I'm sorry, Pattie," I said, putting my arms around her. "I'm so sorry."

That next night, just after we'd finished dinner, the phone rang. George answered it, talked for a few minutes, and then handed the phone to me.

"Listen, why don't you come over tonight?" Maureen said. "I'd love to spend time with you. I'll pay for a minicab to bring you here."

I had to make up my mind fast. My biggest concern was Pattie, but I thought she might want some time alone with George to talk, and it might be good for me to get away for a few hours. Things were tense between Pattie and George.

"Sure," I said. "We're just finishing dinner, so I'll be over in a few hours."

I hung up the phone and explained the plan to Pattie and George.

"I'll drive you," George immediately offered.

"Really? You don't have to do that." I looked at Pattie and we were both thinking the same thing: Was George looking for an excuse to be with Maureen?

"I'd like to visit with Ringo, anyway," George added.

"I'll go too," Pattie said.

I was so proud of her—she was protecting her territory. With all five of us there, it should be a nice, civilized evening, nothing like the night before.

I'd never been to Tittenhurst before. It was night and the middle of winter, so I couldn't see the grounds—I'd heard that the gorgeous Georgian manor house, which John had sold to Ringo, was surrounded by seventy-two landscaped acres—but inside the house looked so cheery with a fire crackling in the living room and the dark lampshades creating little pools of light around the room. Toys were scattered about on the floor, and good kitchen smells (dinner for the kids, most likely) filled the house. Tittenhurst had a warmth and glow to it that made me want to settle right down into the comfy, overstuffed furniture. It was such a contrast to the majestic magnificence of Friar Park.

We sat at the long wooden table in the kitchen, Ringo and George on one bench, Pattie and I facing them on the opposite bench. Maureen spent the entire evening flitting around like a little bird, landing here, then there, jumping up to cook an omelet for Ringo, refilling our drinks, bringing plates of food to the table. Soft music drifted in from the jukebox in the dining room. The lights were dimmed. A bottle of sweet liqueur stood on the table. The kids were all upstairs with Stella, the nanny. It was late, almost midnight, so they were probably all sound asleep.

At one point Maureen went to a side table, opened the drawer, and pulled out a packet of Marlboros, George's brand. Maureen and Ringo both smoked Larks.

George looked up at her as she put the cigarettes on the table next to his hand and smiled. Nobody said a word. I could hear the tick of the clock on the kitchen wall. We sat there in silence, and then George turned to Ringo and said, "You know, Ringo, I'm in love with your wife."

I think all five hearts in that kitchen stopped beating for a few seconds. The room was completely still, no sudden gasps, no deep breaths, no fingers tapping or throats clearing. Absolute silence. I looked down at the table, wanting to reach out to Pattie, furious with George for being so cold and indifferent to her feelings. How could he have said those words in front of her, in front of all of us?

Maureen retreated to the far side of the room and stood by the sink, frozen, staring at the kitchen counter. Ringo looked down at the table. He flicked his cigarette ash in the ashtray. His jaw clenched, and a muscle by his mouth twitched.

We sat there. Waiting. Finally, he looked at George. "Better you than someone we don't know," he said in a steady voice.

I looked at Pattie. Her eyes were wide and unblinking. *This can't be real,* she must have been thinking. *This can't be real.*

I gently touched her arm. "Pattie, let's go into the other room." She nodded as we stood up and walked away from the others into Maureen's little sitting room at the front of the house. I looked around, surprised, even a bit shocked. Filled with Indian tapestries, pillows, and candles, the air thick with incense, the room looked as if Maureen had decorated it specifically for George.

"Are you okay?" I said as we sat by the fireplace on two of the large pillows scattered around the room.

"Oh, that George is such a monster," she said, her arms wrapped tightly around her body, as though she were comforting herself. She didn't cry. We sat there for what seemed a long, long time, staring into the fire.

"There you are!" Maureen said, walking into the room as if she had been looking all over the house for us. "Would you like something more to drink?"

We had another drink or two, and our conversation was civil and polite, as if nothing at all had happened.

"My black suede boots would look fabulous with your skirt," Maureen said as we were getting ready in her bedroom before the big New Year's Eve party.

Maureen's feet were three sizes smaller than mine, but when she gushed about how great I looked in those boots, I figured I could stand the pain for a few hours.

We were all dressed and ready to go, with some time left before the party started. I sat down on the bed, wondering whether I should talk to Maureen about what had happened that night in the kitchen. I was already in the thick of it, so I figured what the hell, I might as well bring it out in the open.

"Maureen, how did you feel when George told Ringo he was in love with you?"

She looked at me, a quick, sharp glance, then sighed heavily. I was relieved, realizing that she wanted to talk.

"Oh, it was dreadful. Absolutely dreadful."

"How did Ringo feel?" My questions felt so intimate, but I was there, I'd seen it happen, and for days we'd all been pretending that the world hadn't been stood on its head.

"He was upset. Very upset. Angry." Maureen fiddled with the seam on one of the velvet tops she was considering wearing that night. She had a way of showing her tension by keeping her hands busy.

A moment passed as we sat together, both of us remembering that night. "Very angry," she added.

Another long silence passed between us. "Honestly, Chris, this thing between George and me, it's not a physical relationship, it's emotional."

I found that a little hard to believe. They certainly acted like they were crazy about each other. With George, how could it not be physical? Why did they shut themselves up in a room at Friar Park and not answer Pattie when she called out to them? I didn't believe Maureen, but I knew that she needed to convince herself that it wasn't lust that brought her and George together but a spiritual connection between two kindred souls. Maybe it was her Catholic upbringing that forced her to deny the truth of what was happening, or the fact that she loved Ringo too much to think that she could have anything but an emotional relationship with another man, or maybe she was just so deep in denial about the whole thing that she couldn't see it for what it was. Or maybe I was wrong. I'll never know. Maureen and I were friends until the day she died, and she never once intimated that her relationship with George was anything more than an emotional entanglement. She always called it "the situation."

"Mo, do you still love Richie?" I asked.

"Of course I love him. You know that!" she said impatiently. "But it's bloody complicated. There's a lot of stuff going on now."

Maureen sighed, took a few sips of her brandy and Coke, and then fixed me with a look. The moment was gone—I swear, I actually saw it go. Maureen was finished with this conversation.

"Maybe you should be with him," she said, a little offhandedly, as though this was the answer to her problems. .

"With who?"

"Richie," she said.

I laughed, softly. She had to be joking.

The New Year's Eve party was an absolute dud. Pattie, George, Elton John, Keith Moon, and Hilary (with his worry beads) were all there, along with Rod Stewart, Ronnie and Krissy Wood, and Neil and Susie Aspinall. Those are the only people I can remember being there. George and Maureen stood in a corner flirting for a while. Later in the night I saw Pattie and Ringo by the fireplace talking quietly together. I just felt so sad.

And my feet hurt like hell.

29

RINGO

February–June 1974

I was sitting at my corner desk at Journeys, a travel agency owned by my good friend Sara that specialized in booking tours for rock bands, working on the Eagles' upcoming tour and grumbling to myself about all the phone calls and paperwork. I was getting so tired of planning rock tours and living vicariously through them. I missed my old life. I missed working directly with the bands.

When the overseas call came through, I was surprised to hear Maureen's voice on the other end of the line.

"Oh, Chris, all hell's broke loose here."

"What's happened?" I asked, worried by the desperate tone of her voice.

"Richie's freakin' out," she said. "He's still really upset about everything. Says he just can't cope!"

"Oh, dear," I mumbled, thinking of poor Ringo pacing the floors of Tittenhurst.

"He's coming to LA next week, he says he needs to get away," Mo sighed. I could just imagine her standing by the phone in her kitchen, dressed from head to toe in black, the cigarette holder tightly gripped between her teeth. "Would you look after him, Chris, make sure he's okay?"

"Of course I will," I reassured her. I could only imagine the pain they were both going through. "Maureen, how are you doing?"

She sighed again. "It's just dreadful. But what the bloody hell am I supposed to do? I've got to keep it together for the children."

Ringo arrived on Valentine's Day. Eileen and I went to a Dylan concert that evening and at the party afterward I spent some time with Ringo. That was fun. I knew from what Maureen had told me that he was in some serious emotional turmoil, but he didn't talk about "the situation," as Maureen liked to call it, and he seemed to be in a great mood. A few days later he invited me to record producer David Geffen's formal party at the Beverly Wilshire and that was even more fun. Bianca Jagger was there, and I walked right past her with my nose slightly up in the air, laughing and talking to Ringo. When I was working for Mick, I always felt insecure around Bianca, even a little inadequate as a woman because she was so stunning and stylish, but with Ringo by my side I had plenty of self-confidence. After the party we went back to Ringo's room and spent the rest of the night talking and drinking. When he went to bed around five that morning, I drove my Toyota to work and slept in my car until the office opened. He flew back to England later that week, I settled back into work, and life returned to normal.

Six weeks later, Ringo returned to LA. I wrote a short entry in my journal that only hinted at the conflicted emotions I experienced when I saw him again. It's almost as if I were afraid to put my feelings on paper for fear it was all a dream. Or, perhaps more truthfully, for fear something might be happening, and I was powerless—and unwilling—to stop it.

April 2: Ringo is in town again. He phoned the day after he arrived. Went to the hotel to get Ringo to go to the Record Plant for a session John and Mick were doing. We danced. R & I definitely were feeling attracted to each other. It was weird and made me feel down. It's this lifestyle. I want the best—all the time. Ringo just represents to me how I want to live. I am lonely. Will he call? Sorry, Mo, I just can't help the feelings.

Let me tell you about that evening at the Record Plant. The control room reeked of cigarettes, Scotch, and beer, with incense wafting around trying like hell to beat out the other odors.

"Hey, Chris," John said, turning to smile at me from his place at the mixing board. I gave him a smile and a little wave of my hand.

"Hi, May," I said, giving May Pang a big hug. May took care of all John's personal and business needs, including coordinating his recording sessions and the artists he was working with, such as Harry and Ringo. She was extremely organized and was one of the few of us who didn't drink or do drugs.

I walked over to the table where the drinks were set up, poured some Coke into a paper cup, adding a big wallop of Scotch, and took a seat between May and Ringo. I put the cup to my lips and tasted the sweetness of the Coke, laced with the burning sensation of the Scotch rolling down my throat. I never did like the taste of alcohol, but I loved the way it made me feel. Warm. Loose. Happy. Confident. The musicians started playing again; they were working on "Too Many Cooks (Spoil the Soup)," a song that wouldn't be released for twenty-five years, when it appeared on the 2007 album *The Very Best of Mick Jagger*.

"Let's listen to that again," John said. "From the top." John bowed his head, his eyes closed, his body moving to the beat.

"How's it going?" I asked May, taking another sip of my drink.

"John is doing such a great job," she said, looking at him with adoring eyes. She was in love with him, no doubt about that, and from everything I witnessed during the weeks I spent with them, he was crazy about her, too. Everyone commented on how happy he looked in LA and called him "the John of Old." I always wondered how they got together, with Yoko right there in the middle, and one day I just came out and asked May. She was very forthright and detailed with her story, giving me the impression that this was her first opportunity to set the record straight. She was working in New York City with John and Yoko as their personal assistant when one day Yoko walked into her office and announced that she and John were splitting up. "If John asks you out, you should go," Yoko told May. It was more of an order than a suggestion. May began to protest because she didn't want Yoko to think she had designs on her husband (and, she told me, she'd never thought about John in a romantic way), but Yoko insisted, telling May that she would rather John was with her than some stranger who might hurt him. Later, May said, she learned that it was John who had been interested in her, and Yoko picked up on it and made the first move.

At the mixing board, John's head was moving to the beat while May started swinging her long legs. I closed my eyes, feeling the music swelling up inside me, knowing that more than anyplace else on earth, this was where I wanted to be. I took another sip of my drink and, like May, started moving my legs to the beat.

I hadn't been paying much attention to Ringo, but in the middle of the song, he stood up and did one of his little dances, bobbing up and down, fingers snapping to his own inner beat. Then, just like that, he grabbed my hand and pulled me to my feet.

"Care to dance?" he said in a proper English accent. Well, now. Ringo had great rhythm and style, pulling me in toward him, pushing me away, holding my hand up high and spinning me, then twirling me around the other way. Once I got over my initial nervousness, I was able to follow him pretty well except for trying to stay upright in my "corkies," the current "in" shoe that consisted of three inches of solid cork that you wobbled around on trying to maintain your dignity. Corkies came in all colors, and I probably had six pairs of them. I was wearing the metallic pink ones, my favorites, that night.

"Hold on just a second," I said, stooping down to unbuckle my shoes and tossing them off to the side of the room. When I stood up, I was the same height as Ringo and we were looking straight into each other's eyes. That's when it happened. I saw *into* his eyes for the first time. It was as if two wires suddenly connected, sending an electrical jolt of attraction right through me. In that instant, Ringo wasn't just a friend, he wasn't just a Beatle—he was a man. A very desirable man.

"Hmmm," he said, pulling me closer. He felt it, too.

We kept dancing until the music stopped and then I went back to my chair and started putting on my shoes. The song was finished, the dance was over, the moment had passed, and it was time to leave.

• • •

On the way out of the studio John asked Ringo if he was going to Roman Polanski's party.

"Do you want to go?" Ringo asked me.

"Why not?" I said, trying to stay casual. I kept hearing Maureen's voice in my head. "Take care of Richie, Chris." I wondered if Ringo was hearing Maureen's voice, too. "Chris will take care of you, Richie."

"Are you coming with us, Ringo?" May called out in the parking lot.

"No," he said, "I think I'll ride with Chris." That made my heart beat a little faster.

It was around 2:00 a.m. when we arrived, and only a few stragglers were left at the party. We walked through the expensively decorated but sterile modern house looking for our host and found him lying on the bed in his bedroom with several women sprawled out around him. The television was on. Everyone looked pretty relaxed—actually, they all looked a little out of it. Roman lifted his head and peered at us.

"Oh, hello," he said, slurring his words slightly and resting his head back on the pillow, "make yourself at home."

Ringo grabbed my hand and pulled me back into the living room.

"That was weird," I said, thinking about how Roman didn't even bother to get off the bed.

Ringo laughed. "Yeah, you'd think he'd be happier to see us!"

We sat on a sofa facing a huge picture window with a fabulous view of the city. For a moment we didn't speak, looking at the city spread out beneath us. Then Ringo turned to look at me, studying my face as if meeting me for the first time.

"You know, I don't really know a lot about you, Chris O'Dell," Ringo said, his knee pressing against mine.

A shiver ran through me. "What would you like to know?"

"Well, anything. I just don't feel like I really know you," he said, reaching for my hand.

I'm not imagining this, I thought, this is happening. Ringo is looking into my eyes, he's holding my hand, his body is touching mine. We talked for three hours, or was it four or five? I have no idea how long we talked. I was in a dream world, nothing else existed in that time and space but Ringo and me. Maureen never once entered my mind.

When we got back to the Beverly Wilshire, John and May headed up the stairs to the loft bedroom that overlooked the living room.

"Man, I'm tired," John yawned. "We're going to bed."

"Night," Ringo said from the bar as he fixed us a drink.

We looked at each other, wondering what came next.

"Let's go sit on the balcony," he said.

We sipped our drinks and watched the sun slowly rise over the Beverly Hills skyline. Then, without a word, Ringo disappeared into his bedroom. I sat on the balcony for a while, wondering what the hell to do. Should I follow him? I waited, hoping he'd come back. Finally, as the sun turned the sky from deep pink to bright orange, I walked into the suite and peeked in his room. He was sound asleep. I stood there, still confused about what to do. I was tired, I'd been up all night drinking, and I wanted to get into bed with him. But I wasn't about to embarrass myself. This was a tricky situation, no doubt about that. I could just imagine Ringo telling John—or, worse, Maureen—the next morning, "Well, I woke up and there she was in bed with me, what could I do?"

I drove home to my little studio apartment in the San Fernando Valley, near Burbank, in a mess of emotions. My mouth felt like cotton and tasted like stale alcohol, my hands were shaking, my head felt as if it was filled with static, like when you're stuck between stations on the radio, and when I finally got home and looked in the mirror, I discovered a new pimple on my face. Oh God. How could anyone, let alone Ringo, find me attractive? I climbed into bed and tried unsuccessfully to fall asleep.

Three hours later the phone rang.

"What happened to you?" Ringo said, his voice playful.

"Oh hi," I said, scrambling to get my thoughts together. "I just thought I'd better come home."

"Are you going to come over to the hotel and then we'll go to the lunch?" he asked.

"Okay, sure," I said. I had forgotten all about Ringo's invitation to go to actor Roger Moore's house for lunch. How the hell was I going to get myself ready in an hour? I felt like shit.

"Are John and May going?" I asked.

"I'm not sure, I just woke up," he said.

John and May didn't end up going, so it was just Ringo and me at Roger and Luisa Moore's house for lunch that day. I have never had to endure a more agonizing three hours. I was in no shape to be social. My eyes were puffy and red, my hands were shaking, and my zit was still there (I couldn't stop thinking about it). What did this elegant, extraordinarily cordial couple think of me, of us? Ringo introduced me as his friend, but Luisa Moore looked at me curiously and asked more than once about Maureen.

We were sitting on the terrace having drinks, engaging in what felt to me like excruciatingly stilted small talk, when the French doors opened and there stood David Niven, drink in one hand, cigarette in the other, looking like he had just stepped off a movie set. *What the hell?* I looked at Ringo, not sure whether to laugh or cry. I was right at home with rock stars but had no idea how to behave around movie stars.

We sat down for lunch in the formal dining room as the butler prepared to serve us. I'd never been served by a butler before. I watched him go from one person to the next with his big silver serving tray and wondered how I was going to be able to transfer the food to my plate. I couldn't hold a steady gaze let alone keep my hands from shaking. Why didn't they just serve us something, like they do everywhere else?

"Here, let me help you," Ringo said. The butler nodded ever so slightly and placed the serving tray next to Ringo, who took the silver tongs and expertly transferred the chicken, niçoise salad, baby potatoes, and green beans to my plate. I sat there with a frozen smile on my face. It was just such an enormous effort to try to hold myself together and act normal. Every so often Ringo reached under the table and squeezed my leg.

After lunch Luisa asked us if we could stay a while longer but, thank God in heaven, Ringo said he had plans that afternoon and had to go.

"That was fun," Ringo said as we drove back to the hotel. "Let's not do it again."

I laughed, then groaned. "I thought it would never end."

"What do you think they're saying about us now?" Ringo said.

"Gosh, I don't know. Do you think they noticed how out of it we were?"

He looked at me sideways, a silly expression on his face and broke into a huge grin. "Who cares? I haven't had so much fun since war broke out," he said, one of his all-time favorite expressions.

We laughed all the way back to the Beverly Wilshire where we fell into bed and immediately conked out.

I spent most of the next three weeks with Ringo at the beach house, a two-story white stucco mansion in Santa Monica that John had rented from Peter Lawford. Ringo's room was on the second floor in a library that had been converted to a bedroom. Hanging right over his bed was a big print of the famous photograph of John-John Kennedy peeking out from under his father's desk in the oval office. President Kennedy, according to the story I heard, was a frequent visitor to the beach house, the site of his secret trysts with Marilyn Monroe. We were all sort of spooked by the legend of Marilyn, especially John, who was convinced that her ghost haunted the house. He said something woke him up every morning, and we all just assumed it was Marilyn.

I was drinking a lot during those weeks, which helped with the guilt about Maureen, and I often encouraged Ringo to get drunk, too. Alcohol made it easier for both of us to dull our feelings and continue the affair, but reality kept finding its way in.

"This is awkward," I said one morning.

"Yes, it is," he said. He seemed depressed. "We should talk."

"Okay."

"I can't do what all my friends are doing. It's not right."

"I know," I said. "It isn't right. But I'm just having a hard time fighting my attraction to you."

"Yes. Well." He opened up his arms to me. "Come here, then, and we can cuddle."

One evening we went to Disneyland with Hilary, Harry Nilsson and his girlfriend Una, and Klaus Voormann and his new girlfriend Cynthia. Ringo held my hand the whole time.

Back at the beach house, Ringo told me we'd better have another talk. "That last one isn't working," he said, putting his arms around me as I snuggled closer.

On Easter morning we turned on the television to watch *Easter Parade*, and he got such a kick out of the word "rotogravure" that he kept repeating it over and over again, as if the word had texture and he liked the feel of it on his tongue.

"Rotogravure," he said, smiling at the television screen, "that's what I'm going to call my next album."

I started calling him Rich. Maureen called him Richie, the world called him Ringo, but Rich was my special name for him, although I never really felt comfortable calling him that. It seemed forced, fake, like I was trying to claim some part of him that didn't really belong to me.

We went to the Beverly Wilshire for dinner with Klaus and Cynthia, to the Rainbow Bar and Grill with Alice Cooper, and at least a dozen times to our favorite bar at the Beverly Wilshire where we both really loved the Brandy Alexanders. On a scrap of paper Ringo wrote a song for me (I added the last line):

> *I've got a girl*
> *with plenty*
> *of charm*
> *She's got nine legs*
> *and big long arms*
> *And when we go to party's she*
> *causes a riot*
> *Because she*
> *dances with 5 guys*
> *You oughta try it.*

Was it real? It was real to me. We comforted each other at a time when we both needed comforting. He was good to me, and always, always kind, and just being with him made me happy. I wanted it to last, but I knew it wouldn't. Ringo and I were always meant to be friends; we just got mixed up there for a while.

Ringo flew back to England for a month, and when he returned to LA, he didn't call me for a few days. "I am accepting the fact that it's all been a fantasy," I wrote in my journal. "It's difficult. But I must be strong. I can handle it."

He called, finally, and we went to a party at the beach house. He was playing poker when Maureen called and asked to speak to me.

"I think Richie is seeing someone there," she said. Her voice on the overseas line sounded hollow. "Do you have any idea who it is?"

Oh shit. I wasn't prepared for that moment. I really didn't think Maureen would ever find out about me and Ringo. Why would she? He wasn't in love with me—I was just a temporary Band-Aid, a friend when he needed one, someone who could console him when his wife, the woman he really loved, was supposedly having an affair with another man.

"Gosh, Maureen," I lied, "I don't know of anything going on out here."

Maureen called Ringo about a week later to tell him she was coming to town. We agreed not to tell her what was going on between us, but we had already started to drift apart. The "situation," as Maureen kept calling it, was becoming too painful. For the first few days after she arrived, I let my answering machine pick up her phone calls (I learned that little trick from Leon), but she just wouldn't give up. Knowing I couldn't avoid her forever, I finally picked up the phone.

"Chris, it's me. Where have you been? I want to see you."

"Hi, Maureen, gee, I'm so sorry, I've just been so busy with stupid stuff." *Shit.* I was so afraid my "ums" and "ahs" and awkward pauses would give it all away.

"Can you come over after dinner tonight?" she asked.

"Sure," I said, knowing there was no way out. I was so conflicted. I wanted to see Maureen because I loved her, but I was afraid because she was so damn smart and intuitive. I feared she'd immediately pick up on the vibes, once warm and loving but now fearful and cooling fast, between me and Ringo. How would I act around him? How would he behave toward me? How would I react if he ignored me or glared at me? What if I stumbled and said something that gave away the whole thing? God, how I dreaded that meeting.

I walked into the lavish marble lobby of the Beverly Wilshire Hotel and headed to the back wall of elevators. My insides were shaking, my breathing was shallow and fast, and I wished more than anything that I could run back to my car and head home to the safety of my little apartment. The elevator came to a halt and as I walked down the wide hallway to the familiar suite—the same suite I'd shared with Ringo—I talked to myself. "Remember, we agreed not to tell her." And in the next second I felt overwhelmed with anxiety, thinking about walking into that suite and pretending everything was normal, just the way it used to be. But then again, maybe she didn't know about Ringo and me. But she was so smart, so sharp, savvy, streetwise. "Okay," I kept talking to myself, saying, "just be yourself, focus on Maureen, forget about Ringo. Stay calm. Don't give it away." In the hallway I knew that I would keep my promise to Ringo and deny that anything had happened.

Maureen opened the door, and we gave each other a hug and a kiss on the cheek. Ringo was sitting on the sofa across the room, looking at the floor.

"Want a drink, Chris?" Maureen asked. Ringo suddenly stood up and walked over to the window, where he stared out at the night.

Boy, did I need a drink. The room was air-conditioned, and the night was cool, but I was beginning to perspire.

"I'd love a drink—Scotch and Coke, please," I said, keeping my voice light.

Just as I was taking the first sip, Maureen asked the question she must have planned for days.

"Are you sleeping with my husband?"

Everything stopped. I looked at her and she stared back with those dark, piercing eyes. "Deny it, deny it" kept running through my head. I was trapped. It seemed like hours went by as I searched for the words

I needed to get out of this situation. Another moment passed and then the silence in the hotel room was broken by the rattling sound of the ice in my glass. My hand was visibly trembling. I caught a glimpse of Ringo, his face ashen but expectant, waiting for my answer. Would I lie and deceive Maureen or tell the truth and betray him? But the ice had already revealed our secret.

I took a deep breath and answered her question. "Yes," I said.

"Well," Maureen said, looking over at Ringo but speaking directly to me, "at least you were honest with me."

I don't know how I drove home that night. My thoughts were chaotic, careening all over the place. Would Ringo blame me for what happened? Would Maureen ever forgive me? Had I destroyed two relationships, all at once? Overwhelmed with guilt and shame, I kept trying to rescue myself by finding someone to blame. Wasn't Maureen the one who started this whole mess with her affair with George? Hadn't she told me to take care of Ringo? Didn't Ringo have some responsibility for me, for my feelings? Then I plummeted back into the shame. Why didn't I have the courage to stick to my agreement with Ringo? Why did I betray him? But I told the truth—how could I not tell the truth? Maureen was my friend. But Ringo was also my friend. I had betrayed them both. I had lost them both. God, I was a mess.

That was Sunday night, June 1, 1974. Monday passed and not a word from either of them. Then, on Tuesday morning at 4:30 a.m., the phone rang.

"Chris," Maureen said, speaking in a very soft voice, almost a whisper, as if she were trying to hide the phone call from Ringo. "Things have gone all awful here. Can I come to you?"

"Of course you can," I said, finally finding my voice. "What's happened?"

"I'll tell you when I get there."

I gave her my address and half an hour later she showed up at my apartment. We talked for hours, sitting at the table in my living room, smoking one cigarette after another, drinking cup after cup of strong, dark tea. I had never seen Maureen in distress before. She was always in perfect control, the one with all the answers or the bravado to pretend she had them. But now she seemed utterly defeated.

"It's bloody awful," she said. "We yelled and screamed at each other. I don't think it can fix itself."

"I'm so sorry, Maureen," I said, "I wish I could make it all go away."

She waved her hand at me as if to say, "Oh don't worry about that, we've got other things to think about right now." I tried to talk about George with her that night, but she vehemently denied having a sexual relationship with him, and not once did she admit that she might have some responsibility for the damage to her marriage. I'm not faulting her, because I truly believe she considered her relationship with George a fling without any lasting significance. Ringo was the love of her life.

"I know 'the situation' got us here," she said. "But that's not what's keeping me and Richie apart. He's just so angry. He won't listen. He won't talk to me."

I tried to console her. Maybe after they'd both had some time to calm down and think, they'd be able to find a way to get back together again.

"I don't know, Chris, I don't know," she said. "This is bad, really bad." She took a sip of tea and looked at me with those dark eyes, her thick makeup smudged from tears and lack of sleep, as if to ask: How could it ever be good again?

She lit another cigarette. "And what about the children?" she said, exhaling deeply. "How am I going to protect the children?" There it was again, that tone of despair and defeat. And yet—she had her children. They were her refuge.

"I need to get back to the children," she said, a tone of desperation in her voice. We called the airlines and she booked a flight to England leaving later that day.

"I'll call you when I get back," she said.

That night I called Ringo. "I'm sorry I let you down," I said.

Silence.

"Are you okay?" I asked.

"I thought we agreed not to tell her."

"I'm sorry," I said again.

I had hoped for something more from that conversation. I wanted Ringo to tell me that everything would be okay, that we would all be just as we were before.

But he was honest enough to tell me the truth with his silence.

30

CSNY REUNION TOUR

June–September 1974

"Chris O'Dell? It's Barry Imhoff. Look, I'm thinking of hiring you as one of the tour managers for the Crosby, Stills, Nash and Young reunion tour. You interested?"

Was I interested? Just a week had passed since Maureen left for London, with Ringo following her a few days later. I was grief stricken, heartbroken, tired of my job at Journeys, and desperately needing a change of scenery. I flew to San Francisco a week later and sealed the deal with Barry, Bill Graham's partner at Bill Graham Presents. After the Stones tour, I figured I'd be ready for anything, but there was no way to prepare for the CSNY tour. It was a frenzy of details, a snowstorm of trivia, a blizzard of complaints. The title "tour manager" encompassed everything from babysitter to mother, secretary, therapist, problem solver, travel agent, maid, and alarm clock. David ranted, Stephen pouted, Graham mediated, and Neil stayed as far away from the madness as he could. It was the Never Ending Tour that went on and on and on, the most dysfunctional gathering of egos in the history of rock and roll.

I should have known. I first met David Crosby, Stephen Stills, and Graham Nash in 1969 when they came to London hoping to seal a deal with Apple Records. Like a hurricane looking for a place to destroy, they blew into the house Graham shared with his agent, Larry Curzon. I was there because Larry let me use Graham's room while Graham was in America recording an album with David and Stephen.

One night we sat around the living room listening to the tape of their prospective album.

"Do you like it?" Graham asked, looking directly at me.

"Man, it's great," Stephen jumped in before I could answer. Smiling in his cocksure way, he passed a plastic bag of cocaine to David. Reaching for the bag, David misjudged the pass and the white powder drifted to the floor, embedding itself in the shaggy tufts of beige carpet. David and Stephen immediately dropped to their knees, frantically trying to salvage the coke, snorting it right off the carpet. I watched in amazement. I'd never seen that kind of drug hunger before.

Five years later they hadn't changed all that much except David and Stephen, both even deeper into drugs, had turned into true spoiled brats, and Graham had taken over the role of the beleaguered older sibling who tried to calm down their tantrums and keep the peace. Neil Young was the smart one. He showed up for the gigs and then disappeared into the night, traveling on his own private bus with his girlfriend Carrie Snodgress and their two-year-old son, Zeke.

I had my first hint of what the tour would be like when I walked out of Barry Imhoff's office at Bill Graham Presents in San Francisco. Sitting in the hallway was my fellow tour manager and new friend, Gary Shafner, one of the nicest guys you'd ever want to meet. Surrounded by boxes, he was leaning over a desk, stuffing something into a cigarette.

"Hey, Gary, what are you doing?" I asked.

"Well," he said, looking up at me with his big droopy beaglelike eyes, "I'm filling up these cigarettes with pot."

"Pot?"

"Yeah, I've been sitting here for hours. This is really tedious work." He could see that I was curious, so he let me in on the secret. "First, you have to unwrap the cellophane around the carton very very carefully, so it doesn't look like it's been opened," he said, showing me as he talked. "Then you take out every pack of cigarettes, remove the tobacco from each of the cigarettes, and replace it with marijuana. Then you wrap it back up, put all the cigarette packs back in the carton, and try to make it look like the carton has never been opened."

"How do you that?" I asked.

He laughed. "Very carefully."

I pointed to the seven cartons next to him. "How long did those take you?"

"A few days," he shrugged. "There are two of us working on it."

"I'm impressed." I didn't know what else to say.

"But that's not all. See these bottles of ginseng?" Pointing to a dozen ginseng bottles lined up in a neat row, Gary looked pretty proud of himself. "There are fifty capsules in each bottle. We emptied out the ginseng in each capsule and filled them with cocaine. Then we put the capsules back in the bottle, stuffed the cotton back in, closed the bottle, and made it look as if it hadn't ever been opened."

At that moment Barry Imhoff walked out of his office and looked at me. "What?" he said in a belligerent sort of way. Barry was an easygoing guy but at times he could be a bully.

"I can't believe you're doing this," I said, marveling at the way tours create their own rules of law.

"Chris, we have to be ready for anything," Barry said with a hint of a smile. He suddenly seemed somewhat amused by the whole thing. "This band is going to want for nothing. We're putting together a whole trunk that has everything they could possibly want: toothpaste, toothbrushes, real cigarettes, fake cigarettes, real ginseng, fake ginseng, razors, special soaps, first-aid items, candles, matches, lighters, you name it, we've got it. If they walk in and say they want something, we'll have it for them."

Well, I thought, there's certainly some very thoughtful planning going on here. That was true of every Bill Graham tour I ever did. They were meticulously organized, every detail accounted for, every possible emergency predicted.

"Now, we can safely get through customs and immigration when we cross into Canada," Barry said, surveying the row of ginseng bottles and the cartons of cigarettes.

"That's good," I said. And there I was once again—caught between fantasy and reality, about to set out on tour with a big-name rock group crossing international borders with cocaine in the ginseng capsules and marijuana in the cigarettes, and not one person, not even the tour managers, thinking there was anything strange about it. I had learned the unspoken (and definitely unwritten) law of rock and roll: we were above the law, no matter what country we happened to be in. At least that's what we thought.

My job, on paper, was pretty simple: waking everyone up in the morning, making sure the luggage was collected and put into the luggage van, herding the band members into limos, checking everyone in at the airport, and double checking to see that they were on the plane in their assigned seats. At the other end, I'd round them up in the airport terminal and steer them to the limos, which took us straight to the next hotel. While the luggage was being delivered to their rooms, I'd inspect the hospitality room to ensure it was set up properly with plenty of food and drink, handle any complaints that might arise, smooth over disagreements, and, finally, when a sense of peace and calm descended upon us, I'd sneak off to my room to hide out for a few quiet moments.

I had no way of knowing how difficult those seemingly simple tasks would be. My only tour experience was with the Stones, and for those weeks I was a guest, a special friend, really, with no routine duties to perform. Sure, I flew from Dallas to LA to get drugs for Keith and from St. Louis to New York to get Mick's camera fixed, and I'd take care of daily personal needs like collecting their laundry at night and making sure the freshly cleaned clothes were delivered to their rooms the next day, or making lists of friends they wanted to include on the guest list for the show that night and calling in the names to the tour office at the hall. Basically I showed up and helped out when Mick, Keith, Bill, or Astrid needed a personal favor. That was always part of the problem on the Stones tour—the tour could have gone on without me. I was a luxury.

On the CSNY reunion tour, in contrast, I was on call twenty-four hours a day, and I never got a day off. Not one. If the guys needed or wanted something, Gary and I had to make it happen *right now.* That was our role. We were there to take care of the band, and whatever the band wanted, they got. Always something, every day, a hundred times a day, something.

I learned how to dance with the demands and make things happen fast. The philosophy on the road is, there's nothing that can't be done (or undone), and I spent a lot of my time getting hotel staff to change rooms, extend room service hours, reopen the restaurants after they'd been closed for hours, clean rooms while we were at the gig, and on and on it went. My phone started ringing days before we opened in Seattle, and it didn't stop ringing for sixty days, until Bill Graham finally put an end to the madness. What time are we leaving, who's picking up my luggage, what kind of hotel is this with no mini-bar in the room, I'm hungry, when do we eat, I don't have an alarm clock, the lightbulb burned out, the television only gets four channels, the walls are too thin, my room is right next to the ice machine, the guy next door snores, the carpet smells like somebody pissed on it, the window doesn't open, and on and on and on it went. Oh and by the way, do you have any of those ginseng tablets and maybe a pack of those cigarettes?

In Seattle (or was it Vancouver, I can't remember) I had a lovely little diversion from the madness when I had breakfast in the hotel coffee shop with a seventeen-year-old writer from *Rolling Stone* magazine. Imagine—a high school kid writing for the premiere rock and roll magazine of the world! His name was Cameron Crowe. He was sweet and adorable, just an angelic-looking kid, but what really stood out about Cameron was his shy personality and his unobtrusive ways. He wasn't the least bit threatening, which meant he could go where other journalists only dreamed of going: onto the bus and into the dressing rooms and hotel suites, getting right into the heads and hearts of the rock-and-roll royalty. (Many years later he'd draw on his experiences to write and direct the movie *Almost Famous.*) Just being around Cameron made me feel good. He was so wide eyed with wonder at the magical experiences he was having that he reminded me of myself in more innocent times.

"Have you worked with any other bands?" Cameron asked me as I sipped my coffee. He took a gulp of his Coke.

"Well, yeah, a couple," I said. I never liked answering that question because I didn't want people to think I was bragging. I was always a little uneasy talking about myself.

"Like who?"

"Well, I worked with the Beatles and the Stones," I said.

"You're kidding?" Cameron said, leaning across the table, a huge smile on his face. Like most people who ask the question, he expected me to name some small band, musicians he'd never heard of before.

"No, I'm really not," I said, reaching for my coffee and thinking how cute he was.

"Do you know you're one of the only female tour managers out there? That's a pretty cool thing, don't you think?"

"What about you, Cameron?" I said, changing the direction of the conversation. "What got you into this?"

"Well," he said, and it was his turn to be a little shy. "I guess it's that I just love music." Uncomplicated, unpretentious, undemanding—that was Cameron. God, I wished he was just a little bit older.

At the Vancouver airport we encountered a little problem. Joni Mitchell was supposed to meet us at the airport, and she was late. (I'd soon discover she was often late.) I used all my powers of persuasion to convince the folks at the airport to hold the plane. We were flying commercially, and we'd booked half the plane, so they were willing to inconvenience the other passengers to keep us happy.

Well, okay, I thought, feeling my confidence muscles bulging a bit. This is real power—I can make planes wait.

"Did you know Eric Clapton is staying in our hotel?" one of the roadies told me when we arrived in Denver.

I immediately called Eric's room, knowing that if Eric was in the hotel, Pattie was, too. Several weeks earlier Pattie had called me with the news that she'd left George and was now with Eric. George was cold, distant, and seemed almost indifferent to her thoughts and feelings, she said, while Eric claimed to be madly in love with her, wrote beautiful love songs for her, and over the years had worn her down (as she put it) with his declarations of love. A choice had to be made, and she chose Eric.

"Chris! How wonderful!" Pattie said when she answered the phone. "I can't believe you're really here! Come up to the suite. We can't wait to see you."

I spent several hours with Pattie and Eric, and that was a very strange night. Eric seemed happy enough to see me at first, but the longer I stayed, the more distant he became. He wanted her all to himself—that seemed absolutely obvious to me—and Pattie wasn't resisting. She was radiant, the happiest I had ever seen her. They laughed and giggled, teasing each other, touching each other, calling each other by their new pet names, "Nell" and "El."

"Why Nell and El?" I asked.

"Oh, it was Eric's idea, a way of keeping me secret," she said, snuggling up to him. "We don't want the press to know I'm on the tour with him." Years later, writing in his memoir, Eric told a different story. By using the nicknames "Nell," "Nelly," or sometimes "Nello," Eric said he was able to overlook the fact that Pattie was married to one of his best friends. "Pattie" belonged to George. "Nell" was Eric's property. Eric even confessed that the nickname might have been a means of relegating her "to a sort of barmaid status so that I wasn't so much in awe of her."

But that night she was still high up on a pedestal. Eric was possessive of her and jealous of me, and I realized that I'd never felt like a third wheel with George, who had always treated me like part of the family, a "sister," as Pattie sometimes called me. With Eric I felt more like a distant cousin, someone he had to put up with for Pattie's sake. I couldn't put my finger on, it but something strange was going on between them. Eric was drinking a lot—maybe that was the problem. Or maybe their fairytale relationship was so new that they didn't quite know how to act when someone from the old days showed up suddenly.

On the way back to my room, I realized that I might be the one who was dreaming up trouble. I wondered if I was projecting my feelings onto Eric. Maybe I was taking my jealousy and putting it into his mind, imagining that he was jealous of me when I was jealous of him. Like Eric, I would have loved to have Pattie all to myself. But with Eric always next to her, adoring her, watching over her, I felt as if I'd lost Pattie. I kept thinking, *Where has my girlfriend gone?*

In New York at the Plaza Hotel David Crosby had a meltdown. I was just starting to unpack my bags when my phone started ringing and at the same moment someone knocked on my door. I opened the door, waved Gary in, and picked up the phone.

"David Crosby is flipping out because he doesn't have cross ventilation in his room," Barry said. "You need to get down there and work it out right now."

"Okay," I said. "Look, Gary's here, don't worry, we'll take care of it."

I hung up the phone and looked at Gary.

"David is having a fit," Gary said.

"Yeah, I heard." David was the baby. When he was upset about something, which was often several times a day, he'd rant and rave, grow red in the face, puff and pout, blow and wheeze, but as soon as he got what he wanted, he'd settle down, happy as could be. Stephen Stills had a slightly different way of showing his anger or displeasure. His mouth would turn down at the corners and he'd whine like a spoiled toddler, stomp his foot, and go off into a corner and sulk. After he'd have his little time-out, he'd apologize in shamefaced embarrassment for his loss of control. Both David and Stephen were doing a lot of cocaine on the tour, which made their moods even more intense and unpredictable.

I knew Stephen better than I knew David, Graham, or Neil, and when he got into one of his moods, I'd stand eye to eye with him and very calmly say, "Stephen, what are you doing?" He'd immediately snap out of it, almost as if he'd suddenly come out of a trance. Graham, thank heavens, played the part of the mature older brother who did his best to keep the youngsters in line. "It's okay, it's okay," he'd say in a soothing tone whenever Stephen whimpered or David had a temper tantrum. Neil just kept to himself and stayed out of the insanity. Smart guy.

"David is ranting and raving, threatening to leave the tour," Gary said, those big puppy-dog eyes wide and frantic. He was getting burned out by all these demands, no doubt about it. Me, too.

"Shit," I said. "He needs to grow up."

Gary and I looked at each other with tired eyes, trying to work up the energy to deal with this ridiculous new crisis. The constant bickering, nagging, complaining, and sudden fits of rage left us feeling exhausted and demoralized. But what could we do? Our job, as Barry had warned us weeks earlier, was to take care of their every need. So we trudged downstairs and, using a slightly apologetic tone, explained to the hotel manager that one of our musicians needed a room with cross ventilation. They were used to special requests at that hotel—it was the Plaza Hotel, after all—and with many apologies and promises to do whatever they could to make our group happy, they assigned David to a corner room with lots of windows and plenty of circulating air.

Gary and I took the elevator to David's room and explained that the management was arranging new accommodations for him.

"But let's go look at the room before we move you," I suggested.

"Fine," he said, sulking and muttering about how this imposition should never have occurred.

We walked down the long, wide halls to the last door on the front side of the hotel. The bellman opened the door, and David stepped into the bedroom of the suite. The curtains flapped in the breeze and the sun shone brightly into the room.

"Perfect!" David said, lying down on the bed with a happy smile on his face. We had his luggage moved right away, before he could change his mind.

A few days later, just several hours before the show started, Stephen called my room.

"Would you come to my suite?" he said.

Shit, I thought, *what could possibly be wrong now?* I was expecting the worst when Stephen opened the door and pulled me by the arm into the room, leading me to the sofa. I reluctantly followed along, wondering what in hell he had on his mind.

"Look," he said, pointing to a big white rock on the coffee table. It was the size of a baseball, or at least that's how big it is in my memory. One damn big rock of pure cocaine.

"Want some?" he said as he sat down on the floor beside the table and started chopping up lines of coke.

"That's cocaine?" I asked, stunned at the size of the rock. I'd never seen anything like it.

"Yeah, and it's really good. I thought you might like some."

"Okay," I said, thinking that I really should do at least one line since Stephen had been so thoughtful to share it with me. I'd been trying to stay away from drugs, knowing that if I started doing cocaine again, I'd never make it through the tour. *But just this once,* I thought, looking again at that big beautiful rock. And oh, that feeling of ecstasy. I hadn't felt that good, that alive, that *normal* in weeks. This tour isn't so bad, I found myself thinking, and for those few minutes, it wasn't.

Everyone's nerves were on edge. The tour sputtered and stalled but somehow managed to keep trudging along even as the relationships between all the different camps deteriorated. Gary, Barry, and I became the scapegoats for most of the problems between the different band members and their individual staffs and crews. We were running around like crazy trying to answer to four different stars and four different staffs, and as people got worn down by the tour, the demands on our time intensified.

Elliot Roberts, the band's manager (and a powerful LA music executive in partnership with David Geffen), was the one steady link with the band members. His primary purpose on the tour was to protect the band's interests. He was a nice enough guy, but he also tended to be emotionally distant and annoyingly arrogant, with a slightly condescending attitude toward those of us who worked for Bill Graham. Elliot and Bill were equals, but Elliot spent most of his time with the musicians at the hotel, while Bill was always one step ahead of us at the gigs, working with the crew to set up the show.

I picked up the phone on the second ring. "Chris. It's Elliot."

"Hi, Elliot," I said, surprised to hear from him. When Elliot needed something, he rarely came to me, the underling, but instead went straight to the top, to Bill or Barry.

"What the *fuck* is going on?" he said, screaming at me about some equipment issue that had nothing to do with me or my job. I had no idea what he was yelling about. All I heard was the shouted threat. "If you don't get this *fucking* fixed, I'm going to have you *fucking* fired."

I held the phone to my ear, having no idea how to defend myself. When he hung up, I stood there for a moment with the receiver in my hand, shaking and close to tears. Taking a few deep breaths, I called Barry Imhoff, who listened to my story and said he'd call me back.

Half an hour later the phone rang.

"Chris. It's Bill. Bill Graham."

"Hi, Bill." *Uh-oh,* I thought. Bill Graham never called me either.

"I understand Elliot Roberts called you a little while ago and was very rude to you."

"Well, yeah, that's true," I said.

"I want you to know that I just spoke to him."

I waited, holding my breath. Was Bill going to let me have it?

"I told him that he has no right to talk to anyone who works for me like that, and if he needs something, he should come to me."

"Okay," I said, breathing a sigh of relief.

"And one more thing." Bill was pissed. "If anybody ever talks to you like that again, you have my permission to hang up on them. No one in my employment should ever be treated like that."

From that day forward, Bill Graham was one of my all-time great heroes.

As the tensions on the tour escalated, so did my drinking. I was burned out from being constantly on the run during the day and sleeping just a few hours a night. Alcohol was my saving grace. I drank to relax and reduce my stress, or so I told myself, and it worked for those few hours, but then the stress just built up again, along with the irritability and the depression. I managed to avoid drugs on the tour, except for those few lines off that big white rock in Stephen's room. But the drinking got bad and then it got worse. I thought I could control it, having stopped several times before then, but years later in Twelve Step meetings I'd learn that when we stop for a while and then start up again, the drinking is just as bad or worse than before. It's like something inside you keeps feeding that addiction, even if you're not feeding it yourself, and it just roars back to life when you start up again.

In Tampa, Florida, not long before that endless tour finally ended, I hit a wall. We always had limos waiting at the airport to take us to the hotel, and I jumped in with Gary and Barry. As soon as we arrived at the hotel, which wasn't quite up to my standards (by this time I was complaining about everything, too), Gary and I did our usual routine of checking out the hospitality room, an important part of the hotel setup because that's where the band and tour staff congregated for food and drink before and after gigs. The seventh-floor suite was a complete letdown, a small, white-walled, crappy junior suite with shitty modern furniture and just one window that let in barely any light because it looked onto a backstreet alley and another building across the way.

We paid for that hospitality suite, just like we did at every hotel, and this one sucked. I took responsibility for it, too, because it was part of my job to take care of all the travel arrangements and make sure everything was set up the way we wanted it. Well, I took one look at that crummy relish plate with the limp carrots and brown-edged celery dumped on a fake silver serving tray, picked it up, and tossed the whole damn thing out the window.

Gary stood there frozen, not quite believing what he had witnessed. "Chris," he said, concerned, maybe even a little scared.

"It was a shitty relish tray," I said. "We can't eat that crap."

Gary chuckled, keeping his eyes on me.

"God, that felt good," I said. I picked up the phone and called room service. "We need a relish tray," I said, not very politely.

"We left something up there."

"Well, it's not here now," I said, hanging up the phone.

Gary was looking out the window at the remnants of the relish tray scattered in the alley seven floors below. "I wonder if anyone will find that silver tray," he said.

"Well, they can have it," I said, and for some reason that just cracked us up.

31

JAMAICA

Fall 1974

I couldn't wait for the CSNY tour to end, but once it was officially over, I didn't know what to do with myself. That's how it goes with tours: the roller coaster comes to a slow halt, the crowds disperse, the gates lock behind you, and you walk away from the deserted fairgrounds, kicking at the empty pop cans and cardboard popcorn boxes, wondering what to do with the rest of your life.

"We might need you for the George Harrison tour in two months," Barry said just before the end.

"Sure," I said, "call me." But first I needed a rest, so I flew to Jamaica to be with Pattie and Eric.

"Tell me about the tour," Eric said, leaning across the table, a cigarette dangling from his fingers. He seemed so relaxed and self-confident that day as we talked on the patio of the exclusive Kingston Terra Nova Hotel, once the home of Island Records owner Chris Blackwell. Maybe he felt more secure now that he had his Layla. He and Pattie traded loving looks as I filled them in on the shenanigans of the last three months. Eric seemed to get a big kick out of all my detailed stories. Over the years, I learned that most musicians enjoy hearing about what goes on with other tours. It's such an odd life, and not one that you share with many people, so when someone really understands how rigorous, ridiculous, silly, and sublime tours can get, it can be entertaining to sit around and trade stories.

Pattie and I spent several hours by the pool where we were joined by one of Eric's backup singers and a couple of the musicians' girlfriends. As I sat by the pool listening to their stories, laughing along with them even as I wondered what was so darn funny, feeling left out when they shared insider comments about the band or the tour they had just finished, I realized I was jealous. For so long it had been just Pattie and me, but now—now that she was with Eric—she'd found a whole new group of friends. I felt out of place. I'd just stepped out of the CSNY world, where I had a purpose, I was in control, and the people, even if they did drive me crazy, were familiar. But sunning next to Pattie in my new bikini, the palm trees swaying in the breeze overhead, I felt insecure and vulnerable. Days before, I was an insider and now I felt like an outsider—and I knew full well what that meant after my experiences on tour. The inner circle is close and tight, and anyone outside that enclosed space is viewed as out of touch and out of sync. Outsiders are considered a distraction from the ordinary routine of things.

When Pattie and I went shopping and got away from everyone else, I felt much better. I wasn't crazy about the town of Kingston with all the goats wandering the dirty streets, the oppressive heat, and the pervasive odor of fragrant spicy food wafting from downtown restaurants intermingling with the pungent stench of garbage that had been cooking on the sidewalks for days. But Pattie and I laughed about old times, shared our own inside jokes, and cracked up when we walked by a McDonald's restaurant and saw goat burgers on the menu.

I was tired that second night, but after dinner and several stiff drinks, Pattie and I were in the mood to keep partying. We asked the bartender to make us a pitcher of Brandy Alexanders that we could take with us to the studio, and off we went. I must have been drunk because as soon as we got there I went straight to the piano in the middle of the studio and started to play, with one finger, the only song I knew how to play—

"Tammy" from the Debbie Reynolds movie *Tammy and the Bachelor*. The musicians and technicians were taking a break, and I figured, Oh, why the hell not. A few minutes later Tom Dowd, Eric's producer, sat down next to me, playing the song with both hands, and I sang along with him. With Tom sitting next to me at the piano, playing one of my favorite old songs, I felt like I was back where I belonged with my trusted friends.

Pattie and Eric joined me in the studio and while Eric put vocals on one of the tracks, Pattie and I proceeded to polish off the pitcher. We sat in a little circle, the three of us, with Eric in the middle in front of the microphone. The tape kept running over and over as Eric laid down the vocal, always looking for "the one perfect take." When Pattie left the studio for a minute during a break, I leaned closer to Eric. I was drunk, of course, which gave me courage and at the same time removed the filter that would have stopped me from making a total ass out of myself.

"You know, Eric, I had a dream about you once when I was living with Leon." Although I was half wasted, I was telling the absolute truth about the dream. "I dreamed that you rescued me on a white horse. You swept through town and saved me. You were my knight in shining armor."

Eric looked at me, eyes squinched together, an odd little smile at the corner of his mouth. I knew exactly what he was thinking: *What the fuck are you talking about?*

"Okay, Chris," he said, laughing at me, not with me, "go have another drink."

But I wasn't quite done embarrassing myself. Listening to Yvonne Elliman, Eric's backup singer, I began to imagine that I had an even better voice than she did. I started singing along, quietly at first, so no one noticed, but the more I sang, the louder I got. Pattie was giggling, which just encouraged me. Finally, Eric turned around and, not unkindly, told us to go home.

We laughed the whole way back to the hotel about how we had gotten kicked out of the studio, and when the car dropped us off, we went straight to the bar to get some more Brandy Alexanders. The bartender was gone for the night, but we finally convinced the night clerk to open the bar, and he let us make our own drinks.

Back in Pattie's room, we started talking about George and how much we both missed him. Pattie loved Eric but still cared deeply about George—there was never any doubt in my mind about that. I once asked her if George or Eric was her "one true love." After some thought, she answered, "Eric." But later, after she and Eric were divorced, she told me that George was the love of her life.

"Let's call him," I said. I honestly had no intention of creating problems in Pattie's relationship with Eric, at least not consciously, but I was definitely feeling nostalgic for the way things used to be. With George, I always felt included, and he was happy to leave me alone with Pattie as he pursued his own interests; but Pattie and Eric were inseparable, and there wasn't much room left for me. I was being left behind and I didn't like it one bit.

"Really? Do you think we should? It would be nice to talk to him," Pattie said. We both started giggling again as Pattie dialed the number. It must have been around nine in the morning in England.

"George. It's Pattie," she said, turning to smile at me. I was so happy to hear her talking on the phone with George as if they were old friends and nothing bad had ever happened between them. The three of us were together again!

I was talking to George when Eric walked in. He stood in the doorway looking at us.

"What are you doing?"

"Oh, we're talking to George," Pattie said very calmly, standing up from the bed and moving toward him, almost as if she were trying to protect me. At the same time, I wanted to protect Pattie, and I said a little silent prayer of gratitude that she had passed the phone to me right before Eric walked in the room. He could blame me for the phone call. I was happy to take the rap on this one.

Eric's jaw was clenched, and his eyes seemed to bore right through us. He'd walked in with an expectant look on his face, clearly looking forward to some private time with the woman he had loved with such passion for so many years. But within seconds his expression changed to anger. Fury. He threw his bag on the bed, fixed me with a deadly glare, and walked into the bathroom, slamming the door.

I looked at Pattie, who was visibly shaken. She came back to the side of the bed and slowly sat down, looking at me with wide, pleading eyes that conveyed both her fear and her helplessness.

I hurriedly ended the phone call. "Hey, George, I have to hang up now, we'll try you back tomorrow," I said as I put the phone in the receiver. My hands were shaking. I needed to get out of there. I picked up my purse, gave Pattie a quick hug, and was headed for the door when Eric threw open the bathroom door and strode over to Pattie, who was sitting on the bed.

"Why the fuck did you call him?" He was even angrier than he had been a few minutes before.

"We just wanted to say hello," Pattie said, keeping her tone light.

"Chris, you better go back to your room," Eric said in a low voice without even turning around to look at me.

"Okay," I said, clutching my purse tighter and getting the heck out of there. "See you guys later."

That night I had the most fitful sleep. I kept having recurring nightmares about strange, frightening people coming into my room, threatening me, and I'd wake up, startled and afraid. "The past is the past," I kept repeating to myself, "nothing is going to happen to you." Those nightmares were based on a real event. Just a year earlier, a friend of mine had been raped in this very hotel, maybe in this very room. "You're safe, it happened a long time ago," I kept reassuring myself, and after a while I'd drift back into a twilight sleep somewhere between waking and dreaming. Early that morning I woke up, the nightmarish fears dissolved by the morning light, but new worries troubling my mind as I remembered bits of the night before and realized that Eric was going to be really mad at me. He'd blame me for the whole thing. He'd probably ask me to leave.

I tossed and turned and finally made up my mind. I'd beat him to it. Eric was going to reject me, I had no doubt about that, so I'd preempt him by making the first move. Somewhere in life I'd learned that pattern worked, and I kept using it because it helped me avoid pain. I'm not sure I really thought about it, but I'd learned that if I left first, before things got ugly or out of hand, I could maintain some control over the situation. I discovered that strategy with my high school boyfriends, and I fine-tuned it with Leon when I moved out of his house hours after he told me we needed some time apart, with George when I announced I was leaving Friar Park before he could ask me to leave, with Apple when I basically forced them to fire me because I never showed up for work, and now I was repeating the pattern with Pattie and Eric. This was another rejection that I could avoid by staying one step ahead of him. That's how I handled everything—work, love, friendship—I stayed one step ahead, seeing the problem before it occurred, adapting and adjusting before I was taken by surprise. Survival of the fittest, I convinced myself. The faster I could get out, the better.

I fell back asleep, then, and slept soundly because I had a plan.

I woke up with a pounding headache and a roiling stomach. My hands shook as I reached for the phone.

"George?" I spoke as cheerfully as possible into the phone.

"Chris?" George said, recognizing my voice.

"I'm so glad you're there, George, it's awful here, I have to get out. Eric is angry with us for calling you last night. Do you think I can come and stay for a week or so, would you be able to pay for my ticket, and pick me up at the airport?" I blurted it all out, and George just said yes, yes, yes, although I did pick up on a little amusement in his tone. What spindly webs we weave.

I called my friend Sara at Journeys, who booked me on a flight late that afternoon, but when I hung up the phone, I was suddenly filled with doubt. I felt like a traitor. I'd only been in Jamaica for two days, and now I was running away from Pattie and Eric, back to George and Friar Park. What was I doing? How could I face them? All these anguished questions kept running through my mind as I packed my bags—as always, I had too damn much stuff—and every time I bent over and straightened back up again, I'd have to run to the bathroom to throw up. It took me a good hour to pack. And then I waited. I couldn't show my face until the very last minute, when I'd scurry out the door like a frightened little rat looking for another dark hole to hide in.

I crossed the reception area, head down, and was almost clear of the dining room when I heard Eric call my name.

"Chris! Come join us!" Eric was smiling, waving me over to the table. Pattie was smiling, too, that little secret smile of ours that said, *Well, we had a little fun last night, didn't we?* I could tell they'd both been waiting for me to show up so they could razz me about my drunken behavior the night before. Fuck!

"How are you feeling this morning?" Eric said. I realized then that Eric wasn't angry with me anymore. But I knew I was about to make him really, really mad.

"Hi," I said, barely managing to say the word.

"Have you had breakfast?" Pattie said cheerfully. She looked fabulous, as always, her hair all done up with the blond wisps framing her gorgeous face, her makeup perfectly done, no wrinkles or bags under her eyes, no shaky hands or quaking insides.

"No, no thanks, no breakfast," I said, just the thought of it making my stomach heave. "Listen, guys, I've got to leave."

"Leave?" they both said at once.

"Where are you going?" Pattie asked in disbelief.

"I'm flying to London," I stammered.

"What?" Pattie said.

"Why?" Eric asked.

"I just have to go." They sat there staring at me. "I have a plane to catch."

"Okay," Pattie said.

"See ya," Eric said.

I hugged them both good-bye and practically ran out the door to the waiting taxi. I *was* a traitor. I had betrayed their kindness, abused their friendship, chosen sides in their famous love triangle, and turned my back on my best friend. I chose George over Eric. Worse, I chose George over Pattie. I didn't mean to do that. I didn't intend to do anything. I wanted to be friends with them all, I wanted it to be like it used to be. I didn't want anybody to be mad at me, and the very last thing I wanted was to hurt Pattie's feelings. But I was embarrassed and ashamed, and I thought Eric would be angry with me, and Friar Park felt safe, George felt safe, so I figured this would work out best. I had really, really, really screwed everything up this time.

Kumar, Ravi Shankar's nephew, picked me up at the airport. When we arrived at Friar Park, George was pulling up weeds in the garden, a trowel in his hand, a smile on his face, the spitting image of Chance the gardener.

"It's good to see you, Chris," he said, wiping his hands on his jeans and giving me a hug, followed by a questioning look. "Are you okay? You sounded really upset on the phone."

"Yeah," I said. "Let's talk about it later."

Friar Park felt different—quiet, empty, lonely without Pattie there. I settled into my room and over the next few days George and I had some good talks.

"How are Pattie and Eric?" he asked one evening after dinner. Kumar had fixed a delicious Indian meal that night, then disappeared into the office on the other side of the house. He was so comfortable there, part of the Friar Park family, just as I had been so many ages ago. Was I still?

"They're fine," I said, telling him about the night in the studio and how drunk Pattie and I had gotten. He got a huge kick out of that story.

"It was strange being with them," I admitted after a few glasses of wine. "I'm so used to you and Pattie being together."

"Things are probably for the better," he said and left it at that. I was hoping he'd talk about how much he missed Pattie and maybe confide that he still felt there was hope for their marriage, but as the days went by, I realized that George had moved on. He'd accepted what had happened, and he never uttered one word of sadness or regret, at least not to me. I almost got the feeling he was a little relieved that the marriage finally had come to its natural end. Neither he nor Pattie had been happy for a long time, but George didn't seem bothered by the way things had worked out. It was almost as if he felt it had been preordained. He just accepted it and seemed to revel in his solitude, spending most of his time in the garden or playing his guitar, with no one else to think or worry about, no need to talk, no set schedule to follow.

The affair with Maureen was over, and Maureen had moved into a cottage in London while Ringo stayed with the children at the house in the country.

"So what's going on with you and Ringo?" he asked me one day as we walked in the gardens, looking at the magnificent green lawn and the profusion of colorful flowers he had planted.

"Oh," I said, my face flushing red, "you heard about that?" Well, of course, I realized—Maureen must have told him.

"Tell me about it," he said, clearly interested in the details.

"Well, it was—awkward," I said. How could I tell the story without getting into all my feelings of guilt and shame? Or the hurt? Ringo was now with Nancy Andrews, who had been my good friend during the beach house days with John and May. Nancy moved in with me when she broke up with Carl Radle. I originally introduced her to Ringo. How could I describe the rejection I felt? One day it was just over, and Ringo and I never talked about it again, but Nancy told me later that she talked to Ringo and expressed concerns about my feelings.

"Chris will understand," Ringo said. He was right. I did. But that didn't make it hurt any less.

I told George the story without all the emotional edging, and he listened intently, smiling in a way that told me he was gently amused by it all. George had this wider perspective on life, believing in the Hare Krishna philosophy that we are all children acting out our problems on this life's stage, getting the nonsense out of our systems before ascending to the state of Nirvana. In this particular drama, George was the first actor on the stage, the one who started it all when he announced to Ringo that he was in love with Maureen, and from that point on, the whole thing had spun out of our control. Ringo and I were together, briefly; Pattie and Eric got together for however long that might last (I had my doubts but also my hopes for her happiness); George and Maureen broke up; Maureen was alone; Ringo was with Nancy; and who knew where it would all end.

• • •

"We're going to a party," George announced a few days later.

"Oh good," I said. The party was at John Entwistle's house—he was the bass guitarist for the Who—but it was no fun at all. In fact, it was probably the worst party of my life. I wandered around, feeling out of place because the only people I knew were George and Kumar. I kept looking for a familiar face, and then, to my complete surprise, I saw Pattie.

"Pat!" I said, edging my way into the group of women standing around her.

Pattie glanced at me for a split second, just a slight movement of her eyes, and then looked away and continued her conversation.

"Pattie," I repeated. I knew I was interrupting the conversation, but this was Pattie, after all. I don't know why, but it didn't occur to me that she might be angry with me, still. I was just so happy to see her.

She stopped again, the conversation trailing off, and slowly turned toward me so that her back was to the group. "Oh hello, Chris," she said with a dead stare.

I felt the blood rushing to my head. I'd never seen her act like that.

"Pattie, are you upset with me?" I blurted out.

"Well," she said, her voice low but her tone sharp, almost cutting, "you left very abruptly. And Eric was very upset that you didn't pay your hotel bill." She turned back to the circle of women, which seemed to close around her, and I knew at that moment how angry she was with me. In Jamaica I had made a choice between her and George, and I had chosen George. I'd turned my back on her, and now—not out of malice or spite but from the fear of being betrayed again and the need to protect herself—she was turning her back on me.

What had I done? Had I lost my best friend? Pattie had never been mad at me, not once that I could remember, and I couldn't bear to think that this moment might mark the end of our friendship. I was frantic to find George and get out of there. Searching through the crowded rooms, I ran right into Eric.

"Oh, God," he said with a smile that looked more like a sneer. "Look who's here."

He drew back from me, almost as if he found me repulsive, and once again I ran away, looking for George. Finally, I found him and I pulled at his sleeve.

"We need to leave," I said.

"Okay," he said. He'd had enough of the party.

On the way back to Friar Park, I fought back tears. "Pattie and Eric are really mad at me," I said.

"Yeah," he said. He seemed to know all about it.

"Did Eric talk to you?" I asked.

"He mentioned it," George said with a shrug.

"Oh shit." If Eric was angry with me, he would make it difficult for me to smooth things over with Pattie. He might try to come between us. He might even tell Pattie to forget about me.

Clapton Is God—I remembered the graffiti all over the London subways and storefronts. I felt the power of Eric Clapton coming between me and Pattie, and it terrified me. He could take her away from me.

"Don't worry," George reassured me, steering the Mercedes around a steep bend, "it will all blow over soon."

One night during that trip to England, I stayed with Maureen at her London apartment. We talked for hours, drinking Scotch and smoking one cigarette after another. I told her what had happened with Pattie and Eric. She shook her head, the same gently amused smile on her face that George had when I told him the story of what happened with me and Ringo.

She took the cigarette holder out of her mouth and tapped it against the ashtray before speaking the words that summed up all of it, every last ounce of it. "It's all gone to hell in a handbag, hasn't it?"

32

GEORGE'S TOUR

November 2–December 20, 1974

"When you get back to LA, would you go to Dark Horse and take a picture of Olivia?"

"You want me to walk in there and take a picture of her?" I said, not hiding my surprise. Olivia Arias was the secretary at Dark Horse Records, George's record company in America.

"Well, I've been talking to her on the phone a lot," he said, a little sheepishly. "You know, we really have a connection. Sometimes we talk for hours. I just want to know if she's as beautiful as she sounds."

Oh brother, I thought.

"Okay," I said. "I'll do it."

I wasn't happy about that little task, though, because I still hoped that Pattie and George might get back together. But I figured that by saying yes, I had a bargaining chip. George's American tour was just six weeks away, and while Barry Imhoff had talked about hiring me, no one had officially offered me the job. I really wanted to be part of that tour. After just a week of lazing around, I missed the excitement and nonstop action of the tour life. So I jumped right in.

"George, I still don't know if Barry Imhoff is going to hire me for your tour. Would you talk to someone about it?" I had a hard time asking George for favors, fearing that he might think I was taking advantage of our friendship. But being part of this tour was really important to me.

George looked perplexed. "Why wouldn't you be part of the tour? But, sure, I'll talk to Denis, no problem." Denis O'Brien was George's manager at the time.

I called Barry the next day, but before I had a chance to mention the tour, he brought up the subject himself. "By the way, O'Dell, when are you coming back? I need you to start working on the tour."

I flew back to LA and even stopped by Dark Horse Records to meet Olivia, a stunning Mexican-American girl with long dark hair and big brown eyes. But I never did take her picture. I couldn't imagine any other woman in George's life but Pattie. And if he really wanted to meet Olivia, he could walk into her office and introduce himself. Which is exactly what he did. From all accounts, it was love at first sight.

I thought touring with George would be easy after the chaos of the CSNY tour, but trying to keep two bands with two crews from two different continents with two different cultures happy was a real organizational feat. First, there was George's band of nine musicians, along with their wives and girlfriends who joined the tour at various points along the way. Add in Ravi's band of fourteen musicians (no wives or girlfriends), the cook Ravi brought along from India, the two road crews, the tour staff and crew, Olivia, Kumar, George's father, and various and sundry friends and hangers-on, and the grand total ended up being somewhere around 120 people schlepping from one city to another.

Then there were the three portable kitchens, which went everywhere with us. I had to hand it to Bill Graham for figuring out a way to honor Ravi's request for Indian food at every stop along the way. Two of the kitchens closed up to the size of a large equipment container, and one of those was installed in the hospitality suite where George's band and the tour staff stayed, while the other kitchen was set up in the hotel where Ravi's band stayed (usually a less expensive place than George's hotel). The third kitchen was actually a small truck retrofitted into a fully functioning kitchen that went with us to all the gigs.

Every time I walked into the current hotel's hospitality suite—morning, afternoon, late at night, it didn't matter—I took a deep whiff of the heady mixture of sweet and pungent spices and felt grounded. George felt that way, too. He hated touring. The noise, the crowds, the pressure, his high expectations, and the feeling of being so vulnerable standing all alone on the stage kept him on edge, along with the still-fresh memories of the Beatlemania years when crazed fans mobbed them everywhere they went. George didn't want to be the center of attention; he wanted to be alone with his thoughts, sheltered in the quiet solitude of Friar Park.

But the soothing and familiar fragrance of Indian food, along with his good friend Ravi's presence, helped him relax at least for a few hours a day. I loved watching George wander into the hospitality suite and go straight to the portable kitchen to fill his plate with curries and chutneys. As he sat on the couch and ate quietly by himself, there was a prayerful presence about him. Food, meditation, solitude, silence—George held on to the spiritual realities that helped him get through the stress of being on the road.

He seemed so happy in those days, especially when he was with Olivia. I was surprised to see how affectionate he was with Olivia, holding hands, heads touching as they talked, snuggling up next to her at every opportunity. I'd never seen George be very demonstrative with Pattie, but she sometimes talked about how gentle and loving he was at the beginning of their marriage. Most marriages, as I would learn soon enough, start off with a honeymoon stage, and when the passionate physical stuff starts to ebb, the emotional connection changes, too. Either we learn how to nurture it or we lose it, but losing it can take a very long time.

I liked Olivia, but she had two insurmountable disadvantages. She wasn't Pattie. That was the big one. But I was also jealous of George's attention to her. For all the years I had known George and Pattie, I never worried about intruding on their private space. George always included me in conversations and often turned to me when he was troubled about something, needed some advice, or just wanted to hang out. But Olivia was his new love, and he was clearly head over heels, spending all his spare time with her and creating a little invisible wall that separated them from the rest of us.

I was happy for him, but I missed the way it used to be.

On December 13, just a week before the final show at Madison Square Garden, we played two shows at the Capital Centre in Largo, Maryland. We were all so excited because we were spending two nights at the infamous Watergate Hotel where a botched burglary brought down a presidency. I enjoyed a "lie-in," as Pattie would have put it, sleeping until almost noon and then propping myself up in my queen-size bed in my junior suite to watch a soap opera. It hit me then, as it sometimes did, that I had the best job in the whole world.

Hmmmm, I smiled, sinking deeper into the down pillow and soft satinlike sheets. This is the life.

The next day when I arrived backstage, there were Secret Service agents everywhere. Earlier that day George, at the invitation of Jack Ford, son of President Gerald Ford, went to the White House to meet the president and during that visit George invited Jack and his sister Susan to the evening show. Well, that will be cool, I thought. I did my routine walk-around, making sure I knew exactly where everything was located—the dressing rooms, the tour office, and the box office (to make sure the seats I'd reserved were being held). I wandered through the hall to get a feel for the audience, as I always did, and nodded my head, one professional acknowledging another, at the Secret Service men with their walkie-talkies. The seats continued to fill up as Ravi and his band opened the show, never losing his concentration even as people talked and laughed in the audience. That always irritated me, but Ravi never seemed bothered in the least.

After watching Ravi's band for a few minutes from the side of the stage, I walked back to the dressing rooms to see if anyone needed my help. I'd discovered early on with the CSNY tour that the most important part of my job before the show was creating a positive environment. I laughed, nurtured, mended, listened, and entertained in the half hour before the show, always fixing myself a drink and thoroughly enjoying the party atmosphere.

That night I was joking around with saxophonist Tom Scott when the door opened and Jack Ford walked into the room. George welcomed him and went around the room, introducing him to everyone. When he got to me, he said, "Jack, this is an old friend, Chris O'Dell. If you need anything, see her." I thought Jack was adorable, a little shy but at the same time very self-assured. After the show we had a party back at the hotel and I had a great time flirting with him.

The next morning on the plane, I settled in next to George and Olivia. "So, what did you think of Jack Ford?" I asked casually.

George looked up from his book. "He seemed nice." A smile suddenly crossed his face as he caught my true meaning. He put his book down.

"What did you think about him, Miss O'Dell?"

"I thought he was cute." I laughed.

George always got a big kick out of my flirtations—he loved playing my big brother, checking out all my boyfriends—and he did his best to fix me up with Jack Ford, who apparently lived up to George's standards. Nothing ever came of it, but I did, briefly, have some fantasies about living in the White House.

On December 15, just five days before the tour ended, we played Nassau Coliseum and everyone was excited because John Lennon was coming to the show. That morning in the hotel Barry took me aside.

"Since you know John, I want you to bring him to the hall," Barry said. "I'll organize a car and driver, but you're in charge of him."

I hadn't seen John and May since my days with Ringo at the beach house, and I was excited to spend some time with them before the show. When I showed up at their East Side apartment around six that evening, May greeted me with a big hug. I looked up to see John, dressed in a T-shirt and jeans, standing at the top of the stairs to the apartment's second level.

"Hey, Chris," he said, smiling down at me, "come up, come up. Gotta tell us all the gossip."

That made me smile. John wasn't usually one for small talk.

The apartment was sparsely furnished with a TV and king-size platform bed in the living room ("it doubles as a couch for guests," May said), but they both seemed so proud of their "home."

"Chris, come look at this terrace," she said, pulling me toward the French doors and the huge terrace overlooking the East River and the FDR Drive.

"Greta Garbo lives there," John said, pointing toward the building closest to the river.

"Have you ever seen her?" I asked.

"Occasionally, on the street when she's taking a walk," he said, already distracted. He walked back inside the apartment. May laughed. She seemed so happy.

"Chris! Come here, you have to see this!" John called out. He was pointing at the television and as I watched he started switching channels, stopping now and then to check out a program. "You won't believe this, there's just fucking amazing stuff here."

John Lennon had discovered cable television, and he was getting a huge kick out of it. Watching him, I realized that I'd never seen him that relaxed, even when he was lying out by the pool at the beach house, eyes closed, glass of ice water in his hand, contented smile on his face.

We had dinner at a tiny neighborhood restaurant about a block away from their apartment where they knew they wouldn't be bothered; they ate there so often they didn't even have to look at the menu.

"Wanna drink?" John asked.

"Sure," I said. "I'll have a Brandy Alexander."

"You're joking," John laughed, not unkindly. "You're not still into those, are you?" I knew what he meant: *You're not still hanging on to the past, are you?*

"Yeah, I'm still into them," I said, figuring I might as well be honest. I still was clinging to the memory of my time with Ringo.

John gave me a concerned look. I knew what that meant, too. *Let it go, Chris. It's over.*

•   •   •

We watched the show from the side of the stage, my favorite place of all because you can see the musicians and the audience all at once. John smiled and tapped his foot the whole time, like a proud older sibling watching his kid brother score a touchdown. After the show I went to my room to change my clothes and found a message from Maureen. She had just arrived from London and was waiting in the lobby. When I'd invited her to join me in New York, she was hesitant and noncommittal. Her divorce had just been finalized, and she was feeling fragile and insecure, trying to adjust to the freedom she never really wanted. But here she was at the hotel, and her timing couldn't have been better—George and John were right next door in the hospitality room.

Watching her tiny figure moving down the hallway toward me, I was suddenly overwhelmed with emotion. She was her usual vision in black, dressed from throat to ankle in layers of velvet and lace. Her pale white skin contrasted starkly with her dark clothing, and for a moment I imagined I was watching a tiny, beautiful vampiress floating down the corridor toward me. Oh, she was so little, so fragile and vulnerable. And so alone. I was filled with sadness and shame, feeling her loneliness like a cold draft that filled the hallway, wishing I could turn back the pages of time.

We hugged tightly, kissed each other's cheek, and settled down on the bed to talk. She was obviously exhausted from her transatlantic flight, but the nighttime had always been the right time for Maureen, so I knew she'd find a way to push through the exhaustion.

"Do you want a drink?" I asked.

"Oh, yes. That would be lovely."

I took her hand and gave a gentle little pull. "Let's go to the hospitality suite; it's only next door, and you can say hello to George and John."

"John is here, too?" Maureen said, a little anxiously.

"He was at the concert tonight with May."

Maureen closed her eyes for a moment, sighed deeply, and lightly touched her forehead. "No, no," she said, almost apologetically. "I'll just wait here, it will give me time to catch my breath. I'm knackered." She began rummaging through her black velvet purse, which I took as a sign that she was distressed. Maureen was such a paradox—a real force of nature, brutally honest and wholly herself, but also deeply shy and accustomed now to living in the shadows. She didn't like people looking at her, talking about her, especially now that she wasn't with Ringo, because he always made her feel safe. She could always hide behind Ringo.

"Okay, I'll go get the drinks and be right back." I stopped at the door and turned around. "Scotch and Coke?"

"Jack Daniel's and Coke," she said, smiling at me. She had changed drinks from the old Beatle standard and for some reason that brought home to me the fact that everything had changed.

The hospitality room was filled with people, but the music was soft and low, and everyone was talking quietly in little groups. George and John were deep in conversation—I didn't see May or Olivia, so they must have both called it a night—and I didn't want to intrude. I made my way to the bar, fixed two drinks, and headed back to my room.

"Hey, Chris, where are you going?" John said when I walked past.

"Maureen just flew in from London, and she's exhausted," I explained. "We're just going to talk in my room."

"Maureen is here?" they both said at the same time.

"Maybe I'll pop in later and say hello," John said.

Maureen and I settled into the pillows on the bed and talked. Mostly about Ringo.

"It was the drugs that caused the breakup," she said. "I always thought Richie was strong enough to deal with any drug. All those years he never let any drug ever get hold of him and when he thought it was, he'd stop immediately. I always admired that about him. But cocaine changes your brain. It made him paranoid. God's honest truth. It changed his brain. I hate cocaine."

We looked at each other for a moment. I was thinking about all the pain that she had been through, and remembering my role in causing some of it, but I think she was long past recriminations.

"Have you seen him?" I asked

"Just when he comes to see the children."

"Was the divorce difficult?" I said, knowing she wanted to talk but afraid to upset her.

"I've gone through madness," she said, leaving it at that.

We were halfway through our drinks when there was a knock on the door. It was George.

"Hello, Mo," he said, giving her an affectionate kiss on the cheek. "It's good to see you. What are you doing in New York?"

"I just wanted to get away. Sorry I missed your show tonight."

"Yeah, me, too," George said. "How long are you here?" I was struck by the friendly but somewhat formal way they talked. Who would have guessed at the passion that once consumed them and contributed to the ruin of their marriages?

"Don't know. Probably not long. The kids are with Stella, and I need to get back." Stella was the nanny who had been with the family since their first child, Zak, was born.

There was another knock on the door, and John walked in. He kissed Maureen on the cheek, and then gave her a big hug.

"When did you arrive?" he asked.

"A couple of hours ago," she said, looking over at me to make sure that I felt included in the conversation. "I came to see Chris."

We talked for at least an hour that night, George and John standing by the fireplace in my room, drinks mostly untouched on the mantel, Maureen and I sitting on the bed, our backs propped up against the pillows. After a while George and John sat down in the overstuffed chairs, settling back to listen as they talked about the old days, the good times, the "remember whens."

"Remember when we stayed in this very hotel and watched the fans screaming in the streets below?" John said.

"Yeah, we were hiding in the bathroom," George laughed, "never knowing if someone would climb through the window."

Maureen laughed, too, remembering. I sat on the bed with my legs folded underneath me, watching them, feeling a sense of wonder at the strength and intimacy of the connection that would always exist between them. I was an observer, not quite one of them, but close enough to be included. They were in *my* room at the Plaza Hotel. Imagine that:

George, John, and Maureen, three of the original group, reminiscing about old times in my hotel room. I held that moment close, framing it for later, knowing that it was one of those moments that if someone had said, *Chris, one day you will be in this exact place at this exact moment,* I would have told them they were crazy.

The final show was on December 20, and there was tension in the air as George and his band prepared to ascend the stage at Madison Square Garden. Ravi had just come offstage after performing to a less than enthusiastic crowd, and we were all a little nervous about this final show of shows.

"Paul's in the audience," Barry Imhoff whispered. "Here are his seat numbers. Go out and find him, see if he wants to come backstage."

"Paul McCartney?" I asked in surprise.

"No, Paul Revere, you schmuck." Sometimes Barry could be a real jerk.

This was Barry's half-assed idea, I knew that much. George would have figured that if Paul wanted backstage passes, he would have asked for them. But I had my orders and headed into the audience in search of Paul. I should have trusted my gut feelings.

Standing on the main floor some twenty rows from the stage looking at a sea of unfamiliar faces, with just minutes to go before George walked onto the stage, I searched for the seat numbers that Barry had given me. Two complete strangers were sitting in those seats. I looked back at the numbers and back at the faces, trying to figure out what was going on, and then I recognized Paul and Linda. They were in disguise, wearing wigs and makeup. Paul had a fake beard. I never would have recognized them if I hadn't known exactly where they were sitting.

I pushed my way past the people in the row behind, stepping on toes, excusing myself over and over again until I was directly behind them. I leaned down and touched Paul on the shoulder.

"Hi, guys," I said.

They jerked around, startled.

"Do you want to come backstage?" I said, and I knew from the looks on their faces that I had screwed up.

"Chris. Shhh," Linda whispered.

"Go away, Chris," Paul added, "before anyone knows we're here."

I backed out of there as fast as I could, trying not to step on feet, humiliated, furious with Barry, and angry with myself for not following my instincts. There I was with a tour pass proudly dangling from my blouse, announcing to the world that someone important might be in that row. I should have known better. I made a mistake and even now the memory makes me want to turn back the clock to the moment when Barry gave me the seat numbers and asked me to find Paul.

"No, Barry," I should have said, "I'm not going out there. If they want to come backstage, they know the way."

33

SANTANA

September–October 1975

The first stop was Birmingham, England, and the last stop was Paris. In between there were thirty gigs in twenty-six cities including London, Glasgow, Frankfurt, Copenhagen, Vienna, Zagreb, Belgrade, Zurich, and Amsterdam. Everywhere we went, even in smaller cities like Leverkusen, Linz, and Saarbrücken, Santana drew huge crowds. I loved that band. In all my days of touring, I never worked with sweeter, kinder, more humble, or hardworking people. Earth, Wind & Fire, the opening act, put on a dazzling show full of fabulous dance numbers and spectacular lighting effects, and although that group of musicians was a lot more demanding than Santana (and definitely not as humble), I became a big fan.

Bill Graham joined us halfway through the tour, and the more time I spent with him, the more I liked and admired him. I'll never forget a magical fall night in Munich, when we had drinks with Carlos at an open-air restaurant in the town's main square, and Bill talked about his childhood in Germany during the war. His parents died in the concentration camps, but he escaped to Paris and eventually to America. "I swore I'd never come back to Germany," he said, looking up at the spires of St. Peter's Church and the twin steeples of the Frauenkirche, "but here I am. And it is very, very beautiful."

It was beautiful, that night in Munich's Marienplatz, and there were other beautiful nights in other beautiful cities, but I was not happy. I was the advance person on this tour and my job was to keep one step ahead of the band, flying ahead to the next city to make sure everything was set up for their arrival. As soon as they arrived at the hotel, I'd hand over the keys to their rooms and jet out to the next town. That might sound glamorous, jet-setting all over Europe, but it wasn't. I spent the days working my butt off and the nights staring out my hotel room window at city streets that all looked the same. I didn't speak the languages, I ate all my meals by myself, and I spent most of my evenings alone in my hotel room yearning for a familiar face. I didn't like being separated from the band, the odd woman out. During those long, lonely days and nights, I often thought about Charlie Watts on the Stones tour, remembering how he'd stay up all hours of the night creating exquisitely detailed drawings of his hotel rooms. He hated being separated from his wife. He told me he'd drawn sketches of every hotel room he'd slept in.

When Santana played London's Hammersmith Odeon, I ran into Pattie and Eric. Almost a year had passed since the debacle in Jamaica and that awful night at John Entwistle's party. I was on my way to the hospitality room from the stage area when I passed by the backstage door.

"Hey, Chris," Ray, Santana's road manager, called out to me. Standing next to Ray were Eric and Pattie. "Would you take them up to the hospitality room so Eric can see Carlos?"

"Sure," I said, trying to calm the quaking that started at my toes and worked its way up to the top of my head. My smile, it seemed, was frozen on my face.

"Well, look who's here," Eric said, giving me a sincere smile. He must have forgotten all about Jamaica, I found myself thinking. But not Pattie. As I led them up three flights of stairs to the hospitality room, she kept her eyes focused on the stairs, completely ignoring me. I trudged along with an aching heart, wondering why my best friend (she may have given up on me, but I would never let her go) wouldn't even say a few friendly words to me. She must have decided I wasn't the kind of person she could trust.

That was a long, silent walk up those stairs and at one point I turned around to assure Pattie that we were almost there. She looked up at me, leaning forward slightly and squinting her eyes.

"Chris! Is that you?" she said. "Oh! I can't believe it! Sweetie, I am so sorry I didn't recognize you—I can't see a thing without my glasses!"

And just like that, we were friends again.

The last stop on the Santana tour was Paris. We stayed in a fabulous little hotel, and my room was up in the attic. I loved that room under the eaves with the little windows that opened up to the sky.

Two days before the tour ended, Barry Imhoff called.

"Hey, O'Dell, how are things going? Tell me about the tour." Barry and Bill Graham had parted company by then, and Barry had started his own promotion company. I might have completed two sentences about my experiences on the Santana tour when he interrupted me.

"Hey, look, I want you back here. I need you for the Dylan tour."

"Dylan?" I said. I had to gather my wits about me. Bob Dylan?

"Look, I want you to get on a flight as soon as that thing is over and get your ass to New York." I heard his emphasis on *that thing* and knew he was trying to steal me away from Bill Graham. I didn't have anything planned after Santana, though, and I knew Bill would support me. In fact, he'd tell me I was crazy if I didn't jump at a chance to work for Bob Dylan.

"Okay," I said, only briefly thinking about the fact that I wouldn't have time to go back to LA to pick through my wardrobe and get a change of clothes. Oh well.

I called Bill to tell him the news. He wasn't the least bit upset and, in fact, he suggested we fly back to New York together.

"I'll upgrade your ticket to first class and pay the difference," he said. I offered to book the tickets, but he said he'd handle everything. Now I was really excited. I loved flying first class, but how many people get to fly first class from Paris to New York seated next to legendary rock promoter Bill Graham?

Two days later we arrived at the airport to discover that there were no seats available in first class.

"But I booked first-class tickets for both of us," Bill said a little gruffly. He gave me a smile that said, *Don't worry, I can fix this.*

The ticket agent was flustered. Even if you didn't know who Bill Graham was, he was intimidating. "I'm sorry," she stammered.

"It's okay, don't worry, I'm fine in coach," I said.

"I booked both tickets in first class," Bill repeated, as if the woman hadn't heard him the first time.

She flushed red. "I'm very sorry, Mr. Graham, but we don't have a first-class ticket for you, either."

Bill was notorious for losing control and raging at people, and he put on a pretty good show that day, but even Bill Graham couldn't produce two first-class seats out of thin air. Our seats were in the center section in the back of the plane, and I have never seen anyone so miserable. He had the aisle seat, but he could not get comfortable. He got up, he sat down, he paced the aisles, he stretched, he sighed, he complained. The food was fucking awful. There wasn't enough fucking leg room (that was worth at least ten fucks). The seats were too fucking small. The toilets had a fucking line. The service was fucking lousy. Fuck this, fuck that.

That fucking flight was six hours of fucking hell.

Bill's limo was waiting at the curb. Stretching out his legs and leaning back against the soft leather with a dramatic sigh, Bill told the driver to drop him off at the Plaza Hotel before taking me to my destination. An hour or so later the limo dropped me off at the Rolling Thunder Tour offices near Grand Central Station, and the next tour was about to begin.

Bob Dylan stood by the door of the coffee shop, dressed in jeans, vest, and leather jacket. He had a raggedy, loose feel about him, as if his joints didn't quite fit into their sockets. He walked toward our table, shoulders hunched, fingers hooked into his jeans pockets, a reflective, loose, free sort of shuffle. So that's how a poet walks, I thought. Not that I knew all that much about poets.

I was sitting at a booth in the Gramercy Park Hotel coffee shop with Bobby Neuwirth and my fellow tour organizer Gary Shafner, drinking coffee and wondering what to order for breakfast. It was great to be working with Gary again, and Bobby was one of my favorites. An old friend of Dylan's and a gifted songwriter (he cowrote the Janis Joplin song "Mercedes Benz"), Bobby was responsible for assembling the backing band on the tour. He was kind to everybody and at the same time wasn't afraid to give anybody shit. You just had to love him for that.

Even after the long flight from Paris to New York, I was feeling good. I'd gone to bed early the night before and wasn't suffering from the usual jet lag. That's one of the good things about flying west—you wake up early and you don't feel so stuck in a time warp. I was also back in my element. As much as I appreciated the music and professionalism of Santana and Earth, Wind and Fire, I was thrilled to be working with a large tour again, and Dylan was the legend, the one musician that even the Beatles idolized. Touring with Dylan represented the full circle, an act of completion—now and forever I could say that I had worked with the Big Three.

Bob strolled over to our booth in his loose, gangly way and pulled up a chair. I took a deep breath. I was definitely in awe of Bob Dylan. As Derek put it once, "The Emperors were the Beatles in London. The Pope was Dylan in New York."

"Hey, Chris," Bobby Neuwirth said, "have you met Bob?"

"Yes, we've met a few times," I said.

Dylan raised an eyebrow at me.

"We met at the Isle of Wight when I arrived with the harmonicas and again at George and Pattie's suite at the Bangladesh concert."

"Oh yeah," he said. "Oh yeah." That was one of Dylan's quirks—he'd repeat things twice, almost as if he had to hear himself say it a second time in order to know that he'd said something at all.

"So how are you?" he said, putting his elbows on the table. "Are you on this tour?"

"Yeah," I said, amused that he had no idea I was working for him. "Barry hired me."

"Cool," he said. "Cool." Like I said, Dylan is a man of few words and most of those words are repeated. He'd take a word and use it well, or he'd take a word and use it twice. That was his way.

Dylan and Bobby started talking, and I faded into the background. I was good at that.

Gary and I took a last sip of coffee and were getting ready to leave for the tour office when I noticed a blond, good-looking, fresh-faced guy in a plaid checkered jacket walking toward the table. I was immediately attracted to him. He looked like he was still in college and it was obvious he wasn't part of the rock-and-roll scene—he just had too much of the farm boy look to him. His face was smooth and clear, innocent and wide eyed in a way that you didn't see too often in the rock-and-roll world. He hadn't been traumatized by the lifestyle, that was for sure.

He sat down next to Dylan, and they started talking about a film. I listened in, hearing bits and pieces and trying to figure out the relationship. Dylan talked to him as an equal, clearly deferring to him a lot. "Do you think we should . . ." Dylan said, leaning toward him and creating a space that included just the two of them, shutting the rest of us out.

Out on the street, hailing a taxi, I asked Gary who he was.

"Oh, that's Sam Shepard. He's a playwright. He's written a bunch of plays, and people say he's got great talent. He's writing the script for the film Bob is making about the tour."

I looked back over my shoulder, just to get one more look at him. He was so young. And so damn cute. As always, I could just hear Maureen laughing at me. "You've got to be kidding me!" she'd say, taking a puff of her cigarette and exhaling it in amused disgust. "Cute! What kind of word is that?"

Starting a new tour is like beginning a new job, and those first few days are always the most stressful. My insecurities unfailingly flared up and didn't settle down until I began to feel comfortable with the band, the road crew, and the rest of the tour staff. I put up a good front by acting confident and being assertive, but the truth is that in the beginning I felt awkward and out of place because I was the new kid trying to win them over. "Who's she? What's she doing here?" people would be wondering, and I had to walk right up, introduce myself, and let them know why I was there and what I could do for them. I had just a few days before the tour officially began to figure out who was close to Bob and who wasn't, who might cause trouble and who I could call on for help, who drank too much and who abstained, who was sleeping with who, and on and on it went.

I slipped into my job. I use the word *slipped* knowingly because that's exactly what I would do, just sort of slip into situations and conversations, picking up the vibe of the tour. I had to figure out where the trust could be built, and the way I did that was to talk to the band members and roadies, find out their likes and dislikes, discover what interests we might have in common, and do everything I could to simplify their lives while on tour. "How's it going?" I'd say. I didn't want to jump in too fast. If somebody needed something, I'd get it for them. If one of the band members said, "I need a Coke," I'd say, "I know just where to find one." If I ran into someone in the lobby who told me they couldn't sleep all night because of a faulty air conditioner or a noisy next-door neighbor, I'd say, "Let me deal with that." If someone needed to talk, I'd stop what I was doing and listen. I made myself useful, and I was always watching, always aware of what was going on around me.

I didn't see much of Bob Dylan the week before the tour began. He'd appear and then disappear, and you wouldn't have a clue where he came from or where he went. But when he was there, with you, talking to you, he was really *there,* focusing all his attention on you. One night, just before we left on tour, I stayed late in the tour office typing up some changes to the itinerary, a page-per-day schedule that listed the hotels, show locations, time, and travel distances. The detailed itinerary was a top-secret affair—only Bob, Louie Kemp, Barry Imhoff, Gary Shafner, and a few key members of the tour personnel (myself included) knew the whole itinerary. The band and the rest of the touring company received the schedule in segments, just a day or two before the next show. The point was to create an aura of mystery around the tour and attract media attention. The tickets went on sale a few days prior to the concert and were advertised solely through posters and handbills. That strategy worked wonders—they sold out within hours.

I heard someone walk into the room and, assuming it was Barry Imhoff or Gary Shafner, I kept pounding away at the keys of the electric typewriter.

"Hi," Bob Dylan said, pulling a chair over to my desk and slumping into it. "So have you seen George lately?"

Startled by his voice, it took a few seconds for me to respond. "Not since his tour a year ago," I said.

"I really like George," he said, reaching into his jacket pocket and pulling out a cigarette.

I nodded my head. I liked George, too.

"So, I was thinking about it. I remember you from the Isle of Wight." He turned his head and smiled at me, sideways. "I can't believe I forgot my harmonicas. That was cool when you flew in on the helicopter."

"Yeah, that was pretty cool," I agreed. I wasn't really sure how to talk to Bob, so I just followed his lead.

"That was a weird show," he said. "I hadn't performed in a long time, and I was pretty nervous."

"You didn't seem nervous," I said, hoping to reassure him.

"Yeah?" he turned his head to the side and looked at me, narrowing his eyes, measuring my honesty. Then he seemed to relax. "Well, that's good. But I sure felt it."

He laughed, then, almost shyly, and averted his eyes. "I'm glad you're on the tour," he said. "Any friend of George's is a friend of mine."

34

ROLLING THUNDER

October 1975–Spring 1976

Once the buses and campers rolled out of Gramercy Park in New York City, heading to Plymouth, Massachusetts, for rehearsals and the first two shows at the War Memorial Auditorium, we all got wrapped up in the excitement. The Rolling Thunder tour felt like a three-ring circus with extra added attractions. Actors and actresses, poets and playwrights, friends and family members joined us at various stops along the way. Joan Baez was with us the whole time, Joni Mitchell joined the tour for the last three weeks, Allen Ginsberg made several appearances, Bruce Springsteen, Patti Smith, and Mimi Fariña attended the New Haven concert on November 13, and Woody Guthrie's ghost haunted every concert when Bob would sing the very last song, "This Land Is Your Land." Sideshows included a visit to Jack Kerouac's grave in Lowell, Massachusetts, a Native American sunrise ceremony at Niagara Falls led by Rolling Thunder himself, and the prison concert for Rubin "Hurricane" Carter in Trenton, New Jersey, where fans actually tried to break into the prison to see Dylan perform.

Every night I'd write, copy, and distribute a newsletter (I started writing newsletters on George's tour a year earlier), letting everyone know what was happening the next day. *Wake-up call at 10:30 a.m., luggage pickup at 11:15 a.m., meet in lobby at noon, buses depart at 12:15, arrival in Worcester, Massachusetts at 4:00 p.m., show at Memorial Auditorium 8 p.m.* I added little jokes and bits of gossip to the newsletter to liven it up, things like "Who was seen sneaking into room 232 last night?" or "Who stole the bottle of Scotch out of the dressing room?" Then people started slipping juicy little notes under my door telling me that so-and-so did this-or-that, things started to get out of hand, and I had to tamp it down. When I refused to print some gossip about my relationship with playwright Sam Shepard, there was a fierce outcry about censorship. Eventually that blew over.

I almost always had a boyfriend on tour. That was just the way it was. You can't travel with a group of people who you see every single day, virtually every hour of the day, for weeks or months without finding someone who you find attractive. But it was more than mere attraction. Touring is filled with the stress of packing and unpacking, moving from city to city, and going from show to show, all the while existing on a few hours' sleep. Relationships on the road are an outlet. You're giving, giving, giving, and what do you get back? The music. The excitement. The adrenaline rush of it all. But it's exhausting and somehow you have to relax and let go of the tension.

A young, single woman on tour with a lot of men is going to find someone to spend her nights with. But I learned early on in my touring career that I had to draw a firm boundary between excitement and commitment. If I got too involved—if I wasn't careful—a tour romance could take over my world. When it got to the point where I was spending too much time picking out an outfit, fussing with my makeup, or holding my breath with anticipation because I couldn't wait to get to the show to see some guy and then holding it again until the show was over because I couldn't wait to be alone with him—well, if it got to that point, I was too far gone. I couldn't forget my role, my job, my career. I couldn't make another person my main concern when my absolute first priority was my work.

Nevertheless, tour romances were a way of life. On the Crosby, Stills, Nash and Young tour I fell for Guillermo, an adorable Argentinean who was Stephen Stills's roadie. Guillermo taught me that you can brush your teeth and blow your nose at the same time you're taking a shower. *God,* I thought, *that is so damn efficient!* That's how you have to think on tour if you're going to get any sleep at all. On George's tour I had a crush on Jack Ford, and on the Santana tour I got involved with German rock promoter Mike Scheller (who would come back into my life several years later). And now, on the Dylan tour, Sam Shepard was making my heart beat faster. There was something about that farm-boy innocence, the shy, self-effacing way he had about him that really got to me. I knew he was married, but, well, this was a tour, after all, and we both knew the relationship would end when the tour was over, so somehow I convinced myself it would be okay. I should have known better.

"I don't know what I'm doing here," Sam said one night, about a week into our romance. We were staying in a charming inn in Springfield, Massachusetts, and just the day before he'd celebrated his thirty-second birthday.

"It's really weird," he said, shaking his head in a confused way. "Bob wants me to do a script for a film, but everything is so disorganized and chaotic. I don't know how to relate to all this stuff."

"Stuff?" I said.

"You know, this rock-and-roll lifestyle." He hung his head, his long, lean body slumping forward a bit. Sam was born in Illinois, studied agriculture at a junior college, and his first play was titled *Cowboy.* He loved horses, wide open spaces, and having lots of time to himself to think and write. He was disciplined, made deadlines, showed up for work on time. And he was accustomed to interacting with actors and directors, not roadies and rock stars. The tour was much too loose for him, too spontaneous, a play with a hundred scenes going on at once, and he was just one person out of a cast of hundreds. He didn't have the foggiest idea how to make it work.

"You know, nobody shows up to film when they're supposed to, and it's almost like I should write the dialogue after it happens," he said. "It's so different from the way I usually work."

"But Sam," I said, remembering a conversation from a few days earlier and trying to get a smile out of him, "you told me you wanted to be a rock-and-roll star."

"Yeah," he said, shaking his head in that little-boy way of his, "but I just wanted to play music. I didn't want to do *this*."

A few weeks later, we were in Niagara Falls for two shows. After the evening show I looked all over the place for Sam. I couldn't find him anywhere. He wasn't in his hotel room. He didn't answer his phone. Nobody had seen him.

The next morning I was headed downstairs for breakfast when I heard someone call out, "Have you seen Sam?"

"Oh yeah, he was hanging with Joni Mitchell all evening," someone else said.

Joni Mitchell? I thought. My heart was sinking. When I saw Sam later that morning, I ignored him. He looked guilty. A few nights later in Rochester, New York, he didn't show up at the hospitality room after the show. That was where I'd usually meet him and then we'd spend the rest of the evening together.

Oh no, I thought, maybe this thing with Joni is more than a flirtation. I went up to his room and knocked on the door.

"Who's there?"

"It's Chris."

Ten seconds. Thirty seconds. A minute passed.

He finally opened the door and then retreated to the bed where he lay down, hands underneath his head, looking at me with a sweet little smile. I sat down at the foot of the bed, my back to the door.

"What's going on, Sam? Why aren't you downstairs?"

"I'm tired. I've just been lying around here."

Behind me I heard the door to his room open and close.

"Oh, what's that?" he said, all innocent like, looking over my shoulder.

"Sam, who was here?" I knew perfectly well who it was. Joni had been hiding in the bathroom, and when my back was to the door, she sneaked out behind me.

"No one," he lied.

"You know what?" I said on my way out the door, "You're a shit."

As we were loading up the bus the next day, I took a seat up front, on the couch just behind the driver. The band members were getting onboard, settling in for the ride, when Bobby Neuwirth suddenly jumped on the bus, full of his usual piss and vinegar. He stopped right in front of me.

"Hey, Chris," Bobby said, looking down at me and talking loud enough for everyone in the front of the bus to hear. "You know Sam's having it on with Joni. You need to take care of yourself."

The blood pulsed through me, turning my face scarlet and making my stomach twist and turn. I slunk down in my seat, mortified. My ears were burning, and all I could hear was the pounding in my head. Bobby and a few others stared at me for a few seconds, uncertain how I'd react. Then they shuffled off to their seats.

My thoughts were spinning as fast as the tires. How crazy is this? I kept thinking. Here I am having an affair with a married man, and now he's sneaking around with someone else. What could be worse than a guy who cheats on his wife with you and then turns around and cheats on you? With Joni Mitchell, of all people—how could I compete with her? Everyone in the band knew, and they were trying to tell me to get out of the situation. Shit. I was fucked. Busted.

Okay, Chris, I thought, taking a deep breath and staring out the window, this is a tour romance after all, and it will end because tour romances always end. The tour doesn't need this kind of drama and you don't either. I was talking to myself. It was one thing to have a tour romance if it replenished you and gave you something fun to do every night, but this was a bad situation, too many people were involved, and if the band knew about it, then everyone knew about it.

I wasn't about to screw up my job for some guy. By the time the bus pulled into the next town, I'd made up my mind. I withdrew from the competition. Joni could have him.

Things settled down. I ignored Sam, avoided Joni whenever I could, and concentrated on doing my job. Several days later in Bangor, Maine,

I knocked on Joni's dressing room door. The tour was leaving for Canada right after the show and I had to let everyone know what the plans were. Sam, to my great delight, was going back to New York for a while.

"Come in!" she called out. She was sitting at her dressing table, the classic backstage table with the lightbulbs all around the edges of the mirror, getting ready to go onstage. I said a pleasant hello, asked her how she was doing, handed her the itinerary, and prepared to leave.

"Chris," she said, "can you sit down for a minute?" She motioned to a chair by the wall. Well, I didn't feel like sitting down. It was awkward being with her, and I wanted to back out of that room, fast. But I sat down in the chair.

"Has the show started yet?" she asked.

"Yeah, T-Bone Burnett's doing his song right now." Joni always came on midway through the show.

"How are you doing?" she said, putting her makeup on the table and swiveling in her chair to look at me. Oh, shit, I thought. She wants to have "a talk." I wasn't real comfortable with that idea. All I wanted to do was get out of there.

"I'm fine," I said cheerily.

"You know, I really admire the way that you're handling this thing," she said. Of course, I knew what "thing" she was referring to.

"You just seem so confident and able to deal with this," she said. "I really respect that. I wish I could do the same."

I was stunned. Here we were, two women vying for the same guy, but instead of doing that catty, competitive female "I've got him," or "I hate you for having him" thing, she was being real. *Real.* That really got to me.

Of course, we both knew deep down that neither one of us "had" Sam—if he could cheat on his wife with me and then cheat on me with Joni, he was going to cheat on Joni sometime, too. What a crazy, conflicted situation: we were both head over heels for a man who had a wife waiting for him at home.

"Joni, you have no idea how much I appreciate what you just said," I said.

And that's as far as we went with it. A few days later Joni sang the song "Coyote" for the first time. It's a song about Sam Shepard and how he had "a woman at home and another woman down the hall" and he wanted her anyway. I was the woman down the hall. I loved the lines Joni wrote about how we licked our wounds and took temporary lovers, using "pills and powders" to get us through the drama.

She was right. I had my pills, my powders, and my whiskey to help me through the drama of those hard days and nights. I knew I had to march forward—the show must go on.

But that thing with Sam hurt like hell.

35

DANCING WITH DYLAN

November 1975

The backstage of the Civic Center in Augusta, Maine, looked like every backstage of every other hall we ever played. I followed the musicians into their dressing room, a cavernous area with bare white walls and tile floors. The local promoter had done his job, following the contract requirement to set up a table with alcoholic beverages, sodas, and snacks of cheese, cold cuts, and crackers. Just having the food there helped with the pre-show nerves although Dylan, his band members, and the other musicians along for the ride on the Rolling Thunder Revue tour rarely ate much of anything before a show. They might grab a piece of cheese as they walked past the table, toss back a shot of whiskey, or pick up a beer and carry it around, but the big meal always came after the show, when we returned to the motel.

I walked by the snack table and picked up a few carrots and a piece of cheese. I was hungry—no, I was starving. I hadn't eaten all day. If I had to sum up in three words a day on the road with rock musicians, I'd say "anxiety run wild." From the time I woke up until the time I finally fell asleep, adrenaline was pumping through my body, helped along by maybe a dozen cups of coffee and a pack of Marlboros. After several weeks on the road, on the go from morning to night and on call twenty-four hours a day, seven days a week, I had the feeling that if I stopped moving, I'd crash completely.

I grabbed a few more carrots and slumped down in the chair next to singer-songwriter T-Bone Burnett, the guitarist who sang one of my favorite numbers of the show, Warren Zevon's "Werewolves of London."

"Hey, Chris, what's in the newsletter for tonight?" joked the lanky Texan with the smooth, throaty voice.

"I'm not telling," I said, and we both laughed. He knew that I'd never reveal the contents of the nightly newsletter before I distributed it.

He gave my arm a friendly little push, we talked for a while longer, and then it was time to make my way around the room. That was my pre-show routine, checking in with the musicians to see if they needed anything, joking around with them, and generally trying to create a relaxed atmosphere before the show.

On this particular night, with just a little over a week left on the tour, everyone was in a mellow mood except for Rob Stoner, the bass player. Intense and always slightly on edge before a show, Rob took his job as bandleader seriously. I put my hand on his arm as I was leaving the room, hoping that a simple touch would help calm him down a little. He looked up and smiled, appreciative of the attention.

I was walking down the fluorescent-lit hallway, headed for the women's dressing room, when Gary Shafner came running toward me.

"Chris!" Gary said. He seemed slightly out of breath. "Bob needs you in his dressing room."

"Okay," I said, changing my direction. Reassured that I was on top of it, Gary hurried off on another errand. Gary was always in a rush, and the dark circles under his eyes told the story about how little sleep he was getting at night. If I ever needed to find him, no matter what time of the day or night, Gary was awake and nearby, ready and willing to help in any emergency. I don't know what I would have done without him.

I knocked on Bob's door.

"Hi, Chris," Louie Kemp said, opening the door just a few inches, looking at me almost suspiciously, and then opening the door a little wider to look from side to side, checking out the hallways. *Oh geez,* I thought, *here we go again*. I wanted to grab Louie by the shoulders, force him to look me in the eye, and say, "Hey, Louie, this isn't the CIA," but I did what I always did, waited patiently for him to allow me entry into the hallowed halls of Bob's dressing room. Louie was Bob's childhood friend turned advocate and protector, the keeper of the door, the loyal sidekick who made sure that Bob was protected from the riffraff and received the royal treatment he deserved. Louie was always chasing after Barry Imhoff, the tour promoter. With his monotonous droning voice, wiry energy, and unpredictable growl, Louie was like a dog at Barry's heels, barking and yapping about every little detail that did or didn't or might or might not go wrong. Louie's obsessive overprotectiveness sometimes drove me crazy.

"Hey, Chris, come on in," Bob called out. Louie stood aside and I walked over to the couch where Bob was sitting. A makeshift dressing table stood against the opposite wall, and several fold-out chairs were scattered haphazardly around the room. Dressed in a black leather jacket, black vest, scarf, and white shirt, Bob was strumming his guitar and looking at a copy of the set list, which detailed the order of the songs for the show.

"Hey," Bob said, looking up from the list, "could you sew a button on a shirt?"

"Sure," I said. The shirt was draped across the chair next to him with one of those travel sewing kits sitting on top. I began threading the needle.

"So, hey, Chris, what's going on?" Bob asked. I knew he wanted me to share any little gossip I might have heard about the tour from the other musicians, the promoters, the roadies, or the actors, poets, and filmmakers who were accompanying us or dropping in along the way. He was just checking in. In some ways he reminded me of George with his childlike curiosity about all the goings-on around him.

"Everything is great, I love the show," I reassured him, keeping my voice cheery and animated. Bob wasn't one to be coddled, and he was more aware than anyone of the complicated dynamics of this tour, but if there were problems to discuss, we'd talk about them after the show, and, in most cases, Louie would take care of them.

I tied a knot in the thread, made sure the button was securely fastened, stood up, and handed Bob the shirt.

"There you go, all done," I said, feeling extra proud of my handiwork. I wasn't exactly the domestic type.

"Hey, thanks," he said, absentmindedly reaching for the shirt. His mind was elsewhere as he lit a cigarette and became absorbed in a discussion with Louie about journalist Larry "Ratso" Sloman, who was pissed off because the local security person didn't allow him backstage. They were laughing about the whole thing when I left them.

In the ten minutes I'd spent in Bob's dressing room, the atmosphere in the hallway and dressing rooms had changed dramatically. It felt to me as if a guitar string had been tuned just a little too tight and that taut energy found its way under everybody's skin, setting our nerves on edge. Roadies hustled around on the stage double checking the electrical wires and sound equipment. Musicians gathered at the side of the stage, mentally gearing themselves up for the show. Gary Shafner appeared and just as suddenly disappeared, big rings of perspiration under his armpits. The lights in the hall were dimming, and we all knew what that meant. The show was about to begin.

I waited until the band was onstage and then went to one of my favorite places to watch the performance, just in front of the barricades that prevented overly enthusiastic fans from jumping onto the stage. I have to admit that sometimes, standing there, I'd feel a slight twinge of grandiosity, that feeling of being "important" and somehow set apart. From my position right below and off to the side of the stage, I'd watch Bob do his reckless saunter up to the microphone and feel the wave of excitement that swelled from the front row to the balcony as people in the audience realized that the guy with his face painted white and his hat pulled down low over his eyes was Bob Dylan. I'd watch the band play the songs I'd heard so many times, outdoing themselves on some nights and other times making mistakes that only those of us on tour would notice—like when one of the musicians forgot to come in for a solo or somebody messed up on the lyrics. Often they'd smile that knowing smile at one another, aware that the audience really didn't catch the mistake.

After a while I'd head backstage to relax, flip through *People* magazine, make a few phone calls, and have a few drinks. But on that night, like most other nights, I made sure to be out front again when Bob sang my favorite songs, "One More Cup of Coffee," "Sara," and "Just Like a Woman." I had watched the show so many times that by the end of the tour I'd memorized (and could imitate almost perfectly) Bob's movements and mannerisms—the way he'd lean toward the microphone when he sang "Just Like a Woman" in such a sweet, moving voice, and then swing back away from the mike, swiveling on his right foot in a big sweeping motion with his guitar held high as he turned to face the band. His phrasing on that song was so childlike and the way he sang, "Just like a little *gurll*," always made me smile.

In the bus on the way back to the hotel, we were on our usual after-show high. Everyone talked too fast, laughed too loud, and drank too much from the well-stocked bar at the front of the bus. Believe me, that bus was designed for comfort. From front to back there were couches lining the walls, a kitchenette with a little table, bunk beds, and a tiny bathroom. Nobody was using the bunks that night, though—we were all too revved up.

Gary was waiting for us in the hotel lobby and directed everyone to the hallway leading to the hospitality room where the food and booze were set up. I helped Gary direct traffic and then escaped to my room for a few minutes to unload all my stuff. I always carried a big purse filled with itineraries, a notebook for jotting down bits of information, and the jewelry, watches, wallets, and other items the musicians gave me for safekeeping when they went on stage.

Checking myself out in the mirror before leaving the room, I said "oh God" out loud. Mascara was smudged under my eyes, and my face looked drained of color. I spent a few minutes primping. It was my time to relax and have fun after the show, and I wanted to look good. After dabbing a little sandalwood oil (a favorite fragrance from Friar Park days) on my wrists and neck, I went downstairs to join everyone for an hour or so before going to bed. It was already after midnight.

I couldn't believe the size of the room the motel staff had set aside for us. In most motels or hotels, we were given a small hospitality suite for the after-show gathering, but that night we met in a huge conference room complete with tables, a dance floor, and music playing on the loudspeakers. One long table was filled with chafing dishes with chicken, roast beef, potatoes, and vegetables, and another table was loaded up with just about every kind of booze you could imagine along with mixers, sodas, and buckets of ice.

Bob showed up with his wife, Sara, and his mother, Beatty Zimmerman. I adored Beatty and often wondered how Bob could be related to her—she was such a joyful, silver-haired lady, so warm and affectionate, so social and uninhibited. He was the moon, it seemed, to her sun. "How are you?" she'd say, looking up into your eyes (she couldn't have been much more than five feet tall), her hand clasping yours. "Is everything okay? Are you enjoying yourself?"

Sara, like Bob, was much harder to read. She tended to avoid big groups, standing off by herself or engaging in one-on-one conversations, usually with Bobby Neuwirth, Sam Shepard, or Louie. She seemed much more comfortable with men than women. Sara had the biggest, saddest eyes. She always appeared serene and composed, but I sensed a tension underneath, a kind of anxiety or shyness that separated her from the rest of us. Watching her at these gatherings and thinking back to the first time I'd met her at the Isle of Wight, I'd find myself thinking that she was becoming more and more like Bob. She had the same aura of mystery and elusiveness. When she was talking to you, or more likely listening to you, you felt that she was right there with you—like Bob. But when she wandered off, you kept your distance, respectful of her privacy. Her boundaries were clear and firm, just like Bob's.

We ate and drank, and although I was dead tired from the nonstop activity of the day, I didn't want to leave. The music added to the party atmosphere, and I was having too much fun watching Bob joke around with the other musicians and listening to the bantering back and forth. Winding down after a show is not about having a serious conversation. Someone might say something like, "Hey, did you notice when Mick's guitar string broke in the middle of the song?" or "Did anybody else think that it took a while for the audience to warm up tonight?" but that was about the extent of it. The show was over, we had another show in a day or two, and it was time to relax, forget about our jobs and the stress of the day, and enjoy ourselves for a few hours.

I remember looking at my watch around 2:00 a.m. and noticing that the only people left in the room were Bob, Louie, Mick Ronson, Bobby Neuwirth, and Gary Shafner. We were all sitting at a round table, which was littered with ashtrays, wineglasses, and dishes that were, for the most part, scraped clean. A slow song was playing in the background when Bob turned to me and reached for my hand.

"Wanna dance?" he said. I just stared at him for half a second, suddenly feeling nervous and a little flustered. I'd never seen Bob dance before. My heart started pounding, I could feel the blood rushing in my ears, and I remembered how I used to feel at those junior high school dances when a really cute guy walked up and asked me to dance, and all sorts of thoughts went rushing through my head like, Are my hands sweating? Am I going to step on his toes? Does he like me? Do I like him? And the worst of all, Did somebody dare him to come over and ask me to dance?

"Oh," I stammered. "Okay."

I put out my hand and he pulled me close, his arm around my waist, holding me tight. I literally felt the room spinning, for in that moment I feared that all my professional rules were at risk, especially my One Big Rule about romances on tour: *never* get involved with the Big Guy. My job was to smooth things over, not complicate matters, and I had a reputation to protect. I wasn't willing to risk my career for a one-night stand with the star of the show.

But there I was on the dance floor of the Howard Johnson's motel conference room in Augusta, Maine, with Bob Dylan's cheek next to mine. I wasn't thinking about how famous he was (or that his wife, Sara, and his mother, Beatty, were asleep in their rooms upstairs) but only how incredibly sexy he was. My brain, at least the part of it that's responsible for impulse control, was on hold while my hormones were going bonkers. As I was trying to sort out my emotions, Dylan's bad-boy image stimulated a schoolyard fantasy. I imagined Bob Dylan as the leather-jacketed rebel smoking a cigarette in the schoolyard, the one who stands off to the side by the chain-link fence with his hands in his jean pockets, looking with a sly, knowing smile at the cute cheerleader who suddenly finds herself swooning because he's looking at her, and he knows something she doesn't know, and she knows she's supposed to stay away from him.

I felt Bob's breath on my neck, his hair against my cheek, his lips brushing lightly against my ear.

"You smell good," he whispered.

I smiled, happy that I'd remembered to dab some sandalwood oil on my neck before I left my room.

"Thank you," I said. What else was I going to say? What do you say when someone says you smell good? I couldn't say he smelled good. He'd been onstage all night under those hot lights. He didn't smell bad, but I couldn't say he smelled good.

When the music stopped and we released the hold we had on each other, I looked around the room. We were alone. I thought about his wife upstairs, and I knew at that moment that if she hadn't been in the motel that night, I might have ended up in bed with Bob.

"I guess I'd better go," I stammered.

Bob smiled, that sideways grin that said, "I know that you know I'm making a pass at you, and you know that I know that you're interested," and then he gave me a little kiss, not quite on the lips, and we said good night.

The next day, it was as if nothing had happened. Around noon I walked down to the lobby. Bob and Louie appeared to be having a serious conversation, and I kept my distance, watching them out of the corner of my eye. Bob didn't even notice I was there, and I found myself admiring him for his ability to tune out the world around him. He would literally look *through* you and when that happened, you felt pretty insignificant, as if you didn't even exist. He wasn't trying to be mean or cruel, it was just that he got lost in thought. Sometimes, though, I think that freezing stare was his way of telling people to keep their distance. "Stay away," it said, loud and clear.

I wondered what it would be like to be able to look through people like that, to get so deep inside your own head that you didn't notice all the little details going on around you. I couldn't afford to lose my focus, of course—I was a detail person, it was part of my job description. I had to be aware of everything, attentive to everyone's needs, and as a result I spent an awful lot of my time watching and waiting—waiting for the band to straggle downstairs and get on the bus, waiting for the bus to get to the next town, waiting for the luggage to arrive, waiting for the show to begin, waiting for the show to be over, waiting to do whatever it was that someone needed done.

So I was standing in the lobby waiting for Bob to finish his conversation with Louie when I decided to play a little game. I stared off into space, pretending to be lost in my own little world. After a while Bob noticed me, but I ignored him, looking around the lobby as if I didn't recognize a soul, mimicking his pattern of freezing people out as if they didn't exist. I looked in his direction and stared right through him.

He was watching me, his head cocked to the side, eyebrows pulled together in a *What's-up-with-you?* kind of look. I think he knew I was playing some kind of game, because he looked amused as he walked toward me.

"Hi, Chris," he said. "Aren't you talking today?"

"Oh, hi, Bob, I didn't see you there," I said. *Gotcha!* I thought. I wish I had a picture of the look on his face. He nodded his head and smiled; if he'd had a hat on, I think he would have tipped it at me. It felt good to be back on solid ground after the night before, to know our respective roles and yet feel comfortable enough to be playful with each other. As I waited in the lobby for the next leg of the journey, I felt proud of myself for proving once again that I was adept at dealing with famous people with complicated egos. I wasn't afraid of them or overawed by their stardom. I could see the person behind the cloak of fame, but— and this was key—I never, ever forgot that the cloak was there. The strategy I followed was to be patient, waiting and watching, noting their likes and dislikes, observing the way they interacted with others, and then adapting my behavior to match theirs. When I had demonstrated my worth and proved I could be trusted, I stepped out of the shadows and felt comfortable being myself.

Many years later my son Will, eleven or twelve years old at the time, told me how he made friends at his new school. "I watch the kids I want to hang out with, and then I begin to act like them until they accept me," he told me. "Then I can act like myself again."

Gee, I thought, I wonder where he learned that!

We all had our picture taken in a big group photo before the last show at Madison Square Garden, and Bob gave each of us the same parting gift—a medallion. Mine was engraved with an eagle, wings spread, head bowed, and embedded with two gemstones, a topaz on the left representing the sun setting and an opal on the right depicting the moon rising. The words "Rolling Thunder Revue 1975" were engraved on the back of the medallion. Dylan handed out the gifts individually, personally thanking each of us for our part on the tour.

I flew back to Los Angeles a few days later, once again at loose ends, but not in any real hurry to seek full-time employment. Just as I was getting used to sleeping in my own bed and reconnecting with old friends, Barry Imhoff called.

"Okay, O'Dell," he said in his growly way, "Bob's going to do another tour and we want you there."

I thought about that for a minute. I'd done two tours back to back, Santana and Rolling Thunder, the Sam thing had gotten my emotions all roiled up, and just thinking about going on the road again made my bones ache. But, then again, this wasn't any old tour.

"I really need more money, Barry," I said. My price for the other tours was five hundred dollars a week and thirty dollars per diem for a total of seven hundred and ten dollars a week. Now in 1975 that was pretty good pay. But at that stage of the game, I figured I'd done all these tours, and I hadn't had a raise in a long time. I wanted more money, and if I didn't get it, I wasn't going to do the tour.

"How much?" he asked.

"Seven hundred fifty a week plus per diem."

"Well, I can't pay you that."

"Well, then, I can't go on the tour."

"Come on, O'Dell, don't be a schmuck."

"Sorry, Barry, unless you pay me seven hundred fifty a week, I'm not going."

"I can't do it," Barry grumbled. We said an amiable good-bye, but I had some doubts about whether I'd done the right thing. I was kind of sad about not going on the tour, but at the same time it felt good to stand up for myself. I deserved that raise. I'd gained a lot of experience in the last two years, and I was one of the only females around doing this kind of work. I'd done major tours and pulled them off. With that experience should come some money.

Halfway through the tour, Barry called again.

"Okay, O'Dell. We need you."

"Will you pay me $750 week plus per diem?"

"Yes, yes," he said rather impatiently, "just get your ass on a plane and get out here. Things are kind of crazy."

It was a bizarre tour that never really got off the ground. The carnival was over, and I for one was glad to see it end.

A few years later when I was working again as a travel agent, Bob was on tour again. I'd done all the travel arrangements for the tour and decided to fly to the East Coast and see how it was going. I convinced Maureen to fly to New York and attend the concert with me. Maureen adored Bob Dylan, and I had a little fantasy going on in my head about getting them together. By this time Bob and Sara had split up, and I thought Maureen and Bob might make an interesting couple. Bob invited us into his dressing room when he heard Maureen was there, and I thought my little plan might work. But after the concert, when I tried to talk Maureen into going to the hotel bar where Bob and a small group of people from the tour were meeting to unwind, Maureen shook her head.

"No, no. I'll just stay in my room," she said as she filled her glass with Jack Daniel's and Coke and stared at the television. "You go. Don't worry about me." I tried my best to talk her into it, but Maureen had become even more reclusive after the divorce and in the days that followed in New York, I realized how deeply depressed she was, drinking, chain-smoking, staying in her room most of the day.

So I went to the bar by myself, had a few drinks, and ended up talking to Bob. We were deep into a conversation about something, I have no idea what, when he asked me for a cigarette. Fifteen minutes later he asked me for another cigarette. And then another, but by that time I was out.

"You want to go to my room?" Bob asked. "I have some cigarettes there."

"Sure," I said.

I think I knew what was going to happen. We walked into the bedroom and I sat down on the bed. He disappeared for a moment and came back holding a picture of himself. He looked really young with his little-boy face surrounded by beautiful curls. I'd guess the picture was taken when he was in his early twenties.

"Somebody gave this to me the other night," he said, handing the photograph to me with a perplexed look on his face.

I took the photograph and studied it for a moment, then looked up at him. I wasn't sure what he wanted me to say.

"Did I really ever look like that?" he said. "Was I ever really that person?"

I found the whole thing kind of weird. I didn't know Bob well enough to understand what he was asking, but it seemed to me that he felt as if he were looking at someone else. I wondered if he wanted me to connect the Dylan in the present—the person I had come to know— with this young man in the photograph. Did he want to talk about the time that had passed? Did he want to be reassured that he really was the same person who was framed in the picture? I almost got the sense that he wanted to go back in time, back to the beginning, before he was so famous. Or maybe it was just Bob Dylan's way of making small talk.

"Well, you were a lot younger then," I said hoping that would end the conversation.

He put the picture on the night table next to the bed and sat down next to me. "I'm tired," he said. "Wanna lie down?"

And it just kind of went from there.

36

PATTIE'S WEDDING

March 1979

After all the mega tours—the Stones, George Harrison, CSNY, Santana, Dylan—I kept wondering what might come my way next. That's how I was back then—a typical Pisces, floating down the stream and letting the currents pull me along, trusting that life would take me where it wanted me to go, knowing that something interesting might be waiting just around the bend. I never tried to push the river.

So, from 1976 to 1979, I settled down in LA and led a relatively quiet life. I had a new boyfriend, Bernie Gelb, who I met on the Dylan tour, and we lived together in a beautiful house in Nichols Canyon. I adored Bernie, although he did have one big problem—he loved cocaine. But then, didn't we all?

I patched up my friendship with Ringo, who was living in Beverly Hills with Nancy Andrews. Nancy and I had been good friends during the beach house days, and we even lived together for a few months. She knew how I felt about Ringo when she started dating him, but what could I do? I'd betrayed Maureen and now Nancy had betrayed me, or so I felt, and when you're messing around with someone's husband, you can't get all high and mighty about morality. It was what it was, a complicated human mess.

One good thing came out of that situation, though. In the divorce petition Ringo cited his adultery with Nancy Andrews. That upset Maureen, who told me she wanted my name to appear on the divorce decree, not Nancy's. That way the whole affair would have stayed in the family, in a sense, a terrible and deeply consequential indiscretion between friends, but not a sordid external affair with a beautiful stranger who didn't know Maureen and thus could not understand her deepest feelings. I think those are the thoughts that might have been going through Maureen's mind when she mentioned Nancy's name on the legal papers, although I can't be certain because she never wanted to talk about the divorce after it was finalized. But I will never forget that winter night at Tittenhurst when George told Ringo he was in love with Maureen. "Better you than someone we don't know," Ringo said. When you're betrayed by someone you love, at least you know they'll feel guilty about it, and there's some small comfort there.

Guilt might have played a role in my renewed friendship with Ringo. Slowly and with some caution, we began to trust each other again, returning to the casual days of old when we could laugh and tease each other. Hilary, Ringo's financial adviser and my great friend, wanted to help get me started in my own business and decided to lend me ten thousand dollars of his own money. We needed a name and after many suggestions, Ringo came up with Brains Unlimited. I organized tours and booked studios while my partner Tina Firestone planned parties and weddings. Our biggest event was Harry Nilsson's wedding. We eventually paid back Hilary, but the business folded because, as Hilary jokingly claimed, "each time you or Tina got your period, things would come to a grinding halt."

I helped out with a few tours in those years. The John Denver tour was the most forgettable. John was filming a television special and touring Australia, and I organized the travel. While he and his people were great fun, the television crew ruined the experience for me. I've never met a rock musician who had one-tenth the ego of those TV cameramen. After the tour I met Bernie in Sydney and we vacationed in Fiji. I was so drunk at the Fiji airport that the immigration people told Bernie that if I didn't shut up, they were going to put me on a flight back to Sydney. The only good thing that came out of that vacation was my amazing suntan.

Touring with Jennifer Warnes on her first headliner tour following the phenomenal success of her hit single "The Right Time of the Night" was great. She was fun to work with and a real professional. Smart, sweet, and blessed with a laid-back personality and a great sense of humor, Jennifer devoted a lot of energy to making sure that we all got along and had fun on the tour. We used to joke about how she was usurping my job duties. And, man oh man, could she sing! She'd stand there on stage with her granny glasses and golden blond hair, looking like an innocent choirgirl, and in a sumptuous alto voice belt out one song after another. Jennifer's good friend Leonard Cohen compared her voice to the California weather, "filled with sunlight" but with "an earthquake behind it." She's still singing her heart out.

The Ronstadt tour was a big deal because Peter Asher hired me to be Linda's tour manager and gave me control over every last detail of the tour. Once upon a time, I'd been his secretary and now I was managing one of his top star's tours. That was a thrill. I can't be absolutely certain, but I think I may have been one of the first female tour managers ever in the history of rock and roll. The Ronstadt tour was a true on-the-road, no-frills tour, just a small troupe traveling on a converted bus from one town to the next, up and down the East Coast, and I was the ultimate authority on everything from sound checks to collecting (and counting) the money at the box office. I ran into a few problems with the head roadie, who didn't like the fact that a "chick" was in charge—and, believe me, there was no respect attached to that word—but we worked through our difficulties and ended up with grudging respect for each other.

One evening we all decided to go out for dinner. We didn't have a show that night, so it was a holiday of sorts, and we all sat around drinking, laughing, telling stories about being on the road. Linda didn't drink, but she was more fun that the rest of us combined. I didn't drink much on that tour, either, because I couldn't afford the hangovers the next day. I'd have a drink at the gig or a few drinks after the show, but I was always careful to stay in control.

We'd just finished dinner when Linda announced in a little-girl voice that she wanted dessert.

"Okay," I said, feeling a little bit like the mom.

"I can't make up my mind," she said, after looking at the menu. "Should I have the chocolate cake or the mousse or the pie or the ice cream?"

The waitress waited patiently.

"Okay," Linda said, looking up from the menu with a big smile. "I'd like one of each, please."

We all just sat there for a second. "Anybody else?" the waitress asked very sweetly, but we said no, thanks, we were just fine.

She returned a few minutes later with eight or nine desserts and arranged the dishes in front of Linda, who very daintily took a bite of each. I remember thinking that was a little decadent, sampling every dessert on the menu. Funny, isn't it, that snorting up five hundred dollars' worth of cocaine in one night with Keith Richards didn't seem decadent at all, but ordering every dessert on the menu seemed like the height of self-indulgence.

I never expected the call from Pattie. I was living in an apartment in the Brentwood district of LA and waiting to hear from Bernie, who was in New York scouting out jobs and a place for us to live. He'd lost his job as Joan Baez's manager, I wasn't doing much of anything, and we decided to give New York a try. Why not? I was always up for something new.

Pattie had been in town for several days, staying with her friends Rob and Myel Fraboni. We'd just spent an afternoon together, talking mostly about Eric's excessive drinking and belligerent behavior. I was so angry with Eric when she described the way he belittled and mistreated her. Here he was, finally with his Layla, and he was treating her like shit.

"Chris, guess what—I'm getting married!"

"You're what? To who?"

"Well, to Eric, of course!" I could just imagine her smiling on the other end of the line, enjoying the surprise. I was completely flummoxed, thinking back to the conversation we'd had just the day before when she said she was sick and tired of the way Eric was treating her. The relationship wasn't working, she said.

"Eric?" I repeated. "What happened?"

"Yes, Eric!" she said, almost as if she didn't quite believe it would ever happen. "He called today and I was at the beach, so he told Rob to call me and tell me that he wanted to marry me."

I had to think about that for a moment. Eric asked Rob to ask Pattie to marry him? He used a go-between to propose marriage to the woman he loved so much that when she refused his advances, he locked himself up in his house for three years and almost killed himself with heroin? What was wrong with this picture?

Pattie was chattering on. She seemed so blissfully happy that there was no way I was going to say anything to upset her.

"When is the wedding?" I asked, lifting my voice to convey excitement.

"Four days," she said.

"Four days?" I repeated. "Where?"

"Chris! You're not going to believe this—we're getting married in Tucson."

"Tucson? Why Tucson?" I just couldn't stop asking questions. Tucson was my hometown, of all places. It was all so completely unexpected and spur of the moment. I hoped—I had to believe—that Pattie knew what she was doing, and once again I had to remind myself that there was no way I could express my concerns, as loving as they were. I was not going to do anything that might negatively affect her bright mood.

"Eric's tour starts in Tucson the day after we're married, so he thought that would be the best time for the wedding."

My heart was sinking fast. This was all on Eric's timetable—he was fitting his wedding in at the beginning of his next tour. He might as well have been cramming in a haircut or a dental appointment at the last minute.

"I want you to fly to Tucson with me," Pattie was saying.

"I wouldn't miss it for the world," I said, deciding at that moment to put all my emotions in a deep freeze. Pattie needed me to be joyful with her, and so that's what I would be.

From that moment on, as always with Pattie, I felt like I was on a big adventure. It didn't matter if we were at Friar Park preparing the evening meal, at the beach in Santa Monica planning our next shopping spree, or flying to Tucson for her wedding—we laughed and held on for the ride. The ceremony took place at a tiny church on the south side of Tucson. Pattie looked stunningly beautiful in a cream-colored silk dress that clung to her slender body and then flared out, ending just below her knees and showing off her gorgeous long legs. When Pattie, her sister Jenny, and I arrived in the limo, all the roadies were standing around in their tuxedos, a scruffy bunch all combed and fluffed and flossed for the occasion. We oohed and ahhed as they kicked the gravel with their sneakers and pulled at their tight collars, blushing with pride and embarrassment.

"I want you to be my bridesmaids," Pattie told Jenny and me just before the ceremony. We were helping her get ready in a back room of the church. I would have loved nothing more than to walk down the aisle and stand at the front of the church with the best friend I would ever have. But I couldn't do it. I was afraid of Eric's reaction. I imagined that he would be at the altar, hands clasped, smiling with pride and joy, and then catch sight of me and whisper or even say it loud enough for everyone to hear, "Oh no, what is *she* doing here?" I don't know why I annoyed Eric so much, but it seemed that every time I visited with Pattie, Eric would get drunk and say mean things to me; then the next day he'd treat me like an old friend and act as if nothing had happened. Jenny told me that he was rude and nasty to her, too, lots of times, but he was always careful not to take it too far with Jenny—she was, after all, Pattie's sister. I knew it all stemmed from some kind of perverse jealousy; Eric wanted Pattie all to himself. I understood that, sort of, because I was jealous of Pattie's attachment to Eric since it took her away from me. But having some insight into the situation didn't make it any easier for me to imagine walking down the aisle and having him sneer at me.

"Pattie," I said. "I think it would be better if I was your bridesmaid in the pews."

She smiled knowingly at me. "Okay, sweetie."

I sat down next to Rob and Myel Fraboni on the bride's side of that sweet little church, and the musicians and crew sat across the aisle on the groom's side. The ceremony was so personal and private, with the light filtering through the simple stained-glass windows in the tiny church, casting a golden glow over everyone—the dust particles floating in the light seemed like sparkling fairy dust—and everyone was smiling and happy, and it was perfect.

At the reception Pattie told me that Eric wrote my name in the wedding book as one of the bridesmaids. That made me happy, and I warmed a little toward Eric that day. But I also knew I had to keep up my guard because that's how it always was with Eric. I'd retreat when he was mean to me, move a little closer when he was nice, then retreat again when he lashed out at me, and on it went. It was always a push-pull with Eric. But Pattie loved him, and he loved her, and I wanted them to be happy ever after.

A few years later, when things were going bad between them, I asked Pattie who was her greatest love—George or Eric. "Eric," she said, hesitating for only a second.

But, as I said, that would change.

Four months later I was walking down Park Avenue in New York City, wondering once again what I was going to do with my life. Bernie and I had completed the move to the East Coast, arriving in the heat and horrendous humidity of mid-August. I spent hours cleaning the Midtown one-bedroom basement apartment Bernie had rented for us, scrubbing the toilets, scouring the sinks, cleaning the floors on my hands and knees. Sometimes I'd hang out with May Pang or Pierre, a makeup guy I knew from a Stones tour. Bernie was always off somewhere visiting relatives or making business contacts.

I was bored and seriously depressed. I didn't feel any connection to New York. It was too big, too busy, too dirty, and I didn't feel safe there. It didn't feel like home. I looked up at the tall buildings on Park Avenue and I missed London. All I could think about was going back home to England, the only place where I felt I belonged.

Back at the apartment, I dialed Maureen's number. Like me, she was adrift, living with her kids and Stella, the nanny, in her house in Ascot, outside of London. Like me, she was depressed, mourning the end of her relationship with Ringo, and wondering what to do with her life. Like me, she was feeling fragile and vulnerable. I'd be safe with Maureen.

"Chris!" she said, immediately recognizing my voice. "How are you? Are you okay?"

"I'm okay," I said in a way that told her I was anything but. "Look, Mo, I was wondering—would you mind if I came over and stayed with you for a bit?"

"Sodden hellfire, you might as well be miserable here as there," Maureen said. We had a good laugh over that one. So once again, I ran away from my life. I never seemed to run *to* anything. I was always running *away*.

Maureen was in a dark, dark place. She was nocturnal, staying up most of the night and sleeping much of the day. She always wore black, that hadn't changed, but she was wearing tight jeans now and layering her clothes as if to protect herself from a sudden chill wind. The windows in the front rooms were heavily draped, and the lighting was even dimmer than I remembered. She was drinking heavily—later she told me that during that difficult time in her life she'd "put away comfortably half a bottle of brandy a night"—and her behavior was increasingly erratic and bizarre.

One night I woke up, startled by a noise from downstairs. I crept down the stairs and found Maureen in the dining room, standing on the third or fourth rung of a six-foot wood ladder, paintbrush in one hand, cigarette holder firmly gripped between her teeth. She had already painted half the wall dark green.

"Maureen, what the hell are you doing?" I said as I stood in the doorway watching her.

She turned around, leaning her hip into the ladder to steady herself, and gave me a look that said, *Well, what does it look like I'm doing?* Cigarette smoke drifted above her, rising toward the ceiling.

"Painting," she said simply.

• • •

Everything about that visit was bleak and sad. Maureen talked about Ringo constantly, and many of her stories dated back to the time they met, outside the Cavern when she was sixteen years old.

"He'd just that week joined the Beatles," she recalled. "I was just a kid. I used to go down to the lunchtime sessions when Pete Best was with them, changing my school uniform around, trying to make it look like a frock. They'd do a gig, I'd see him afterward, he'd ask me to dance. He was six years older than me. I had to learn how to smoke. I mean, I got a girlfriend to teach me how to smoke. I used to pay her ten ciggies a day, for Christ's sake, to teach me to smoke right."

At one point Ringo broke up with her. "I went apeshit," she told me. "All I did was sit on the end of my own bed and rock. That's all I did. That's it. Honest to God. Meanwhile, those four days when he hadn't phoned me, I knew he was with the Ronettes. They'd arrived in London and I bleedin' knew he was with the Ronettes. Think about it. Sixties. In London. The Beatles. And the Ronettes were in town. Now work it out with a pencil!"

But after those four days he came back to her. "Are you ready for this line? He said to me, 'I had to test our relationship, Maureen, whether I needed you or whether I didn't.' And I fell for it hook, line, and sinker. It's not a bad line to use, actually. He said, 'You can't teach an old dog new tricks.' And that's how I got myself where I am right now—with three kids."

One evening I walked into the kitchen and asked Stella if she knew where Maureen was. I hadn't seen her all day.

"She's upstairs in her room," Stella said. She was peeling potatoes at the sink, preparing the children's meal. Maureen and I usually didn't eat with the children, who would have their supper around six in the evening, far too early for us night owls. We'd barely finish our coffee and toast by midafternoon (if we bothered to eat at all) and often we'd skip dinner entirely.

I knocked gently on Maureen's door.

"Come in," she called out. She was sitting in the middle of her bed with the plush velvety spread gathered around her, cigarette in hand, drink on the bedside table, talking on the phone.

"It's Chris," she said into the phone. Then she turned to me and mouthed, "Richie."

I sat down on the side of the bed.

"No, Richie, I need money. The children have to eat." The rough edge to Mo's voice didn't match the tortured look in her eyes.

"Okay. Hold on a minute." She covered the phone receiver with her hand. "He wants to talk to you."

"Me? Why?" I didn't want to talk to Ringo. I had a bad feeling just looking at the expression on Mo's face.

She shrugged and handed me the phone, reaching for her drink.

"Chris." He was angry. "What are you doing there?"

I had never heard that tone in his voice before. When Ringo was drinking heavily, he could be verbally combative at times, even slightly belligerent. But on the phone he was talking to me as if he despised me, as if I had done something unforgivable.

"I'm visiting Maureen." I was pissed off that he was taking this derisive tone with me. I hadn't done anything to deserve his contempt.

"Listen, Chris, Maureen doesn't have very much money," he said, still using that scolding tone of voice. "And you're eating the children's food."

I heard the slur in his words then and knew he was drunk and probably high on cocaine, too. I'd heard from friends in LA that he was doing a lot of coke. But that didn't excuse his behavior. How dare he accuse me of eating the children's food? Where did that come from?

"Are you kidding me?" I raised my voice a little. I wasn't afraid of him.

"Look, I'm just upset." He sighed and I imagined him putting his head in his hand, eyes closed, trying to calm himself down. I didn't have much sympathy for him at that moment.

"Okay, well, rest assured I won't eat your kids' food. Talk to you later." I handed the phone back to Maureen, who quickly ended the conversation.

"He has no right talking to my guests like that," she said, finishing her drink and lighting another cigarette. I noticed my hands were shaking. After everything Ringo and I had been through, how could he talk to me like that, as if I were a servant or, worse, a freeloader taking advantage of his family's hospitality? And if Maureen was hurting so much for money, why hadn't she said something to me?

"What was that all about? Why was he so angry with me?"

Maureen shrugged her shoulders, an apology of sorts. "I told him I needed more money," she said.

"Am I really eating too much of your food?"

"No," she said. "Of course not."

But there I was, in the middle again, with no power and few defenses, an easy target for Ringo to focus on. It was all so horribly complicated. Maureen wanted Ringo back. Ringo was involved with another woman. Money was tight, there were kids to feed, Maureen and I were both drinking too much, and oh, it was a mess. I couldn't take any more of it.

I had to leave, I knew that, but where could I go? Going back to New York or LA seemed like moving backward, and what did I have to go back to? London was too expensive, and, except for Maureen, all my friends and business contacts from the Apple days were gone. Derek had six children now and he'd moved his family up north; I rarely heard from him. George and Olivia were still at Friar Park, but they had a son now, one-year-old Dhani. Pattie was touring somewhere in America with Eric—the last time I saw them was in Philadelphia, and Eric, as usual, acted like an absolute jerk.

I didn't have anything else to do, so I kept going east, ending up in Frankfurt, Germany. There are times in my life that seem to be black holes, where memory disappears and only a few flashes of light illuminate the passage of time. The years between 1979 and 1983 were full of darkness and shame brought about by my ever-worsening addiction to alcohol and drugs. I call them my lost years.

37

LOST YEARS

1979–1983

I settled in Frankfurt and resumed my romantic and working relationship with rock promoter Mike Scheller, who I first met on the Santana tour. For the next four years I worked with a number of bands, including Phil Collins, Queen, Led Zeppelin, Grateful Dead, Frank Zappa, Santana, Fleetwood Mac, Crosby, Stills, Nash and Young, Boston, Electric Light Orchestra, and lesser-known artists such as Italian recording artist Angelo Branduardi and the English postpunk band Echo and the Bunnymen. Along the way, in airports, hotel lobbies, and trips back to England, I reconnected with Mick Jagger, George Harrison, and Eric Clapton, and I stayed in close touch with my three best friends, Pattie, Maureen, and Astrid.

But for most of those years I drifted, lost, alone, depressed. I'd lost my identity somewhere along the way. Everything I'd once called family was all torn up or shuffled around. Pattie was with Eric. Eric was in deep trouble with alcohol. George was with Olivia. Ringo and Maureen were divorced. Ringo was living with Barbara Bach. Bill and Astrid were having problems. My memories from that period of time are all mixed up. The best I can do is to tell the stories that come back to me now like dreams, fragmented yet still somewhat whole in my mind. These bits and pieces of memory are out of sync. They connect with each other only in the larger story they tell about my deepening depression, my loss of self, and my spiraling drug addiction.

Mike and I drank a lot, but it was a new level of drinking. We'd mix schnapps with beer or wine and top it off with cocaine. That was our evening routine for a while, and then it became an afternoon ritual. After a while, the first thing we'd do in the morning was pop a beer.

I was in a bad state. Mike would often stay late at the office, and I'd lie on the couch in our apartment and cry. I just felt so—useless. It was the same feeling I had when I moved to Los Angeles with Leon. I was someone's old lady, and that was the beginning and the end of my identity. I had no sense of purpose, no goals, no role to play except being Mike's girlfriend, and I hated my dependence on him, but I didn't know what to do. I'd lie on the couch, feeling sorry for myself and listening to the Eagles' new album, *The Long Run*. I loved the song "I Can't Tell You Why" because the lyrics described my life perfectly. I'd stay up all night, wanting to hold tight to Mike but loathing myself for being so needy, loving him, hating him, tearing myself apart, tearing us apart, oh so lonely but with no idea why I was so utterly miserable or what I could possibly do to turn my life around.

Everything had changed. I couldn't go backward and I couldn't go forward. Loving Mike, knowing that he loved me, wasn't enough. I needed work, a job, something that would give my life meaning and purpose. My work had always shaped my identity, but with nothing to do and no set routine to follow, I was getting perilously close to the sense that I had no value.

Well, I couldn't go on living like that. I had to do something, so I decided to learn German. I bought a book and a tape and spent hours studying and talking to myself. *Lieben. Ich liebe dich. Du libst mich.* To love. I love you. You love me.

It was a start.

Mike sent me on tour, first, with Angelo Branduardi, a tiny elflike man with a long, crooked nose, heavy-lidded eyes, deeply etched smile lines, and a swirling halo of curly hair. Angelo was an old soul. His music, so positive and hopeful, evoked memories of long-ago times and faraway places where people believed in fairies and witches, and the line between good and evil was finely drawn. Every time I watched him onstage, the audience spellbound, I thought about Pattie's comment comparing musicians to Pied Pipers with adoring crowds following them wherever they go.

We traveled by bus through the German countryside, and the highlight of the day was stopping for a meal. The rumbling would start at the back of the bus, *mangiamo, mangiamo,* let's eat, let's eat, and soon they'd be chanting the refrain, just like little kids moaning and groaning in the backseat, endlessly repeating, "I'm hungry, when are we going to eat?" until finally the bus stopped, and they'd all pile out, barely able to contain their excitement. *Mangiamo, mangiamo!*

I couldn't speak Italian, and the band and crew didn't speak much English, so we couldn't communicate very well, which was frustrating at times. But I did learn a few choice Italian phrases. *Fuck you. Let's eat. Let's go.* Now that I think about it, those words pretty much sum up the touring experience.

Phil Collins was not like any rock star I'd ever met. "How are you?" he'd always say, putting the emphasis on "you." A round-faced, happy guy with gentle eyes and a great smile, he made you feel good just being near him. Phil was so unusual because he never displayed that nervous, hypersensitive, high-strung side that so many musicians have, the "I'm the star, take care of me" attitude that almost defines the rock star personality. He wasn't a big drinker and didn't use drugs as far as I knew, so maybe that explains some of it. Truthfully, though, I think he was just one of those people who was born happy and, at least for the time I knew him, hadn't figured out how to ruin it.

When Queen arrived in Cologne, Germany, for their tour, Mike sent me to the airport to greet them. I was in the lead limo, two limos following behind us, and we hit a huge traffic jam on the autobahn. After what seemed like hours of frantic pleading with the limo driver, I finally talked him into pulling onto the shoulder and driving on the grass divider, right past all the traffic, but we were late and I was freaking out because Queen was a big group, and they were used to being pampered. I knew exactly what I was walking into when the limo pulled up to the curb. Deep shit. I walked into the terminal and the whole group of them, tour staff included, glared at me. They were pissed.

I was not a popular person that day, and I didn't like that feeling one little bit. I wasn't used to being unpopular on tour; I was the one who made people laugh, who kept up their spirits, poured their drinks, took care of their problems, and made sure they were fed, slept well, and woke up on time. After a few days, though, things began to loosen up. Roger Taylor was the first to be nice to me and then slowly the others came around as they started to trust me and have faith that I wasn't going to screw up again.

Queen was such an exciting band to watch, so tight and together. With most bands, even with the Stones and Dylan, I'd stand out front or on the side of the stage, listen to a few songs, and then go backstage and relax with a drink and a magazine, skipping most of the concert. But I never missed a song with Queen.

I have two strong memories of that tour. One day Roger Taylor, Mike Scheller, and I were at a restaurant when a friend who worked at Deutsche Grammophon walked in and handed me a beautiful boxed set of Beatles albums. Roger knew I had worked for the Beatles and he watched me intently for a moment as I looked at the individual albums and repeated some of the song titles.

"Wait a second," he said, leaning across the table. "Your last name is O'Dell, right? Chris O'Dell? Are you *the* Miss O'Dell in the George Harrison song?"

"Yeah," I said, feeling a little embarrassed. When I was touring with other bands, I didn't like to bring up my connection with the Beatles or the Stones. Oh sure, every once in a while I'd throw it in as a power play if someone was ignoring me or treating me like shit. But for most of my touring years, I was reluctant to even talk about my past because it felt like bragging or one-upmanship. I didn't want to take away from the present moment; my job, after all, was to make each group feel that they were special and unique, the entire focus of my world for the time we were together.

"Wow, I didn't know that! You're famous!" Roger lifted his glass to me, and I saw the change in his face, the subtle shift in his attitude as he realized that I had worked for the Beatles and become close enough to George that he had written a song about me.

My second favorite Queen story took place in Munich after the final show. The local promoter invited us to a popular club, which he'd reserved just for the band, road crew, tour staff, and friends. What a wild night. In the midst of all the fun, Freddie Mercury asked me if I had any coke. Well, I just happened to have some with me.

"Yeah," I smiled. "You want some?"

We found a broom closet, shut the door, snorted a few thick lines, told a few good jokes. It was a lot of fun. I love to tell people that I was the one who put Freddie Mercury back in the closet.

During the Fleetwood Mac tour I was standing in a hotel in Cologne talking to Lindsey Buckingham and John McVie when who should come strutting into the lobby but Mick Jagger. He walked straight toward me and gave me a big fat kiss on the cheek. Lindsey, who was in absolute awe of Mick, looked at John as if to say, "Who is this chick we're touring with?" I smiled to myself. Mick gave me instant credibility, and that felt good. Touring with the bands, big and small, in Germany, I was always slightly on the outside, a stranger the musicians and road crew got to know in the days or weeks of the tour, only to be forgotten when the tour was over. But once upon a time, I'd been on the inside, and Mick Jagger had not forgotten me.

Led Zeppelin, the Grateful Dead, Crosby, Stills, Nash and Young, Electric Light Orchestra—I remember bits and pieces of those tours. I loved ELO, which surprised me because I'd dismissed them as a sort of "bubblegummy" group. I remember raving to George about the band and feeling happy when George told me later that I was the one who had turned him on to Jeff Lynne, who would become one of his closest friends. Led Zeppelin wasn't my kind of band, a little too hard-rocky, but I thought Robert Plant was beautiful with his blond corkscrew curls. I kept wishing he'd make a pass at me.

Bobby Weir of the Grateful Dead told me a really sad story. My old friend Frankie from the Hells Angels' days at Apple shot herself in the stomach. "She got really weird," Bobby said, shaking his head in amazement. "She lived through it, but man, it was strange." I couldn't quite believe the story; the bubbly, fun-loving Frankie I knew wouldn't shoot herself. What went wrong? I'd never seen her act depressed. What had she been hiding? Perhaps the depth of her emotions was masked by her drug use. It never occurred to me then that the drugs might have caused the depression. Back then we all equated drinking and drug use with fun and craziness, wacky behavior for sure, but not depression—drugs took you up, not down! We were just so damn clueless about drugs, even as people all around us were dropping off the face of the earth.

Eric Clapton stopped in Frankfurt on his way back from Poland, and I decided to surprise him at the airport.

"What the fuck are you doing here?" he said, half laughing, half serious when he saw me waiting outside customs and immigration.

"I thought you'd like a welcoming committee." I had expected his reaction, steeled myself for it, and figured I'd power right through it. He was married to my best friend, so I couldn't exactly ignore him. We went back to his hotel for a few hours and had a good talk.

"You know, Chris, sometimes you make me so angry," he said after we'd both had a few drinks.

"Well, that's pretty obvious," I said. Nothing like the truth.

"Yeah, I was writing in my journal just the other day," he said, "about how I really love you, but I can't stand it when you and Pattie are together."

I'd always known, deep down, that Eric was jealous of my friendship with Pattie, but it sure felt good to hear it from him.

Frank Zappa came to town for an outdoor rock festival, and it was raining so hard that the band had to leave the stage. Water and electricity do not mix. I'd had a lot to drink that day, and for some reason I got it in my head that I could entertain the crowd until the band returned. I walked to the front of the stage and started clapping my hands. People in the front rows were laughing and clapping, which encouraged me to continue making an ass of myself until I finally got bored (not to mention drenched) and left the stage.

The next morning I woke up feeling so sick—physically, mentally, emotionally, spiritually—that I knew it had to stop. I went to a Twelve Step meeting and for the first time, in German, I admitted that I was an alcoholic. *"Ich bin ein Alkoholerin,"* I said. I stayed sober for three weeks that time and when I started drinking again, Mike was clearly relieved. He missed his old drinking buddy.

Mike went bankrupt, and Pattie suggested that I ask George for a loan. I flew to England and spent several days at Friar Park before I found the courage to bring up the subject. I just kept thinking about the time, that long-ago spring at Friar Park, when George got into a little rant about taxes. "I have to earn a hundred pounds just to buy a pack of ciggies," he said. "The government takes the fucking rest."

"So you wanted to talk to me," George said. We were in the kitchen drinking tea, just like the old days, but on this particular morning I was feeling terribly uncomfortable. George didn't like parting with his money, and he liked even less people who took advantage of him. Would he think I was using him somehow? Would my request for a loan threaten our friendship?

"Yeah," I said, not sure how to start.

"Well, let me tell you this, Chris," George said, trying to ease my discomfort. "Whatever you want, you've got it."

I was so grateful to George for making it easier for me and stumbled around trying to explain why I was asking him for the loan. "If I were able to invest in the company," I said, "I'd be an equal partner and then maybe I'd be able to set aside some money for my future."

"How much do you need?" George said. He didn't really want an explanation.

"Six thousand pounds."

George smiled. "Well, it turns out that I have that exact amount up-stairs. I just sold a car."

He walked upstairs and came back with a money bag holding ex-actly six thousand pounds.

"I'll pay you back," I promised.

"That would be okay, but the truth is, I don't want this to come be-tween us," George said. "I do have one favor to ask, though. Don't go around telling people I gave you money because then everyone will be lining up outside my door."

I will always regret asking George for that money. Years later we talked about that day and I told him how sorry I was that I'd put him in such an awkward position.

"I never should have asked you for a loan." I paused, feeling a little ashamed. "And I never did pay you back."

"Oh, Chris." He laughed. "That wasn't a loan, it was a gift. Don't worry about it."

I flew back to Germany with the bag of cash, and Mike and I registered a new company, which we called Modern Sounds Concerts. But noth-ing could save us at that point. The drinking and drugging got worse than ever, and Mike and I were miserable together, shouting at each other when we were drunk, refusing to talk to each other when we were sober, incapable of getting along but afraid to face life without each other. We both knew it had to end.

My touring days were coming to an end, too. I knew for sure that I was done, over, finished, kaput when Mike asked me to work with groups that I had never heard of before. Like Echo and the Bunny-men.

One night one of the Bunnymen, sweating profusely after the show, asked me to fetch him a towel. Now if he had been George or Mick or Bob—or Angelo, Roger, Phil, Frank, Lindsey, or Freddie—I would have gotten him a towel and probably been happy to do it. But a Bunny-man?

"Get your own damn towel," I snapped.

I was at the end and I knew it. Mike's concert promotion business was headed into bankruptcy for the second time (and, with George's loan, I owned half of it). We were drinking all day and all night, and every morning I'd wake up with a searing hangover, unable to think clearly, my emotions veering wildly out of control. I had no goals for the future, no purpose in the present, and I couldn't go back to the past. I was drained, despairing, lost. My eyes were wandering, looking for someone to replace Mike, always a bad sign because the only way I knew how to break up with a boyfriend was to find a new one. I missed my closest friends—Pattie, Maureen, Astrid—and I missed my old life where anything seemed possible. Life in Germany had gotten all "too real," as Ringo might have put it, and I had had enough of reality.

Time to leave. Time to end it with Mike. Time to get the hell out of Germany. Maureen invited me to stay with her in England, but first I decided to take a little vacation to visit Astrid. We had stayed in close touch, and whenever the Stones toured in Europe or the States, I'd try to find a way to meet up with them and spend a few days with her. The years had taken their toll on Astrid and Bill's relationship, as he grew weary of her drug taking and she got fed up with his womanizing. After sixteen years together, they were breaking up and Astrid had isolated herself in their house in the South of France. The view from the villa, set high up on a hill in the quaint village of Saint-Paul de Vence, took my breath away. From the windows in my sky blue room I could see the town of Nice far off in the distance, and beyond, extending to the horizon, south, east and west, the sparkling Mediterranean Sea.

38

ARISTOCRACY

1984–1986

One night, as if in a dream, my prince arrived. Astrid had invited a few of her French society friends over for dinner, and I had escaped to the sofa in the living room. Dozens of lighted candles danced around me, the moon drew a silver pathway across the patio, and a warm breeze blew gently through the open French doors. I was alone and feeling grateful for the solitude when he stepped into the room. Slim and blond, boyishly handsome, with an energetic spring in his step and a bright, beautiful smile, he walked right over and shook my hand.

"Hello," he said in a clipped British accent, "I'm Anthony Russell."

I was immediately drawn to his warmth and down-to-earth, friendly manner. He was so sure of himself, almost (but not quite) to the point of arrogance, and I found his self-confidence intoxicating. I couldn't take my eyes off him. Several nights later he returned, and we drank our way through a bottle of brandy as he told me about his delightfully eccentric aristocratic family. The Russell family, he explained, holds the title of the Duke of Bedford, a noble rank first created in the fourteenth century. His father was a baron who served in the House of Lords, and he held the honorary title of the Honorable Anthony Russell. I was impressed. What American isn't impressed by a proper English title?

But there was more to Anthony than a privileged background. He loved music and after his boarding school days he had played in a band and even auditioned for John Hammond at Columbia Records. That experience ended in disappointment, Anthony confided with a wry smile. Hammond, who had discovered Bob Dylan, told Anthony that he wasn't "hungry" enough. So this handsome, confident, privileged man with his good breeding and polite manners was a frustrated rock star! I thought that was kind of ironic.

"So, tell me about your music life," he said as he opened another bottle of brandy, poured each of us a glass, and then cut up a few lines of cocaine.

"Oh," I said, feeling a little tentative and afraid of sounding like I was bragging, "I've worked with a lot of people in the business."

"Like who?"

"Well, the Beatles," I said. Anthony nodded his head, encouraging me to continue. "And the Stones."

"I know Mick Jagger," he said. "We often see him socially. But I love the Beatles. They really are my favorite band."

I took a sip of brandy and snorted a line of cocaine, wondering how he could be more perfect. I encouraged him to tell me more about his family. I was fascinated by the aristocracy, and Anthony's connection to that world brought up visions of stone mansions in the English countryside, butlers and maids in uniform, and horseback riding on the moors. I loved the shocking story about his paternal grandmother, Cristabel, and his father Geoffrey's "virgin birth." In the scandal that came to be known as "the Ampthill Baby Case," pregnant Cristabel claimed she was a virgin, and gynecological examinations confirmed that her hymen was intact. According to one account, Anthony told me with a bemused expression on his face, Cristabel claimed she had become pregnant when she took a bath and used a sponge containing her husband's semen.

His father was conceived on a sponge! But that's not all. Claiming that Geoffrey could not possibly be his child and that his wife was an adulteress, John Russell filed for divorce, but plucky Cristabel (who allegedly rode across the Sahara desert on horseback in her seventies) refused to grant the divorce until her husband succeeded to his title as the third Baron Ampthill, at which point it looked as if her son's claim to the title was secure. Phew. Anyway, Geoffrey held on to his title as the fourth Baron Ampthill through several nasty court battles and continues to serve in the House of Lords.

That luscious little tale delighted me—it was so quirky and eccentric, so paradoxically ignoble, so rich and sumptuous with detail that I felt as if I were listening to an aristocrat's version of *News of the World*, the popular English tabloid sometimes dubbed "Screws of the World." But my favorite stories of all were Anthony's memories of growing up in Leeds Castle in Kent—"the loveliest castle as thus beheld in the whole world," according to Lord Conway, a historian of castles. Anthony's maternal grandmother, Lady Olive Baillie, an heiress to the New York Whitney family fortune, bought the castle in 1926 and spent thirty years restoring it. When Lady Baillie died, she left the castle to a private trust but included a provision allowing her daughter Susan, Anthony's mother, to live in the Maiden's Tower, which once upon a time housed the Royal Maids of Honour to Henry VIII's first queen, Catherine of Aragon. One of Catherine's maids was Anne Boleyn, who would become Henry's second queen and the mother of the future Queen Elizabeth I.

Anthony spent most of the weekends and summers of his childhood at Leeds Castle. When he stepped out of the bath, a butler would be there to hand him a towel. All the toilets were decorated to look like thrones. His grandmother, Lady Olive Baillie, dined daily on pheasant. Drinks were served at eleven in the morning, sharp. On the weekends, Lady Baillie invited artists, politicians, film stars, and fellow aristocrats to visit, and Anthony and his brothers would be brought down to the sitting rooms during tea to say hello to everyone. Once he showed up in a cowboy outfit with a gun and holster and the delighted guests repeatedly encouraged him to draw the gun. Those tearoom visits were often the only time during the day that he would see his parents.

As the days and weeks flew by, Anthony and I found less time to talk about the past because we were too busy squeezing every possible drop of life out of the present. When I returned with him to England, our days were filled with dinner parties, charity events, and long weekends

visiting fabulously rich friends at their country estates. My favorite
weekends of all were spent with Astrid and her new boyfriend, Mi-
chael, along with an assortment of Anthony's other jet-setting friends,
at John Hervey's estate in Sussex. The Seventh Marquess of Bristol, John
was well known for his flamboyant lifestyle, outrageous appetite for
alcohol and other drugs, and numerous homosexual liaisons (later he
claimed to have used over two thousand male prostitutes). At age
twenty-one he had inherited five million pounds, along with Louisiana
oil wells, an Australian sheep station, a helicopter, a bunch of fancy
cars, and 160,000 acres of land, but he would lose it all because of
drugs and die at age forty-four.

We didn't know the sad end to the story, of course—we couldn't
even guess at the sad endings to so many of our stories—and we always
had a grand time at Ickworth House, strolling around the magnificent
grounds, playing tennis on the clay courts, taking helicopter rides
around the countryside, shooting quail, playing poker, drinking expensive wines and liqueurs (dinners were always followed with a snifter of
brandy). Meals were formal affairs with butlers circling round, silver,
china, crystal, and place cards. Like most Americans faced with a formal English setting, I was seriously confused about which fork and
knife to use, but Anthony charmed me out of my embarrassment.

"A true gentleman doesn't care which knife or fork one uses," Anthony whispered, his eyebrow raised in amusement, "because after all,
it doesn't really matter, does it?"

I adored him in that moment. But I couldn't help thinking that all
this elegance, all these titles, all this money was like the fairy tale where
the handsome prince sweeps his beloved off her feet. Was this real or a
fantasy? Would we live happily ever after?

That night, as we played billiards, Astrid put her arm around me.

"Hmmm," she said, leaning in close to whisper in my ear, "I think he
really likes you."

Was this it? Was I in love? Yes! I was sure of it, so when Pattie invited
us to spend the weekend at Hurtwood Edge, I could hardly wait to in-

troduce my handsome new boyfriend to my beautiful best friend. Pattie's sister Jenny Fleetwood and her friend, drummer Ian Wallace, were also at the house that weekend and after drinking most of the day and evening, we sat down at the kitchen table to feast on one of Pattie's gourmet meals. Her cooking had changed now that she was living with Eric and no longer a strict vegetarian. I smiled as I cut my steak, remembering the days at Friar Park when I'd go to the village with Pattie and steal away to stand outside the butcher's shop and drool over the meat hanging in the window.

The wine was flowing, the food was exquisite, and we were all flushed and happy when Eric interrupted the conversation, a strange smile on his face. He'd been grumpy and morose most of the day, so when we saw that he wanted to join the conversation, we stopped talking and waited. I was sitting next to him and turned slightly in my chair to convey my interest in what he had to say.

"I'm surprised, Chris," he said, slowly swiveling his head to look at me, "that it took you so long to get to the aristocracy."

There was an awkward silence and a terrible moment when he seemed to look right through me, a sardonic smile lifting one corner of his mouth, the expression in his eyes conveying his delight at successfully humiliating me in front of my new boyfriend. Anthony, with his impeccable manners, laughed, and everyone else followed suit.

Pattie and Eric were having big, awful troubles with their marriage. Eric was gone a lot, touring and recording, and Pattie spent much of her time with Anthony and me in London. She'd become quite fascinated with our friend Will Christy, a tall, handsome photographer who worked for *Vogue* and other high-fashion magazines. Will was so sweet and gentle with Pattie, and it was so wonderful to see her with someone who treated her the way she deserved to be treated. The four of us became great friends and had a lot of fun together.

One spring weekend when Eric was home, Pattie invited us to spend a few days at Hurtwood Edge. Eric was sober, and when Eric was sober, Anthony, Pattie, and I walked around on eggshells. Of course, when

Eric was drunk we also walked around on eggshells, so it didn't really matter if he was drunk or sober. We simply avoided him and spent most of our time in the kitchen, preparing meals and drinking wine. The drunker we got, of course, the louder we got, and any little thing would get the three of us laughing hysterically. I never really thought about Eric's feelings at the time, but now I wonder how he ever put up with us. Most of the time he'd play his guitar in a different room of the house, sit huddled up on the den sofa and watch television (never taking his eyes off the screen), or head out the back door with his fishing gear.

It was our second day at Hurtwood Edge. Dinner was over, Anthony was reading the newspaper in the kitchen, Eric was strumming his guitar in the den, and I followed Pattie into the basement and watched as she moved the clothes from the washer to the dryer.

"Eric is being so silly," she said, absentmindedly shoving a new batch of clothes into the washer. "He's hardly even talked to me this weekend. I don't know what to do."

"He doesn't know about Will, does he?" I asked.

For a moment she stared blankly at some point on the basement wall, almost as though she hadn't even heard the question.

"Oh, Chris, would you talk to Eric?" she whispered, almost pleading with me. "Would you tell him that he's going to lose me if he doesn't start paying more attention to me?"

"You want me to tell Eric that?" I asked incredulously. "Why would he listen to me? He doesn't even like me."

"Go on," she said with a little smile, "you can do it."

I hesitated, not exactly thrilled about the idea of warning Eric that he might lose Pattie if he didn't shape up. But I steeled myself, thinking that this was an opportunity to do something really brave to help my best friend. She needed me, and I was drunk enough to think that I could help save her marriage. I took a big gulp of wine from the glass in my hand to fortify me.

"Okay," I said, smiling back at her, "I'll do it."

I marched straight into the den where Eric was watching something on television and absently strumming his guitar. I sat down on

the opposite couch, pretending for a moment to check out the TV program.

"Eric, I need to talk to you," I said, surprised at the confidence in my
voice. Alcohol will do that for you.

"What?" he said, as if I had just taken his attention away from something really important.

"I'm worried that you're going to lose Pattie," I said, pushing bravely
on. "I really think it would be good if you spent more time with her."

He looked at me with such intensity that I found myself holding my
breath.

"What has this got to do with you, Chris? My marriage is none of
your business."

He was right about that, but I was feeling smug and a little self-
righteous because I knew something he didn't: Pattie was already pulling away from him and focusing her attention on Will Christy.

"Yeah, you're right," I said as I stood up and prepared to leave the
room.

"It's none of your fucking business," he repeated.

I walked into the kitchen where Pattie and Anthony were yammer-
ing away. "I don't think Eric appreciated my message," I said.

At that moment Eric came striding into the kitchen. "I have to get
out of here, I can't stand being with any of you," he said, slamming the
kitchen door behind him. We heard the roar of his Ferrari and the
sound of gravel flying as he sped out of the driveway.

"Oh, dear, I think he's angry," Anthony said in the understatement of
the year. My heart was beating faster than normal. The last thing I
wanted to do was face Eric when he returned.

"I think we should leave," I said.

Pattie looked shaken. I don't know what she had hoped for when
she asked me to speak to him, but this was definitely not what she expected.

"Yes, that might be best," she said, her voice trembling.

Anthony and I were upstairs packing when suddenly all the lights in
the house went out. We made our way back downstairs to the kitchen,
suitcases in hand.

"What happened?" Anthony asked.

"I've no idea," Pattie said. I couldn't see her very well in the dark, but her voice was high and thin. We were all spooked.

"We can't leave you like this," I said, reaching out for her hand. "We're staying until the lights come back on."

"Do you think perhaps Eric had something to do with this?" Anthony asked. We were drunk enough that it seemed plausible, and we started laughing at the idea of Eric childishly turning off the lights and plunging us into darkness. Wouldn't that be just like him? We gathered close together, drinking and giggling until the lights came on about fifteen minutes later. We kept giggling and drinking until we heard the *vroom-vroom* of the Ferrari engine. Then we all froze.

Eric threw open the kitchen door and marched right up to me, a belligerent look on his face.

"You know," he said, his voice a low growl, "there I was driving along the country roads, trying to decide where to go and how to handle this situation when I suddenly thought, Wait a minute—this is my house. You're the one who needs to leave, not me."

"Fine," I said, my chin up, eyes cold, unwilling to apologize to him. "But remember, I was only trying to help you."

"I don't need your fucking help."

We hurriedly gathered up our suitcases and threw them in the back of Anthony's leased Mercedes. Pattie and Eric stood in the back doorway watching us, but there was no happy waving, no cheerful calls telling us to come back soon. As I looked back at him standing there with Pattie at his side, I was suddenly overwhelmed with anger. And I'd put up with his behavior for too long.

As we started down the drive, I leaned out the car window. "Fuck you, Eric Clapton!" I yelled, flipping him off. "Fuck you!"

I can't tell you how good that felt. I sat back in the car seat, gave Anthony a triumphant little smile, and turned to watch the trees go by with the moon speeding along behind them. I felt powerful, bold, deliciously wicked, almost as if I had told Buddha or Krishna or God to fuck off. Wasn't that what Eric's rabid fans had spray painted all over the Underground stations in London? "Clapton Is God"?

Well, Eric Clapton was no god to me. He was a royal pain in the ass.

Despite the fact that Eric's tantrums kept us apart, often for weeks at a time, Pattie, Anthony, and I became a close threesome. Pattie adored Anthony. A kinship quickly developed between the two of them, rooted in a great sense of playfulness and humor. Pattie respected Anthony's aristocratic background and polite manners, and Anthony, like most men, found her charming, childlike nature beguiling. Pattie would get that little-girl grin and poke fun at Anthony, "Stop that, you silly boy," she'd say. They really were like two children, living in their own world, talking for hours, throwing their heads back at the same time and laughing from some deep joyful place. I often felt like a pragmatist caught between two free spirits, trying to hold down the kite lines as the wind kicked up.

Maureen got along well enough with Anthony, although they were complete opposites, the Liverpudlian daughter of a ship's barman and the son of the fourth Baron Ampthill. But she was not happy about the changes she saw in me after I started dating Anthony. Not long after we returned from France to England, Anthony flew to his apartment in New York and I spent a few days with Maureen. We had just finished dinner and were hanging out in her large sitting room, the thick curtains drawn tight, lamps lit up all around the room. I was sipping on a brandy and Coke, telling her how much I liked Anthony and my exciting new life. She just snort of sniffed and dismissed him with a wave of her hand.

I felt I had to defend him. "But he's so cute," I said.

"Cute!" I knew she hated that word, and I instantly regretted using it. But the contemptuous tone of her voice surprised me.

"He's good looking and great fun to be with," I said, listing his other attributes. "He seems to like me a lot and he makes me laugh. And he's got money—that has to count for something."

Maureen just rolled her eyes. Her next statement made me realize that Anthony wasn't the main issue.

"Chris," she said, flicking the ash from her cigarette holder, straightening her back, and fixing me with a look, "the trouble with you is that once you meet a guy, you turn all your attention to him. You forget all about your friends."

Maureen had it right. Every time I got involved in a new romance, I disappeared into the relationship. I stopped calling my girlfriends. I couldn't seem to find the time to meet them for lunch or drinks or dinner. If it came to a choice, I put my boyfriend's needs and desires first because . . . well, because I assumed that I needed a man to bring me lifelong happiness and fulfillment. Sure, I put the guy first, but in my experience that's what most girls did. I was distracted by Anthony, no doubt about that, but who wouldn't be enchanted by a handsome, charming, and witty aristocrat? Wasn't it time for me, in my late thirties, to think about settling down with a man who was good and kind to me? Maureen, it seemed to me, was doing precisely the same thing now that she was seriously involved with Isaac Tigrett, one of the original owners of the Hard Rock Cafe. Although Isaac clearly adored Maureen, some of her good friends (me included) worried that she was just another sample of the rock memorabilia that filled his restaurants, a rare and unique possession that once belonged to one of the Beatles. Maureen's new mantra, which she often repeated with a flip of her dark brown hair, streaked now with red, was "Just give me furs, jewels, and property, thank you." She knew that material possessions would never fill up the hole left by Ringo, but she was also a realist. If she couldn't have Ringo, at least she could have safety, security, comfort.

Maybe those thoughts came into my head because I was jealous of Maureen's relationship with Isaac for the same reason she was upset with me for focusing too much attention on Anthony and neglecting my friends. Isaac took her away from me in much the same way that Anthony took me away from her. But while Anthony was fond of Maureen, Isaac didn't hide his disapproval of me. One night at Maureen's house, Isaac got drunk and started lashing out at me for my affair with Ringo.

"How can you consider yourself a good friend when you slept with her husband?" he asked me. I never much liked him after that.

•　　•　　•

"Chris?"

I had been sound asleep. It was the middle of the night and Anthony was sitting on the side of the bed with a piece of paper in his hand. His expensive Turnbull and Asser shirt was wrinkled and his eyes were bloodshot. He'd been drinking

"What? What is it?" I mumbled, still half asleep.

"Here," he said, handing me the paper which was decorated with designs he had drawn. Anthony was a pretty good artist. In block letters in the middle of the paper were the words, written in large, bold letters, "WILL YOU MARRY ME?"

"Are you serious?" I said.

"Of course I am, old bean," he said. I loved that expression from the first time I heard John Jermyn use it during one of our wild weekends at his country estate, and ever after that, it became one of Anthony's favorite terms of endearment.

"Yes," I said. This was all I ever wanted, more than I had ever hoped for. He *was* my Prince Charming. I gave him a big kiss and fell back to sleep. He stayed up the rest of the night, drinking and snorting coke.

The next few months were all about the wedding. When Anthony called his father with the good news, Geoffrey's response was, "Can I call you back?" He never did, which absolutely crushed Anthony, although he never let on. But Susie, and Teddy, his stepfather, were much more diplomatic about it all. Susie even offered to pay for the wedding, which, she insisted, would take place at Leeds Castle. Since both Susie and Anthony were intently focused on doing the wedding in "the proper way," they did most of the planning. I simply followed along, loving every minute of it.

Anthony and I were married in the chapel of Leeds Castle at five-thirty in the evening on June 22, 1985. Pattie was my matron of honor, my sister Vicki was maid of honor, and Maureen acted as my witness, signing the marriage license. Will Christy was Anthony's best man. We invited just twenty people to the wedding—my parents and my sister, Anthony's somewhat larger family, Astrid, Carolyne Waters, Maureen, Isaac, and of course my great friend Hilary. We invited more than two hundred friends to the exquisite sit-down dinner in the old banquet rooms of the castle, and after dinner we danced to a live band in a huge tent set up on the grass between the castle and the Maiden's Tower. Ringo and Barbara Bach, who were now married, were there along with Steve and Nicole Winwood, Angie and Mike Rutherford, Peter Asher and his new wife, Wendy (Peter and Betsy divorced in the late 1970s), lots of Anthony's aristocratic, jet-setting crowd and one of my very best high school friends from Tucson, Linda Mignery. I invited George and Olivia and Paul and Linda, but they never responded, which hurt my feelings. Derek wrote with apologies that he was unable to attend; I hadn't seen him in almost a decade.

We honeymooned in Paris in a fabulous suite at the Ritz-Carlton and then flew to the south of France for two fabulously romantic weeks. I was so happy. At long last, the fairy tale had come true. I married my Prince Charming in a real castle with rock stars and aristocrats cheering us on, and I was now the Honorable Mrs. Anthony Russell, a member by marriage of the British peerage.

39

WILLIAM

1986–Present

"I think I'm pregnant."

Anthony looked across the table at me, hesitated for a moment, and then stretched his mouth into a baby whine. "Waaahhhh!"

I wasn't sure what that meant. A moment passed before he reached across the table and held my hand. "Are you sure, old bean?"

"I think so," I said, suddenly feeling nervous about the whole thing. Anthony didn't seem to be taking this too well, but then again it must have been a shock as we'd only been married two months. He smiled, squeezing my hand, and changed the subject.

I hadn't planned on getting pregnant, but now that I was, I desperately wanted this child. I'd discovered soon enough that marriage wasn't going to change me from the inside out. We were still having lots of fun, but the newness was fading a bit—so now I had a new fantasy, the hope that being a mother would change the direction of my life and help me become the person I'd always wanted to be. But who was that person? I was thirty-eight years old but still felt at times like a child. I did a pretty good job of convincing other people that I was self-assured and self-sufficient, but inside I felt uprooted and disconnected even from myself. I longed for stability, security, serenity. I yearned to belong to something, to feel part of something. I wanted to find a place that I could call home.

I stopped using alcohol and all other drugs, including cigarettes (I was so proud of myself), and Anthony actually joined me for a while. When he started using again, I continued to abstain. I felt an intense and over-whelming gratitude that I'd been able to get pregnant at my age, and I was not going to lose this child.

Telling Pattie was one of the most difficult things I have ever done. For years she had wanted to have a child, first with George and later with Eric. With Eric she went through two bouts of in vitro fertilization treatments and all the while Eric refused to cut down on his drinking and smoking, both of which can affect sperm count. When Eric told her about his infatuation with a beautiful Italian woman, Pattie was devastated, but when he told her his mistress was pregnant, she said she thought her heart would disintegrate. For twenty-one years she had tried to have a baby and now her husband was having a child with another woman. In private she told me she was "disgusted" with his behavior. That was the ugly beginning of the terrible end of their great love affair.

That was also the very first time I felt I had something that Pattie wanted desperately but couldn't have. I didn't like that feeling. For all the years we had been friends, we shared everything with each other, but I could not share this with her. I felt I had betrayed her somehow, and I didn't know how to console her. I knew she was suffering, but as always she kept her feelings locked up deep inside her, showing only happiness for me and joy in my good fortune. That's the kind of friend she's always been.

On May 10, 1986, Anthony's thirty-fourth birthday, and not quite eleven months from the first anniversary of our wedding day, our son was born. His hair was silky white and his eyes, barely open, were al-most transparent blue. I looked in his eyes and felt a shock of recogni-tion. He felt so—*familiar.*

I know you, I thought. I think I might have said the words out loud.

"Have you decided on a name?" the nurse asked.

"William Odo Alexander," Anthony said, looking with pride at his son. Odo was a family name, dating all the way back to Odo William Leopold Russell, the first Baron Ampthill also known as Lord Odo Russell, born in 1829 and the first British ambassador to the German Empire. I listened as if in a dream, knowing that of all the magical moments in my life, William's birth was the one true miracle.

We hired a nanny to help us out for the first month or so. When William cried in the middle of the night, she'd bundle him up and bring him to me. I felt guilty having someone else take care of him all the time, and I even found myself wishing that I could have my baby to myself. But after she was gone, I didn't know what to do with him when he wouldn't stop crying or refused to sleep. I felt so horribly inept.

I'll never forget the first night after the nanny left. William woke up in the middle of the night and he was inconsolable. Anthony and I took turns walking with him in the upstairs hallways, back and forth, back and forth, both of us feeling completely helpless. How do you stop a baby from crying? I looked down at the infant in my arms, his face bright red, his tiny body rigid with frustration or hunger or whatever emotion he was feeling, and I realized I had no idea what to do with him. Within a few weeks we hired an au pair to help us out.

I loved Will with all my heart, but I was not the kind of mother I had dreamed of being. I knew that too well. I knew it when I slept in until noon and depended on the au pair to take care of my son. I knew it when I had hangovers that lasted three days and felt so sick in body and soul, so full of guilt and shame and self-loathing, that I could barely get out of bed. I knew it when Anthony and I would get into drunken shouting matches in the middle of the night. I knew it when the au pair would give me a sympathetic but almost fearful look when I finally made it downstairs the day after those awful fights, which had undoubtedly disturbed her sleep. I knew it when I held William with trembling hands and feared that I might drop him. I knew it when I looked in the mirror and saw a face that I didn't recognize staring back at me.

I started drinking again three weeks after Will was born. I never really intended to quit forever, and Anthony wanted his drinking partner back. I also began using cocaine again and I'd wake up with the most excruciating migraine that would last for days. I didn't want to let Anthony down by not partying with him, and yet I wanted to be there with my son. I felt so torn. I tried to quit on numerous occasions, but Anthony and our friends would say, "But, Chris, you're much more fun when you're drinking." Those words kept me going for months.

When William was six weeks old we had our first real social outing together as a family. With our baby strapped into the child carrier in the backseat, Anthony and I chatted excitedly as we drove in our Mercedes station wagon to Ringo and Barbara's house in the country. Ringo was one of Will's godparents; he and Barbara visited us at the hospital right after William was born.

We spent the entire day and evening drinking and drugging and finally left the party around 8:00 p.m. The fog had rolled in, and we drove along the unfamiliar country roads to the motorway, unable to see more than a few feet in front of us. Frightened, I turned to look at William, this precious, beautiful little baby with his white hair and delicate features, sleeping soundly, oblivious to the fact that his life was in the hands of his drunk, cocaine-addled parents.

What the hell are we doing? I thought. I was almost forty years old and I knew that William would be my only child. What would I do, how would I live if anything ever happened to him? I looked over at Anthony, his hands clenching the wheel, his neck strained forward, and realized he was even drunker than I was. At that moment I realized that Anthony and I didn't have a clue how to be parents.

Chris, you need to stop, I told myself for the millionth time. I even made a promise to myself, but I broke it the very next day.

One morning when William was about eighteen months old, I realized I was done. I couldn't get out of bed. My head pounded, my stomach heaved, my insides felt twisted up, my hands shook. Memories of the night before flashed through my mind. Anthony and I had been partying and when we came home, we had another of our drunken fights.

We yelled at each other, he pushed me, I pushed back, I started to cry, he kept yelling, we continued drinking, and finally we both passed out.

I forced myself to get up and walk to the study, where I stared at the phone for the longest time. I was just so desperately sick, so terribly ashamed, so completely helpless. I dialed Astrid's number. She had been clean and sober for almost four years.

"Hi, it's me," I said in a weak, helpless voice. "Would you go to a meeting with me today?"

"I'll meet you at the one in Chelsea, off the King's Road," Astrid said. That day, the first day of what is now twenty-one years of sobriety, marked the beginning of a long journey back home to myself.

I was powerless, however, to control Anthony's drinking. Fearing for our marriage and our child, hoping to escape the heavy drinking and drugging going on all around us, I talked Anthony into moving to LA. He tried so hard to quit, and once he even stayed clean and sober for a month. But at the end of those long, difficult weeks, he got drunker than ever. "I'm celebrating my month of not drinking," he said, trying to break the tension with laughter.

After a year we moved to Tucson because I wanted to be close to my family. Wherever we went, Anthony's addiction followed. I could tell when he was going to get drunk before he did. I saw the look in his eyes, the energy beginning to build up, the mood change, and the distance beginning to form between us. And the music—always the music, blaring at all hours of the night. I had spent half my life loving music and now something that I had always looked to for solace and inspiration became a daily dread, almost an evil presence in my life. I began to prefer the sound of silence.

One morning, three years after we moved to Tucson, the truth hit me. *I don't have to do this anymore,* I realized. Anthony and I separated and eventually divorced. I grieved for a long, long time. He was my best friend. We had a child. We were a family. But addiction tore us apart.

I went back to school, and over the next ten years earned a college degree and a master's degree in counseling psychology. Those degrees are proudly displayed on my office wall, along with a framed photo that shows me, Ken Mansfield, Maureen, and Yoko sitting on the Savile Row roof, huddled up against that massive chimney with its four red chimney pipes. I think of that photo as a degree in and of itself—the official certification of my involvement with the Beatles in the years before they broke up. Framed photographs of Mick Jagger, Keith Richards, Ringo, Bob Dylan, Pattie, and Maureen complete the picture. I think of them as my degrees of Good Luck, Great Friends, and Being in the Right Place at the Right Time. They are, in truth, my degrees of Life.

A few months ago, Will stopped by and we spent a few hours going through my photo albums and scrapbooks.

"Mom, it must have been cool to be in that crowd and know that they trusted you," he said.

I looked at my son, now twenty-two years old, and almost the exact age I was when I flew to England and started working for Apple, his hair still blond, his easygoing personality so like mine.

"It was cool," I said, smiling at the way he used the same word I loved to use so many years ago.

"Sometimes I wish I could go back in time, just to see what it was like," he said. I smiled, remembering when he was seven years old and we were watching a black-and-white film. "Was life in black and white back then?" he asked.

He flipped through the pages of the scrapbook and stopped at a photo of him and Ringo sitting together at a table on the patio of a Tucson hotel. The photograph was taken in 1992, when Will was six years old.

"People can't believe that he's my godfather." William had never known Ringo as a Beatle, of course. The first time he remembers seeing Ringo was on television, when Ringo was the station master on *Shining Time Station* and appeared to be just a few inches tall. When Ringo and Barbara visited us in Tucson, Will was terrified to see him as a normal-size person, and he hid behind my legs.

Will picked up another album, flipped through the pages, and pointed to a faded newspaper photograph of me and George. "When was that taken?" he asked.

"In 1969," I said. "It's from an article in a Dublin newspaper about how the Beatles' popularity was slipping."

Will laughed. "They're still pretty popular," he said.

I thought, then, about what George had said, more than three decades ago, as he stared out the window on a frosty December morning at Friar Park, just before he confessed to Ringo that he was in love with Maureen. "You're the lucky one, Chris," George said.

And I remembered something Ringo had said to me, just a few years ago, when a reporter kept questioning him about the past and what life was like being one of the Beatles. "Don't they understand I've had a whole life since then?"

"You know, when I was young, I thought you were famous," Will said.

"No, I was not famous," I said, laughing softly at the idea.

He stared out the window for a moment, looking at the desert sunset with the mountains in the distance and the clouds all pink and gold crossing the sky.

"Why did you come back to Tucson, Mom?" he asked.

"To be with my family," I said without even a moment's hesitation. "To get back where I belonged."

AFTERWORD

Many of my friends are no longer with us and I wish to pay tribute to their lives.

Maureen Starkey died of leukemia on December 30, 1994. She was forty-eight.

Derek Taylor died of cancer on September 8, 1997. He was sixty-five.

George Harrison died of cancer on November 29, 2001. He was fifty-eight.

John Lennon was murdered on December 8, 1980, two months after his fortieth birthday.

Harry Nilsson died on January 15, 1994 of alcohol-related heart disease. He was fifty-two.

Billy Preston died of drug-related kidney disease on June 6, 2006. He was fifty-nine.

Mal Evans was shot by police in Los Angeles in a drug-related incident on January 5, 1976. He was forty.

Neil Aspinall died of cancer on March 24, 2008. He was sixty-six.

Denny Cordell died of cancer on February 18, 1995. He was fifty-one.

Linda McCartney died of cancer on April 17, 1998. She was fifty-six.

Doris Troy died of emphysema on February 16, 2004. She was sixty-seven.

Carl Radle died on May 30, 1980 from a kidney infection caused by alcohol and other drug use. He was thirty-seven.

Bill Graham died in a helicoper crash on October 25, 1991. He was sixty.

Ron Kass died of cancer on October 17, 1986. He was fifty-one.

Where Are They Now?

Peter Asher lives in Los Angeles and still works in artist management. Peter and his wife, Wendy, have a daughter, Victoria, who is the keyboardist in the band Cobra Starship and known as Vicky-T. Peter and I remain close friends.

Eileen Basich lives in Los Angeles and is one of my dearest friends.

Pattie Boyd lives in England, has written a *New York Times* bestseller, *Wonderful Tonight,* and is a highly respected photographer. She is still, and will always be, my best friend.

Peter Brown resides in New York City and is a partner in a public relations firm.

Leslie Cavendish is living in England. The last time I saw him was in the late eighties but, sadly, we've lost touch.

Eric Clapton opened a drug and alcohol treatment center in Antigua and is still making music. We haven't been in contact since he and Pattie divorced.

Crosby, Stills, Nash and Young—in the eighties I toured again with CSNY in Italy and Germany. As difficult as the 1974 Reunion Tour was, I'm very fond of every member of the band.

Richard DiLello and I email quite often. He lives in Los Angeles and is married with one daughter. He writes screenplays for television and film and is considering writing volume two of his rock-and-roll memoirs.

Terry Doran and I saw each other in the seventies but then drifted apart. He is living in England and we keep in touch through Pattie.

Bob Dylan and I kept in touch after the Rolling Thunder Tour but eventually lost contact. The last time I saw him was at a concert in Tucson in 1996. He still stared right through me.

Hilary Gerrard is still a free spirit and still works with Ringo. He remains my dear, dear friend and we speak often.

Jim Gordon has been incarcerated in the California prison system for more than twenty-five years for murdering his mother.

Astrid Lundstrom has lived in Tucson for almost twenty years, and she is still one of my closest friends.

Paul McCartney and I last saw each other at the private opening of *Love* in Las Vegas in 2006.

The Rolling Stones will always be one of my favorite bands. I try to catch their shows whenever they tour in Arizona, and I have deep affection for Mick Jagger, Keith Richards, Charlie Watts, and Ronnie Wood. Today, my strongest relationship is with Alan Dunn, their longtime friend and logistics chief.

Linda Ronstadt returned to her hometown of Tucson for several years, and, during that time, we saw each other often. I toured with her again in 2006.

Anthony Russell is happily remarried to Catherine. They live in Los Angeles and France.

William Odo Russell lives in Tucson and loves music and sports. One day he will inherit the title of Lord Ampthill.

Leon Russell lives outside Nashville with his family. We stay in touch.

Gary Shafner and I have had no contact since the eighties. I wish I knew where he was.

Carlos Santana and I lost contact after the tour.

Ringo Starr and Barbara Bach have been good friends to me over the years. They spend their time enjoying life and avoiding the spotlight.

Gary Stromberg has a public relations firm in Los Angeles, and he has written two books on addiction. We speak often. He remains a good friend.

Jennifer Warnes still lives in Los Angeles, where she was born, and we email and phone occasionally.

ACKNOWLEDGMENTS

Memory is a funny thing. Take for instance the story about the guy climbing in the window at Friar Park in the late sixties. There were three of us there at the time, Pattie, Richard DiLello, and me. Pattie's memory is that she went upstairs and saw the guy climbing in while Richard and I stayed downstairs. Richard's memory is that he went upstairs and I wasn't even there. Mine is in this book. All three of us have slightly different recollections. I would like to thank the people who helped me put together some of those gaps or uncertainties in my memory—Jack Oliver, Peter Asher, Eileen Basich, Betsy Asher, and May Pang.

Thanks to my darling friend Pattie Boyd, who has always inspired me with her joyful, openhearted approach to life, and Leon Russell for taking the time to read my book before it was finished and supporting me to tell my story, even if it was difficult for you at times.

Thank you, Astrid Lundstrom, for always being there with memories and friendship.

A special thanks to my friend Neal Preston; you have supported me and been there since the early days with your friendship, honesty, and wisdom. Thank you, Ethan Russell, Peter Blachley, Nancy Andrews, Ed Erbeck, Jim Marshall, and Shyamusundar, for your photographic contributions; and to Cynthia Keltner, Henry Diltz, and Jennifer Warnes for sending me photos which I sadly did not have room for.

Thanks so very much to Ringo, Bruce Grakal, and Apple Corps Ltd. for permission to use the On the Roof photo.

Thank you to my dear friend Hilary for always being there, for encouraging me to finish my degrees, and for letting me stay in your apartment in New York. I love you.

Thank you to Sonja Stupel and Laura Brinkerhoff, my two friends who have only known me as the person I am today and have supported me and encouraged me to follow my dreams. And a special thank you to all my clients who put up with my erratic schedule and always wanted to know how things were going "with the book."

My family has supported me through all the stages of my life. My mom has always been the positive voice in my head, telling me anything is possible. My dad introduced me to country music, Elvis, and Jerry Lee Lewis and drove me to Los Angeles when I wanted to "run away from home." My sister, Vicki, always loved to hear about my experiences and continuously shows me the value of "sisterhood." I love you all, and I thank you all from the bottom of my heart.

Thank you, my darling son, William, who has brought meaning to my life. When I told him it might be hard for him to read some of the book, he said, "But, Mom, you were just a kid then. It was years ago." And to Joshua, my stepson—who at seven years old reminds me what it's like to be innocent and endlessly curious.

My love, my life—my husband, Morrise, has supported me through this whole project, always encouraging me to keep going, even when it was difficult for him because he had to share me with the past. One morning, when I was really down, he left me this note: "I didn't know the girl Chris and I don't know if we would have fallen in love. But I do know and am very much in love with the woman." Thank you, my darling.

As have many things in my life, this book came together almost of its own accord. Throughout the years, there has always been a Circle of Women of three around me. In high school Becky, Terri, and Patty, my three closest friends; then Pattie, Maureen, and Astrid. And now the Circle of Women involved in this book.

I read *Under the Influence* years ago and the book impressed me so much that the name Katherine Ketcham stuck with me. When William Moyers told me that she was co-writing his memoir and that I should consider her if I ever wrote mine, I was impressed and made a mental note to myself. Two years ago, my old friend Ken Mansfield said, "Chris, you should write your book." I emailed Kathy and she told me she was too busy. So I sent her one of my stories. She emailed to say that she was intrigued. We started working together and spent the next two years chained to our computers. She pushed, I pulled. She said, "Go deeper," I said, "Leave me alone." But she won and it worked. She touched my heart and I began to see my life coming alive on the pages. No words could ever express the gratitude I have for her writing, her passion, her hard work, and her friendship.

A big special thanks to her family—her husband, Pat, who so willingly and lovingly supported her through every day of the last two years, and her children Robyn, Alison, and Ben, who shared their mom with me so that I could share my story with you.

Thank you, William Moyers and Ken Mansfield, for helping to make this happen.

The circle widened when Kathy introduced me to Linda Loewenthal, her agent at the David Black Literary Agency in New York. Linda has been an inspiration throughout the planning and writing stages of this book, bringing calm and objectivity when they were most needed. Her enthusiasm, wisdom, good humor, positive attitude, and compassionate support helped us through a long and often challenging process. Linda is a writer's dream agent and a good friend.

The completion of the circle came with Trish Todd, our supremely talented and always helpful editor who believed in this book from the beginning. She loved it just the way it was and trusted us to bring together a book of substance and interest. Her insightful suggestions and steady guidance have helped us all along the way.

Thank you to Marc Gompertz, Stacy Creamer, Chris Lloreda, Marcia Burch, and the rest of our family at Touchstone. You have been an inspiration to us with your enthusiasm and kindness. And a special thanks to Danielle Friedman, who has always had the answers.

And lastly, thanks to Kathy's friends: Katherine Farley, her daughter Laura, Candy Cohen, and Marilyn Dickinson; and to Keith Farrington, who invited me to speak to his History of Rock and Roll Class at Whitman College. The past continues to live on in the present.

INDEX